THE COMPANION GUIDE TO * Br. G. Guides*

SOUTHERN GREECE

R.W.J. Morper.

THE COMPANION GUIDES

GENERAL EDITOR : VINCENT CRONIN

*It is the aim of these Guides to provide a Companion,
in the person of the author, who knows intimately
the places and people of whom he writes, and is able to
communicate this knowledge and affection to his readers.
It is hoped that the text and pictures will aid them
in their preparations and in their travels, and will
help them to remember on their return.*

The Guides to Rome, Venice and London are available
in paperback in the *Fontana* edition.

THE COMPANION GUIDE TO

Southern Greece

Athens, the Peloponnese, Delphi

❧

BRIAN DE JONGH

COLLINS
ST JAMES'S PLACE, LONDON
1972

William Collins Sons & Co Ltd
London · Glasgow · Sydney · Auckland
Toronto · Johannesburg

To
Pamela L. Pawson

First published 1972
© Brian de Jongh 1972
ISBN 0 00 211124 1
Set in Monotype Times
Made and Printed in Great Britain by
William Collins Sons & Co Ltd Glasgow

Contents

❧

Contents

Illustrations

❧

Note for the Traveller

❧

Southern Greece consists of Athens, Attica and the Peloponnese. The rest of the country, island archipelago apart, falls under the natural geographical headings of Central, Northern and Western Greece. Nevertheless the traveller in Southern Greece is unlikely to wish to omit Delphi, the most impressive single Classical site (outside the Athenian Acropolis) and no more than three hours' drive from the capital, from his itinerary – although the oracular seat lies well within the boundaries of Central Greece. It has therefore been thought fit to include Delphi, together with a description of the approach to it from Athens, in this volume. Historical homogeneity is not thereby destroyed. The country around Delphi – the olive groves, the terraced vineyards, the broken coastline – possesses much of the character of Southern, i.e. Mediterranean, Greece, as opposed to Continental Greece. A further point in favour of its inclusion is that this volume thus constitutes a modest attempt to cover the ground, that is to say Classical Greece, described by the first, most informative and entertaining of all Greek guides, Pausanias.

Introduction

❧

'Other countries may offer you discoveries in
manners or lore or landscape; Greece offers you
something harder – the discovery of yourself.'
LAWRENCE DURRELL,
Prospero's Cell.

PRIMARILY, this book is meant to help the traveller in the
Peloponnese and the southern part of mainland Greece to
identify the surviving monuments of the Mycenaean, Archaic,
Classical and Hellenistic ages and look at them in terms of
their historical context against the background of their
natural setting. The sightseer's ability to view things through
the prism of the past is essential in all places, at all times;
nowhere more so than in Greece, where devastation, whether
from natural or unnatural causes, has periodically swept the
country, reducing cities, citadels and sacred enclosures to
shapeless heaps of limestone slabs and truncated marble
columns. But beneath the hard rocky soil the continuous
discovery and excavation of ancient tombs, filled with gold
ornaments and priceless pottery, are constantly reminding us
of the wealth, ingenuity and density of the population that
inhabited the coasts and valleys of this mountainous country
in the pre-Christian era.

Many masterpieces of ancient sculpture have come down to
us in a relatively good state of preservation, and Greek
museums are filled with bronze and terracotta figurines, often
of the utmost sophistication, together with a wide range of
ceramics in the form of painted vases, goblets and pitchers.
But the temples, palaces and monumental gateways, the civic
and commercial buildings, the public baths, gymnasia,
theatres and floor mosaics of antiquity are, with some
notable exceptions, in a very fragmentary condition. Goths
and Vandals, and other invaders who should have known

better, have wrought even greater destruction than the chronic earthquakes. The Acropolis, it is true, still dominates the centre of Athens, the Delphic oracle can still be identified in one of the grandest settings in the world, and the Olympic Games relived among the rubble of an idyllic pine grove on the banks of the Alpheius. The wounds left by the wars of totalitarian Sparta still scar the fields and hillsides, and long lines of demolished fortifications recall the civil strife unleashed by the truculent successors of Alexander the Great. The names of poets, philosophers, sculptors, architects and statesmen still spring readily to the lips of the humblest modern Greek. There can hardly be a town in the country that does not possess a Pericles Street, a Themistocles Square, a potholed village lane named after one of the great tragedians. Mythology is mixed up with history and many of the ancient legends are repeated in Byzantine superstition and modern folklore.

But antiquity is not the whole story. I have therefore attempted to give a rough general picture, in guide-book form, of the continuity of the Greek achievement in the southern part of the country during a period of three thousand years: to draw attention to the Byzantine churches, mosaics and frescoes, the medieval keeps and machicolated towers that represent the legacy of less illustrious but equally turbulent ages. New protagonists enter the scene. East Roman emperors, Crusaders and Western adventurers, pashas, patriots and party politicians. But the character, though not always the genius, of the people survived intact. In the nineteenth century the Greeks were the first Balkan people to defy Turkish tyranny and, with foreign aid, to gain their independence. Subsequently they have fought in two Balkan and two World Wars, have been subject to endemic political instability and have thwarted two major Communist bids to seize power by armed force. In 1922 they suffered what they still call 'the catastrophe', when over a million Greeks were expelled from their ancient homes in Asia Minor and had to be assimilated into a population little more than five times that number. Resilience is a quality no one can deny them.

Placed at the crossroads of East and West, they are a racially mixed people – in many regions the Slav invasions of the sixth century and the Albanian inroads of the seventeenth have left their mark on the physical traits of the inhabitants. For all their powers of endurance, they sometimes betray symptoms of the lingering malady that afflicted the subject peoples of the Ottoman Empire: the apathy, corruption and nepotism that thwart the smooth working of the modern administrative machine. Periodically, however, the wind of reform sweeps the air, and a backward peasantry is rapidly being replaced by an urban bourgeoisie. Hire-purchase, self-service, parking problems, suburban development, washing-machines, television and air-conditioning are becoming increasingly absorbing preoccupations. Nevertheless the Greeks retain a curiously intuitive sense of history (especially their own). Incurably conservative (but not reactionary), they possess a sense of humour – and of the ridiculous – which is very captivating. They can be rowdy, pushing and prodigiously egocentric. As business men they are shrewd, even wily – the careers of their hard-headed shipowners have become modern legends. They also have their poets. From Solomos to Seferis it is a notable record. The clarity and brilliance of the light preclude the fostering of false illusions and woolly-minded-ness. A Greek, though open-hearted, can be as hard as the light in which he dwells. The landscape, for those who fall in love with it, is a source of imperishable enchantment. The constant interplay between these elements – history, light and landscape – impinge so subtly on the traveller's sensibility that he will suddenly find himself confronted with that ultimate discovery that Lawrence Durrell calls 'the discovery of yourself'. It is very exciting. But make no mistake about it. The edges are sharply outlined, like a Greek limestone mountain or a fifth century B.C. frieze. There are no half-tones. The brilliant refractory light hits you in the face – straight between the eyes.

The best way to see the country is undoubtedly by car. The broken coastline, from whose cliffs and beaches islands are always visible, provides an infinite variety of landscapes. The distances are not great. Like all countries in which the sea makes profound inroads into the land mass, and whose interior is seamed with narrow plains between successive mountain ranges, the road, asphalt or dirt, is the best, if not only, approach to the ruined sites. The main roads are good;

and even some of the out-of-the-way places are accessible by
tracks which are only impassable in the muddy season (early
spring and late autumn). The principal towns are linked by
bus services, and motor coaches cover the conventional
classical and medieval sites in a series of tours ranging from
one to five days. On the other hand, Greece, a geological
upheaval in which a god with the most perfect sense of form
must have taken a hand, is not a land of railways. The
mountain massifs, a final extension of the Dinaric Alps,
running north to south, and crossed east to west by passes at
extremely high altitudes, preclude the development of an
extensive railway network.

I have chosen to start in Athens, which seems to me
logically, historically and geographically correct. It is, after
all, the pivot, a capital of over two million inhabitants in a
country of eight. From Athens the circular tour of the Peloponnese, richest of all regions in major ruins, is easy to
accomplish. From Athens again I wind up the east coast (with
deviations into and around the Parnassus massif and its off-
shoots) to Delphi. Beyond the mountains that encircle the
'navel of the earth', the character of the country changes.
Less Mediterranean, more continental, it falls outside the
context of this book.

Finally, what to see? That is up to the traveller's choice,
interests and tastes. But among the classical sites of the
Peloponnese, I think it would be a mistake to ignore the
ruins of Frankish castles overhanging strategic gorges which
debouch into fertile sun-drenched plains. They are among the
most substantial ruins in Greece, undeservedly little known,
and not always adequately described. Nothing too could be
more attractive than the Byzantine churches in acacia-lined
village squares or hidden among cypress groves surrounded
by kitchen gardens. Of the monuments of the Ottoman period
little is left. On the whole, Greeks dislike being reminded of it.
During those four long dark centuries it is only in Northern
Greece that any semblance of the old creative tradition
lingered on – in folklore, the handicrafts and rural architecture. The volatile southern Greek, as easily dejected as he is
elated, seems to have been more deeply affected than his
northern compatriot by the miasma of inertia and indifference
that blanketed the country with the arrival of rapacious

pashas and fanatical imams. Since the establishment of the modern Greek state, following the War of Independence of 1821–32, hardly a building worth mentioning has been raised in any part of the country. Literature alone has undergone a renascence. True continuity is virtually only found in the character of the people and in their conduct of affairs, both public and private.

CHAPTER ONE

Athens: The Acropolis

❦

Syntagma Square – The Royal Gardens – The Monument of Lysicrates – The Theatre of Dionysus – The Odeum of Herodes Atticus – The Propylaea – The Temple of Niké Apteros – The Parthenon – The Museum – The Erectheum – The Areopagus – The Pnyx

ON Christmas Eve, 1809, Byron and his escort entered Attica through the pass of Phyle. As the pack-animals wound down the stony scrub-covered hills, one of the guides suddenly cried: 'My Lord! My Lord! The village!' In the distance, a cluster of hovels nestled at the foot of a fortified rock in the middle of the plain, encircled by a ring of earthworks no higher than a garden wall. Mosques and minarets rose above the domes of Christian chapels, shaded by a few mangy cypresses. It indeed required a poet's imagination to associate this Turkish 'village' with the city of Pericles. Its inhabitants, decimated by the plague, numbered little more than five thousand. At the last census (1971), the population was two and a half million.

The centre is Syntagma Square, midway between the hump of the Acropolis and the taller pinnacled crag of Lycabettus which overlooks the sprawling ellipse of the modern town. The square, lined with hotels, travel agencies and air terminals, has a very up-to-date air. Historically, it is without roots. The names that spring so easily to the mind, as one approaches Athens and its Acropolis, ring rather hollow, for there is little here to recall the past. At night the skyline is bright with illuminated signs: TWA, BEA, KLM, Air France, American Express. The Grande Bretagne, with a loggia overlooking the square, is the oldest and best hotel in Greece, its bar and lounges the rendezvous of high-powered tycoons and politicians out of office – dapper little men in dark suits with

ATHENS

Lycabettus

FUNICULAR RAILWAY

American School
of Archaeology

British School
of Archaeology

ch School of
aeology

LOUKIANOU STREET

IOANNIS GENNADIOU ST.

Evanghelismos
Hospital

KOLONAKI
SQUARE

VASILEUS ALEXANDROU

Benaki
Museum

Koumbari
Street

Byzantine
Museum

VASILISSIS

SOPHIAS AVENUE

SPYRO

Old
Parliament

IRODOU ATTIDOU STREET

Officers'
Club

CONSTANTINOU AVENUE

YEORYIOU MERCOURI

AGMA
ARE

Royal
Gardens

Royal
Palace

VASILEUS CONSTANTINOU

sian
rch

VASILEOS

Zappeion
Gardens

Byron
Monument

VASILISSIS OLGAS AVENUE

Stadium

mple of
Zeus

Ardettos

Callirrhoë

ARCHIMEDOU

ARA PAVLEOS

LLIRRHOIS AV

ENLARGEMENT of The PLAKA

ADRIANOU STREET

MNESICLES ST.

VENTZELOU

Tower of
the Winds

LYSIUS STREET

THRASYBULUS

EROTOCRITOU

PHLESSA ST.

Demotic
School

Ayioi
Anarghyroi

PRYTANEION ST.

Metamorphosis

St. Nikolaos

0 200 400 600
es
ds 0 200 400 600

nut-brown complexions. From Syntagma Square streets branch out in all directions, their suburban tentacles encroaching on the foothills of limestone mountains that enclose the plain on three sides, with the sweep of the Saronic Gulf on the fourth.

Café tables spread across the pavements of the square. The kiosks – a focal point in the life of the shopper in Greece – are festooned with foreign newspapers, magazines and paperbacks, with just enough room for the salesman to sit perched on a stool, smothered by stacks of airmail envelopes, films, soap, aspirin, after-shave lotion and other useful articles. Above the east end of the square, beyond the orange trees and crowded benches, rises an austere war memorial, in front of which children feed pigeons, flanked by a large bleak nineteenth century edifice, once the royal palace, now the Parliament House, frequent scene of rowdy political brawls that send press circulation figures skyrocketing. Politics are the breath of life to large sections of the population. Personalities are rated higher than policies, and loyalty to the man of the moment is sometimes so fanatical that its only outlet lies in acts of violence. Interim periods of dictatorship (repressive or otherwise) are accepted as part of the pattern. The site was chosen in 1834 by Otho, a nineteen-year-old Bavarian prince, the first king of modern Greece, because of its salubrious air and the proximity of a spring, now blocked up. Somewhere around here, in a little oasis of green shade, was the Lyceum where Aristotle taught logic to a people already glutted with the excitements of artistic and literary creation. To the south the Parliament House is skirted by the Royal Gardens (open to the public), a pleasant refuge from the glare of summer, laid out by a Prussian landscape gardener in the service of Queen Amalia, King Otho's pretty, ambitious wife. Despotic tendencies and misjudgement of the Greek character soon estranged the German sovereigns from their subjects, and in 1862, dejected and embittered, they sailed away into unlamented exile, setting a precedent which more than one subsequent monarch has been obliged to follow. But the leafy arbours and aromatic shrubberies of the Royal Gardens remain an enduring memorial to Queen Amalia's romantic tastes. Exotic plants were imported by caïque from Marseilles and the palm trees in the Sanctuary of Apollo at Delos were uprooted on the Queen's instructions and replanted in one of the royal glades.

The Acropolis area and its built-up slopes form a ragged, somewhat elliptical circle. This is the 'city of Theseus'. Around it extends the 'city of Hadrian', which merges into the modern residential quarters. One can therefore walk from Syntagma Square, in little more than half an hour, to most of the main archaeological sites, strung out like an irregular garland round the Acropolis.

The term 'archaeological' must be stressed, because, after the fall of the Roman Empire and the shock of the Gothic invasion of Greece in 395 A.D., ancient Athens never recovered. The city itself was spared destruction by Alaric, but he ravaged the rest of Attica so thoroughly that Gibbon, quoting a contemporary philosopher, says 'Athens resembled the bleeding and empty skin of a slaughtered victim.' While paganism was being swept away in the triumphant surge of Christianity, the civilised world was busy regrouping itself round the new capital at Constantinople. Throughout the Byzantine, Frankish and Turkish periods, Athens was relegated to oblivion. The spirit (and some of the genius) of the ancient city had found a new refuge on the shores of the Bosphorus. There, at the Byzantine court, in a heady atmosphere of Orthodox ritual and oriental splendour, it produced a rich and hybrid civilisation destined to last another thousand years. Athens, more than most European capitals, lacks historical continuity, and it was not until after the War of Independence ended in 1832 that the city, emerging from the apathy and debasement of four centuries of Ottoman subjection, began to recall its illustrious heritage and that a new little capital, laid out by German town-planners, gradually grew up on the site of the Turkish 'village'. Instinctively, one turns to the archaeological sites, to the shattered monuments of the Classical, Hellenistic and Roman periods, and every natural impulse cries out: 'The Acropolis first!' The ancient theatres lie on the way. It can all be seen in a day (morning and afternoon visits). But two days spent on and around the famous little rock are unlikely to be regretted.

Let alone its associations – mythological, historical, artistic – the Acropolis is always physically omnipresent. Consciously

or not, one is constantly looking up to see if the colonnades of
the Parthenon or the porches of the Erectheum are still there,
outlined against a sky, which, for weeks on end, can be an
astonishingly vivid blue. The walls and bastions that Byron
observed from the pass of Phyle still dominate the cream-
coloured modern blocks on the periphery of its slopes. A
sense of intimacy with this gleaming hump of limestone is
quickly acquired; and equally quickly taken for granted.
Athens without the Acropolis is unthinkable; not only would
the skyline be different, but also the entire town-plan, ancient
and modern, would probably have developed otherwise – if
indeed at all.

There are several approaches. An obvious one, which the
traveller may do well to follow, begins at the BEA terminal at
the south-west corner of Syntagma Square. There is much on
the way that is historically irrelevant, though not without
charm. If you follow Amalias Avenue, on the left lie the Royal
Gardens, on the right the Church of Ayia Sotira of Lyco-
demus, an attractive brickwork edifice, the first of several minor
masterpieces of Byzantine church architecture in Athens.
Founded in the eleventh century, restored in the nineteenth,
it is now the church of the Russian community. Right of the
Anglican Church of St Paul, built of granite imported from
Aberdeen, the narrow passage of Kydathenaion Street crosses
two minute squares with wispy shrubbery: a crowded quarter,
full of tavernas, churches and dimly lit cafés. At night touts
and pimps pullulate in the narrow streets. During the day
stylishly dressed young men stroll self-consciously along the
pavement outside the café opposite the Ciné Paris. From
within, the rattle of dice on a backgammon board is followed
by the echo of raised voices. Sudden altercations, mysterious
eruptions of mock-violence, are a familiar feature of café and
street life. But differences are quickly resolved. Beneath all the
bluster there is a wonderful aptitude to forgive and forget.
Pharmacis Street, left of the Ciné Paris, leads to the cruciform
Byzantine Church of Ayia Aikaterini (St Catherine) in a
sunken square. Two ancient columns stand in front of a little
garden. The building has unfortunately suffered from tasteless
restoration.

A few yards away is the **Choragic Monument of Lysicrates**
in another minute square surrounded by crumbling houses.

The monument is a fantasy: a cylindrical drum of marble on a square stone base, with six Corinthian columns engaged under the architrave. The roof was once decorated with lush acanthus leaves, on whose tips rested a bronze tripod: the prize won by the impresario Lysicrates in 334 B.C. for supplying the best boys' choir in a theatrical competition. The tradition is not altogether dead. The standard of Greek choral ensembles, particularly the National Choir (State Opera), is high. One is sometimes astonished by the quality of tone produced by a group of workmen singing a popular tune in a taverna. As soloists they are, with some obvious exceptions, less gifted – an unexplained paradox in a people as aggressively individualistic as the Greeks. Women's voices in particular tend to be strident. The mutilated frieze of the monument represents the episode of Dionysus' capture by Tyrrhenian pirates and the tricks he played in order to confound them. For the preservation of the monument much is owed to the French Government which bought it in the seventeenth century. A Franciscan monastery was built around it, and this architectural extravaganza, restored in the nineteenth century, served as the monks' library. Tomatoes were grown for the first time in Greece in the monastery garden, and Byron lodged here in the winter of 1810–11; he read much in the library, organised boxing matches between Catholic and Orthodox schoolboys and drank with the Mufti of Thebes and the Kaimakam of Athens. Behind the alleys – Byron Street, Shelley Street, Tripod Street – the east wall of the Acropolis rises sheer above a warren of hovels and maisonettes.

From the Choragic Monument Byron Street leads into Dionysiou Areopaghitou Avenue which ascends towards the Acropolis. On the right lie scattered marble slabs and truncated columns: fragments of the Sanctuary of Dionysus. One has entered the area of '*ta archaia*' – of 'ancient things.' A relative hush is perceptible. Motor coaches filled with tourists trundle up the hill. The tremendous weight of antiquity, which has done so much to fashion the mind and character of the modern Greeks, begins to impinge; so does the vast tragic void in Athenian history, the cumulative effect of Byzantine neglect, Ottoman oppression and Western

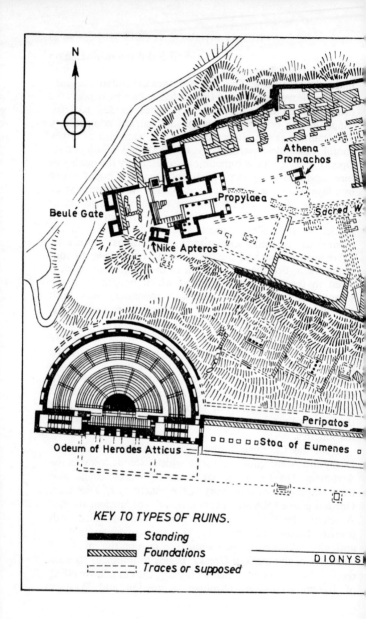

N

Athena
Promachos

Propylaea

Beulé Gate

Sacred W

Niké Apteros

Peripatos

Odeum of Herodes Atticus

Stoa of Eumenes

KEY TO TYPES OF RUINS.

Standing

Foundations

Traces or supposed

DIONYS

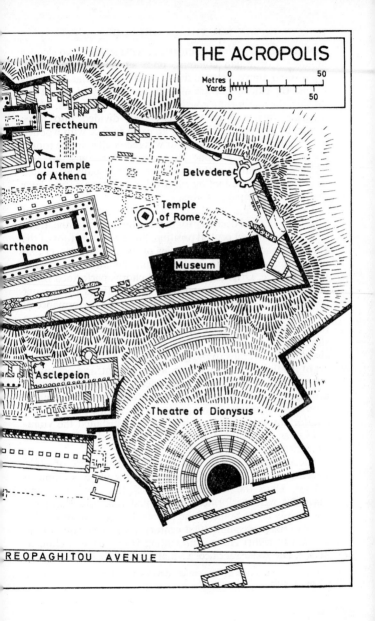

THE ACROPOLIS

Metres 0 _____ 50
Yards 0 _____ 50

Erectheum

Old Temple of Athena

Belvedere

Temple of Rome

Parthenon

Museum

Asclepeion

Theatre of Dionysus

REOPAGHITOU AVENUE

spoliation during fifteen centuries of 'village' life. Two slender
unfluted Corinthian columns, once surmounted by votive
gifts, stand above a grotto in the south wall of the Acropolis
behind the ruined **Theatre of Dionysus**. Hollowed out of the
hillside, the auditorium consisted of seventy-eight tiers, whose
diameter increased as they ascended, divided into three
sectors by diazômas. Originally an earth surface with wooden
tiers for distinguished citizens, it was remodelled in the fourth
century B.C. into a stone structure by Lycurgus, an able
financier and patron of the arts. Nero, more usually associated
with the wholesale looting of Greek art treasures, was later
one of the principal restorers.

The theatre is a good example of the Greek practice of
utilising a natural declivity for carving out an amphitheatre in
some dominant yet central position. Situated at the foot of the
citadel, it once commanded a view of the shrubby groves and
undulations of the plain. Today nothing but an urban expanse
meets the eye. Originally actors and chorus performed in the
circular orchestra, surrounded in Roman times by a water
conduit which enabled it to be flooded for the performance of
mock naval battles. In the centre was the god's altar on a
raised platform, marked by a large diamond-shaped paving
stone, around which the chorus revolved in stately measures,
chanting dithyrambs to the god. With the development of the
art of the theatre, a proscenium, a narrow platform occupying
a segment of the orchestra, was added as a stage for the main
protagonists. The acoustics were improved by the placing of
inverted bronze vessels on pedestals at various points in the
auditorium where they received and redistributed the vibra-
tions of sound. Painted scenic props were used and the actors
wore large grotesque masks.[1]

The tiers may be less well preserved than those of other
Greek theatres, but the significance of the place is infinitely
greater. Here the tragedies of Aeschylus, Sophocles and
Euripides were performed for the first time and European
drama was born. Some of the figures depicted on the marble
frieze of the proscenium (first century A.D.) are worth looking
at: (left to right) Hermes presenting Dionysus as a child to
Zeus, a Dionysiac sacrifice, a squatting Silenus, the wine god's

1. For a description of mechanical devices used during performances,
see pp. 164-65.

licentious old pedagogue. The throne of the high priest of Dionysus, with its decoration of lions, griffons and, very appropriately, satyrs and a bunch of grapes, is easily identified in the centre of the front row. The concave seats, reserved for archons and priests, once shaded with awnings, are extraordinarily comfortable. The earliest theatrical compositions were accompanied by dancing, mimed scenes and impassioned dialogues. The annual performances, which formed part of the Great Dionysia, were held with much pomp in the spring sunshine, to the accompaniment of flute-playing and the banging of cymbals and drums. The audience did not only seek entertainment; they were genuinely moved by religious exaltation and the desire to honour the licentious young god. During the festival all work in the city ceased, a general moratorium was declared, law-courts were shut and prisoners released from jail. Abstinence from wine was considered a mark of disrespect to the god, and bawdy colourful processions wound through the streets.

From the highest tier of the theatre a row of cypress trees leads westward between the ruins of the Asclepeion – a sheltered sanctuary for the sick, dedicated to the god of healing – and the Stoa of Eumenes, the work of a philhellenic king of Pergamum in the second century B.C., which consisted of a double colonnade and served as a foyer during intervals between the successive trilogies which lasted all day. From the stoa one regains Dionysiou Areopaghitou Avenue and mounts a broad modern stairway to the **Odeum of Herodes Atticus**, the gift of a wealthy public benefactor of the Antonine era to the people of Athens. The cedar wood roof has vanished and thirty-two tiers have been restored with marble facings. The stone facade of three stories is embellished with arches. When floodlit it creates an effect of Roman splendour, the arched openings allowing for an interplay of light and shade, glowing and mysterious, absent from the classical simplicity of the monuments on the Acropolis. The contrast is striking – yet the two styles complement each other, as Greek and Roman architecture often do. In front of the semi-circular orchestra, a chequer-board of black and white marbles, rises the stage and behind it the skene (the stone or marble back-cloth to a stage) consisting of a colonnade with niches for statues, surmounted by a narrow ledge reserved for actors who impersonate the gods. A festival, very different from the Dionysia, is now held every summer (August–September) in the restored theatre, which was used by the Turks as a stable and later as a redoubt guarding the defences of the Acropolis. Apart from a cycle of ancient drama, the festival includes performances by the world's leading orchestras, operatic and theatrical companies. Its tourist attraction is obvious. Acoustic imperfections are redeemed by the setting: especially the mellow glow of the arched skene and a glimpse of a floodlit projection of the west pediment of the Parthenon above the massive Cimonian wall. The impression made by the trumpet solo in the Leonora No. 3 Overture echoing across the ruins could not be more dramatic. The Dionysos restaurant (international cuisine, expensive) is conveniently situated on the opposite hill.

From the Odeum one ascends to the Acropolis which has the shape of a polygonal lozenge with a flat top and is five hundred feet high. 'There is but one entry,' says Pausanias. 'It affords no other, being precipitous throughout and having a strong wall.' As one climbs, one is conscious of a feeling of isolation; at the same time, of being at the heart of things, of one's proximity to the city and of one's remoteness from it, of an atmosphere that has become unusually rarefied. The perpendicular surface of the other sides is honeycombed with grottoes and defended by strong walls, of which the earliest, below the Temple of Niké Apteros, are called Cyclopean, but are also attributed to the Pelasgians, the first inhabitants of the Attic plain.

The origins of the Acropolis, as those of Athens – it is impossible to separate the one from the other – go back to the ancient, often conflicting, myths of the Pelasgian age. If Cecrops, an earth-born creature, half-man half-snake, was the first king to recognise paternity, to invent the institution of marriage and found the city, Erectheus (or possibly Erecthonius? – the genealogy is very muddled), whose body also ended in a tail, is even more a key character in Acropolis mythology. On the other hand, Theseus is too ubiquitous, both in legend and literature, to be dismissed as a mere mythological hero who slew a bull in Crete and had a lot of love affairs with well-born ladies whom he did not always treat impeccably. Apart from exploits, sexual and martial, he is credited with having united Attica into a single administrative unit and established Athens as its capital. In the sixth century B.C. the tyrannical Peisistratae embellished the town and its citadel with temples and public buildings. But it required the democratic reforms of Cleisthenes, followed by the repulse of the Persian invasion, for the full impact of classical art to be felt. Studded with sculptural and architectural masterpieces, the Acropolis then emerged as the symbol of the inspiration and skill of a galaxy of artists whose object was to exploit the brilliant light of Attica in the most subtle architectural forms ever imagined. Conditioned by their landscape, the Greeks looked at objects in contour and relief. There is no shifting perspective, no hazy diaphanous background. Clarity is the keynote. This is nowhere more apparent than on the Acropolis.

During the miraculous years of the fifth century B.C. Athens, an expanding maritime empire, self-assured and flushed with victory, pullulated with outstanding men in every walk of life. In war, Miltiades, Themistocles, Alcibiades, men of infinite resource and ambition, immensely vain, sometimes treacherous. In peace, Aristides, justest of Athenians, Cimon, munificent and far-seeing, above all, Pericles, shrewdest of administrators, blessed with an oratorical flair so formidable that Plutarch likens it to a 'dreadful thunderbolt'. In the arts and literature new ideas, new men open up new horizons. In sculpture, Phidias and Myron; in architecture, Ictinus and Mnesicles; in poetry, Aeschylus, Sophocles and Euripides, who transform Attic tragedy, a more or less static form of mime, into living drama. Clarity and enlightenment have become the mainspring of Greek thought. There is now nothing to prevent Socrates from talking and dying in the cause of moral wisdom or to stop Plato from writing about it with consummate artistry. To record this explosion of spiritual and physical creativity there is an Herodotus, a Thucydides, a Xenophon. In everything there is a note of modernity, the stamp of intellectual integrity and the thirst for knowledge. But the Peloponnesian War took its toll and the Golden Age drew to a close with the Spartan victory over an exhausted Athens.

As one ascends the stairway, past a platform crowded with touts, guides and motor coaches, a large pedestal of greyish-

blue Hymettus marble, once surmounted by a statue of a
Roman general in a bronze chariot, stands on the left.[2] In
front rises the **Propylaea**, the entrance way to the citadel, one
of the masterpieces of classical architecture. Commissioned by
Pericles, it was built by Mnesicles, a fashionable fifth century
B.C. architect, who fell off the top of the building in the course
of its construction. He was thought to be fatally injured, until
miraculously cured by the application of a herb suggested in
a dream to Pericles by Athena. Extending across the west side
of the hill, the Propylaea, much of whose complexity of
design is due to the asymmetrical slope of the ground, forms
an entrance hall to the five gates through which men and
horses entered the precinct. The marks of the chariot wheels
are still visible. A costly massive edifice of Pentelic marble, it
consisted of a central gateway with five openings, on either
side of which rise Doric colonnades directly from the stylobate. In the west portico, two rows of three Ionic columns
flank the main passage. The ceiling was coffered and embellished with a gilt star in the middle. The huge doors of the
gateway, which are not all of the same height, were probably of
wood faced with bronze and the loud grating noise they made
when opened is mentioned by Aristophanes. There are two
projections: one to the north, leading to the Pinacotheke,
where paintings were exhibited on boards; the other, less well
preserved, to the south (towards the Temple of Niké Apteros).
In the fourteenth century the first Florentine Duke of Athens
established his chancery here, adding a second story, battlements and a tower; in the seventeenth century the Turks, with
their customary disregard for historical monuments, turned
the marble porticoes into a powder magazine. Struck by a
thunderbolt, the ignited gunpowder blew the entablature sky-
high and the central part of the building caved in. Much of
what we now see standing is the result of laborinos restoration
by modern archaeologists. A more majestic entrance to a holy
precinct can hardly be imagined.

To the right, the **Temple of Niké Apteros** (Wingless Victory)
seems minuscule in comparison. Only 18 by 27 feet, it is a
memorial to the Greek victories over the Persians. Pericles

2. For the uninitiated there is no more handy factual guide-book of
the Acropolis than *A Concise Guide to the Acropolis of Athens* by
Pericles Collas, Cacoulides, Athens.

entrusted the plans to Callicrates, who so constructed the temple, resting on a stylobate of three steps, that its front pointed in the direction of the Parthenon: an effect probably designed to focus the eye on the more imposing building. This exquisitely proportioned little monument, with its eight Ionic columns, composed of monolithic shafts instead of the usual series of superimposed drums, was demolished by the Turks and the materials were used for the construction of a defence wall. A century and a half later King Otho commissioned the restoration of the temple. The original materials fortunately lay at hand, but the greater part of the frieze is so mutilated that it is difficult to identify the headless figures. The east frieze represented the assembly of the gods; the other three are believed to have depicted scenes from the Persian Wars, contrary to the usual practice of portraying mythical feats – the *gigantomachia*, battles between gods and giants – on the friezes of temples.

In prehistoric times the natural bastion on which the temple is built served as a watch-tower from which pirates approaching the coast could be spotted. From here King Aegeus sighted the black sail of the vessel bearing Theseus back to Athens after his expedition against the Minotaur. Theseus had promised his father that, in the event of victory over the Cretan bull, he would hoist a white canvas in place of the original black one. Brooding over his somewhat churlish behaviour to Ariadne, to whom he owed his escape from the Labyrinth and whom he had abandoned in Naxos, he forgot to carry out his promise. Seeing the ominous black sail, Aegeus gave up his son for lost, fainted and fell off the cliff. There is a wide view from the bastion, with a series of hills in the foreground including the Mousaeon crowned by the Monument of Philopappus, raised by a philhellenic Syrian official in the Roman administration, its concave structure adorned with a frieze and turned towards the Parthenon. At the foot of the hill there is a cave, popularly believed (but by no means proved) to have been the scene of the last act in the great *cause célèbre* of the early fourth century B.C., the trial of Socrates. The rock-hewn chamber, it has been claimed, may be the prison where the philosopher, charged with the corruption of Athenian youth by his advanced religious views, drained a cup of hemlock and, as the sun set behind Salamis, died with the words, 'We ought to offer a cock to Asclepius' – a last typically paradoxical sally, implying that death, after all, was the only cure for life. Behind the hills a built-up plain extends towards the sea. A century ago caravans of camels, carrying goods from the Piraeus to Athens, wound slowly along its dusty tracks. Beyond the smoking factories of the Piraeus, Mt Aegaleos tapers off into the sea and Salamis emerges out of the bay. Across the Saronic Gulf, Aegina raises an elegant conical peak against a screen of jagged crenellations formed by the summits of the once volcanic mass of the Methana peninsula.

Returning to the Propylaea, one passes out of the east portico into a vast esplanade littered with the debris of centuries. To the left is the Erectheum, to the right the Parthenon on a culminating terrace crowning the entire precinct. There is no vegetation: nothing but rock and marble; and sky overhead. How often one has seen it all before – in reproductions. But there is one thing one had not anticipated, perhaps: the sheer physical dominance of the Parthenon, with its famous honey-coloured patina and splendid almost squat self-assurance. In the second century A.D. Pausanias described the Sacred Way, which led obliquely up the incline from the Propylaea to the east front of the Parthenon, as a jumble of statues, pedestals and votive offerings. Today nothing remains but the sun-baked bases, the ruts formed by ancient water-ducts, the sockets from which innumerable columns sprouted. At intervals faint incisions in the rock, intended to prevent horses and sacrificial animals from slipping on the hard smooth surface, are noticeable. A little less than midway between the Propylaea and the Parthenon are the foundations of the pedestal of Phidias' gigantic bronze statue of Athena Promachus, whose height equalled that of the Propylaea. The goddess was depicted in full armour, leaning on a lance with a gilded tip. In the sixth century Justinian removed it to Constantinople, where it perished in a fire. As pilgrims passed out of the Propylaea they had a view at a slant of both temple and statue. Here, as in the sanctuaries at Delphi and Olympia, buildings are seldom parallel to each other. Greeks sought symmetry, but not parallelism which they considered monotonous.

The Temple of Athena Polias, tutelary goddess of Athens,

'The Upper City' – walls, temples, gateways, crowned by the Parthenon

The Temple of Niké Apteros. A masterpiece of 5th century B.C. architecture, the work of Callicrates, one of the architects of the Parthenon

The Peplos Koré (Acropolis Museum)

Maiden removing her sandal
(Acropolis Museum)

The Moscophorus or Calf Bearer
(Acropolis Museum)

The South Colonnade of the Parthenon.
The honey-coloured columns mount
skyward, dominating the whole
precinct.

or **Parthenon**, as it came to be known, stands on the site of an earlier temple burned by the Persians on the eve of the battle of Salamis. The new temple was the brain-child of Pericles; Ictinus, assisted by Callicrates, was the principal architect; and Phidias, the greatest statuary of the age, was in charge of the sculptural decoration. The plans were the most ambitious and architecturally daring ever attempted. Little wonder that the building, primarily a place of worship, soon came to be regarded as a national treasury, containing bullion, archives and votive gifts of immense value. It is constructed entirely of Pentelic marble and not one of its forty-six Doric columns is exactly the same height as the other. The slight convexity in the middle of the columns prevents the eye from being automatically carried upwards along the shaft (it moves up and down); the columns thus acquire volume and elasticity and relieve monotony. This all important *entasis*, as it is called, was intended to correct an optical illusion, for a perfectly straight column invariably appears thinner in the middle when seen against a background of bright light. The resultant effect of strength and harmony is particularly evident from either end of the north and south colonnades. Other architectural refinements include the oblique line of the cornices of the pediments and the gradual rise of the stylobate to a point which is highest in the centre. There is, in fact, hardly a straight line in the building. The ultimate effect of all this *entasis*, or convexity, almost invisible to the untrained eye, is to create an impression of a perfectly proportioned edifice growing organically out of a natural eminence.

The sculptures, executed by Phidias and his pupils, and originally painted over in brilliant hues of red, blue, green and yellow – the effect, it is thought, may have been rather gaudy – consisted of ninety-two metopes, a frieze 524 feet long running along the entire circumference of the exterior walls of the cella, and two gigantic pediments, at each corner of which lions' heads projected. The decoration is arranged in three tiers – on, as it were, three different religious levels – embracing the entire cosmos in which the Greeks of the fifth century B.C. had their being. First came the Phidias frieze, representing the procession of the Great Panathenaea: a masterpiece of animation, with men and animals depicted in actual motion. On this level, mortals were shown in the act of worship. The Great Panathenaea, most splendid of festivals in honour of the patron goddess, held in the third year of every Olympiad, lasted several days and included games, sacrifices, cockfights, torch races, recitations and musical contests, culminating in the Panathenaic procession, in the course of which the sacred *peplos*, a crocus-coloured garment, woven by Athenian virgins and embroidered with designs depicting the battle of the gods against the giants, was suspended from a ship with nine banks of oars motivated by a mechanical device and borne to the goddess's temple. The Parthenon frieze depicted every section of the population – on foot, on horseback, in chariots – participating in the procession. Followed by flute-players, sacrificial animals, young men in armour, elderly citizens carrying olive branches and aristocratic maidens bearing baskets filled with offerings, the procession started at the Cerameicus (see pp. 56-58) and ended with the placing of the *peplos* on the goddess's statue in the Erectheum. Parts of the frieze, though much damaged, may be seen on the west front. In the equestrian groups the prancing horses seem to be defying the attempts of the young riders to bridle them. Other plaques are in the Acropolis Museum (see p. 42) and the remaining fifty-six in the British Museum. The angle of vision is very awkward, for the frieze towers forty feet above the spectator, who has little room to manœuvre in the narrow colonnade, where the shadows must have been deepened by the hollows of the coffered ceiling enamelled with stars and rosettes. The detail is best examined in reproductions.

From the human bustle of the frieze we move on to the metopes, which represent the gods and mythological heroes engaged in epic contests with giants, Centaurs and Amazons, symbolical of the victory of mind over matter. These were of inferior quality to the frieze. Thirty-two remain in their original position, between triglyphs, but they are mutilated almost beyond recognition. Other surviving metopes are in the British Museum and the Louvre. There is also one in the Acropolis Museum. Finally, on the highest level, crowning the whole structure, we enter the realm of the divine, the sculptures of the pediments representing two of the most venerable scenes in Athenian mythology: the birth of Athena, when she sprang fully armed from the head of Zeus 'with a mighty shout, while Heaven and Earth trembled before her',[3] and her contest with Poseidon for possession of the city. The most important fragments are in the British Museum. Except for a cement cast of Dionysus and the superb heads of three horses of the chariots of the Sun and Moon at either end of the east front and two headless figures in the west, the Parthenon pediments are now no more than two gaping wounds in a scarred and mutilated structure.

The origins of Lord Elgin's action in removing the sculptural 'plums' of the Parthenon, whether regarded as an act of salvage or vandalism, go back to the seventeenth century, when Charles I, who was fond of sculpture, instructed his Ambassador in Constantinople to carry off as many statues as he could. When these were too bulky to be moved, the Ambassador had their heads severed and transported to England. This, says one Greek author, 'explains the presence of so many fine heads in the West, and so many headless statues in Greece'.[4] Headless statues are indeed an all too familiar sight in Greek museums, but it is the Goths and other barbarian invaders who bear the heaviest responsibility for these acts of senseless savagery. Then in 1687 occurred the famous explosion, when a Venetian army under Morosini, later doge of Venice, was laying siege to the Acropolis. Informed by a deserter of the existence of a Turkish powder magazine in the Parthenon, Morosini, a hard-headed soldier, did not hesitate to place the fate of battles above that of ancient temples. A direct hit set off a tremendous explosion and the central part of the building was blown to bits. Many of the sculptures were scattered round the shattered colonnades. After capturing the city, Morosini wanted to detach some of the horses of Poseidon from the pediment. But he employed unskilled workers and a number of sculptures were smashed. No attempt was made to put them together, and they eventually found their way to a Turkish lime-kiln. In order not to return home without a trophy, the future doge removed two ancient lions, which now guard the entrance to the arsenal at Venice. Morosini's stay on the Acropolis was short-lived. The Turks returned and set fire to what remained of the city. Athens

3. Pindar, *Ol.* vii, 35.
4. Demetrios Sicilianos, *Old and New Athens*, Putnam, London, 1960, translation by Robert Liddell.

and Attica remained desolate for years, the Acropolis a shambles.

Towards the end of the eighteenth century the Comte de Choiseul-Gouffier, a French diplomat and philhellene, instructed his agent in Athens, M Fauvel, 'to lose no opportunity of pillaging Athens'.[5] The sculptures collected by the conscientious Fauvel are now in the Louvre. At this point Lord Elgin, British Ambassador at Constantinople, enters the scene. In 1801 he obtained a firman from the Sublime Porte, authorising him to remove a number of already mutilated sculptures, thought likely to suffer further, possibly irreparable, damage, which were eventually purchased by the British Museum for £35,000. Turkish indifference to the treasures of antiquity was a byword. Slabs of the Parthenon frieze, offered as gifts to foreign travellers, were hurled over the ramparts as the most commodious means of transport. The visible effects of the Morosini explosion clearly indicated the appalling hazards to which the sculptures must be exposed under Turkish trusteeship. Moreover, Lord Elgin's action drew attention to Greece and its sufferings under Ottoman rule. Philhellenism grew fashionable. Byron, referring testily to Elgin's agents as 'classic thieves of each degree', visited Athens in 1809. The publication of *Childe Harold* turned the spotlight on 'this fated soil'. Fifteen years later the poet died, admittedly somewhat disillusioned, in the cause of Greek freedom. His example impressed all Europe. Adventurers and philhellenes hastened to enlist in the Greek army of liberation. The Anglo-Greek love affair had started.

Sometimes the demand for the return of the marbles to Athens grows embarrassingly insistent (the degree of insistence depending on the current state of Anglo-Greek relations). It would certainly be exciting to see the pediments of the Parthenon crown its ancient architrave once more. But when scholars of other countries refer to Lord Elgin as a kind of Nero, Alaric and Goering rolled into one, one is tempted to ask: what about the Aeginatan marbles acquired by Crown Prince Ludwig for the Glyptothek in Munich? What about the Venus de Milo and Victory of Samothrace, long among the chief glories of the Louvre? The French archaeologists

5. Demetrios Sicilianos, *loc. cit.*

neither paid for the statues nor obtained the permission of the (by then) Greek Government to remove them.

The huge cella of the Parthenon is now open to the sky. The interior arrangement can be traced from any ground plan: first (east to west), the pronaos, an outer porch, then the naos, the inner shrine housing Phidias' great chryselephantine statue of Athena, over 40 feet high and adorned with precious stones – probably as garish as it was awesome in the sombre glow of the sacred chamber; then the Parthenon proper, the chamber of the goddess's virgin priestesses, where the treasure and bullion were kept (a nice juxtaposition of religion and finance); finally the *opisthodomos*, a back chamber corresponding to the pronaos.

In the fifth century the temple was converted into a Christian basilica consecrated to the Mother of God (traces of painting are discernible on the interior north-west wall) and Phidias' statue of the goddess was removed to Constantinople. At the conclusion of the victorious wars against the Bulgars in the eleventh century, the Emperor Basil II, after ordering the blinding of fourteen thousand prisoners, paid Athens a royal visit. It was a conspicuous honour, for the city had long been assigned to the provincial scrap-heap. For the first time in centuries a solemn procession – very different from the Panathenaic, with its profoundly human quality and natural spontaneity – wound through the Propylaea to the Parthenon. The imperial cortège was met by dishevelled priests chanting sonorous flatteries of the Emperor and hackneyed clichés about the city's ancient glories. Surrounded by a bodyguard of flaxen-haired giants from Norway and Britain, the warrior-Emperor must have struck the open-mouthed provincials as a bizarre figure – a stocky powerful-limbed Macedonian who suffered from trichosis, his crown, surmounted by a gold cross, tied under the chin by a chain of diamonds. A chasuble glittering with gold and gems covered his long white tunic, from under whose hem peeped the imperial red buskins. Behind him trailed the ritualistic Byzantine court: prelates in gorgeous vestments and bearded courtiers in purple and scarlet uniforms embroidered with gold thread. The Emperor was sufficiently impressed by the Church of the Mother of God to enrich it with a golden dove, hung above the altar, and a gold-wrought lamp whose flame was never extinguished.

After the Frankish conquest of the Levant in 1204, the Parthenon became a Latin church. Two and a half centuries later, after the fall of Constantinople, Athens was visited by the conqueror, Sultan Mehmet II, whose delicate parrot-like features are so subtly reproduced in the portrait by Gentile Bellini, now in the National Gallery (Knolles says his nose was 'so high and crooked, that it almost touched his upper lip'[6]). A cruel, fastidious and intelligent man, student of history and master of five languages, he set a standard of religious toleration in mainland Greece that was maintained – with only sporadic intervals of retaliatory persecution – throughout the Turkish occupation. But he could not resist converting the Parthenon into a mosque, to which a minaret was added. As such it remained until the Morosini explosion, only to suffer further damage during the War of Independence. It was not until 1930 that the restoration of the north colonnade, with the drums, capitals and fragments of architrave left lying about since the seventeenth century, was completed by Greek archaeologists. Thus, in spite of siege, pillage and desecration, the bare bones of Pericles' brain-child, with its honey-coloured columns and the matchless subtlety of its proportions, have survived the vicissitudes of centuries.

The view from the Parthenon embraces the whole Attic plain. It is most spectacular at sunset, when the famous violet light spreads across the bare slopes of Hymettus and for one miraculous moment is reflected in the buildings of the entire city. In summer the Acropolis is open for four successive nights during the full moon period. Figures stumble about between pools of light reflected from marble slabs and fluted drums strewn around the stylobate. Others move stealthily amid the shadows of the colonnades. Gone, alas, are the owls, sacred to the goddess, whose hooting disturbed the slumbers of Lysistrata's friends when the women of Athens seized the Acropolis, barricaded themselves within and refused all further intercourse with their husbands until the Peloponnesian War was ended.[7]

From the east front of the Parthenon you descend to the **Acropolis Museum**, a unique showcase of Archaic sculpture of

6. Richard Knolles, *The General Historie of the Turkes*, Adam Islip, 1638.
7. Aristophanes, The *Lysistrata*.

the seventh, sixth and early fifth centuries B.C. All the exhibits
were found on the Acropolis. In Archaic sculpture – at first
breathtaking, even disconcerting – the males, generally
youths, are nude (a fact attributed to the importance attached
to athleticism since the establishment of the Olympic Games
in the eighth century B.C.), whereas the females are fully
clothed, for it is not until Hellenistic times that Eastern influences cause Greek modesty with regard to the nude female
figure to be swept away in a wave of sensuous opulence. All
Archaic statues, male and female, from the earliest to the
latest, are, whether pleasing in a conventional sense or not,
based on the Greek concept of perfection in shape. Geometry is allied to plasticity. Nevertheless the figures represent
living beings, and a voice seems to speak through the inscription on their pedestals, telling one who they are and who
created them. The kouroi, narrow-waisted youths exulting in
their beauty and athletic prowess, stand rigid, left leg slightly
forward, head and neck very erect. The oblique eyes protrude
and a faintly mocking smile, hinting at a quiet sophisticated
sense of humour, plays about the full sensual lips. In spite of
the ritualistic stiffness of the figures, reminiscent of Egyptian
models, they are, in the words of Sir Kenneth Clark, 'alert and
confident members of a conquering race'. But the best kouroi
are in the National Museum (see pp. 76-77). It is the
reed-like maidens, the korai, presented as votive offerings to
the goddess, that exercise the greatest fascination in the
Acropolis Museum. In their main attributes they differ little
from the kouroi, except that they are fully and stylishly
dressed, and the arrangement of their hair is extremely
elaborate. The korai represent fashionable young women of
Athenian society in the aristocratic age of the Peisistratae,
clad in a skin-tight tunic, the chiton, and a frequently jewelled
mantle, the himation, which falls in symmetrical pleated
folds in front of the breast. In spite of variations in size (most
korai are about three quarters life-size), hair style and details
of drapery, one is struck by the prevailing conformity.

In the entrance hall a large marble effigy of Athena's owl
(No. 1347) establishes the goddess's symbolical authority. To
the left, a charming fourth century B.C. bas-relief (No. 1338)
depicts eight male figures preparing to perform a Pyrrhic
dance. Room I contains part of a seventh century B.C.

pediment (the earliest extant one in Greece) from a small treasury, subsequently destroyed. Executed in painted tufa (traces of red, green and black), it represents the struggle of Heracles with the Hydra, whose innumerable coils are fashioned like octopus tentacles. In Room II the impact really begins to be felt. Fragments of a large primitive pediment from the original temple of Athena (sixth century B.C.) depict Heracles slaying Triton, while a friend of Triton's, a monster with three winged bodies (No. 35), looks on. The composition – what remains of it – is full of vitality, the expression of the three faces one of grotesque whimsicality. The **Moscophorus** or Calf-Bearer (No. 624), representing a man bearing a sacrificial calf to the goddess, is a far more evolved work of art. The austere geometric lines of the man's figure are softened by the gentle, even affectionate, manner in which he carries the calf slung round his shoulders. His locks fall parallel to the calf's hind legs, with the animal's tail extended down his left arm; the muzzle is on the same level as the man's half-smiling lips. The integration between man and beast is complete. The best preserved of four exquisitely carved little archaic horses (**No. 575**) are the two central ones, who turn their heads towards each other, as though engaged – somewhat shyly – in social conversation. Fragments from the early temple of Athena destroyed by the Persians are among the chief exhibits in Room III.

But the greatest enchantments are reserved for Room IV. First comes the **Rider** (No. 590), which formed part of a small equestrian composition, believed to be the work of Phaidimos, greatest of Archaic sculptors. The head is a cast from the original in the Louvre; none the less its charm and liveliness, with the almond-shaped eyes and firm expressive lips set in the familiar teasing smile, make it one of the most attractive in the museum. Particularly decorative are the elaborate bead-like curls across the forehead and the long locks, strung like corals, hanging behind the large ears. But it is the monolithic upward thrust of the torso from the wasp's waist that is most impressive: a perfect achievement of grace and naturalness, in spite of the absence of movement. In the same room are the korai, ranged in a circle on pedestals: formal, architectonic in conception, often haughty, always amused. A world of

aristocratic ease, poise and serenity, destined to perish forever
in the holocaust of the Persian Wars. No. 679, the **Peplos
Koré** (so-called because she is wearing a heavy woollen *peplos*
over her chiton), her bosom framed between parallel plaits of
hair, is a masterpiece of sixth century B.C. Attic sculpture,
also probably the work of Phaidimos. The body, true, is
block-like (in the lower part flat in front and round at the
back), but the head is both authoritative and refined, the
modelling miraculously rounded, the expression cynical, yet
full of a kind of detached felicity. Among her companions,
none are more elegant than **No. 685**, with her exquisitely
formalised drapery, and **Nos. 670, 674, 675, 682.** Fascinating
examples of the Archaic sculptor's genius for animal portraiture are found in the Phaidimos **Running Hound** (No. 143),
a taut sleek creature pursuing its prey, and the little horse
(**No. 700**) – only a fragment of the rider's leg remains – which
has an air of self-assurance no less arrogant than that of the
young scions of the nobility.

Room V is dominated by a larger than life-size koré
(No. 681), as formidable as her sisters in Room IV are
diminutive, and by fragments of a pediment from an older
temple (No. 631) depicting gods and goddesses victorious
over fallen giants in a *gigantomachia*. Showcases in the alcove
contain bases and heads of small statuettes, of which the most
beautiful are those of a bearded man (No. 621) and a gently
ironical koré (No. 641). Passing into Room VI one is suddenly
conscious of a change, a break with the past. We are in the
fifth century. The mocking smile has vanished, and emotion
is reflected in pensive expressions and relaxed attitudes. The
change of mood is most striking in the **Kritios Boy** (No. 698),
a perfect reproduction of the human body, its weight evenly
and naturally distributed. An effortless poise has replaced the
taut formality of the strictly frontal position. But in the
sweeping away of rigid class distinctions, which followed the
fall of the Peisistratae, the Kritios Boy seems to have lost his
sense of humour. A small plaque in low relief (No. 695)
represents a **Mourning Athena**. Emotion has broken through,
and the limbs have grown supple in the process. Again there
is the new distribution of weight, the goddess's body being
slightly tilted forward, leaning on her spear; only the toes and
ball of the left foot touch the ground. No. 689, the **Blond Boy,**

is a typical classical Greek head; a serious-minded youth, not unengaging, rather given to contemplation.

In Room VII there is a well preserved metope (No. 705) from the Parthenon, portraying a struggle between a Centaur and a Lapith woman (remarkable for the modelling of her body in the round) and two fine heads of horses (No. 882) from the Chariot of Poseidon which formed part of the sculptural decoration of the west pediment of the Parthenon. Room VIII is dominated by **fragments from the Parthenon frieze**, stunning examples (notice how shallow the relief is) of crowds in motion, full of dash, energy and liveliness. Here the procession consists of sacrificial bulls (No. 857), young horse-men (Nos. 862, 867, 868), water-carriers (No. 864), a group of Olympians (No. 856), Poseidon, Apollo and a rather buxom Artemis, debating some point of divine importance. **No. 973** (relief from the balustrade of the Temple of Niké Apteros) depicts a maiden removing her sandal. Although her chiton is so thin that the contours of the flesh stand out firm and rounded, deep shadows lurk mysteriously in the folds of the loosely flowing drapery. Finally, in Room IX there is a fourth century B.C. head of Alexander the Great (No. 1331), sensuous, full-lipped, conventionally handsome, and a fragment of a relief depicting a serene authoritative Niké crowning Heracles, while Athena looks on benignly.

From the museum one follows the line of the north-east rampart, past a belvedere overhanging a steep incline once cluttered with mean little medieval houses grouped round the blue-domed twelfth century Church of St Nicholas Rhangabes. Westward, below the walls of Themistocles, extend central Athens and the northern periphery. Beside one rises the **Erectheum**: for some, the supreme moment on the Acropolis.

The temple, completed during the later years of the Peloponnesian War, occupies the site of the holiest place on the Acropolis (by one of those ironical quirks of history, it was in this sanctuary of a virgin goddess that centuries later a Turkish governor lodged his harem). Its origins go back to the beginnings of Attic religion. This is the spot where Athena brought forth the olive tree in her contest with Poseidon for the possession of the city. Here was venerated the ancient olive wood statue of Athena Polias, which fell from heaven, and on which the holy *peplos* was draped at the end of the

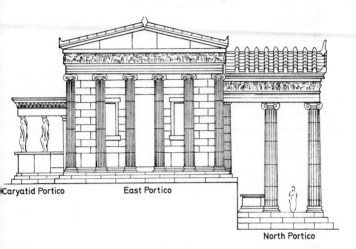

Caryatid Portico   East Portico   North Portico

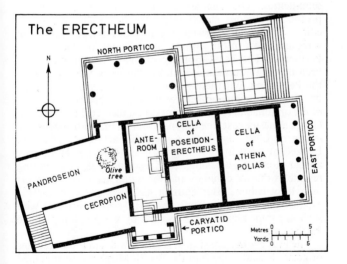

The ERECTHEUM

N

NORTH PORTICO

PANDROSEION

Olive tree

CECROPION

ANTE-ROOM

CELLA of POSEIDON-ERECTHEUS

CELLA of ATHENA POLIAS

EAST PORTICO

CARYATID PORTICO

Metres 0   5
Yards 0   5

Panathenaic procession. Beside it stood a bronze palm tree that touched the roof. The temple is also associated with the cult of the earliest Attic heroes: Cecrops and Erectheus, the sight of whose snake-like feet, when revealed to Cecrops' daughters, filled them with such horror that they went mad and cast themselves over the walls of the Acropolis.

The Erectheum is situated on lower ground than the Parthenon, and its complexity is in sharp contrast to the monolithic grandeur of the larger temple. Built on different levels, on the foundations of the edifice destroyed by the Persians, it had no side colonnades but three porticoes different in size, style and execution. From every angle the spectator obtains a different view: startling, novel, sometimes confusing. The side opposite the Parthenon consists of a blank wall of marble courses, broken at the west end by the **Caryatid Portico**; it is the least attractive, for the architect, probably Mnesicles, had to cope with a sloping site and the inclusion of three separate shrines – those of Athena Polias, Poseidon and Erectheus – the Pandroseion, which contained the ancient olive tree planted by the goddess, as well as altars of other semi-deities. The temple served several purposes, all of profound religious significance. Architecturally, the whole edifice, it has been suggested, was intended as a counterweight – more modest in dimensions and different in style – to the Parthenon. The heavy drapery of the Caryatids may have been meant to harmonise with the fluting of the columns of the Parthenon, but these six hefty maidens, in spite of their brave self-conscious simper, seem to be crushed by the weight of the ornamental roof they support on their cushioned heads. One is a plaster cast, the original being in the British Museum – one of Lord Elgin's least justifiable acts of 'vandalism'. Looked at from a crouching position (from the east), they appear more majestic, silhouetted against the sky, the spacing resembles that of columns and the porch acquires the aspect of a lofty tribune. But nothing really compensates for the expanse of blank wall from which the portico projects with such apparent aimlessness, dwarfed by the proximity of the Parthenon.

The **East Portico** consists of six narrow fluted Ionic columns of great elegance (one is in the British Museum), surmounted by elaborate capitals, the necks of which have a beaded moulding and palmette frieze, followed by an egg and tongue moulding and crowned by an echinus, or cushion, adorned with beads and flutings. Approaching the entrance, the spectator would have had side views of the Caryatid and North Porticoes which broke up the symmetry but not the harmony of the edifice. It is not, however, until one has descended a flight of steps and reached the **North Portico**, through which the chamber of Erectheus was probably reached, that one receives the full impact of this unique and anomalous building perched above the sprawling city, with the long line of Mt Parnes forming a bluish-grey barrier in the north. The portico, although built on a lower level than the other two porches, gives a greater impression of thrust and delicacy, and, both in its proportions and adornment, may be considered one of the most perfect examples of classical architecture. The six Ionic columns (four in front, two on either side) have a slight *entasis* and their bases are embellished with plaited decoration. The beautifully carved capitals, also extremely ornate, are no less elegant. The ceiling is studded with coffers, from which bronze and gilt rosettes once hung (the holes from which they were suspended are still visible), between parallel lines of egg and spoon enrichment. The great doorway, familiar from innumerable replicas, is narrower at the top and has a lavishly ornamented frame. An opening in the floor of the portico reveals a vault in which holes have been bored in the rock: the marks, according to the legend, left by Poseidon's trident when he struck the earth and the sea gushed forth in the course of his contest with Athena. The vault communicated with a crypt under the cella, where the sacred serpent of the goddess dwelt in the Sea of Erectheus, and which was remarkable, says Pausanias, 'for the noise of waves it sends forth when a south wind blows'. During the Turkish occupation it was converted into one of the compartments of the governor's harem, the vault being used as a latrine. The four half-columns on the west wall, between the North and Caryatid porticoes, are a Roman restoration.

One now passes through the Propylaea and descends into the ancient part of the town around the Acropolis. On the right rises the grey flat-topped rock of the **Areopagus**. Here sat the oldest court of justice in the world, first summoned by the gods to judge Orestes for the crime of matricide. At the north-east base there is a fissure that once led to the 'chambers in the rock, lit by the holy torches' of the sanctuary of the Eumenides, whose loathsome attentions drove Orestes, still bespattered with Clytemnestra's blood, from the Lion Gate of Mycenae to the Athenian citadel, where a merciful if somewhat quibbling Athena secured his release by 'Holy Persuasion' of the court.[8] Here, too, Demosthenes was judged for bribery and St Paul addressed the people of Athens on the 'Unknown God'. They gave the apostle a polite but lukewarm reception. Only Dionysius the Areopagite, an erudite councillor, future patron saint of Athens, took up the Christian cause with sufficient fervour to suffer martyrdom. To the south-west, beyond a stretch of ground studded with Aleppo pines, cedars and cypresses, rises the eminence of the **Pnyx**. A rock-hewn platform, about twenty feet high, situated on a semi-circular terrace of the north-east slope, supported by a wall of polygonal blocks, has been identified as the celebrated *Bema*, the tribune from which generations of orators addressed the assembly of the people of Athens in the shadow of the temples of the Acropolis. Nightly performances of *Son et Lumière* (Greek, English and French versions), with splendid floodlighting effects on the Acropolis, are held on the Pnyx throughout the summer.

The road then skirts the north-west bastion of the Acropolis and plunges into the maze of the Plaka – 'old Athens', once gay and picturesque, now full of tourists and brash nightclubs. But it is less confusing to explore the Plaka, the adjacent area of the Agora and the other monuments of the 'City of Theseus' by taking a completely different route, starting from Syntagma Square again.

8.   Aeschylus, The *Eumenides*.

CHAPTER TWO

Athens: 'The City of Theseus'

✤

The 'Little Cathedral' – The Plaka – The Tower of the Winds –
The Roman Agora – Hadrian's Library – Monastiraki – The
Cerameicus – The Agora and Stoa of Attalus – The Theseum –
The Kapnikarea Church

A QUARTER of small shops, offices and churches, dotted with little enclaves of classical ruins, skirts the north slope of the Acropolis. It takes two days to see it all. It is best to walk. Buses are not always conveniently routed, and the distances are short. Taxis are cheap and plentiful.

From Syntagma Square Metropoleos Street descends – much of Athens is built on different undulating levels – into a large square of the same name, where the official Cathedral, constructed with materials plundered from seventy Byzantine chapels, raises its ugly nineteenth century façade. Beside it, somewhat dwarfed, rests the **'Little Cathedral'**, or Panayia Gorgoepicöos (The Virgin who grants requests quickly), a gem of Byzantine church architecture of the twelfth century, whose modest proportions (24 by 36 feet) indicate the humble status held by Athens in the Byzantine world at a time when the Empire's fortunes were at their peak. In style it is cruciform and domed, the drum is slender and elegant, and the exterior walls, which have a glowing ivory-smooth patina, are studded with marble plaques ornamented with crosses, lions, griffons and ox-heads that betray an orientalising influence, probably of Hellenistic origin. On the west front the quaint but charming fourth century B.C. frieze, pilfered from some ancient monument, tells the story of the twelve months of the year, represented by the signs of the zodiac, and the feasts appropriate to them. The decoration is a dotty historical jumble – something that one encounters again and again in Greece – with its ancient steles, Corinthian capitals and Byzantine crosses, to which the coats-of-arms of the Villehardouin and de la Roche families have been added – a reminder of that often forgotten period of Frankish rule, when Athens was governed by the Crusaders and their Latin descendants. Under the de la Roche dynasty Athens enjoyed a brief period of prosperity; but there was little assimilation of ideas or peoples. The French made no positive contribution to the life of the town and there is no record of the construction of a single important church or public building. After them came Catalan bands and Florentine bankers who proved to be even more unpopular masters. The whole of this period of Latin rule lacks verisimilitude. The feudal courts and knightly jousts, the jesters, minstrels, falconers – all the paraphernalia of Western medieval society – seems so out of place and character in the crystalline air of Attica, with its barren limestone hills and ruined pagan sanctuaries.

Metropoleos Square is the best place from which to watch the Epitaphios (Good Friday Procession), when the bier of Christ, heaped with flowers, is borne through the streets at night. The procession is led by the Archbishop of Athens and all Greece, followed by church dignitaries in tall cylindrical hats, flanked by acolytes in red and purple shifts tottering under the weight of enormous banners. Sometimes there are girls in white, like vestal virgins, scattering rose petals in the path of cabinet ministers and detachments of the armed forces. The procession is followed by a shuffling crowd of worshippers, hands cupped round lighted candles. Military bands crash out the funeral march from the *Eroica*. Everywhere there is a smell of stocks and incense. The Epitaphios has one point in common with the Panathenaic procession – the people are part of the procession, not just spectators. The same approach, the same 'mystic union', occurs repeatedly in Greek folklore, which preserves many pagan traditions intact in terms of Christian Orthodoxy.

At the southern end of the square P. Benizelou Street leads into Adrianou Street, the 'aristocratic' quarter of Athens in the eighteenth and early nineteenth centuries, now a maze of cobblers, butchers and undertakers. No. 90 was once the Turkish law-court. George Finlay, author of the monumental *History of Greece from its Conquest by the Romans to the Present Time*, lived with his notoriously ugly Armenian wife in No. 122. Finlay came to Greece in 1823 and stayed with

The 'Little Cathedral' — a gem of Byzantine church architecture whose modest proportions indicate the humble status held by Athens in the Byzantine world.

The Tower of the Winds or Horologium of Andronicus Cyrrhestes is an architectural fantasy created by a philhellenic Syrian of the 1st century A.D. (pp. 53–54).

Byron at Misolonghi. After the War of Independence he was *The Times* correspondent in Athens, where he remained until his death. The house, obviously re-faced, now consists of several shoddy little shops, a dentist's surgery and tax-collector's office. Although the growing pains of a nation just emerging from four hundred years of Turkish servitude did not always arouse Finlay's sympathy, the last two volumes of his *History* (a literary masterpiece), devoted to the War of Independence and its turbulent political aftermath, remain the standard work on the subject in English.

It was in this quarter, below the North Portico of the Erectheum, surrounded by mosques from whose minarets the muezzin called the faithful to prayer, that Caroline, Princess of Wales, driven out of England by her husband's unconjugal behaviour, stayed in 1816 in a house now demolished (between Adrianou and Kyrrestou Streets). Her charitable acts won the affection of the Athenians; she was elected a member of the Society of Friends of the Muses and a medal bearing the head of Athena was struck in her honour. She went sightseeing and visited M. Fauvel, the amiable French Consul, who acted as guide to distinguished visitors (Chateaubriand and Byron owed much of their knowledge of Athens and Attica to his hospitality, scholarship and familiarity with local topography). But for all their aristocratic associations, the houses in Adrianou Street were never distinguished for their interior decoration. Their furniture and ornaments were drab and tasteless. In other parts of Greece the minor arts of embroidery and woodcarving flourished during the Turkish occupation. Not so in Athens. Folklore traditions, so tenacious elsewhere, were unknown here. It was 'village' life *par excellence*. The whole area, though lively, still retains a provincial atmosphere.

At the corner of the Demotic School (neo-classical facade) one turns into Phlessa Street, This is the beginning of the Plaka proper, its steep alleys, which have the most evocative names in the world, criss-crossing the north slope of the Acropolis: Thrasybulus Street, Myron Street, Epaminondas Street, Pelopidas Street, Dioscuri Street, Erectheus Street, Aphrodite Street. But the whole quarter now seems to be earmarked for nocturnal pleasure and the tourist trade. In spite of the garish dolled-up quaintness – smoky bars, shoddy night-clubs and 'arty' tourist shops, with a mass of bogus folklore thrown in – there are still some enchanting spots. Take the tavernas first. These are a very Greek institution, and the ones in the Plaka are among the most popular, though not the best. Greeks do not go to tavernas only to eat and drink; but to indulge in *kephi*, which means to sing and shout and make a great deal of noise; and they expect other people to do so too. Sometimes there are itinerant guitarists. The most popular drink is *retsina*, a white wine to which resin, the glutinous secretion of pine trunks, has been added. To some it is an acquired taste: dry, astringent, with a slight flavour of turpentine. A convivial party is not unlikely to send a brimming carafe (or copper mug) to a table of complete strangers: all the more reason to do so – this is very Greek – if they are foreigners. At all costs the foreigner must be fêted; and in return the Greek flattered. The foreigner must be left in no doubt that Greeks are the best people in the world; and he is expected to say so – fulsomely.

The food consists of *taramosalata* (fish-roe paste), *souvlakia* (pieces of pork or beef grilled on a skewer), stuffed spleen, *kokkoretsi* (chopped liver and sweetbreads twined in guts, highly seasoned with garlic and roasted on the spit), the ubiquitous *feta* (a white, sometimes flaky, goat's milk cheese, which tastes better when sprinkled with pepper, doused in olive oil and served as an hors d'œuvre) and the inevitable tomato salad (in winter replaced by finely chopped cabbage). At the more sophisticated tavernas the food is on more international lines. Among the bottled wines, Boutari red is good by any standard, St Helena white as near to a Chablis as anything in Greece. Some prefer Pallini. Demestica (red and white) is cheap and good. Tavernas, with a few exceptions, are only open at night. The more pretentious ones – 'cosmic' ('social') tavernas, they are called – sometimes have the defects without the qualities of the humbler ones: the noise without the friendliness, and a wider variety of dishes served tepid and invariably garnished with tinned peas and diced carrots. Some of them have floor-shows and dancing.

At the end of Phlessa Street, past the 'cosmic' taverna of Palaia Athena, Erotocritos Street begins. The houses could not be smaller, the alleys narrower. Everything is in miniature. It is like a film set for some Greek island scene. At the top of the rise, Erotocritos Street swerves right and, past the Byzantine chapel of St John the Divine (eleventh–twelfth century), one enters a shady little terrace outside the tavernas of Psathas and Attalus. This is an enchanting place – remarkably peaceful in the daytime – which not even the twang of electric guitars and the hum of polyglot voices can wholly desecrate. The houses are painted with washes of ochre, dove-grey and Siena red; the shutters are green or blue. The narrow tiled courtyards are filled with pots (or whitewashed kerosene tins) of fuchsias, hibiscus and geraniums. From the taverna of Erotocritos ('cosmic') a rough path leads up to O Yeros tou Mouria (The Old Man of the Morea), one of the most popular tavernas in the Plaka. Above towers the floodlit North Portico of the Erectheum; a stream of strollers shuffles up and down a flight of steep worn steps. All round are the roof gardens of more tavernas (very 'cosmic'), their garlands of coloured lamps festooning the night sky.

From this point the steps of Mnesicles Street lead into Prytaneion Street, at the end of which (left) appear the blue domes of the Church of Ayios Nikolaos (St Nicholas) Rhangabes: twelfth century, but so much restored as to retain little of its original antiquity. Above the church a tall building with a glass frontage is the taverna of Tou Vlachou, which commands a superb view of the 'City of Hadrian' and its monuments, with the floodlit pine-fringed summit of Lycabettus crowning successive layers of apartment blocks.

From Prytaneion Street I like to descend into the sunken garden of the Church of Ayioi Anarghyroi (SS Cosmas and Damian), the Arabian twins, patron saints of medicine and surgery, martyred by Diocletian. One of their most famous exploits was the grafting of the limb of a dead Negro on the stump of a white man whose gangrenous leg they had just amputated. The patient henceforth walked with one white and one black leg. The saints are called the *anarghyroi*, the 'silverless ones', because they refused to accept a fee for their cures. The most expensive gynaecological clinic in Athens is now dedicated to their memory. The whitewashed church, to which a porch with four marble columns has been added, was built at the beginning of the Turkish occupation in the form of a single-nave basilica. Among the many scourges endured by the Greeks under Ottoman rule, religious persecution was not one, and George Wheler, the English traveller, counted as many as two hundred churches in and around Athens in the seventeenth century. This show of religious toleration was offset, however, by the cruel institution of a forced levy of Christian boys. The *tournatzimbashi*, generally an Ethiopian slave, visited Athens every four years in order to exact this human tribute, destined to swell the ranks of the Janissaries, the Sultan's *corps d'élite*. The levy, with a few exceptions, was applied throughout the Sultan's dominions. Finlay calls it a 'bold idea' to exterminate Christianity by 'educating Christian children' in the ways of the Prophet and to raise the man-power necessary to police a vast empire of subject peoples. The Sultan was probably aware that the Greeks, given proper Moslem indoctrination, would fill important posts in the military hierarchy and civil service more efficiently than his own less quick-witted countrymen.

The little paved garden of Ayioi Anarghyroi, with its cypresses, oleanders and aromatic shrubs, flanked by a whitewashed house with bottle-green shutters and a wooden balcony, is one of the loveliest in Athens. The feeling of remoteness is complete, the night life of the Plaka an un-reality; the only sound is the hum of bees and insects. The tall house at the end of the garden (entrance from Erectheus Street) is the residence of the Athens representative of the Holy Sepulchre. At the north end of the garden a gate leads back to Erotocritos Street and the focal point of O Yeros tou Mouria. The paradox of this constant juxtaposition of churches and nocturnal pleasure haunts is a feature of the Plaka.

One then enters Thrasybulus Street, passes the tourist shops and night-clubs, ascends the first stairway on the left and reaches the derelict shell of the Old University, screened by a large wild fig tree, scene of the first revival of cultural activity in nineteenth century Athens. The little shaded yard below the crumbling wall, where people sit drinking *retsina* and pecking at chopped-up tentacles of octopus, was once the court leading to the *magna aula* of this modest institution of higher studies. There are more tavernas in this area, where the alleys become so narrow that no wheeled traffic other than vespas and push-carts can manœuvre. From the Old University it is only a few steps up to the Church of the Metamorphosis

(Transfiguration), another charming Byzantine chapel of the fourteenth century, situated below the pines and cypresses skirting the Acropolis walls. The tiny altar is made from the capital of an ancient column. From here the road, now wider, leads round the north-west bastion of the Acropolis to the Areopagus.

For the last time one retraces one's steps to O Yeros tou Mouria and descends the stairway of Mnesicles street, past a group of rather bogus tavernas full of folklore emblems and gaudy wall-paintings, turns left into Lysius Street and, at the end of it, enters the spacious square of the Tower of the Winds, known as Oi Aeridhes (The Windy Ones). The pink- and ochre-washed houses were once the balustraded mansions of the capital's embryo bourgeoisie. The square is now a crowded car-park. A railing runs round two sides of a complex of ancient ruins. At night, when moonlit, it is one of the most romantic places in Athens.

The **Tower of the Winds**, or Horologium of Andronicus Cyrrhestes, rises beside an umbrageous plane tree in a depression below the square. West of it extends the Roman Agora. In 1676 Dr Spon of Lyons, one of the earliest Western scholars to visit Greece, recognising that the tower had no connection with the supposed tomb of Socrates, identified it as an hydraulic clock. Like the Monument of Lysicrates, this octagonal tower is an architectural fantasy, the creation of a philhellenic Syrian of the first century A.D. A bas-relief, portraying the features of the different winds, runs round the eight sides. The north wind blows on a conch, the north-east pours out hailstones from a shell, a rain-bearing southerly squall splashes water out of an urn and a zephyr from the south-west scatters flowers; the east wind bears fruit and ears of corn, and the dreaded north-westerly blast holds an upturned vase. The roof, an octagonal pyramid, was surmounted by a weather-vane in the form of a Triton. Vitruvius says that this bronze Triton held a rod in his right hand that 'He so contrived that it was driven round by the wind, and always faced the current of air, and held the rod as indicator above the representation of the wind blowing.' A small round tower against the east front served as a reservoir for the clock connected by an aqueduct with the spring of the Clepsydra on the Acropolis. The Turks converted the tower into a *tekkeh* (chapel) and for some years it was inhabited by a sect **of** dancing dervishes. The arched gateway and domed cells at the north end of the square led to the *medresse* (Turkish ecclesiastical school), demolished by the Archaeological Society in a fit of nationalist fanaticism. The passage of Diogenes Street, at the north-east end of the square, leads to a decent unpretentious taverna, the Platanos, situated in a shady court.

In the rectangle of the Roman Agora are the ruins of an Ionic peristyle with a double gallery surrounding an interior marble-paved courtyard. Traces of a building with a loggia at the south-east angle have been identified as the Agronomeion, headquarters of the market police. Two arcades run south of the Tower of the Winds. At the west end (Dioscuri Street) stands the imposing Gateway of Athena Archegetes (first century A.D.), with four heavy Doric columns surmounted by an unadorned pediment still intact. The construction of the gateway, a typical example of Greek-inspired Roman architecture, was financed by Julius Caesar and Augustus, a statue of whose adopted son, Lucius, originally crowned the pediment. The subtle refinement and upward thrust have gone, replaced by strength and grandeur. Within the excavation area there is a square brick building with multiple domes and a colonnaded porch, once the Fatih Mosque, built in commemoration of Sultan Mehmet II's entry into Athens after the fall of Constantinople, now a clearing-house for archaeological finds. Beyond the Church of the Taxiarchoi (Archangels) one enters Areos Street.

On the right rises the block of the west colonnade of Hadrian's Library, described by early travellers, with more fantasy than accuracy, as the palace of Themistocles. A single fluted Corinthian column, all that remains of the central portico, stands isolated from the smooth blackened shafts of the colonnade. The façade of the main entrance, charred by fire, is in Aiolou Street, where six Corinthian columns (two survive) supported consoles. Built by Hadrian in the second century A.D., the library possessed a courtyard surrounded by a hundred columns, a pool and garden. The rooms, according to Pausanias, 'were adorned with a gilded roof and with alabaster stone, as with statues and paintings'. All very splendid and very Roman. The library was in turn sacked, burned, converted into a Byzantine church and finally into a bazaar, which became the centre of Athenian life during the Turkish occupation. Early in the eighteenth century a Seminary of Greek Studies was established within the library precincts: the first permanent school to be founded in Athens,

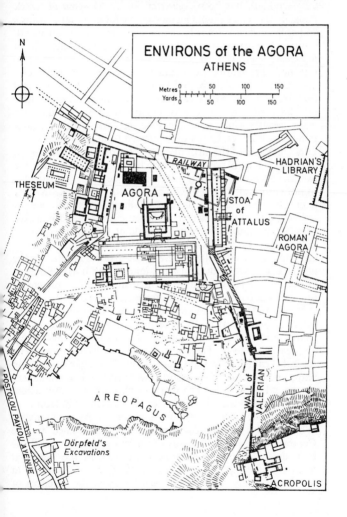

N

ENVIRONS of the AGORA
ATHENS

Metres 0   50   100   150
Yards 0   50   100   150

RAILWAY

HADRIAN'S LIBRARY

THESEUM

AGORA

STOA of ATTALUS

ROMAN AGORA

AREOPAGUS

APOSTOLOU PAVLOU AVENUE

WALL of VALERIAN

Dörpfeld's Excavations

ACROPOLIS

home of Plato's Academy and Aristotle's Lyceum, for over a thousand years. It is now the haunt of stray cats.

A Turkish mosque, the Pazar Djami, in adjoining Monastiraki Square, hub of downtown Athens (railway station and bus terminal), has been converted into a **Museum of Greek Popular Art**. The exhibits include colourful national costumes and folk jewellery (mostly of the eighteenth and nineteenth centuries). Particularly striking is the work of the Epirot *terzidhes*, specialists in needlework with gold thread, who travelled throughout the country, receiving orders for embroideries in gold decorated with designs based on regional folklore patterns. At the east end of the square, in the middle of which rises the unusually tall drum of the modernised tenth century Church of the Panayia (The Virgin), begins Pandrossou Street. Commonly referred to in English as 'Shoe Lane', because of the large display of *tsarouchia*, Turkish-style red slippers with pompons worn by peasants well into the twentieth century, the alley is full of antique shops. Too narrow to hold any traffic, it is often choked with push-carts used by fruit-sellers as a short cut. The whole place is still vaguely redolent of a Turkish bazaar. Hellenistic coins, Attic figurines, rugs, icons, embroideries are on sale at the more expensive antique shops. There is also a lot of Victoriana (opaline vases, egg-cups, etc.) and filigree silverware from Yannina in the north. Prices are high, and bargaining is the norm. Between Greek and Greek it acquires a ritualistic quality. One envies the professionalism and, often, the effectiveness of it.

Right of Monastiraki railway station, Iphaistiou Street, a humble counterpart of Pandrossou, forms part of the blacksmiths' and coppersmiths' quarter. The shops are full of brass and leather objects. There are also some antique shops. The second turning to the right leads to the flea-market, where tin baths and an amorphous assortment of rusty metal appliances are on sale. From the flea-market one rejoins Ermou Street and proceeds west, with a view of the gas-works in front.

Beyond the restored Byzantine chapel of Ayioi Asomatoi (The Saintly Incorporeal Ones) lies the entrance to the **Cerameicus**, a vast necropolis of ancient tombstones. All the best stelae (marble gravestones) are now in the National Museum (see pp. 78-79). The cemetery was destroyed in the first century B.C. when Sulla breached the defences of beleaguered Athens, with, says Plutarch, 'all the terrors of trumpets and cornets sounding'. From here the Roman legions poured into the city, 'let loose to spoil and slaughter, and scouring the streets with swords drawn'. Nevertheless the level of the ground continued to be raised by the super-imposition of more sepulchres. It is now a jumble of broken stelae on different levels, with fosses, corresponding to the ancient alleys, cleaving through the earthworks. The remaining stelae line the right bank of the Alley of the Tombs which begins at the Piraeos Street entrance (now closed): a funeral banquet (bas-relief of Charon); a lion; a bull; a farewell scene (Monument of Korallion); and a replica of the splendid **Monument of Dexileos** (now in the adjoining museum), depicting a young rider overwhelming his foe in a battle against the Corinthians. Class distinctions are preserved, and the graves of slaves are marked by truncated columns. Loutrophoroi (slender black pitchers with two handles), reserved for bachelors, litter the banks of the fosse. A simple and beautiful relief of a maiden bearing a lustral vase crowns the site of the shrine of Hecate. All the graves contained vases mixed with ashes of birds and domestic animals.

Wandering through this ancient necropolis, where the funeral orations of Pericles, Demosthenes, Hyperides and other celebrities were delivered, I am reminded of another cemetery – the Alpha cemetery, its marble tombstones gleaming among cypress alleys bordered with myrtle and plumbago, on the hill above the by-pass to the sea. Here, too, great monuments of Pentelic marble are raised to the memory of poets, statesmen, shipowners. The continuity is obvious. Many of the mausoleums are embellished with realistic sculptures by Chalepas, a fashionable early twentieth century sculptor: marble representations of frock-coated gentlemen and Victorian grandmothers wearing lace caps seated rigidly on wrought-iron chairs, or curly-headed children in what were obviously velvet suits, looking like petrified little Lord Fauntleroys, brooding wistfully over their mortal remains. Sometimes, through the latticed shade, you catch a glimpse of a priest in a tall pill-box hat shuffling in front of a funeral cortège led by undertakers in black suits bearing purple banners.

Besides the Monument of Dexileos, the little museum of the

Cerameicus possesses a collection of Attic vases, figurines and terracotta objects (there is no catalogue): a beast of burden carrying a load of four jars, a round work-basket (?) with a design of swastikas surmounted by four geometric horses, a water jug in the shape of a ship's hull; among the larger objects, a headless rider and a perky Archaic sphinx.

The vestiges of walls at the north-east end of the precinct are those of the Sacred Gate, through which pilgrims bound for the Eleusinian Mysteries passed out of the city, and of the Dipylon, a court closed by a double gate between two square towers, from which the Panathenaic procession started, and was wide enough to allow the passage of two chariots simultaneously. All traffic, entering and leaving the city, had to pass through the Dipylon. A *dromos* (public way) lined with porticoes connected it with the Agora. The Pompeum (only traces of cuttings for doors and marks left by chariot wheels survive), where all the props for the Panathenaic procession were stored, was situated between the Dipylon and Sacred Gates.

On the way back turn right at Monastiraki Square into Areos Street; right again, opposite the west colonnade of Hadrian's Library into Adrianou Street. Crossing the road over the electric railway, you then enter the **agora.** It would be a mistake to expect any of the splendour, complexity or visible ruins of the Roman Forum. One's first impression is of a vast bombed site. This ancient market place, once the social, commercial and administrative hub of Athens, where business was transacted, legislation passed and gossip exchanged, lies in a hollow, littered with ruined fortifications, eroded plinths and truncated columns: a legacy of desolation left by the Heruli, a northern tribe associated with the earliest Gothic invasions.

The pathway follows the route of the Panathenaic procession. On the right rise three giant statues of Tritons with elaborate fish-tails on plinths ornamented with olive branches. This Stoa of the Giants – they were originally six – faced the odeum of the second century A.D. (the orchestra and proscenium are easily identified). The route followed by the Panathenaic procession then reached the vast **Stoa of Attalus,** now entirely rebuilt of Pentelic marble, Piraeus limestone and local clay tiles: the work of the American School of Classical

Studies. The original stoa was commissioned in the second century B.C. by Attalus, a philhellenic king of Pergamum, who founded cities, encouraged the arts and sciences and invented a new kind of embroidery with gold thread. Although destroyed in the Herulian sack, much of the original masonry and materials remained *in situ* and were used in the reconstruction, completed in 1956. The stoa consists of two superimposed colonnades of one hundred and thirty-four columns, the lower Doric, the upper Ionic (Pergamum style). The marbles have not yet acquired the patina of age, and there is a glossy newness about the edifice. But it is a prodigious achievement, and the cool spacious colonnades, once thronged with merchants, travellers and shop-window gazers, are an authentic replica of a market hall towards the end of the Hellenistic era, when Athens, no longer haunted by dreams of imperial expansion, still remained a city of fashion and learning. The sculptures discovered in the course of successive excavations are exhibited in chambers, corresponding to the ancient shops, adjoining the colonnade. They include a colossal headless Apollo of the fourth century B.C. (unnumbered; north end of colonnade, ground floor), a Hellenistic Aphrodite with a headless Eros perched on her shoulder (No. S473), a small but athletic Winged Victory (unnumbered; north end of colonnade, ground floor), a bronze shield (No. B262) captured by the Athenians from the Spartans during the Peloponnesian War, a statue base of the *Iliad* (No. I1628) with an inscription that begins 'I am the Iliad, who lived before and after Homer . . .', a mechanical device called the Cleroterion (No. I3967) for the assignment of public duties by lot, as well as vases, inscriptions, figurines and sherds of different periods. Case 28 contains a collection of *ostraka*, or ostracising sherds, on which members of the Assembly wrote the names of public figures (including Aristides and Themistocles) whom they wished to banish from Athens.

Proceeding clockwise from the Stoa, one passes foundations of public buildings: the Library of Pantainus, which was also lined with shops, on the Panathenaic route (the restored eleventh century Church of Ayioi Apostoloi, slightly to the south of the Library, contains indifferent wall paintings); the central stoa, a milestone bearing the inscription, 'I am the boundary of the agora'; the Tholos, a circular fifth century

B.C. edifice, where dwelt fifty magistrates who constituted a permanent commission to the Senate; the fifth century B.C. Bouleuterion (Senate); and the Metroön, which housed the state archives. A headless statue of Hadrian faces the stylobate of the Metroön. At this point a path ascends to the Theseum which dominates the Agora from a terrace laid out with flowerbeds. Myrtle and pomegranates grow in large clay pots: replicas of ancient vessels found in hollows cut out of the neighbouring rock, once watered by artificial streams whose source was on the Pnyx. The temple is not, of course, a temple of Theseus at all. The origin of the misnomer lies in the fact that the metopes depict the exploits of the Attic hero. It was, in all likelihood, a temple of Hephaestus, god of forges, and the whole vicinity was inhabited by blacksmiths. The din of coppersmiths' workshops in Iphaistiou Street still echoes across this working-class quarter. The tombstone in the north wall is that of an Englishman, for whom Byron wrote an epitaph in Latin, buried here in the early nineteenth century, when the temple was used as a cemetery for foreign travellers.

The temple, of the Doric order, the first in Greece to be built entirely of marble, is dated to the mid-fifth century B.C. (just prior to the Parthenon) and was one of the earliest attempts to restore the monuments destroyed during the Persian invasion. Bronze statues of Hephaestus and Athena Hephaestia, patron gods of industrial workers, adorned the cella. It has thirty-eight columns (six instead of the usual eight on either front) with a pronounced convexity in the shaft. Of the remaining eighteen metopes, ten (east front) represent the exploits of Heracles and eight (north and south) those of Theseus. The pronaos frieze, which is very mutilated, depicts a battle (unidentified) watched by six Olympian deities. Painted decoration is discernible on the palmettes and meander pattern mouldings of the peristyle. The vaulted roof of the interior dates from the fifth century A.D., when the temple, like so many others, was converted into a Byzantine church. Although the best preserved classical temple in Greece, the Theseum is not the most inspiring. The plain Doric style, so supremely effective in Ictinus' monumental plan of the Parthenon, loses much of its vitality in the smaller edifice, one of its worst faults being, in the opinion of a contemporary scholar, 'its unprecedented high entablature . . .

with unduly slim columns'.[1] An air of stockiness, deprived of grace and dominance, prevails. Osbert Lancaster finds 'it produces less effect than many a Doric corn-exchange in an English provincial town'.[2] Its position, lying in a trough between the Acropolis and the western hills, may also account for its lack of an air of authority. Nevertheless, when seen from the upper gallery of the Stoa of Attalus, framed within surrounding shrubberies, it appears startlingly alive in its exterior completeness.

The clockwise route leads down into the agora again. On the left lie foundations of a small temple of Apollo Patroös (fourth century B.C.), followed by bases of columns and fragments of pediments marking the site of the Stoa of Zeus, in whose shade Socrates lectured to students. On the right, parallel to the electric railway, is the site of the Altar of the Twelve Gods, the starting-point for the measurement of all distances from Athens, and beyond it, the main entrance (and exit).

On the way back to Syntagma Square, you may turn left at the corner of Ermou and Aiolou Streets. A pretty flower market extends across the little square of Ayia Irene, beside a church of the same name. Pots of gardenias, oleanders and hibiscus, their scarlet trumpets turned towards the sun, are ranged beside orange trees in wooden tubs and boxes filled with basil; clematis and bougainvillaea trail from trellised bamboo sticks. In and around Ayia Irene there are several cheap rather tumbledown hotels, patronised by impecunious foreign artists and *literati*: the Byron, the Tempe, the Park.

Halfway up Ermou Street there is a charming view of the little eleventh–twelfth century **Church of the Kapnikarea.** One of the best preserved Byzantine churches in the capital, the Kapnikarea is a typical example of the cruciform plan, which was established throughout the Greek mainland in the twelfth century. It is built of stone embellished with brick courses. The little cupola above the additional chapel on the north side is an example of the growing tendency to increase the number of domes. The outer porch with two small columns leading to the door with beautifully decorated marble jambs and lintels

1. A. W. Lawrence, *Greek Architecture*, Pelican History of Art, 1957.
2. Osbert Lancaster, *Classical Landscape with Figures*, John Murray, London, 1947.

has a very coquettish air. The frescoes in the interior are modern, but good. Between the Kapnikarea and Syntagma Square Ermou Street becomes a crowded shopping quarter (drapers, lingerie shops, perfumeries). At the corner of Syntagma Square, Papaspyrou and Dionysos, large pavement cafés get all the morning sun. On summer nights they are the haunt of the chic demi-monde. The circle drawn round the 'City of Theseus' is now complete.

CHAPTER THREE

Athens: 'The City of Hadrian'

❧

Hadrian's Gateway – The Temple of Olympian Zeus – The Stadium – The Benaki Museum – The Byzantine Museum – Mt Lycabettus – The Church of the Holy Theodores – The National Museum – Colonus

IN summer the city gives an impression of dazzling whiteness. The suburbs are blanketed in a metal-coloured haze and there is an almost North African air about the parched plain. A great deal of nineteenth and early twentieth century Athens was demolished in the 1950's. For years the city echoed with the crash of the pickaxe and the grind of pneumatic drills. Row upon row of well-appointed white and cream-coloured apartment blocks, their terraces shaded with bright blue awnings, rose, and still go on rising, from the rubble.

It is best to begin at the entrance to the Royal Gardens under the false-pepper trees, and follow Amalias Avenue as far as the statue of Byron in the arms of a lady representing Hellas. At this point, **Hadrian's Gateway** marks the boundary between the two ancient cities. Two inscriptions on the frieze give the directions: to the west, 'This is Athens, in times past the City of Theseus'; to the east, 'But this is Hadrian's and no longer the City of Theseus' – a quarter of public gardens and residential streets lined with false-pepper trees. Hadrian, whose love of everything Greek went so far as to induce him to be initiated in the Eleusinian Mysteries, not only gave his Hellenic subjects new laws; he also embellished their cities with buildings and statues in the monumental Roman style, a few of which remain to recall the mellow splendours of the second century A.D. Once again the distances are not great and it is easy to walk. All of Hadrian's city can be seen in a day. Another two days are required to visit the museums.

The gateway, with its Roman arch surmounted by a Greek portico, probably intended to symbolise the marriage of the

Greek and Roman worlds, is not one of the happiest achievements of the Emperor's architects. The Emperor himself was
something of an amateur architect: a fact that may account
for its lack of professionalism. Originally, it may have looked
more impressive framed between two Corinthian columns on
either side (their bases are still visible), but it could never have
borne comparison with any of the great triumphal arches of
Rome. The marble arch rests on two square Corinthian
columns. The Greek portico on the upper level has three bays,
the middle one crowned by a pediment. The effect is one of
awkwardness, of something which has not quite come off.
Nevertheless, it remains a landmark, an outpost of traffic-
choked central Athens. The gateway leads to the esplanade of
the **Temple of Olympian Zeus,** supported on two sides by
strong buttresses, of which there were originally a hundred.
The history of the temple, one of the most impressive ruins in
Athens, is a chequered one. It was begun by the Peisistratae
in the sixth century B.C. on the site of an older temple, past
which the waters of Deucalion's Flood are supposed to have
flowed. Work was interrupted by the fall of the Peisistratae
and the Persian Wars, but resumed in the second century
B.C. by a Seleucid king of Syria who would employ none but
the best Roman architects. It was finally completed in 132 A.D.
by Hadrian, who placed a majestic effigy of himself and
a jewelled snake beside the gold and ivory statue of Zeus in the
cella. During the Middle Ages the temple served as a quarry,
and an eccentric Byzantine stylite perched his eyrie on part of
the architrave. In the eighteenth century one of the columns
was pounded into lime by the Turks who used the enclosure
as a recreation ground: a tradition kept up by the Greeks until
recently, especially on the first Monday in Lent – a day now
devoted to picnics, kite-flying and a meatless diet.

The temple, with two rows of twenty columns at the sides,
three of eight at each front, was one of the largest in the
Graeco-Roman world. The Roman architects' attempt to
extend the columns, surmounted by magnificent Corinthian
capitals, to the greatest possible height without giving them an
air of exaggerated attenuation is completely successful. No
Greek architect of the Classical age, to whom man was the
measure of his creation, would have dreamed of going so far.
Nevertheless the original Archaic temple – some of the

a. Cretan amphora

b. Attic krater

Styles of Greek Vase

c. Proto-attic amphora (detail)

d. Attic lecythos

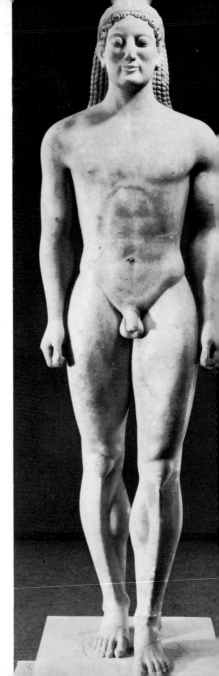

The Anavyssos Kouros
(*c*. 520 B.C.) a strong-
limbed youth, marvellously
self assured, a perfect
embodiment of human
dignity (p. 77).

gigantic drums still lie scattered on the north side of the enclosure – must have been pretty massive, for we have Aristotle's testimony that it was comparable to the Pyramids of Egypt. Of the one hundred and twenty-four columns, only fifteen remain – tall and fluted, their capitals adorned with elaborate acanthus-leaf mouldings. Impressive at all times they seldom look more magical than when floodlit, emerging out of the penumbra of darkness of the surrounding gardens. Two columns, isolated from the rest, are poised like sentinels at the top of Syngrou Avenue, the main highway to the coast

Beyond the temple Vasilissis Olgas Avenue runs between the Zappeion Gardens on one side and a tennis club, swimming pool and playground on the other – the setting of Plato's *Phaedrus*, where Socrates, generally so unbucolic in his tastes, sat on the grass beside the running brook and talked about love, friendship and the art of rhetoric. The area retains something of the parkland aspect that one associates with 'Sacred Ilissus', although it is doubtful that the stream, by whose banks Oreithyia, daughter of Erectheus, was playing when she was abducted by the North Wind, was ever more than a trickle. It is now covered by a wide avenue connecting the north-east residential quarter with Syngrou Avenue and the way to the sea. A clearing between the shrubberies of the Zappeion Gardens reveals the neo-classical porch of a large horseshoe building in which exhibitions are held. It also houses the National Broadcasting Institute. The curve of Vasilissis Olgas Avenue ends in a fork. Vasileos Constantinou Avenue leads to the Hilton, the latest landmark in the expanding skyline, a crescent-shaped palace of marble that might have aroused the envy of Hadrian, and to Vasilissis Sophias Avenue, lined with Embassies and expensive blocks of flats which have replaced the nineteenth century neo-classical houses of the old Athenian families. Beside the Hilton is the Ethnike Pinacothece (National Gallery), filled with Greek nineteenth-century paintings, some Flemish works and four El Greco's, one of which is of considerable distinction: **The Angels' Concert,** an unfinished work, depicting a complex group of swirling figures mantled in draperies that follow the contours of their contorted attitudes. A wooden door, beautifully carved with blooms within diamonds, typical of the high standard of the eighteenth-century Northern

Greek woodcarver's art, is worth noticing. At this point Ioannis Gennadeiou Street leads up the slope of Lycabettus to the fine neo-classical building of the Gennadeio Library, which possesses a collection of rare books on Greece, Byronic relics and Edward Lear water-colours.

South-east of the fork of Vasilissis Olgas and Vasileos Constantinou Avenue lies the **stadium,** capable of accommodating upwards of sixty thousand spectators, built in a wide ravine of the pine-clad hill of Ardettos in the fourth century B.C. Five centuries later its forty-four tiers were faced with marble at the expense of Herodes Atticus, a public-spirited millionaire of the Antonine era. An idea of the magnitude of the work is obtained from Pausanias, who says 'the greater part of the Pentelic quarry was exhausted in its construction', and from the fact that as many as a thousand wild beasts took part in the gladiatorial shows and Roman circuses over which Hadrian presided. In the Middle Ages the stadium was reduced to a quarry. Later travellers describe it as overgrown with corn, the crumbling diazômas as grazing-grounds for goats. In 1895 a modern Herodes Atticus, George Averoff, a wealthy cotton merchant, financed the reconstruction and refacing of the tiers with Pentelic marble, and the first revived Olympic Games were held here the following year. The liberality of the late M. Averoff did not stop there. He also donated the nation with a prison and a battleship.

From the highest tier of the Stadium there is a good view of Hadrian's Athens and its twentieth century extension. Irodou Atticou Street, a cool shaded way, mounts gradually from the stadium to the new Palace on the right. *Evzones*, members of the King's bodyguard, young giants wearing skin-tight white breeches, blue tunics and red skull-caps with black tassels, stand at attention by the Palace gateway, impervious to the click of tourists' cameras. Farther up, on the left (I Koumbari Street) is the **Benaki Museum.** Two generations of a family of cotton magnates from Alexandria have dedicated themselves to the assembly of this impressive collection of icons, jewellery, silverware, woodcarving, embroideries and relics of the War of Independence which provide a fascinating commentary – historical, ecclesiastical, sometimes plain 'folksy' – on the continuity of the Greek tradition (particularly in the popular arts), with its various geographical extensions and counter-influences. Wandering through the spacious high-ceilinged rooms of this former private residence, one is constantly being reminded, as one turns from bejewelled weapons to gorgeous chasubles, from religious paintings to lavish textiles, of the proximity of Italy in the west, of Islam in the east.

Room A contains relics of the War of Independence (No. 955 is Byron's portable writing-desk). 1821, the year the war broke out, is a decisive date, for the final Greek victory over the Turks revealed the first symptoms of that long malady which, a century later, was to dispatch 'The Sick Man of Europe' to a timely grave. Large canvases of battle scenes by Greek nineteenth century artists recall the swash-buckling manner of Delacroix's imitators. Ecclesiastical objects from various parts of Asia Minor fill Room B. No. 31 is a gorgeously embroidered banner from the Pontus. Room Γ is devoted to Byzantine and post-Byzantine works: an elaborate icon-stand in gilt carved wood; a large sixteenth-century icon of the Transfiguration (No. 123); a **St Anne and the Virgin** (in a scarlet mantle), painted by Emmanuel Tzanes, an important iconographer of the sixteenth-century Cretan School (No. 126); the **Hospitality of Abraham** (No. 64), a fourteenth-century symbolical representation of the Holy Trinity (the relaxed attitudes of the figures are unusual in a Byzantine icon, and the subtle shading of reds and blues is rendered with great sophistication). In the Presentation at the Temple (No. 68) the solidity and arrangement of planes in perspective might have been inspired by Piero della Francesca.

In a way, the Benaki Museum is a curtain-raiser – the Byzantine Museum another – to the great religious art of Mistra, where late Byzantine art flourished during the fifteenth century. In its earliest forms (mosaic, sculpture) Byzantine art is the first manifestation of an important Christian medium of aesthetics; but throughout its long history it remains, while profoundly Christian, the prisoner of a paradoxical dualism. Two major contrasting influences are constantly at work: the Hellenistic tradition, translated into terms of Christianity, and the tradition of the Orient, associated with Sassanid Persia, whence came the arts of enamel and cloisonné. The figures, more and more gorgeously robed, remain immobile, hieratic, their rigid elongated limbs the prey of a paralysing formalism. Only towards the end is a slight loosening of the iconographic straight-jacket discernible. The humanist teachings of Gemisthus Plethon, most influential of Byzantine philosophers, reveal an intimate connection with Italian thought, a more humane depiction of the liturgical figures becomes perceptible, and the sense of impending doom – for the Turks were closing round the God-Guarded City – seems to infuse a more dramatic quality into the stately cycles of the iconographer's handbook. A rustle of drapery, a twitching of the limbs transforms the figures into identifiable living beings (see frescoes at the Pantanassa, Mistra, pp. 215 -17). The appeal of despair to the West, though politically fruitless (for the nations watched Constantinople fall and Graeco-Roman civilisation perish as though nothing could have been of less account to them), had generated its counter-influences. Giotto had died in 1336, Dante fifteen years earlier. The breath of the Renaissance was in the air. Byzantine painting could not remain wholly unaffected by the new currents.

Room E contains objects of Turkish provenance of the sixteenth and seventeenth centuries. The show-piece is a restored **seventeenth-century reception room** from Cairo, with a mosaic floor, fountain and cascade from which water trickles into a small basin. The tiles are Persian, the inscriptions Cufic, the atmosphere cool and redolent of a grand Moslem house. On the walls sixteenth-century velvet fabrics from Brusa, chiefly used as cushions, have floral designs of brightly coloured tulips and carnations. Upstairs in Room Z there are two sixteenth-century icons of the Nativity (Nos. 516, 518) and the 'Miracles of the Holy Girdle' (No. 1150) with pronounced Venetian influences. The chink has been opened. The light has entered. After the Turkish conquest of Crete in 1669, a large number of Cretan artists emigrated to the island of Zante, still under Venetian rule, where the humanising influence of Italy was close at hand. Henceforth the iconography of the Ionian Islands becomes progressively more Italianate.

More relics of the War of Independence in Room H include an unusual painting of 'The Battle of Karpenisi' (No. 646). The painter was an illiterate peasant. His aerial view of the set-piece battle is crude and childish, but the imaginative quality of the detail is full of charm and fantasy. Room K contains two early El Greco's. The first (No. 1542), a much mutilated icon of St Luke painting the Virgin, is of purely historical interest, being the only extant work of Greco's in the style of the Cretan school of iconography; it was painted before he left his native Crete for Venice. The other (No. 1543) is an Adoration of the Magi, an early work, belonging to the period of the artist's apprenticeship in the workshop of the aged Titian, whose guiding hand is discernible in the architectural background, the approach to foreshortening and the balanced grouping of figures – technicalities until then unknown to the young Greek. In Room Λ there is a large seventeenth century bed, its curtains and pillows embroidered with threads of light green, brick red and Prussian blue. The jewellery in Room N ranges from gold cups of the 3rd millenium B.C. to French gold snuff-boxes. Case 106 contains a collection of rare Byzantine jewellery.

The Chinese ceramics in Room Ξ (Neolithic, T'ang, Sung, Ming), displayed against a background of sumptuous carpets from Isphahan and Samarkand are part of the Eumorphopoulos Collection. In Room I there is a comprehensive selection of **embroideries** (mostly seventeenth–eighteenth centuries) from the islands and Epirus. The most elaborately worked pieces were usually reserved for household objects, such as pillow-cases, bedspreads and valances. The origins of Greek island needlework, a genuinely popular art, go back to the church embroideries of Byzantium. This probably accounts for the conservatism of the designs, repeated again and again, and handed down from one generation to another. The patterns vary considerably from island to island. No. 3 in Case No. 149, cushion cover of a vessel with flower-decked sails against a background of sky filled with hoopoes and carnations, is an outstanding example. Cretan embroideries possess a rich oriental quality, with the frequent introduction of bird designs, especially peacocks. In the basement there is a magnificent collection of national costumes.

Koumbari Street leads into Kolonaki Square (more officially Philikes Hetairias Square) on the slope of Lycabettus. The little garden in the middle, laid out with flowerbeds and orange trees, is the haunt of foreign nannies and their Greek charges. The centre of a smart residential quarter, the square retains an atmosphere of old-fashioned intimacy trying to come to terms with the impersonal modernity of sheet-glass windows, bright red sports cars and blocks of luxury flats. Three sides are lined with confectioners, where chic Athenians sit for hours in the spring and autumn sunshine, interlarding their conversation with Anglo-American slang and outdated French expressions. At Boccola's the speciality is *loukou-mádhes*: small fried cakes of dough, served very crisp, drenched in honey and sprinkled with cinnamon. From Kolonaki Square you turn into Neophytou Vamva Street (corner of the British Council) and regain Vasilissis Sophias Avenue. On the left, just beyond the large isolated block of the Officer's Club – debased neo-classical style of the 1930s – is the **Byzantine Museum.**

Preceded by a rectangular court with a marble fountain flanked by two cypress trees, the main building (a rectangular block with a double loggia designed in 1840) was the *hôtel particulier* of Sophie de Marbois, afterwards Duchesse de Plaisance, an eccentric French lady born in Philadelphia, Pa., who lived in Athens during the reign of King Otho. She suffered from religious mania, worshipped Moses, and was mean to her guests – she liked to receive visiting men of letters, to whom she recited French poetry for hours on end – but liberality itself where public works were concerned. Stray dogs were another of her passions. The Byzantine Museum might well be visited (or revisited) *after* the traveller has been initiated into the iconographic and theological complexities of this thousand-year art at the more important sites of Daphni, Hosios Loukas and Mistra (not to mention those in Northern Greece) – for it is not in Athens that Byzantine art and architecture make their greatest impact. The amorphous objects, many of a liturgical character, dis-played in the Byzantine Museum then fall into place more easily and their significance is more quickly grasped.

Room I (ground floor) contains early Byzantine sculpture: No. 92, a boy bearing a calf, reminiscent of the Moscophorus in the Acropolis Museum; No. 93, Orpheus, his head crowned by an eagle, playing on his lyre to the animals; No. 95, a crude but charming Nativity, with two Giottesque papier-mâché trees on either side of the crib; a fourth century marble table of prothesis with a sculptured relief of animals divided into sections by four human heads. Nostalgia for the pagan past is still evident. But in spite of the crudity of execution, the sculptor draws his inspiration, full of ingenuous spontaneity, from the emotion with which the Christian revelation fills him. More sculpture (plaques with crosses, Byzantine eagles and effigies of the Virgin) crowd Room 2. Room 3 is in the form of a reconstructed but not altogether convincing Byzantine cruciform church with marble revetments. In Room 4 there is an iconostasis with elaborate woodcarving, twelve panels representing scenes from the life of Christ and a canopy surmounted by a colourful model of a Byzantine church painted with floral designs and scenes from the life of the Virgin. The first room (right) on the upper floor possesses illuminated manuscripts and icons. Among the latter: a Crucifixion (No. 157) with a star-studded background; a Virgin and Child framed within a sequence of the twelve feasts (No. 177); a beautiful fourteenth century **Crucifixion** (No. 169) with the elongated columnar figures of an anguished Virgin and St John in brown and dark blue garments and the houses of Jerusalem depicted in a narrow band along the lowest section of the panel. On the walls of the second room hang fragments of thirteenth century church frescoes; in the third room are displayed censers, chalices, sprinklers and charming little diptychs and triptychs. The fourth room is full of church vestments, together with the celebrated **epitaphios** from Salonica, an exquisitely embroidered fourteenth century fabric depicting the Lamentation over the Body of Christ. At once a technical *tour de force* and a masterpiece of one of the minor arts, it is composed in three panels, with the outstretched body dominating the middle one; the figures are woven with gold and silver threads, stencilled with blues and greens, against a gold background.

On the way out, it is worth looking at the wing on the right which possesses more icons, glittering with golds and reds and blues, of all periods: a St Andrew (No. 1545); an austere seventeenth century St John the Baptist (No. 1578) with chestnut-coloured wings outstretched against a background of gold and green; a seventeenth century Descent into Hell (No. 1210), in which a scarlet-robed Christ is surrounded by prophets and kings; a sixteenth century Virgin and Child (No. 1582), known as the **Panayia Glycophilousa** (The Sweetly Kissing Virgin), which looks like the archetype of all Duccio's madonnas. Duccio, however, lived some three hundred years before the Glycophilousa was painted. But like other Italian primitives, he was not uninfluenced by Byzantine models in Italy. Nevertheless it is difficult to imagine a Duccio of the sixteenth century – say a Caravaggio or a Correggio – composing a head of the Virgin in the manner of the early fourteenth. Yet the painter of the Glycophilousa – moving and tender as she undoubtedly is – is content with a slavish copy of an infinitely earlier model. In contrast to Italian artists, with their restless unfettered genius, open to every new trend in fashion and technique, most Byzantines and post-Byzantines remained with their feet firmly planted on the well-trodden paths of iconographic tradition.

Loukianou Street, the first to the left opposite the Byzantine Museum, mounts steeply up Lycabettus, past the British Embassy residence – once the home of Eleutherios Venizelos, Greece's greatest modern statesman, liberator of Crete and architect of the victorious Balkan Wars. At the end of the street a paved path zigzags up to the summit of the pinnacled crag. The funicular starts from the corner of Aristippou and Cleomenous Streets. At Easter a Resurrection service is held in the whitewashed chapel of St George which crowns the peak, and soon after midnight a long candlelight procession winds down the hill like a trail of glow-worms. Immediately below the chapel there is an expensive restaurant. The view embraces the whole of the plain and the Saronic Gulf, with the Megarid and the Isthmus in the west, the distant hump of Acro-Corinth at the gateway of the Peloponnese, and, beyond it, on a very clear day, the peak of Cyllene, where Hermes, god of thieves, was born and committed his first theft.

The limits of Hadrian's Athens have now been reached. The National Archaeological Museum – a journey back in time, for one starts with Agamemnon, spans a dozen centuries and finishes before Hadrian was born – lies at the other end of the town. The walk from Syntagma Square leads through the main shopping quarter. First Stadiou Street. On the left is the expensive Athenée Palace Hotel; and Kolokotronis Square, with statues of Tricoupis, the nineteenth century statesman, and an equestrian Kolokotronis, hero of the War of Independence, caparisoned as though he were the god of war himself; then Klauthmonos Square, 'The Square of

Weeping,' so called because it was under its bedraggled
acacias that a group of disgruntled civil servants once staged
a demonstration of protest against their dismissal and wept
so loudly that the authorities, moved by pity, reinstated them.
At the north-west end of the square lies the **Church of Ayioi
Theodoroi** (The Holy Theodores), eleventh century Byzantine,
built of stone with brick courses and an exterior Cufic frieze.
Cruciform in plan, with a tall drum (a feature of the small
Byzantine churches in Athens), its proportions are exquisite.

From Klauthmonos Square Korais Street leads into E.
Venizelou Street, more commonly known by its original
name of Panepistimiou (University) Street, which, together
with parallel Stadiou Street, forms the main axis of central
Athens. Immediately facing one rises an imposing group of
neo-classical buildings. From left to right: the National
Library, faced with a Doric portico; the University, with a
painted colonnade; in front of it, statues of Korais, champion
of linguistic reform, and Gladstone, whose government ceded
the Ionian Islands to Greece in 1864; finally, the Academy,
with a portico and pediment, and statues of Plato and
Socrates seated on either side of the entrance. All three
edifices were built of Pentelic marble on plans drawn up by
nineteenth century Bavarian architects. The group of buildings
is dominated by two tall fluted columns crowned with statues
of Apollo playing his lyre and Athena armed with lance and
shield. The traffic blocks, the creeping line of blue and yellow
buses, the impatient pedestrians fulminating against the red
lights – all the stridency of a modern Mediterranean street –
seem to enhance the incongruity of this splendid display of
neo-classical panache, with Lycabettus, its fantastic conical
peak rising out of a sea of apartment blocks.

For years the University was the scene of violent disturb-
ances provoked by the controversy over the linguistic question:
the purist out-of-date *katharevousa* versus the 'vulgar' more
contemporary *demotiki*, which had assimilated large numbers
of Italian and Turkish words and idioms and played havoc
with time-honoured canons of syntax and grammar. The
controversy reached proportions bordering on a state of
undeclared civil war: families were split in two, and 'demoticists' and 'katharevousists' assaulted each other in public.
In the end the more dynamic 'demoticists' won. Their victory,

which had a stimulating effect on Greek literature, has, on balance, been vindicated by the success of Kazandzakis' novels and the prestige acquired by the poetry of Palamas, Sikelianos and, above all, Seferis, whose career as a poet-diplomat – Ambassador in Ankara and London, translator of T. S. Eliot into Greek – was crowned in 1963 by the Nobel Prize for Literature.

Between the University and Syntagma Square there are several landmarks among the shops of Panepistimiou Street: the Bank of Greece, the Catholic Cathedral of St Denis the Areopagite, the neo-classical mansion (now the Supreme Court of Appeal) in which Heinrich Schliemann, excavator of the sites of Troy and Mycenae, lived with his beautiful Greek wife, and two large cafés (with restaurant) called Flocca and Zonar: the heart of cosmopolitan Athens. Parallel to Panepistimiou Street runs Academias Street, with more shops, offices and a modern little opera house, the *Lyriki Skene*, where in 1942 an as yet unknown plump young girl with a haunting deep-throated voice, called Maria Callas, made her début in *Tosca*. In the opposite direction from the University, Panepistimiou Street descends towards Omonoia Square, the centre of a network of crowded commercial streets and a station on the electric railway which links the Piraeus and the northern suburbs with the capital. At night all this quarter is a bit louche; there are some scruffy night-clubs, cafés and cheap hotels. The National Theatre, whose annual season (November–April) generally begins with a play by Shakespeare (still the biggest box-office draw in Athens) is round the corner in Ayiou Constantinou Street.

From Omonoia Square Patission Street, a long straight avenue, penetrates into another world: the residential area of Patissia, a dreary urban extension dating from the inter-war years: now the mecca of the new bourgeoisie. The first large building on the right is the marble Polytechnic School. Beyond it a wispy public garden with some tired-looking palm trees forms a frontage to the **National Archaeological Museum**. It should be entered as one climbs the Acropolis, in the spirit of a pilgrimage. Here are some, if not most, of the greatest ancient sculptures in the world, monumental and diminutive, Archaic, Classical and Hellenistic, and a collection of painted vases, ranging from huge amphoras to delicate lecythoi, so vast and varied in execution and detail that imagination boggles at the ingenuity of the ancient potter's skill. Smaller objects, daggers, jewels, figurines, death-masks, shields, ornamental boxes, inscriptions, even toys, fill in the gaps, so that one is able to obtain a picture – hazy and confused perhaps, but still whole and in the round – of man's tastes and occupations, of his changing attitudes to religion, sex, death, recreation and athletics from Mycenaean to Roman times. The existing arrangement of the exhibits is not ideal; the rooms are not always numbered (nor are some of the exhibits); one is inclined to get lost; and there is as yet no complete catalogue. The best I can do is to describe the principal objects in the order in which I last saw them.

Immediately facing the entrance is the Mycenaean room, filled with gold objects excavated from the royal shaft tombs at Mycenae. Later archaeologists, notably Wace and Papadimitriou, complemented the work of Schliemann, and the Mycenaean room, with its two annexes, now contains a comprehensive collection of the accessories of life during the Neolithic, Cycladic and Mycenaean civilisations of the 3rd and 2nd milleniums B.C. The quantity of gold objects is breathtaking; equally astonishing is the degree of sophistication achieved by jewellers, potters and goldsmiths of this prehistoric age. On a sweltering day in July 1876 a group of workmen, digging through successive layers of soil on a hill above the Argive plain, disclosed a deep vertical shaft in the rock. Schliemann, his wife and the local ephor peered into the pit. It was Frau Schliemann's eye that first caught the gleam of gold. The excavation of the grave circle began. Its yield was one of the most sensational in the history of archaeology (see p. 142).

A pedestal, on which the gold death-mask of an Achaean king of the fifteenth century B.C. is placed, faces the entrance to the Mycenaean room. Schliemann, inclined to dramatise, believed it to be Agamemnon's mask. Kissing it reverently as it was raised from the soil, he telegraphed to the King of Greece: 'I have gazed on the face of Agamemnon.' No. 384 is a **libation cup** in the form of a bull's head with gold horns and muzzle and a gold sun composed of strap-shaped petals on the brow. The bull-taming scenes on the **Vaphio gold cups** (Nos. 1758, 1759) illustrate the perfection achieved by representational art in the Mycenaean age. In the first wild bulls are hunted with the utmost vigour, in the second they are set to pasture in the shade of embowering trees. Two cases, on either side of the entrance, contain precious objects dating from 1500 to 1200 B.C.: gold necklaces and bracelets, terracotta animals, goblets ornamented with spiral designs, silver and alabaster vessels, rings, shells, daggers, amethysts and seal-stones. The love of beautiful objects must have been strong among the Mycenaeans. The tentacles of an octopus, the dreaded sea-monster which has haunted the Mediterranean imagination from the earliest times, writhe round a large amphora on the left wall. No. 3908, a crude but charming statuette, in the left annexe (exhibits of Cycladic provenance) represents a male figure seated on a throne, playing an unidentified musical instrument – possibly a harp. In conception and execution, it might be an object from a contemporary exhibition of abstract sculpture. Its date is c. 2400–2200 B.C.

Back in the entrance hall, one proceeds clockwise into the first of six halls devoted to Archaic sculpture. An air of essential masculinity prevails. The powerful-bodied kouroi (young men, often athletes, later soldiers), huge monoliths hewn out of the crystalline rock, represent a monumental image of man. The design is fixed, the planes flat, but the body is still structural and the dimensions spatial. Left foot forward, they are vigorous, enigmatic, sometimes reticent, always self-confident, and of heroic mould. The statues, which were either wholly or partly painted, were often placed on tombs or in the neighbourhood of temples, probably in groves. The most striking of the earlier kouroi is No. 2720 (late seventh century B.C.), 'The Colossus of Sunium' (he was found near the Temple of Poseidon at Cape Sunium). The cast of his features, set and wooden, is distinctly Egyptian, the conception architectonic. But there the comparison stops. For no Rameses possesses the muscular tension or freedom of pose enjoyed by this giant Greek youth. No. 3686, of a later date, is more evolved. The formal stylisation is there, but the excessive stiffness is less evident; the hair is more elaborately arranged and there is a vestige of a smile on the lips, which have grown more full and sensual. No. 12, the Ptoion Kouros (c. 540 B.C.) is even more evolved, taut and alert, with a smile half-arrogant, half-compassionate. But it is No. 3851, the

Anavyssos Kouros (*c.* 520 B.C.), a strong-limbed youth, marvellously self-assured, a perfect embodiment of human dignity – he is a warrior, not a god – that dominates the scene. Traces of red paint are visible on the coral-shaped locks that fall down his shoulders from the head-band, and the whole surface of Parian marble has a roseate glow. His smile is more radiant than that of any other kouros. The modelling is opulent, the tension just about to break, the taut powerful limbs to experience the ecstasy of movement with which classical art will bless the human body. No. 1959 is a relief of a running hoplite (end sixth century). The limbs, in spite of the stylised posture, are now articulate. The marble **reliefs of two statue bases** (Nos. 3476, 3477), originally built into the walls of Themistocles, carry the development further, and depict scenes from the palaestra: boys playing with a cat and a ball; boys playing hockey. The Marathonian soldier of Aristocles (No. 29) represents the transitional period between late Archaic and early Classical sculpture.

In the next two halls we pass into the fifth century. The Archaic smile, iron self-control and taut muscular strain have gone. All is fluency and pliability and perfection of detail, with a constant interplay between tense and relaxed attitudes which both enhances the rhythm and allows the body to achieve a greater variety of aesthetic forms. Realism has substituted symbolism and sculpture has begun to describe and idealise. In the **Eleusinian votive relief** (No. 126), Demeter presents an ear of corn to her protégé, the youth Triptolemus, who is commanded to instruct man in the cultivation of the earth, while Koré crowns him. The **young athlete crowning himself** (No. 3344) is another work of Attic perfection. In spite of the low relief the flesh has the resilient quality of youth; the boy's thoughtful expression reflects the solemnity with which victory on the race-track fills him. Scenes from the palaestra inspire some of the greatest Greek sculpture. The athlete, the symbol of youth and health, is the film star, the pop singer of his day. His victory at the games, preceded by sacrificial rites, is an act of dedication to a god. In ancient Greece athletics cannot be divorced from religion; and the athlete becomes a focal point. That he was often vain, spoilt and insolent, the physical animal *par excellence*, is more than probable. But as such no sculptor dared to depict him. As the centuries and Olympiads succeed one another, the adulation grows hysterical. Bribery and corruption inevitably become rife, and by the time of the Roman conquest Pindar's ideal athlete who 'goeth in a straight course along a path that hateth insolence' is a mere delusion.

Turning to No. 1732, one is confronted with a remarkable personification of a breeze in the form of an (now headless) effigy of a zephyr. The bronze **Poseidon** (No. 15161), a work of the mid-fifth century, drawn up from the sea-bed off Cape Artemisium, represents the god larger than life-size, his left arm outstretched, his right hand holding a trident (which is missing) about to be hurled. Nothing better expresses the Greek concept of a god as a physically perfect man than this springy, superbly healthy Poseidon. His presence is that of a deity, his pose of a man we all know: strong, arrogant, probably a bully. God-head in terms of human flesh. And Homer's gods, one recalls, were often more human than his heroes. Zeus is a far more likeable person than Achilles.

The next six rooms (the first three separated from the others by a rectangular hall) contain the stelae (marble gravestones) that lined the alleys of the Cerameicus and other ancient necropolises. The scenes represented are intimate family affairs. The departing soul, which has a remote other-worldly expression, is often depicted in the act of shaking hands with its next-of-kin. Grief is borne with dignity and restraint – with heartbreak just below the surface. Some critics find the scenes over-sentimentalised. Executed by some of the best sculptors of the fifth–third centuries, the stelae must, in some instances, have cost the bereaved families a small fortune. Every visitor has, or will have, his own favourites. Among the ones I never like to miss are **No. 717,** an athlete raising his hand in a farewell gesture, his youthful escort leaning mournfully against a marble plinth; **No. 3624,** a girl looking at her jewels for the last time; **No. 718,** a woman stroking the head of a kneeling child; **No. 3790,** a servant girl holding up a baby in order that the departing mother may cast a last look at it; **No. 869,** a hooded old man taking leave of a hunter, whose dog and little escort crouch at his feet (believed to be the work of Scopas, one of the most distinguished sculptors of the fourth century); **No. 2583,** a mourning siren with wings and bird's feet, her face contorted with grief;

No. 13400, a little Negro groom (his features tense with concentration) trying to bridle a frisky horse.

At the end of the long rectangular hall the famous **Jockey Boy** (No. 15177), a second century B.C. bronze, gallops through the air. A lively little creature – he has even more dash than his earlier prototype, the Negro groom – he too was fished out of the sea off Cape Artemisium. There are also some fine Roman copies of older Greek statues. In No. 1826, the Diadumenos of Polycleitus (the original was of bronze), an athlete is depicted crowning himself with the laurel wreath of victory; in No. 218, the Hermes of Andros, the most mischievous of the Olympians, is represented in one of his more responsible roles – that of conductor of souls to the Underworld. The small but full-lipped mouth has an almost Praxitelean perfection – and sulkiness. In the room on the left are terracotta and bronze figurines. No. 16546, Zeus about to hurl a thunderbolt, is almost a replica in miniature of the Poseidon of Artemisium, but perkier, more stocky.

The last hall is reserved for a series of masterpieces. First the enormous **Piraeus Apollo** (unnumbered), the earliest of all extant bronze statues (sixth century B.C.). He was discovered at the Piraeus in 1959 by a group of workmen repairing a sewer in a main thoroughfare. Other sculptures, which formed part of this unexpected cache, are now in the Piraeus museum (see p. 87). They are believed to have been abandoned near the port, as a result of some sudden alarm, by plunderers about to ship them to Rome. The Apollo is in a good condition, except for a crack down his left thigh. The detail is of a coarser texture, less elaborate, less finished – especially in the treatment of the hair – than that of most bronze statues. Yet few others convey such a positive impression of achieved symmetry and balance or possess more of the formal dignity associated with Archaic sculpture. All the familiar Archaic features are there – the protruding eyes, the full lips, the left foot forward – but there is also an air of melancholy concentration which is absent in the confident young kouroi, bursting with physical health and the joy of life. This truly hieratic Apollo is as holy an image as anything in Greek art, and he takes his place, beside the Charioteer at Delphi and the Poseidon of Artemisium, among the Greek sculptor's supreme achievements in bronze.

Beyond the Apollo there are more bronzes: the **Marathonian Ephebe** (No. 15118), possibly by Praxiteles, discovered by a fisherman at the bottom of the sea-bed in the bay of Marathon, and the **Hermes of Anticythera** (No. 13396), sometimes described as Paris. This hefty young man with somewhat effeminate features is, in fact, holding some obviously round object (the apple?), now missing, in his right hand. Both are works of technical perfection of the fourth century; but there is a slickness, even an impersonality, about them that conjures up a vision of an efficient sculptor's workshop where equally polished models are run off the line in a steady stream. Both young men are entirely physical; they may reflect the pleasure experienced by the Greeks in the beauty of the human body, but they have no interior life. Of the two, the little ephebe, slightly wistful, is the more moving. Less spectacular, but more compelling, are two bronze heads, one (Hellenistic) of a **bearded philosopher** (No. 13400), with piercing inlaid eyes and a face of remarkable intellectual power, and No. 14612, a man of the first century B.C., known as the **Man from Delos** – a meditative creature with weak undecided mouth and anguishing doubts. Finally, turn to the **Tegean head** (No. 3602), believed to be by Scopas, representing Hygeia, goddess of health. The almond-shaped eyes glance downwards, and the curved lips are slightly open. The neck is slender and the rounded chin beautifully modelled. In the complete harmony of its forms, this oval face crowned by soft wavy hair is the personification of serenity, a perfect expression of idealised beauty in Parian marble.

The second floor of the museum (staircase in the long rectangular hall) possesses the enormous collection of **painted vases.** The evolution of Greek painting from the earliest times can be traced in these products of the potter's workshop. The exhibits are displayed chronologically, but the absence of a catalogue is a handicap. First there are the vases of the Geometric period (twelfth–seventh centuries), ornamented with superimposed bands; then the Archaic period (seventh to mid-sixth centuries), characterised by orientalising features, such as lotus flowers, palmettes, sphinxes and other animals. These are followed by Attic vases of the sixth century. The bands have now disappeared and the ornamentation consists of mythological scenes (figures in black). Figures in red on a

Poseidon (mid-5th century B.C.). Nothing better expresses the Greek concept of a god as a physically perfect man than this springy, superbly healthy Poseidon. (p. 78).

Tegean Head. Believed to be by Scopas representing Hygeia, goddess of health. She is the personification of serenity, a perfect expression of idealised beauty in Parian marble. (p. 80).

black background appear in the fifth and fourth centuries. The drawing is now exquisitely fine. The white ground lecythoi, with a black base and neck, and figures painted in light shades, are a feature of fifth century Attic vase-painting. The array is so vast that one can but pick out a few obvious specimens: No. 1002, the Nessus amphora (on the neck Heracles grapples with the Centaur Nessus); No. 4082, black-figured Greek and Trojan archers fighting with Javelins; a black krater with red figures representing Theseus in combat with the Minotaur (unnumbered); No. 1452, a loutrophorus (red figures on a black background); No. 1170, another loutrophorus, portraying a procession of horsemen and pedestrians at a maiden's funeral. Among the lekythoi, Nos. 1761, 1929, 1967, 2020.

The Epigraphical Department has a large collection of historical inscriptions, and the Numismatic Museum contains cameos as well as Greek, Roman and Byzantine coins. Both are situated on the ground floor of the main museum building (entrance from Tositsa Street).

From the Museum, one last pilgrimage. Epirou Street, then Neophitou Metaxa Street, lead westward to the SEK (State Railways) or Larissa Station, the terminal of all trains from Western Europe and the north. The station has an air of Balkan dereliction, with a dimly lit waiting room filled with depressed-looking soldiery bound for remote frontier posts. A little to the south there is another station – the SPAP (Peloponnese Railways) Station. From there Lenorman Street cuts across a sprawling working class quarter, called Colonos, dominated by a flat rocky mound: the site of the ancient deme of Colonus, birthplace of Sophocles, immortalised in his *Oedipus at Colonus*. A marble slab and loutrophorus on the summit mark the graves of two philhellenic German archaeologists. There is no memorial to the greatest dramatist of antiquity.

It is a barren stony place, with a few shrubby pines and lusty cactuses, the box-like houses of suburban Athens spreading for miles around, the Acropolis just visible in the south. The plangent twang of *bouzouki* records echoes from a little shack: the local taverna. One looks in vain for some sign of the sacred grove, with 'its dark avenues and windless courts', where the aged Oedipus, victim of the most appalling fate ever visited by gods upon man, finally comes to die. The 'seat of natural rock', to which he is led by the long-suffering Antigone, can still be discerned; but the 'deep arbours, ivy, dark as wine and tangled bowers of berry-clustered vine', live on only in the chorus of the Elders of Colonus. Sophocles, too, was a very old man when he wrote the *Oedipus at Colonus*. It was his last play. A deeply religious work, it is full of nostalgia for the beloved birthplace. The story – probably apocryphal – is that he died at the age of ninety, choked by a grape pip, before he could see it performed.

Attica

✤

ATTICA is in the form of a triangular peninsula, washed on
two sides by the Aegean Sea. Athens stretches across the
southern end of the central plain. Its main features are rock
and purity of light. The soil is poor, the substrata so solid and
imporous that it is less subject to earthquakes than most of
the country. The coastline is broken by barren promontories
and sandy beaches fringed with Aleppo pines. Ruined
sanctuaries and whitewashed chapels – miniature replicas of
Byzantine cruciform churches – shelter in the folds of rocky
valleys. Sheets of pale grey asphodel, the immortal flower of
Elysium, spread across the hill-sides, and dusty paths are
lined with aloes and wild fig from whose pliable wood theatre
seats, garlands and other ornaments were made in antiquity.
The streams are mere trickles, dry in summer – Strabo, writing
his *Geography* in the time of Augustus, noticed that even
thirsty cattle, let alone men, looked askance at them. Goats,
for centuries the peasants' sole source of wealth, browse among
parched shrubs. Everywhere there is the pungent scent of thyme
and wild marjoram. In spring the boulders are speckled with
round apple-green tufts of *Euphorbia acanthothamnos* and
other varieties of spurge, and the hard ground is covered by
clusters of grape-hyacinths and little mirror orchids with
yellow-bordered blue petals. In autumn there are deep pink
cyclamen, and golden crocus-like sternbergia whose favourite
habitat seems to be around country graveyards. The landscape
may not be the most beautiful in Greece, but it is seldom

without interest. The bone structure is bold and uncom
promising, and the Saronic Gulf, ample and serene in it
contours, one of the loveliest in the country.

An anti-clockwise route is the most practical.[1] First come
the Piraeus. A headland, five miles from Athens, from whicl
nothing now separates it but a flat built-up area of factories
warehouses and suburban houses, it has three harbours
which, in ancient times, possessed nearly four hundred ship
houses (sheds with sloping ramps situated on the water's edge)
One of the great ports of the Eastern Mediterranean and th
main industrial centre of the country, it is a shabby colourles
place: a complex of breweries, soap and spinning factories an
metallurgical foundries. Unlike Athens, the Piraeus had n
organic growth. It has no mythological associations. Fo
centuries the open roadstead of Phalerum, a mile and a hal
away, served as an anchorage. But in the early fifth centur
B.C., Themistocles realised the use to which the headland an
its three sheltered ports could be put. Sea-minded and far
sighted, he built the harbour (encircling it with walls mor
formidable than those of the Acropolis) and created a fleet
Above all, he won the battle of Salamis. But his extravagan
vanity aroused the jealousy of his political rivals. Ostracise
by the Athenians, he went over to the enemy and died
satrap of the Persian king. The pattern is not unfamiliar
The harbour was completed by Cimon, and Pericles built th
Long Walls connecting the capital with its port.

At the end of the Peloponnesian War, when Athens -
brilliant, democratic, volatile – submitted to the superio
power of totalitarian Sparta, Lysander ordered the destructio
of the Piraeus, as well as the demolition of the Long Walls. I
was the end of the imperial dream. During the Middle Ages
the Piraeus was no more than a fishing village, known a

1. Most of the roads are good. Motor coaches go to the obviou
places – to the 'sights'; but their itineraries necessarily omit some of th
remoter spots. I throw out the following suggestions for whole or hal
day trips by car (the former marked with an X), always starting fror
and returning to Athens: (1) X The Piraeus–Sunium–Thoricus–Brauron
Mesogeia villages (a long day); (2) X Daou–Pendeli–Marathon
Rhamnus; (3) Mt Pentelicus–Kephisia–The Amphiaraion; (4) Achar
nae–Mt Parnes; (5) Deceleia–Oropus; (6) Acharnae–Phyle; (7
Kaisariani–Mt Hymettus; (8) X Daphni–Eleusis–Eleutherae–Aegos
thena (a long day).

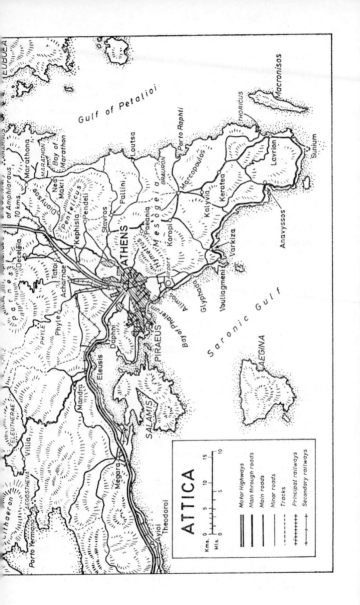

Porto Leone, guarded by a colossal marble lion, on which Harald Hardraada, the giant Viking in the service of the Byzantine emperor, engraved a runic inscription in the eleventh century. Later the lion was removed to Venice. South of the railway station is Karaiskaki Square and the anchorage for island steamers. Twice a day, at noon and sunset, listing and overcrowded, flotillas of these small craft – converted yachts, former channel steamers, flat-bottomed St Lawrence river boats and trim modern hydrophoils bound for every island in the archipelago – nose their way cautiously out of the harbour, which, in the days of Athenian maritime supremacy, held four hundred triremes.

For dinner at the Piraeus there is the taverna of Vasilaina (corner of Aitolikon and Vitolion Streets). Various fish courses include little fried dumplings stuffed with the insides of *echinous*, the ubiquitous sea-urchins that infest the rocky coasts of Attica. From the main harbour it is about twenty minutes' walk to the more attractive Pashalimani (The Pasha's Harbour), a crescent-shaped expanse of calm water lined with cafés, once the battle station of the Athenian triremes. Parts of the corniche beyond the Naval Hospital (south) are buttressed by fragments of ancient walls restored in the fourth century B.C. by Conon, the distinguished Athenian admiral. North-east (Canaris Square) is the site of the Skeuotheke, a great arsenal which, says Pliny, contained arms for one thousand ships. Near the harbour, in Philhellinon Street, are the ruins of a little Hellenistic theatre, in which performances of folk-dances were until recently given by the Dora Stratou Company in summer.[2] The performers, natives of Aegean islands and Epirot mountains, are not professional dancers, and the music and striking costumes are authentic. The girls move in stately fashion; the men leap and shout '*Op-pa!*'. The orchestra consists of clarinet (the player sometimes displays extreme virtuosity), reed pipe, *lyra* (the ancient lyre), various types of drums and violin. The origins of some dances go back to mythological times: the *Pentozali*, for instance, supposed to represent Athenian youths and maidens winding through the Cretan labyrinth; the *Sousta*, danced by Achilles round the

2. The performances, accompanied by a commentary in Greek, English and French, are now held in a new open air theatre below the Acropolis in Athens.

funeral pyre of Patroclus, after 'he had picked up the dark dust in both his hands and poured it on his head'. There is nothing bogus about these dances; they are as genuine, as firmly rooted in the life of the peasants as the dances in the *bouzouki* tavernas along the Phalerum coast are an emotional expression of the urban working classes.

Beside the theatre a small **Archaeological Museum** possesses two impressive larger than life-size bronze statues of Athena and Artemis. The figure of Athena (helmeted) is poised and relaxed, the head of Artemis a typical example of the fourth century B.C. perfectionist style that recalls the Marathonian Ephebe and Hermes of Anticythera in the National Museum in Athens.

A winding corniche, parts of whose sides are pock-marked with grottoes and niches for votive offerings, leads to the third and smallest harbour facing the sweep of the bay of Phalerum. **Tourcolimano** (The Turkish Harbour), the ancient Munychia, is composed of tiers of white houses clinging to two sides of a natural amphitheatre, with a bluff (site of the fortress built by the tyrannical Hippias in the sixth century B.C.) crowned by the Yacht Club, on the third. Yachts, caïques, *trechandiria* (fast-sailing fishing-smacks), motor launches and dinghies crowd the oily waters of the miniature harbour; the water-front is lined with open-air (indoor in winter) fish restaurants. Pedlars of clams and pistachio nuts jostle with sailors, waiters and smart Athenian ladies stepping out of glossy American cars.

From the top of the hill above the harbour, called Castella, which Strabo says was 'hollowed out and undermined in many places, partly by nature and partly by the purpose of man . . .' there are fine views of the three harbours, of Salamis and the Saronic Gulf. All around cheap modern blocks are going up daily; here and there survive traces of neo-classical architectural fantasy: peeling rosette-bordered casements and flaking spiral balustrades – sometimes a ruined Caryatid porch. Compton Mackenzie lived here in 1916. Greece, although officially neutral, was split in two by pro-German and pro-Allied factions. Foreign diplomats and intelligence officers, of whom Compton Mackenzie was one of the most colourful, spent their time backing one military junta against another, fomenting one *coup d'état* to forestall another. In the

end the Greek people paid for it – with war, revolution, the
burning of Smyrna and the eviction of their compatriots from
Asia Minor. Compton Mackenzie gives an exciting, ironical
and sometimes angry account of all this tragic muddle in
First Athenian Memories and its sequel, *Greek Memories*.

The corniche winds down to the bay of Phalerum, where the
Athenian triremes were anchored in the days of the Peisistratae, and past the jetty where Eleutherios Venizelos sailed for
Crete in September 1916 to proclaim the Provisional Government and bring Greece into the war against the Central
Powers: an action which raised the fatal issue of monarchy
versus republic, destined to bedevil Greek politics for the next
half century. At Phalerum was born Demetrius the Phalerian,
the orator-politician entrusted by Cassander with the administration of Athens at a time when the unity of the Hellenistic
world was being undermined by the rival ambitions of
Alexander the Great's successors. At first the Phalerian filled
his high office with such conspicuous success that a grateful
Athenian people erected three hundred and sixty statues to
him. Then popular favour swung against him, and, on the
arrival of the glamorous orgy-loving Demetrius Poliorcetes
with a hostile fleet off Munychia, the Phalerian lost his nerve.
His growing dictatorial ways had lost him the affection of the
people, and he was forced to flee from the city (307 B.C.). So
great was the revulsion of feeling against him that his statues
were demolished and turned into chamber-pots.

Several *bouzouki* tavernas border the coastal road between
the shallow sea and a stretch of low-lying ground, often
flooded by the autumn rains. Here orchestras of *bouzouki*
players (the *bouzouki* is a large mandolin with a particularly
plangent tone) sit stiffly on a stage and play to an audience of
solemn-faced diners. The food is not always good and the
uninitiated are inclined to be over-charged. Soon after midnight
(this is the best time to go, and order wine and fruit, having
dined elsewhere) the local clientèle begins to turn up: soldiers,
mechanics, garage hands, podgy little grocers on their night
out. As soon as they start to dance (sometimes remarkably
well), the atmosphere undergoes a breathtaking change. All is
now zest and enthusiasm, the music louder, the *bouzouki*
soloists more dashing and inventive in their improvisations.
The solemn-faced diners, who follow the dancers' steps with

the eye of professional ballet critics, go so far as to order more drinks (generally *crème de menthe*). The music, Anatolian in origin, brought to mainland Greece by refugees from Asia Minor, is invariably in the minor key. The tunes are stylised, the lyrics confined to the themes of self-pity, the faithlessness of the loved one, the hard lot of the underdog, the anguish of homesickness. Of all the dances, the *zeibékiko*, a *pas seul* danced by a man, is the one nearest to the Greek heart. Its main features are complicated acrobatics, scything movements of the arms, repeated slapping of the ground and symbolical gestures connected with sex and Mother Earth. The *hassápiko*, the 'butchers' dance' (*pas de deux*, *pas de trois*) is more professional – and more interesting. It has a restrained hieratic quality, and the dancers are ranged laterally across the floor, like figures in a shifting frieze. The expression on their faces, fixed and utterly detached from their surroundings, reminds one of the kouroi and korai and the National and Acropolis Museums. The *tsiphteteli* is little more than a glorified belly dance performed by a man. The orchestra includes a plump oriental-looking little lady who bangs on a tambourine and moans into a microphone. The amount of noise she is capable of making is astonishing.

Past the *bouzouki* tavernas lies the Race Course. At right angles to it, Syngrou Avenue leads back to the centre of Athens. Beyond the Race Course the coastal road passes (left) a spacious military cemetery overlooking the sea. The slope is dotted with graves of British Commonwealth soldiers killed in the Greek campaigns of the Second World War and the December 1944 revolution when British troops, a month before greeted as liberators with ringing speeches and garlands of flowers (just like Olympic victors), were reluctantly drawn into a murderous five weeks' battle with Greek Communist-led Resistance forces.

After Alimos, the ancient Halimus, home of Thucydides, and the airport the beaches begin. At Glyphada there are bungalows, the fashionable Astir *plage*, a night-club, good (and expensive) fish tavernas; at Cavouri, green with pines, the Cape Zoster of antiquity, smart villas; at **Vouliagmeni**, the most attractive, two pellucid bays fringed with pines and red cliffs. The Astir Hotel is first class, and there is a sheltered anchorage for yachts (with a club-house and all necessary

facilities for yachtsmen), and a warm fresh water pool with
mineral properties, emerald green in colour, backed by a
forbidding slate-grey cliff. On the isthmus between the two
bays the foundations of a sixth century temple of Apollo are
embedded in the sand. Varkiza comes next: a strand of fine
white sand, with a hinterland of rolling vine country, followed
by a fiord-like inlet approached through a tunnel of rock;
then the headland of Lagonisi, with its beaches, Xenias Hotel
and expensive bungalows; and Anavyssos, once the haunt of
smugglers, on the edge of a salt marsh, where the great
stocky-limbed kouros in the National Museum (see p. 77),
representing the youth Kroisos, was discovered in 1936. His
face, it will be remembered, was perhaps the most engaging of
the kouroi, his smile the most radiant. But no Kroisos roams
the streets of the fishing village now. Most of the inhabitants
are of Albanian origin.

After Anavyssos comes **Sunium,** the southernmost promontory of Attica, with its temple, hotels and villas. The hills
behind the steep pine-clad coastline, where there is quail-
shooting in autumn, are bare except for bushes of sage and
juniper, with a new purity of contour that indicates the
proximity of the Cyclades – Keos and Kythnos are clearly
visible. An isolated rocky headland, surrounded by vestiges of
an ancient semi-circular wall, is crowned by the fifth century
B.C. **Temple of Poseidon,** built on massive substructures
necessitated by the conical rise of the ground. The work of the
architect of the Theseum, its columns – fourteen of the
original thirty-eight are standing – are Doric but more slender
than usual. They lack *entasis* and consequently look somewhat
fragile, almost like stilts. The flutings, too, are fewer in
number, and this also probably detracts from the stolidity
associated with the Doric order. The dimensions are almost
identical to those of the Theseum, except that here the architect has increased the height of the columns. As nothing
remains above the architrave of the south colonnade it is
difficult to judge what impression the building as a whole may
have made when crowned by metopes, cornice and pediments.
In view of the spectacular nature of the position, the increased
height should have added something to the upward thrust so
singularly lacking in the Theseum. The marble out of which
the temple was built came from a local quarry: very white and

without the mellow patina that the Pentelic crystalline lime-stone acquires. Column-bases are disfigured with the scratch-ings of innumerable signatures, including Byron's. It was here, on 'Sunium's marbled steep', that the poet, appalled by the fate of Ottoman-enslaved Greece, asked for nothing better than to acquire the form of a swan and so 'sing and die'. An expanse of sun-dazzled sea extends unbroken towards Crete, and on a clear day, Milos, whence came the Venus in the Louvre, is visible. From below, the temple glistens white as a wedding-cake on its perpendicular cliff. Sunium, the Acropolis and the Temple of Aphaea (on the island of Aegina) form an almost perfect triangle; and many west-bound fishing boats still keep up the ancient tradition of following the course of the temple-crowned triangle – south from Sunium to Aphaea and thence to the Piraeus – instead of hugging the coast (the obvious route).

The inland route back to Athens passes through Lavrion, the ancient Laurium, where zinc and manganese are now mined in place of the silver that contributed so much to the wealth of ancient Athens. By the second century A.D. the deposits had been exhausted. About one kilometre north of the dusty little mining town, surrounded by slag-heaps and melancholy silhouettes of abandoned chimneys, a branch road (right) leads to the extremely ancient site of **Thoricus,** a Cretan naval station during the Minoan age. Later it was fortified by the Athenians and served as an important military outpost guarding the maritime approaches to the silver mines. On the slope of the hill, overlooking the fields and slag-heaps, are the remains of a fourth-century B.C. **theatre,** unique in shape and construction. Following the declivity of the hillside, the cavea is elliptical instead of semi-circular: a typical example of Greek ingenuity in adapting architectural conventions to the requirements of nature. Originally it must have been little more than a place of entertainment for garrison troops. Macronisos, the barren island running parallel to the coast between Lavrion and Thoricus often provides an asylum for political prisoners. Beyond the branch to Thoricus, the road climbs a steep pass and descends slowly into the plains of the Mesogeia.

The Mesogeia is the loveliest part of Attica, an undulating vine country, streaked with olive groves and dotted with sugar-loaf hills. In the east, a chain of mountains, snow-capped in winter, infinite in their variety of forms, suggest the proximity of another world – the mountains of Euboea. Byzantine shrines are scattered about the countryside. The most interesting are the eleventh-century Church of the Taxiarchoi (The Archangels), believed to have been built on the foundations of an early Christian basilica (the marble shrine behind the iconostasis is supported by two fluted columns with capitals adorned with floral designs), Ayios Petros (St Peter's), where the narthex connects with the main shrine through a triple arcade and fragments of Greek, Roman and Early Christian art have been discovered, Ayios Yiorghos (St George's), domeless, in its olive grove, divided into five sections by transverse walls (one of which is in the form of an iconostasis) – all within easy walking distance of the main road.[3] The east coast has a succession of sandy beaches. One of the most attractive is Porto Raphti, an almost circular bay, its entrance little more than a mile wide, guarded by a sugar-loaf islet crowned by a Roman statue.[4] This sheltered anchorage is the ancient Prasiai, whence the sacred embassies sailed to Delos.

The red soil of the Mesogeia is the richest in Attica, the villages the most prosperous. In Byzantine times most of the land was owned by the Church; consequently the peasants welcomed the Frankish conquest because the taxes they paid were no longer sent to Constantinople but retained by their new French overlords who sank the revenue back into the land. The present inhabitants are of Albanian origin, and some still speak an ancient Albanian dialect. Descendants of seventeenth-century immigrants, imported to cultivate a countryside rapidly becoming depopulated under Ottoman maladministration, they continue to dwell in their original settlements, mostly in Attica and the Peloponnese. This desperate Turkish bid to repopulate one of the most impoverished domains of the empire corresponds with the nadir of Greek servitude and abasement. The settlers were soon

3 For the Archangels, the traveller should ask the way at the village of Kalyvia, for St Peter's and St George's at Marcopoulo. Also he should not omit to inquire where the keys can be obtained, in case the churches are locked, as they are likely to be.

4. The branch road to Porto Rapht i is at Marcopoulo.

assimilated (the Greeks are quick at assimilating foreign elements and have always treated their minorities well). Today the farmers and wine-growers of the Mesogeia are among the most loyal of Greek citizens. In 1806, Chateaubriand, victim of a sunstroke caught while partridge-shooting in the hills, stayed in an Albanian hut at Keratea, the first village north of Lavrion. He was delighted with the relative abundance of birds – hoopoes, wood-pigeons, crows and jackdaws, as well as the red-legged partridge – and wrote eloquently of the dignity of the barefoot seventeen-year-old Albanian girl, whose hair was '*chargé de médailles et de petites pièces d'argent*,' and sang '*à demi-voix*' as she waited on him.[5]

At Marcopoulo, famous for its bakeries which produce the best country bread and *paximadia* (crisp rusks flavoured with aniseed) in Attica, there is another fork to the east (besides the one to Porto Raphti). It leads past a Frankish tower of the thirteenth century into a shallow valley, where an orchard of fig trees winds towards a marshland and the sea. The swamp, bordered by low hills, is the site of ancient **Brauron,** where Orestes and Iphigenia landed after their dramatic escape from the 'howling shore' of the Taurians, so vividly described by the Messenger in the *Iphigenia in Tauris* of Euripides.

The story of Iphigenia is one of the key-myths in Greek literature. It was at Aulis, farther up the coast, that the Mycenaean princess was sacrificed by Agamemnon, when Calchas, the court seer, prophesied that the Achaean fleet would remain alternately becalmed and storm-bound until the King's daughter was sacrificed at the altar of Artemis. But the sacrifice was not consummated. The chaste and, in this instance, compassionate Artemis snatched the girl from the pyre and wafted her in a cloud to transpontine Tauris, where she was installed as high priestess in the goddess's temple until rescued by her brother. The motions of the sacrifice having been gone through, a favourable wind arose and the Achaean ships sailed for Troy and its chastisement. Agamemnon's readiness to sacrifice his daughter in the national interest was not forgiven by his wife, Clytemnestra, whose maternal instincts were outraged by this cynical act of political expediency. Further impetus was thus provided for the calamit-

5. *Itinéraire de Paris à Jérusalem.*

ous sequence of adultery, murder and matricide that dogged the house of Atreus and produced some of the greatest literature in the world.

The sanctuary, site of an old Neolithic settlement, was consecrated to the worship of Brauronian Artemis. One day one of the goddess's pet bears was killed by an angry mob for eating up a little girl. Enraged by this act, Artemis demanded that all girls in Attica between the ages of five and ten should henceforth enter her service and worship at her Brauronian shrine, where they were called 'bears' and obliged to perform a ritual dance, dressed in saffron-coloured robes in imitation of bearskins. The Brauronian festival was celebrated every fifth year, and no Athenian girl was allowed to marry unless she had participated in it. On one occasion, the Pelasgians, who had settled on the island of Lemnos after being driven out of Attica on account of their indecent assaults on Athenian girls, made a raid on the coast, seized a number of little 'bears' celebrating the Brauronia, and, according to Herodotus, 'sailed off with them to Lemnos, where they kept them as mistresses'. Recent excavations on the marshy site have revealed a fifth-century B.C. stoa with a marble stylobate. At its north end there is a series of small rooms, in which the girl-priestesses were probably lodged. Little remains but foundations of the Doric Temple of Artemis, to which Iphigenia may have brought the holy image of the goddess, pilfered from the Taurian temple. A series of late **fifth century B.C. reliefs** of exquisite perfection, portraying sacrificial rites in honour of the goddess, are displayed in the little museum. Seldom have the billowing folds of women's garments been reproduced with such virtuosity. North-east of the sanctuary, on the side of a hill covered with sheets of pink and white anemones in early spring, are the ruins of an Early Christian basilica and a round building, believed to have been a baptistery.

After joining the main road again one reaches Paeania, most northerly of Mesogeian villages, where there is a modern church in the main square decorated with frescoes by Kontoglou, a contemporary painter who has turned to Byzantium of the Palaeologue epoch for his models. Every inch of wall space, dome, apse, pendentives, squinches and narthex, is covered with frescoes of saints, prophets, warrior angels, Fathers of

the Church and all the familiar scenes from the lives of Christ
and the Virgin. The great compositions of the *Dodecaorton*,
the Twelve Feasts, with which the traveller will soon become
familiar, are as stylised as anything in the great Byzantine
churches of Daphni, Hosios Loukas and Mistra. The skill in
imitation is so remarkable that one is inclined to ignore the
technical virtuosity. In terms of pure pastiche, the Paeania
church is a *tour de force*.

Close by is the charming taverna of Kanakis, where in fine
weather lunch is served in secluded little boscages surrounded
by fields of Paper-White-Narcissus. In spring the scent of
orange blossom and lilac is intoxicating. The food is simple:
hors d'œuvre (olives, pickled aubergines, fried chicken livers,
home-made sausages), grilled chicken, *souvlakia*, honey and
nuts; and a resinated rosé wine called *kokkineli*. Opposite the
taverna rises a sugarloaf hill terraced with vines and kitchen
gardens, crowned by stately pines. The immediate background
is formed by the screen of Hymettus, steep, bare and desiccated, gashed with rocky ravines: rather cruel-looking. This
side of Hymettus has none of the rounded smoothness of the
western flanks which often make this extraordinary mountain
look like a huge grey elephant sprawling across the plain.

It was in the deme of Paeania that Demosthenes, son of a
sword-maker, was born. Although Theopompus considered
him fickle and unreliable by nature, Plutarch insists that he
was 'admired through all Greece, the King of Persia courted
him, and by Philip himself he was more esteemed than all the
other orators'. He then goes on to describe how the author of
the *Philippics* acquired his oratorical virtuosity. Greatly
impressed by 'the proper mien and gesture of Satyrus', a
contemporary actor, 'he began to esteem it . . . as good as
nothing for a man to exercise himself in declaiming, if he
neglected enunciation and delivery. Hereupon he built himself
a study in under-ground . . . and hither he would come constantly every day to form his action and to exercise his voice;
and here he would continue, oftentimes without intermission,
two or three months together, shaving one half of his head,
that so for shame he might not go abroad, though he desired
it ever so much.' But while perfecting his oratory, Demosthenes was learning little about practical statesmanship; his
Philippics may be among the greatest works of rhetoric in

Greek literature, but they failed to unite the Greek city states against the threat of Philip of Macedon. For in their twilight years, darkened by the shadow of Philip's invincibility, the Hellenic states no longer had the will to sink their petty differences in the common interest.

At Stavros, north of Paeania, there is a fork. The westbound road leads back to Athens, skirting the northern ridge of Hymettus, crowned by the little Byzantine Church of St John the Hunter (twelfth with seventeenth-century additions), recently divested of its homely whitewash and rather too stylishly restored. A whole circuit of south-east Attica has been completed: a long drive.

*

The eastbound road from Stavros cuts across the northern Mesogeia to the Euboean channel and the field of Marathon. At Pallini a branch road leads to the pine-fringed beach of Loutsa. At Pikermi, where there are two good tavernas (game in autumn and winter), a track climbs up to the Monastery of Daou-Pendeli, concealed in a lonely pine forest. Osbert Lancaster calls the church (twelfth century, restored in the seventeenth) 'A dotty triumph of provincial art'.[6] It is, indeed, a curiosity, with numerous arches and six domes, the tallest surmounting the narthex which is on a different level from the main hexagonal body of the church. Possibly Armenian and Georgian influences, although seldom encountered on the Greek mainland, have been at work here. The monastery is said to be haunted. I remember once standing in the court in front of the narthex taking photographs. A friend who was with me remarked: 'Why don't you take a photograph of that old nun making signs to you? You know what pleasure it gives them.' I glanced up. No nun was within sight. My friend was not given to hallucinations, and did not believe in ghosts.

Beyond the turning point to Daou-Pendeli, the road crosses the gulley where a party of distinguished English and Italian travellers, driving back from a visit to the battlefield of Marathon in 1870, were kidnapped by brigands. The incident was not without political repercussions. Jobbery and in-

6. Osbert Lancaster, *Classical Landscape with Figures*, John Murray, London, 1947.

Boys playing hocky. Relief from the base of a statue originally built into the walls of Themistocles. (p. 77).

Karytaena. One of the many Frankish castles perched on crags that dominate the desolate but grandiose Arcadian scene.

The Temple of Poseidon, Sunium (5th century B.C.), is the work of the architect of the Theseum and stands in a spectacular position on the southernmost promontory of Attica.

Attica — a small Byzantine Church.

timidation were still normal practices in Greek politics and brigands had their representatives in Parliament, their contact-men in the government. The inept British Minister in Athens lost his head; Gladstone, then Prime Minister, was too romantically philhellene to act decisively; the ransom was not paid, and the male members of the party were murdered in the most cruel circumstances. International opinion was outraged and Queen Victoria telegraphed from Osborne to Gladstone to express her horror at 'this terrible Greek tragedy'.[7]

The road continues to dip down towards the sea: a wide bay, the bay of **Marathon**, scimitar-shaped, the waves often flecked with white horses raised by the north-east etesian wind. Opposite rise the mountains of Euboea, denuded of vegetation, without a village in sight. From the narrow coastal belt roll the pine-covered hills across which the runner, according to the apocryphal story, raced to Athens to announce the outcome of the battle, only to die of exhaustion on reaching the stadium. It was from the summit of one of these spurs that the anonymous traitor flashed a shield to warn Datis, the Persian commander, that the capital was left without troops. This was the signal for the fleet to sail round Cape Sunium and attack Athens from the sea, while the army of Miltiades was still twenty-six miles from the scene.

Marathon (490 B.C.) was the first of the three great battles which the Athenians waged with such extraordinary success against the immensely superior power mobilised by Darius for what historians believe may have been an attempt at a great Asiatic invasion of Europe. Under the leadership of Miltiades, a resolute and brilliant tactician, the Greeks fought with tremendous dash, and, 'charging at the double,' quickly spread confusion among the heavily armed Medes, who were bogged down in the marshes. The battle was won on both wings, the Persian centre remaining unbroken until the end. Nevertheless it is difficult to believe, as Herodotus claims, that the Greeks lost under two hundred men to the Persian six thousand four hundred. Their victory also owed much to Persian over-confidence and to Datis' refusal to throw into the battle a mass of troops reserved for the protection of the fleet. The effect of the victory – neither as important nor as decisive

7. Romilly Jenkins, *The Dilessi Murders*, Longmans, London, 1961.

as Salamis (for the Persians came again, ten years later, in redoubled strength) – was immense in terms of morale, and every Athenian, as Grote says, was strengthened by a swelling of 'the tide of common sentiment and patriotic fraternity . . .'

The site is now a reclaimed marshland; in the middle of it stands the Soros, a mound raised over a floor on which archaeologists have found traces of charcoal and human bones: the bones of the Greek dead. Pieces of flint have been identified as fragments of arrow-heads used by Persian archers. Although Herodotus says the battle was fought close to a swamp, all around the Soros the land is now arable, with vineyards and olive groves criss-crossed by ditches filled with clusters of Rose of Sharon narcissus in early spring. There is a consecrated feeling about the place: a haunted atmosphere, according to Pausanias, who says: 'At Marathon every night you can hear horses neighing and men fighting. No one who has expressly set himself to behold this vision has ever got any good from it . . .' On one side rise the wooded spurs of Pentelicus, on the other flow the blue waters of the channel. Nobody has described the scene more succinctly than Byron in the hackneyed line, 'The mountains look on Marathon, and Marathon looks on the sea.' Northward extends the lovely crescent-shaped beach of Schina, fringed with tall pines.

About half a mile before the village of Marathon, a turning-point to the right leads across a bleak stretch of scrub-land to the site of **Rhamnus**. The terrace was a sacred enclosure, supported on two sides by a retaining wall composed of blocks of dazzling white marble. The foundations of the larger of two edifices have been identified as those of a temple of Nemesis. Doric in style, probably the work of the architect of the Theseum and Temple of Poseidon at Sunium, it contained a colossal statue in Parian marble of the goddess wearing a crown ornamented with effigies of deer and little victories, an apple branch in her right hand, in her left a cup embossed with figures of Ethiopians. The statue is believed to have been executed by Phidias, who chose, however, to give the credit for it to a favourite pupil. There is some reason to believe that the temple was never finished, for the three steps of the stylobate have not been smoothed and a number of drums of the columns lying about the site have not been fluted. The smaller temple, almost contiguous to the larger, is sometimes described as that of Themis, an offspring, according to Hesiod, of the marriage of Uranus (Heaven) and Ge (Earth). It may, alternatively, have been an earlier shrine of Nemesis, destroyed by the Persians. If so, the goddess took a swift revenge for this act of desecration by ensuring the Persian defeat at Marathon: one of those typical examples in Greek mythology of gods participating in (and often confusing the issue of) battles between mortals.

From the sacred enclosure one descends a steep glen to a pebbly shore dominated by a knoll. A massive fourth-century B.C. stone wall, almost gold in colour, emerges out of the evergreens: the remains of the ancient township of Rhamnus (the name was derived from the prickly buckthorn shrub which grew all over the hills and had emetic and purgative properties). Within the acropolis, thick with brushwood and tangled vines, there are vestiges of watch-towers, barrack-rooms, cisterns and the cavea of a theatre. Clearly a garrison was stationed at Rhamnus – presumably to guard the entrance to the Euripus. The upland valley, the sacred enclosure, the lonely glen, the crumbling fortifications and deserted shore have an austere quality which few can fail to associate with the goddess of retribution. One marvels at the Greek genius for exploiting topographical features to enhance a religious idea. Of Rhamnus, Christopher Wordsworth, the nineteenth century traveller, says: 'We recognise, therefore, in this place one of the most interesting specimens to be found on the soil of Greece of those Sacred Enclosures, which, from their elevation and retirement, gave additional beauty, dignity and sanctity, to the Temples contained in them.'

Rhamnus is a dead-end. Beyond it extend the waters of the channel and the coast of Euboea. One may, however, return to Athens by another road (fork at Nea Makri, two kilometres south of the battlefield) which skirts the northern slopes of Pentelicus as far as Dionysos and thence, through the pine-woods and villas of Ekali, to Athens.

*

Next comes northern Attica. The residential suburb of Psychico, much favoured by foreign residents, is succeeded by Philothei, equally suburban, less fashionable, named after St Philothei, a well-born nun of the sixteenth century who owned vast lands and founded a convent, a hospital and a workshop for weaving (from the profits of which she bought Greek girls out of Turkish harems). A determined hot-tempered woman, she had a poor opinion of Athenians whom she once described in a letter as 'a people without religion, decision or shame, wicked and reckless, with mouths open for insults and reproaches, grumbling, barbarous-tongued, loving strife and trouble and gossip, petty, loquacious, arrogant, lawless, crafty, inquisitive and wide-awake to profit by the misfortune of others'.[8] The Turks, envious of her wealth and incensed by her sharp tongue, finally seized her while she was conducting a midnight service and beat her to death. The Church subsequently canonised her. From Philothei one enters the working class suburb of Nea Ionia, where it is worthwhile looking at the twelfth-century **Omorphi Ecclesia** (The Beautiful Church) which has a pretty octagonal drum. Much of the original structure has been spoilt by later inelegant additions. The interior is decorated with frescoes (possibly fifteenth or sixteenth century) which are pleasant rather than remarkable. The windows are attractively adorned with Rhodian plates.

Back on the main road, one turns right at the eighth kilometre from Athens and cuts across a cultivated stretch of the central Attic plain, rapidly becoming urbanised, to Mt Pentelicus, a bluish pyramid, scarred with the ravages of two and a half thousand years of marble quarrying. It is one of the loveliest of Attic landmarks. At the end of the road, Pendeli, one of the richest monastic establishments in Greece, is surrounded by plane trees. Streams trickle down the sides of the mountain. In summer the whole place, an outpost of suburbia, is a vast holiday camp with tents and wooden shacks on the high ground above the maisonette belt, where the eccentric Duchesse de Plaisance (see p. 70) owned several summer residences, of which the most easily identified is the unfinished 'Castello de Rododaphne', now no more than a gloomy neo-Gothic shell, where she was once attacked by brigands, led, according to the gossips, by her lover, the notorious robber Bitsis. In these former rustic retreats, the Duchess also entertained her distinguished friends, among

8. Demetrios Sicilianos, *Old and New Athens*, Putnam, London, 1960, translation by Robert Liddell.

whom one of the closest was the lovely Jane Digby, successively Lady Ellenborough, Baroness Venningen, Countess Theotoki and wife of an Arab Emir. The two women must have made a strange contrast: the Frenchwoman small, tense and emaciated, in the white cotton robe and veil (worn in the Hebrew style) which she affected; the Englishwoman large, florid, with beautiful features and eyes which Edmond About described as blue as the sea.

The slopes above the monastery are seamed with disused quarries: a lunar landscape of white rubble. Mountain goats browse among tufts of heather and thyme which fail to conceal the centuries-old cicatrices. One cannot approach Pentelicus without a feeling of veneration. The very stuff of the mountain, its actual bones and marrow, has furnished the raw material for some of the greatest works of sculpture and architecture in the world. 'Of Pentelic marble' – the label is familiar enough from museum catalogues. Distinguished for its opaque quality, as opposed to the snowy whiteness of Parian, Pentelic marble contains an admixture of iron which accounts for the fact that, when exposed to the inclemencies of the weather, it acquires a warm honey-coloured patina.

North-west lies Kephisia, where old Athenian families spend the summer in pseudo-Gothic, pseudo-Islamic, pseudo-Hellenistic villas set amid shady gardens where nightingales sing. There are also plenty of hotels. To Kephisia Herodes Atticus retired to mourn the death of his wife Regilla and plan new acts of munificence for the people of Athens. It is also the country of Menander, the comic poet. In I. Metaxas Street, just off the main square, there is a famous confectioner's where an astonishing variety of exotic home-made jams are sold. Jam plays an important part in the ceremonial of Greek hospitality, as visitors to peasant houses will soon discover. Shortly after one is seated, the jam pot, covered with a lace cloth (sometimes with a beaded fringe) arrives on a tray, surrounded by glasses of water containing spoons. One removes the spoon, sips some water, wishes good health to one's host, helps oneself to a spoonful of pistachio nut or morello cherry jam and replaces the spoon in the glass of water. A second spoonful is not offered. The jams include walnut, aubergine, bergamot and mandarin. Rose petal is disappointing, its flavour resembling that of cheap scent. A great favourite is mastic: a sticky white substance, not unlike toffee in texture, composed of boiled sugar flavoured with mastic. It is not served in a jam pot, but in a spoon already submerged in a glass of water (hence its name, *ypovrychio*, i.e. submarine).

North of Kephisia extends a hilly countryside below the wooded spurs of Parnes, with terraced vineyards and olive trees on the slopes of rolling hills and cornfields and vegetable plots in the cup-shaped valleys. To the right there is a glimpse of an artificial lake, one of the main water supplies of the capital. The dam of Pentelic marble, completed by American engineers in 1926, prevents the streams that flow down the mountain sides in winter from escaping through the numerous gulleys into the Marathonian plain.

To the west is the village-stronghold of Aphidnae, associated with the earliest history of Attica. It was one of the twelve townships that Theseus is supposed to have united into a single administrative unit, and the place to which he brought Helen, still a child, after abducting her from her father's court at Sparta. To Aphidnae then came her brothers, the intrepid Dioscuri, in pursuit; but they found her still unravished, for Theseus, growing old, had curbed his waning desires in deference to her tender age. George Finlay, the historian, had a farm here in the nineteenth century.

Beyond Aphidnae the pinewoods become thicker, more luxuriant. There are entrancing views of the Euboean channel which begins to contract as it nears the Euripus. A few kilometres beyond the village of Calamos is the **Sanctuary of Amphiaraus,** the Argive seer, who, after taking part in the abortive war of the Seven against Thebes, was swallowed up in the earth, together with his chariot. The sanctuary is situated in a secluded gulley shaded by pine and plane trees. The wind rustling the pine branches is laden with the scent of resin; the only other sound is that of a stream, its banks overgrown with maidenhair, trickling down to the sea. Pausanias calls the sanctuary a 'dream oracle', and consultants purified themselves by sacrificing to the god before lying on the ground under an animal skin. When they were asleep, their questions were answered in a dream.

The ruins are easily identified: on the right, the substructure of a large altar; behind it, the foundations of a fourth century

B.C. Doric temple *in antis*, with the base of the cult statue in the middle of the cella; next, the opening of a spring, sacred to the seer, from which he reappeared from the Underworld, and into which pilgrims threw coins as a thanksgiving. The curative properties of the waters are described by Erasistratus, the late fourth century B.C. physician who invented a new interpretation of the science of anatomy. Numerous bases of statues litter the terrace above the altar. Beyond them a marble bench, supported by marble feet, where consultants sat while waiting to be allocated sleeping quarters, bordered one side of a long and impressive early fourth century B.C. stoa, which had a façade of forty-one Doric columns and was separated into two galleries by a row of seventeen Ionic columns. Here the consultants slept and were visited with oracular dreams. In a pine-clad declivity behind the stoa is the most charming ruin of all: a miniature **theatre,** famous for its acoustics. The proscenium, judiciously restored, is embellished with eight Doric half columns of grey Hymettus marble. Five seats for high priests, admirably preserved, are ranged in a semi-circle round the orchestra (a full circle contrary to the usual practice of slicing off a segment to make room for the projecting proscenium). Here, as elsewhere, one observes how the Greeks never failed to pay homage to the Tragic Muse. No garrison town, no health resort or remote rural sanctuary was without its little theatre, on whose stage strutted actors in the festive costumes of worshippers of Dionysus, their faces concealed behind a variety of masks – tragic, comic, satiric.

*

Another road from Athens to the north runs across the plain between banks of oleanders to the village of Acharnae, where ivy, the symbol of the god Dionysus, grew for the first time. During the Peloponnesian War, Acharnae, which furnished three thousand hoplites (one tenth of the Athenian infantry), occupied a front line position, being only a few miles from Deceleia, whence the Spartan outposts descended into the plain, plundering and burning the farms. Acharnae is now almost wholly inhabited by descendants of seventeenth century Albanian settlers, and there is no sign of the jolly charcoal-burners, 'as their own oak and maple, rough and tough', of Aristophanes' *The Acharnians*. In the cafés it is not uncommon to hear the older generation chatting in the harsh Albanian dialect of the original seventeenth-century *Skipetars*. Beyond Acharnae the road ascends Mt Parnes, the highest though least beautiful of the mountains enclosing the Attic plain on three sides, where ancient Athenians came to hunt bears and wild boar. About two thirds of the way up the firs begin. Just below the summit, where there are ski-runs, there is an agglomeration of sanatoriums, roadhouses and chalets amid the dark conifers. It is all rather Swiss. There is also a modern luxury hotel with a swimming pool, situated on a ledge commanding a spectacular view of central Attica.

A branch road from Acharnae follows a westerly course to the village of Phyle. Beyond the Monastery of the Panayia ton Kleiston (The Virgin of the Closed Defiles), probably of Byzantine origin, but with later additions, clinging to the side of a precipice, a rough road climbs the lonely defile. In front extend escarpments, contorted rock formations and deep crevices; behind there are views of Athens and the plain against the backcloth of Hymettus. The pass of **Phyle** (over 2000 feet high) is dominated by a small triangular plateau surrounded by a ring of fourth-century B.C. fortifications, with remains of ramparts and square towers (and one round one) dominating the point of intersection of numerous gorges. These fortifications, which replaced an earlier fortress, guarded the shortest route into Attica from Boeotia. In winter there are treacherous snowdrifts and many mountaineers and shepherds have lost their lives in the unsuspected chasms. The quadrangular masonry of the walls, nearly ten feet thick, is well preserved (in some places sixteen courses can be distinguished), particularly on the east side. An interesting point about the two entrances (south and east) is that they were built in such a way as to expose the attackers' right shoulders, unprotected by shields, to the defenders within. The final ascent to the fortress is precipitous. From here Thrasybulus, who played such a distinguished part in the final stages of the Peloponnesian War, descended into the plain to deliver Athens from the infamous dictatorship of the Thirty Tyrants.

Yet another north-bound road leads to the thickly wooded area of Tatoi on the foothills of Mt Parnes. This is the ancient deme of Deceleia, through which Mardonius marched the

Persian army when he evacuated Athens after the battle of
Salamis. The taverna of Leonidas (specialities: brawn, chicken
pie, sucking pig and game in season) is one of the coolest spots
in Attica, and on August nights it is crowded with Athenians
escaping from the stifling air and burning pavements of the
city. The Greek royal family have a summer palace here and
a graveyard for their kings amid the most luxuriant pines in
Attica. Beyond the palace, on the spine of the mountain,
there are vestiges (twenty minutes' hard climb from a little
taverna surrounded by plane trees) of the famous Spartan
stronghold of Deceleia, which, says Thucydides, 'was meant
to annoy the plain and the richest parts of the country . . .'
After the pass of Ayios Mercurios the road descends in loops
to Malakassa, where it joins the national highway and whence
a branch road leads to Oropus on the Euboean channel. By
this time the outline of Euboea, which extends from the
promontory of Sunium in the south to the Pagasitic Gulf in
the north, has become increasingly familiar. There is a comfortable feeling of omnipresence about Euboea. Its peaks are
nearly always visible behind the mainland ranges, and the blue
streak of the channel is encountered again and again along the
coasts of Attica, Boeotia and Phthiotis. From Oropus, a
historic bone of contention between Athenians and Boeotians,
a ferry-boat crosses the channel to the opposite shore and site
of ancient Eretria. All this country, on both sides of the
channel, produces a delicious green fig.

*

Before leaving Athens, it would be a mistake, I think, not to
take one last look at Hymettus, smooth and elephantine, most
homely and familiar of Attic mountains. The road from the
centre of Athens cuts across the working class suburb of
Kaisariani, a Communist stronghold in the 1944 rebellion –
the 'Stalingrad of Greece', it was called – and enters a verdant
little valley in a fold of the mountain: an oasis of cypress, olive
and plane trees. It was from here that Edward Dodwell, an
early nineteenth century amateur archaeologist, drew one of
his charming 'Views of Greece', in which the Acropolis,
surrounded by nothing but a huddle of shacks, is seen rising
out of the bare plain. Today the eye meets with a sea of

cream-coloured buildings. At the head of the valley, under a large plane tree, a spring gushes forth: a fertility spring, according to superstition. Ovid describes it in *The Art of Love* – 'Near the purple hills of flowery Hymettus there is a sacred spring and ground soft with green turf: trees of no great height form a grove; arbutus covers the grass, and rosemary, bays and dark myrtles are fragrant; nor is the thick foliage of the box-tree lacking, or brittle tamarisks and thin lucerne and the cultivated pine.' It has not changed much, in spite of suburban encroachment. Above the spring is the **Monastery of Kaisariani,** with its church, dedicated to the Presentation of the Virgin, built in alternating courses of brick and stone. An eleventh century foundation, for long inhabited by monks who kept beehives, it has undergone considerable restoration. The wall paintings in the narthex, apse and pendentives are of the post-Byzantine period. The marble lintel of the doorway of the refectory is finely carved. Kaisariani is not important in the history of Byzantine church architecture, but its elegant little drum and cupola, its warm red brick roofs, even its somewhat incongruous seventeenth century campanile, all shaded by pine branches, compose into a charming spectacle of rusticity on the fringe of the suburban belt. It is not surprising that Athenian families often sought shelter here during the Turkish occupation to escape from the plague. They could not have chosen a more agreeable refuge.

Above Kaisariani the steep mountain-side is covered with stunted shrubs: cistus, juniper and terebinth; and the aromatic sage, thyme and lavender, which, together with the grape-hyacinth and purple crocus of spring, feed the famous Hymettus bees. Hymettus honey, with which Plato's mouth was said to have been filled at birth, is now produced throughout Attica; but the Greeks believed that the first bees in the world came from Hymettus. Beyond the monastery the road climbs past the pretty little Byzantine Church of Asteri to a bleak summit in the form of a plateau commanding an immense panoramic view of the whole of Attica and the islands of the Saronic Gulf.

*

The road to the west, to Corinth and the Peloponnese, crosses a ridge of hills from which there is an incomparable view, best seen at sunset, of the city spreading round its rocky hills under the 'violet crown' of Hymettus. Chateaubriand wrote lyrically of the impact made on him by this famous scene.[9] The road now joins the Sacred Way to Eleusis, once bordered with tombs of illustrious citizens. Today there are petrol stations and scruffy suburban residences – also the forbidding walls of a lunatic asylum. On the left the red brick dome of the church at **Daphni** and the tops of three cypress trees appear above the high walls with which the Crusaders encircled the monastery; within it they established a Cistercian community in the thirteenth century. Dedicated to the Virgin, Daphni is one of the most important Byzantine monuments in the country. The church is of the middle eleventh century, the mosaics of the late eleventh, a golden age in Byzantine art – the age of the Comnene dynasty which held the stage for a century and, rare in Byzantine history, succeeded in passing the throne from father to son for three generations.

The interior of the church is a classic example of eleventh century church architecture: a wide squat dome and drum, supported by four pendentives, the four arms of the Greek Cross plan meeting in the central square, the sanctuary in the apse behind the iconostasis, the narthex in the west front.

The mosaics have suffered from negligence and desecration; some have been restored; but enough survive to illustrate the perfection achieved by Byzantine mosaicists of the best period. Mosaic floors were common enough in the Hellenistic, Roman and Early Christian periods. In the fifth century mosaic portraiture appears at Ravenna and Salonica. The new medium was quickly developed, with only a temporary break during the Iconoclast period (726–842), when the representation of all divine and saintly forms was banished from religious art. In the Daphni mosaics the strictly formalistic style seems to have become more articulate, to be imbued with a dawning humanism. The large compositions are now rendered as pictures; the draperies are more subtly modelled and the austere frontal position has given way to a slightly oblique view of the stylised faces; the number of scenic representations has increased, that of single figures diminished. The new art has become less monkish. The influence of classical reliefs, both in the flowing drapery and the nobility

9. Chateaubriand, loc. cit.

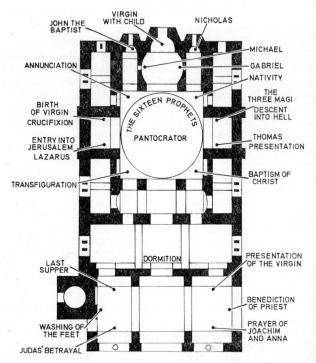

Ground plan of the Church, Daphni.

of expression of the faces, is evident. The mosaics at Daphni, an imperial foundation, are thoroughly Constantinopolitan in character.

On entering the church, one's first impression is of a large expanse of whitewashed walls. There seems to be little of the Byzantine 'gorgeousness' that the Benaki and Byzantine Museums promised. But each of the extant compositions merits careful examination; each is a work of art. The iconographic disposition is not haphazard, but strictly liturgical and symbolical, for the Church is a visual image of Heaven, and the iconographer the servant of the theologian. It therefore helps to have an idea of the iconographic arrangement mosaic or fresco) of a typical Byzantine church interior in one's mind. One then knows what to look for. The dome is Heaven, where Christ – not the gentle saviour, but the image of the invisible Almighty – reigns in glory. He is surrounded by guardian archangels, fully armed. Below them are the apostles or prophets who announced his coming. In the central apse, behind the iconostasis, the Virgin holds the Child. She, too, is flanked by archangels. We now descend from heaven to earth. The walls are covered with portraits of saints, monks, ascetics and Fathers of the Church. Above them – on high panels, and in the squinches below the pendentives – unfold the great scenes from the lives of Christ and the Virgin, the *Dodecaorton* (The Twelve Feasts): namely, the Annunciation, Nativity, Presentation in the Temple, Baptism, Raising of Lazarus, Transfiguration, Entry into Jerusalem, Crucifixion, Descent into Hell, Ascension, Pentecost and Dormition of the Virgin (the order in which these are placed may vary from church to church). Particular prominence is given to the Crucifixion and Descent into Hell which reveal the mystery of the Resurrection. Other scenes from the Gospels are often added, generally in the narthex. Each cycle, each group of saints possesses a special significance in the overall decoration of the church, which represents a profound theological truth to the worshipper.

At Daphni (as elsewhere) it is best to start in the narthex, where narrative tendencies are observed in the Betrayal, the Washing of the Feet and the Presentation, and then pass into the main body of the church, where the new 'humanism' is particularly evident in the **Transfiguration** in a squinch below the dome. The figure of Christ may be static, but it possesses an other-worldly majesty. The **Crucifixion** and **Descent into Hell**, compositions of great poise and balance, are placed in lateral panels in the choirs. The Virgin in the Crucifixion is the personification of grief and bereavement, her mouth slightly turned down at the sides, her almond-shaped eyes contracted as though to hide a film of tears. She is one of the most moving figures in the whole of Byzantine mosaic decoration. In the Descent into Hell the figure of Hades, on whom Christ is treading, recalls a Roman copy of some ancient reclining statue: unmistakable evidence of the classical past that inspired Byzantine mosaicists of the eleventh century. The drapery of the angel with enormous wings in the **Annunciation** also flows with an almost classical limpidity Note the fine splendidly-robed figure of the **Archangel Michael** in the sanctuary – he is the true 'captain of the heavenly host' – and the hieratic though wonderfully alive faces of the saints in the vaults, as well as those of the Jews who welcome Christ at the gates of Jerusalem. A general lightness of tone, an almost pastel quality, prevails in these jigsaw puzzles of thousands of tesserae, pink, blue and green, on gold backgrounds. But it is the formidable **Pantocrator** in the dome, one of the greatest portraits in Byzantine, if not in any, art, that dominates the whole church – a terrifying Messianic vision. Depicted in bust, Christ raises one hand in blessing, the long bony fingers of the other clasping a jewel-studded Book of Gospels. The face, with the superbly arched eyebrows and the mouth of a man who is, beyond all things, decisive, if not unforgiving, is austere, eastern, implacable. There is not the slightest concession to tenderness. It is a Christ of Nemesis. In the Daphni Pantocrator the whole of Byzantine civilisation comes into focus. He is worlds removed from the humanity of the Christ of Italian and Western art.

Beside the monastery there is a tourist pavilion, and in the pinewood above it an annual wine festival is held in August-September. Every wine produced in Greece – from the harshest Attic *retsina* to the sweetest Samian vintage – may be tasted for the price of an entrance ticket. There are snack bars, a restaurant, some rather bogus folk-dances, and a lot of noisy young men taking advantage of unlimited (virtually free drink. The red brick dome and roofs, the stone course and arched windows of the floodlit church provide an impressive background.

Beyond Daphni the road descends towards the landlocked bay of Eleusis. On the right are the foundations of a temple of Aphrodite and a piece of rock hollowed out into niches for votive offerings. Fragments of white marble chiselled in the form of doves, the goddess's sacred birds, were found at the foot of the rocks. The crescent-shaped bay is sealed off from the open sea by the pine-clad island of Salamis. The battle, culminating point of the second Persian invasion (480 B.C.) was fought in the narrow strait between the eastern tip of the island and the coast, where Mt Aegaleos tapers off into the sea. Xerxes, after entering an undefended and deserted Athens and destroying the temples on the Acropolis, placed his throne of gold on a 'high hill' commanding the narrows, where the vermilion-coloured triremes of the Greek allies lay at anchor, their leaders at loggerheads as to what action they should take. Only Themistocles, a sea-minded Athenian, was unflinching in advocating a naval trial of strength. Employing both cunning and eloquence, he persuaded his allies, although considerably outnumbered, to fight on ground of his own choosing. Having lured the Persian fleet into the narrows, he chose the best time of fighting, says Plutarch, 'for he would not run the prows of his galleys against the Persians, nor begin the fight till the time of day was come, when there regularly blows in a fresh breeze from the open sea, and brings with it a strong swell into the channel; which was no inconvenience to the Greek ships which were low-built, and little above the water, but did much hurt to the Persians, which had high sterns and lofty decks . . . as it presented them broadside to the quick charges of the Greeks . . .' By the evening the issue was decided, and the splintered hulks of the Persian ships littered the rocky coast. The words of the oracle had been fulfilled. Athens and Greece had been saved by 'wooden bulwarks'. The command of the sea had been won.

Themistocles and Xerxes may be the chief protagonists of the drama of Salamis; but the names of the three tragic poets also figure among the lesser *dramatis personae*. Aeschylus fought in the battle, an epic account of which he gives in *The Persians*; the youthful Sophocles, famed for his beauty, led the chorus of naked boys round the trophy, with a lyre in his hand; and Euripides was born on the island, some say on the day of the battle. Until recently another important poet, the late Angelos Sikelianos, notorious for his Apollo-like profile and eccentric habit of wearing ancient Greek dress, lived in a whitewashed cottage in the pinewoods near the Monastery of Phaneromeni, writing a sensuous lyrical verse which in some respects is an embodiment of the Hellenic spirit in a twentieth-century context.

One follows the Sacred Way taken by Athenian pilgrims bound for the celebration of the Eleusinian Mysteries, once lined with statues, shrines and votive monuments, now a broad highway running across the Thriasian plain, bordered by soap factories, cement works and oil refineries. To the right, a few yards from the sea, there is a natural reservoir of salt springs, the Rheiti, fringed with reeds, the haunt of wild fowl since time immemorial: an incongruous sight in this agglomeration of industrial installations. Ancient writers believed that the waters flowed beneath the ground from the Euripus. They were sacred to Demeter and her daughter, whose myths haunt the whole of this stretch of country. Just before entering **Eleusis,** birthplace of Aeschylus, a road to the left leads to the ruins of the sanctuary: least inspiring of ancient Greek sites, yet second only to Delphi in religious significance. The ground is flat and featureless; Parnes in the background does not present its most impressive aspect; and smoke trails from factory chimneys in the vicinity.

The Thriasian plain was the first to be sown with corn when Demeter, goddess of fertility, in the course of her wanderings in search of her daughter, Koré, abducted by Hades, presented Triptolemus, son of the king of Eleusis, with the precious seed. The boy proceeded to spread the boon of cultivation to mankind, travelling across the world in a chariot drawn by serpents provided by the goddess. Demeter had a spiky character, was quick to take offence and often vindictive. One of Hades' gardeners was punished for gossiping about her by being pushed into a deep hole, which she sealed with a rock. She turned another young man into a lizard because he laughed at the greedy manner in which she drank barley-water. Triptolemus was better brought up and never mocked his divine patroness.

Below a rocky ledge, close to the sea, extend the ruins of the principal seat of worship of Demeter and Koré, in whose honour the Eleusinia, most sacred of Greek mysteries, were celebrated every September and attended by thousands of pilgrims from all over Greece. Some scholars believe the earliest sanctuary may have been a prehistoric one dedicated to the Cretan Mother goddess. The holy edifices, whose jumbled foundations we now see, were built, rebuilt or refashioned by the Peisistratae, by Cimon and Pericles (after the Persians had destroyed the sanctuary), by Lycurgus in the fourth century B.C. and by the Antonine Emperors in the second A.D., when initiation into the Mysteries was very fashionable among Roman patrician families. Literally

Daphni — The Pantocrator, one of the greatest portraits in Byzantine art, dominates the whole church. (p. 110).

Daphni — The Nativity — one of the Dodecaorton (The Twelve Feasts) unfolding the great scenes from the lives of Christ and the Virgin (p. 109).

Daphni – The Virgin in the Crucifixion is the personification of grief and bereavement. She is one of the most moving figures in the whole of Byzantine mosaic decoration (p. 109).

othing remains standing, for Alaric and his Goths seem to
ave gone about their usual work of destruction with un-
recedented thoroughness. Moreover, the successive recon-
tructions and restorations on different levels over a period of
ight hundred years make it very difficult to identify the
oundations.

The sanctuary area is shut in by cement factories, by the low
idge of an acropolis and by the sea. Left of the Great
ropylaea, an Antonine reconstruction, is the opening of a
vell, once the fountain around which the Eleusinian women
erformed ritual dances, to the accompaniment of a chorus
hanting praises of Demeter. Next comes the Lesser Propy-
aea, also a Roman construction, which had an astonishingly
pulent decoration. On the cliff to the right two caves are
receded by a little walled-in terrace. This is part of the
anctuary of Hades. The caves represent the entrance to the
Underworld and the exit from which Koré emerged every
pring to bring light and fertility into the world again. The

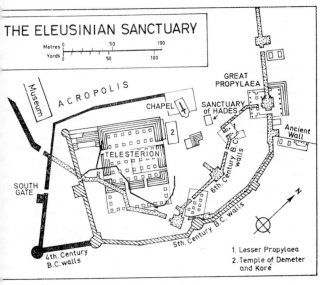

THE ELEUSINIAN SANCTUARY

Metres 0 — 50 — 100
Yards 0 — 50 — 100

MUSEUM

ACROPOLIS

CHAPEL

GREAT
PROPYLAEA

SANCTUARY
of HADES

Ancient
Wall

2

TELESTERION

6th. Century B.C. walls

SOUTH
GATE

6th. Century B.C. walls

N

5th. Century B.C. walls

4th. Century
B.C. walls

1. Lesser Propylaea
2. Temple of Demeter
and Koré

outline of the god's temple is discernible in front of the
larger cave. Returning to the Sacred Way, one reaches the
platform of the Telesterion, where the Mysteries were performed. Bases of columns are easily identified. The fifth-
century B.C. interior consisted of six rows of seven columns,
believed to have been Ionic, surrounded by tiers (those on the
west side are well preserved), on which as many as three
thousand people could stand. It had an upper story, where the
hiera, the holy objects connected with the ceremony of
initiation, were kept, crowned by a wooden roof, the first of
its kind to be placed on cross-rows of columns (an Egyptian
idea). The ruins of this extraordinary building, a square with
a prostyle east portico and a forest of intersecting interior
colonnades, are now no more than a mass of shattered blocks
of masonry from successive restorations. It is useless to look
for the place fashioned into a topographical representation of
the Underworld, furnished with all kinds of grisly objects
symbolising the infernal landmarks of Tartarus, where
initiation took place. Were the site less hemmed in by urban
development and had the landscape one bit of the grandeur
of Delphi or serenity of Olympia, it might have been easier
to visualise the spectacular almost barbaric spectacle and to
speculate on the religious exaltation experienced by the
initiates, or *mystae*, as they proceeded in torchlight procession
to the Hall of the Mysteries.

The administration of the Mysteries was in the hands of two
sacerdotal families who provided the hierophants (revealers of
the Mysteries), heralds, torch-bearers and other officials.
What form the rites took, it is impossible to say. The *mystae*
all swore a solemn oath of secrecy. Yet it seems strange that no
indiscretions should have come down to us. Pausanias, usually
so garrulous, remarks rather pompously: 'The things within
the wall of the Hierum a dream forbade me to describe.'
Strabo is equally cagy. The concensus of opinion is that the
Mysteries probably consisted of fertility rites, accompanied by
speculations on life after death and on the relation between
man's destiny and natural phenomena. The revelations took
the form of a sacred drama of the story of Demeter and her
daughter's annual emergence from the Asphodel Fields of
Tartarus. The *mystae*, carrying a statue of Demeter's son
Iacchus, adorned with garlands of myrtle, were followed by

thousands of spectators and hangers-on, and Herodotus does not consider it unusual that as many as thirty thousand people should be seen proceeding along the Sacred Way from the Cerameicus to Eleusis. The publication of the Edict of Theodosius at the end of the fourth century A.D. brought an end to the celebration of this extraordinary religious performance. It was the last nail in the pagan coffin.

North of Eleusis the road traverses a rugged sparsely-populated countryside. In March the *Anemone blanda*, with its sky-blue strap-shaped petals, grows profusely in the scrubland of the valleys below Mt Cithaeron. Although sacred to pleasure-loving Dionysus, Cithaeron is an austere, even grim-looking mountain. Its contours are not elegant, but the steep slate-grey slopes, sprinkled with silver firs, and the lonely brushwood country at their foot, were reputed to be the haunt of Pan, god of shepherds, half-goat, half-man, lively, lusty, sometimes cantankerous, who created the first pipes from the bed of reeds into which the nymph, Syrinx, whom he pursued in vain, was transformed. Here lions, bears and wild boar had their lairs, and stags roamed the forests. As one descends into a deep sunken valley, the remains of a stone tower rise immediately on the right. It was probably part of a system of ancient watch-towers along the frontier between Attica and Boeotia. In spring the fields are carpeted with pink and mauve anemones; snakes glide among the bushes and reeds by the stream below the tower. At the village of Oinoe a side road ascends to the Monastery of Hosios Meletios, a Byzantine foundation, considerably restored, situated on a little mountain ledge among plane and poplar trees. Beyond Oinoe the entrance to a narrow pass is screened by a steep eminence crowned by ruined fourth century B.C. ramparts: the fortress of **Eleutherae,** which guarded Attica and the Megarid from invasion from the north. It failed to do so in 1941, when British Commonwealth forces retreated through the defile after a vain attempt to hold up the German panzers. The fortifications are well preserved, particularly the north wall (eight feet thick and built in regular courses), dotted with square towers provided with two gates in the lower story and loopholes on the upper. The best view of the enceinte is the backward one, from the north, as one climbs up the defile which ends in a bleak plateau, whence the road descends in hairpin bends into the Boeotian plain. Eleutherae was the birthplace of Myron, one of the most lauded sculptors of the fifth century B.C.; unfortunately none of his original statues has survived, and we are only able to judge the quality of his work from innumerable Roman copies of his Discobolus and from the thirty-six epigrams in the Greek anthology extolling his famous effigy of a lowing cow which adorned a large open space in Athens.

Just before Eleutherae a road to the left climbs to the mountain village of Villia and descends in a series of wide loops between pine forests to the little harbour of Porto Yermano on an inlet of the Halcyonic Gulf. There are enchanting views of the calm expanse of water, with the Boeotian mountains forming a screen to the north. At the end of the descent, the remains of the fortified acropolis of **Aegosthena** are scattered among the pine-woods. To the left of the road rise admirably preserved fourth century B.C. ramparts and the ruins of fifteen square towers, larger than those at Eleutherae, complete with gates, posterns and windows. The most impressive section, with four large square towers projecting from a curtain wall, is on the landward side, although the fortress must originally have been built as a defensive post against invaders from the sea. Many of the towers, especially those erected towards the end of the fifth century, were designed to carry a wooden catapult from which stones were hurled and arrows slung at attacking forces. Along the placid pebbly shore there are some modest tavernas. Brightly painted rowing-boats lie upturned on the narrow strand; children, crouching in their shade, fasten sprats on to fishing-hooks. In summer the fields and olive groves, littered with blocks of ancient masonry, are crowded with campers, the beach infested with horseflies. The sun shimmers on the pellucid sea and a haze screens the wooded spurs of Helicon that ascend abruptly from a barren deserted coastline.

CHAPTER FIVE

The Approach to the Peloponnese:
Megaris, The Isthmus and Corinthia

❧

*Megara – The Scironian Cliffs – The Canal – Isthmia – The
Heraeum of Perachora – Corinth – Acro-Corinth – Sicyon –
The Stymphalian Lake – Nemea*

THE journey from Athens to Corinth, including deviations to
Isthmia and Perachora and the ascent of Acro-Corinth, is
easily accomplished in one day. The Sicyon–Stymphalia–
Nemea deviation requires another half-day.

From Eleusis the coastal highway continues westward, with
backward views of the landlocked bay of Salamis, its hidden
entrance guarded by a string of cone-shaped islands. The road
then skirts Megara, its whitewashed houses terraced on the
slope of an escarpment. Here were born Theognis, the elegiac
poet, and Byzas, founder of Byzantium; here, too, every
spring were held the Megarian Games, a feature of which was
the kissing contest between youths, at whose conclusion, says
Theocritus, 'whoso sweetliest presses lip upon lip, returns
laden with garlands to his mother'. Modern Megarian
festivities are of a more conventional nature, and on the
Tuesday after Easter peasant girls, wearing national costumes,
silver coins dangling from their caps, link hands and perform
the shuffling measures of the *trata* dance in the main square,
believed to be the site of the ancient agora. Beyond Megara it
is advisable to take the old road to Corinth (the distance is
only a bit longer than the highway; it is more interesting,
and it overlooks the sea). All this coast is haunted by the
myths of the youthful Theseus and his journey from Troezen
to Athens, in the course of which he rid the countryside of
several disagreeable characters. The corniche, known as the
Kaki Skala (The Evil Stairway), overhanging coves of crystal-
clear green water, is hewn out of the side of the lofty Scironian

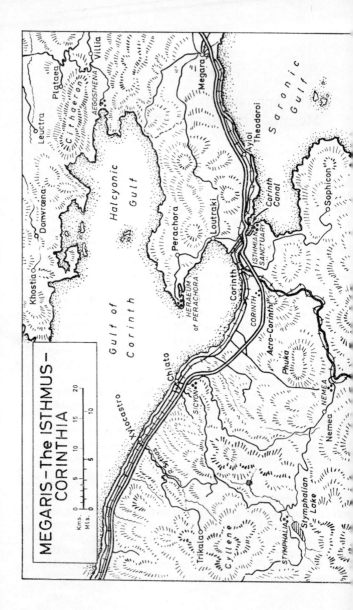

MEGARIS—The ISTHMUS—
CORINTHIA

cliffs, so sheer that Strabo describes them as leaving 'no passage between them and the sea'. The epithet 'evil' is perhaps a legacy of the days when this rugged stretch of country was infested by robbers and the traditional hunting-ground of Sciron, the mythological brigand who had an unpleasant habit of divesting travellers of their belongings, obliging them to wash his feet and kicking them over the cliff into the sea, where an enormous turtle, lurking in the under-water rocks, devoured them. He finally suffered a similar fate at the hands of Theseus. Beyond the Scironian cliffs pine trees – a particularly vivid shade of emerald green – fringe a long beach of white shingle called Kineta, dotted with tavernas and camping sites. The currents are strong in this part of the gulf, which begins to contract as the opposite shore of the Pelopon-nese draws nearer, and even at the height of summer the sea is relatively cold. At the village of Ayioi Theodoroi, the ancient Crommyon, where Theseus slew Phaea, the Grey Sow, which fed on human flesh, there is a good taverna (Nikolaos, 23 Athinon-Corinthou Street), where the specialities are chicken roasted on the spit and quince and mandarin pre-serves.

One rejoins the highway by the toll-gate. The sandy alluvial soil of the Isthmus lies ahead, cut by the **Corinth Canal,** a dead straight ribbon of water between high banks of sand and calcareous rock. Three and a half miles long, no more than 320 feet wide, the canal was completed in the late nineteenth century by French and Greek engineers. It shortens the journey from the Piraeus to the Adriatic by nearly two hundred nautical miles. The project had been contemplated more than two and a half thousand years before: first by Periander, Tyrant of Corinth; later by the Roman Emperors. In 67 A.D. Nero went so far as to import thousands of Judaean prisoners to undertake the work. The Emperor himself hacked out the first handful of earth with a golden axe. The project, however, was abandoned when he was summoned to Gaul to suppress the revolt of Julius Vindex.

Just before the bridge across the canal there is a fork: one road leads to Corinth and the Peloponnese, the other to Perachora. To visit the site of the Isthmian Sanctuary one takes the road to Corinth first, turning left just beyond the bridge, and crosses the windswept treeless plateau of the

Isthmus, an earthquake country, covered with silvery-grey thistles and stunted shrubs. Washed by two seas, the Saronic in the east, the Corinthian in the west, it is fittingly sacred to Poseidon, Earth-shaker and god of the sea. There are no signs of the pinewoods where Sinis, the Pine-Bender, waylaid travellers and tied their arms to two bent branches which, when released, flew apart, tearing the victims in two. But Sinis met his match in Theseus, who, after meting out the same punishment to him, heard a rustle in the undergrowth and caught sight of a girl flitting across the wood. He gave chase and found Sinis' daughter roaming distractedly among the wild asparagus. They fell in love at first sight; and in due course she bore him a son.

On this southern (Peloponnesian) bank of the canal extend the ruins of the **Isthmian Sanctuary,** where the Isthmian Games were held every four years. Within a peribolus (a few fragments remain on the north side, once lined with statues of famous athletes) are traces of the fifth century B.C. Temple of Poseidon. More interesting is the triangle of the starting line of the stadium (south side of the sanctuary, between the temple and the road), with the starter's pit and sixteen shallow grooves for cords crossed by bronze staples to keep them in position clearly marked. From here the starter, in his pit, could release the cords connected with the posts simultaneously. Absolute fairness, to which Aristophanes refers in *The Knights*, was thus ensured. Nearby are the remains of water conduits and basins. West of the sanctuary there was a theatre, of which only the retaining wall and the foundations of the proscenium remain. The place is flat and treeless, shelving down in terraces to the sea. But it has an airy quality and it faces the apex of the Saronic Gulf, where one can see tug-boats preparing to pilot ships through the canal. There is nothing to suggest that Isthmia was ever more than a place where great sporting events were held. It had neither the religious significance of Delphi nor the panhellenic spirit of Olympia, but during the festival it was a scene of considerable animation, with touts, conjurors and fortune-tellers swarming around the stadium. Plato wrestled here as a youth, and Dio Chrysostom describes Sophists arguing, poets declaiming, lawyers applauding athletes crowned with the victorious pine branch.

South of the sanctuary are the remains of a fortress built by Justinian in the sixth century: part of the defensive system of the Isthmian wall, which crossed the Isthmus (east to west), originally built in 480 B.C. by the Spartans, who meant to put up a last-ditch-stand here against the Persians if the outcome of the battle of Salamis failed to turn the scales against the invaders. In some sectors (east of the Byzantine fortress) as many as eight or nine courses of fifth century B.C. masonry are visible. Returning to the fork, one continues along the road to Corinth. At the western end of the Isthmus before reaching Corinth a branch road (right) leads to the port of Poseidonia, the western entrance to the canal, where there are traces of the ancient Diolchus, the paved road across which boats were hauled on rollers from one sea to the other: a short cut used, among others, by Octavian during his pursuit of Antony and Cleopatra after the battle of Actium.

On the north side of the bridge across the canal, the road continues westward along the mainland shore, passing through Loutraki, a popular spa for liver and kidney ailments. A long promontory of bluish-grey limestone with a crenellated ridge projects into the gulf, terminating in the **Heraeum of Perachora.** Before reaching the tip of the headland one passes a tree-fringed lagoon. Traces of ancient masonry begin to appear, and there is an Archaic cistern with a subterranean stairway leading to the water level. The Heraeum, a sanctuary of the goddess Hera, is first heard of in the Geometric period. Its history develops with that of Corinth, for its strategic position, commanding the western maritime approach to the Isthmus, is obvious. Climbing down the south side of the headland, one passes the foundations of the eighth century B.C. Temple of Hera Limenia, of a Hellenistic cistern, of a fifth century B.C. stoa, a Classical altar with triglyphs and, to the north of it, the wall of a Geometric apsidal temple of Hera Acraia. West of the latter there is a little paved esplanade and the foundations of an Archaic temple, also dedicated to Hera.

It is a remote place: a land's end, crowned by a lighthouse. The little cove at the bottom of the site, the Sacred Harbour, is ideal for deep water bathing. Above rise the steep brush-wood foothills of Gherania – the hill of cranes – so-called because at the time of Deucalion's Flood, Megarus, a son of

Zeus, floundering in the turgid waters, heard the cry of cranes which led him to the top of the mountain and to safety. To the north the Halcyonic Gulf, with its porpoise-shaped islets is bounded by Helicon; somewhere to the west is Delphi on a bastion of Parnassus. When the sea is calm, schools of dolphins, friendliest of animals to men, always ready to carry gods and mortals on urgent errands across the ocean, follow in the wake of steamers, bounding in the wash. To the south across the narrow waters of the Corinthian Gulf, the Peloponnesian ranges rise above a fertile coastal belt.

One returns to the pivotal point of the canal bridge and proceeds to Corinth: a dusty garrison town, subject to disastrous earthquakes. The complex topography – the isthmus the two seas, the mainland, the miniature subcontinent – now comes into focus. Corinth is clearly the gateway to the Peloponnese. There is no other land approach. The ruins of **Old Corinth,** one of the most celebrated cities of antiquity, lie to the south, packed into a confined area, superimposed with Roman structures.

All east–west maritime traffic (and vice versa) was alway at the mercy of the occupants of Corinth and its 1800-foot-high citadel. Its position, therefore, tended to make mariners of it inhabitants: the men who founded the colonies of Syracuse and Corcyra in the seventh century B.C. and who, according to Thucydides, built the first triremes. Their naval enterprise assured the city's commercial pre-eminence, its wealth being increased by the fertility of the coastal plain which extends in a crescent-shaped sweep of vineyards, citrus orchards and olive groves from the base of Acro-Corinth to the foothills of Sicyon. Wealth promoted luxury, and the Corinthians acquired the reputation of being the most licentious people in Greece. With Aphrodite as patron goddess, the emporium pullulated with prostitutes – *hetairae* they were called – often women of refined accomplishments, dedicated to the art of venal love and to a religion, which in fact it was, for they were all priestesses in the temple of Aphrodite. Among the most illustrious was Lais, the modelling of whose bosom was so perfect that painters from all over Greece came to Corinth to reproduce its divine forms on their boards. Prostitution in Corinth, like paederasty throughout Greece, was not considered a vice, but an accepted way of life. To abjure either would, for a beautiful girl in Corinth or a handsome youth in any Greek city state, argue considerable eccentricity.

The myths refer to the city as once ruled by Sisyphus, a trickster condemned to pay for his rascalities by eternally pushing a huge boulder up a hill in Tartarus and then watching it roll down to the bottom. It was under the vigorous Periander, of the Cypselid dynasty (seventh–sixth centuries B.C.) that Corinthian trade and navigation began to flourish. Government remained oligarchical. The well-fed pleasure-loving merchants showed little interest in the ideals of political democracy. But the growth of the democratic Athenian empire aroused their jealousy; consequently Corinth associated herself with the Spartan cause and emerged with considerable benefit from the Peloponnesian War. Eclipse came two and a half centuries later, when the Achaean League, of which Corinth was a member, was foolish enough to flout the growing might of Rome. The Corinthians went so far as to pour excrement on the heads of the Roman ambassadors from their windows. For this senseless affront they paid with massacre and the sack of their city by Mummius. Corinth literally ceased to exist. The paintings, for which the city was famous, were carried off to Rome, only a few being retained to serve as boards on which Polybius saw the consul's legionaries, squatting at street corners, playing at dice. In 46 B.C. Julius Caesar made amends by rebuilding the city, and, when visited by St Paul a century later, it was a flourishing Roman colony. The key position of the city, at the crossroads of the Roman world, had assured its rebirth. But the Corinthian sky, unlike that of other Greek city states, was never lit with the radiance that emanated from a creative sophisticated intelligentsia. Throughout history Corinth remained in virtual intellectual obscurity.

The ruined site extends across a plateau at the foot of Acro-Corinth, facing Sicyon and the wooded Achaean coast. One has the impression, as at Isthmia, of terraced ground shelving down towards the sea. Only here the view of the desolate Phocian mountain ranges is infinitely grander than anything the Saronic Gulf, for all its enchantments, can offer. The shambles of the ancient agora is dominated by seven massive Doric columns of porous limestone, crowned by flat capitals, and once covered with stucco, which formed part of

the **Temple of Apollo,** one of the oldest in Greece, built in the
'Golden Age' of Periander on a raised platform and originally
enclosed within a rectangle of monolithic pillars. The southern
end of the temple esplanade was bordered by the north-west
stoa, of which only the stylobate is preserved. Across the
central open space of the agora, paved in Greek times with
large pebbles, in Roman with marble slabs, and bordered by
shops and small temples, one can distinguish a large base
with six stone courses: the Bema, or Roman Governor's
tribune, placed in front of the fourth century B.C. south stoa,
a once magnificent two-story building, whose outer colonnade
alone consisted of seventy-one columns (not one survives),
crowded with shops and taverns, where merchants discussed
market prices and local politics.

This was the scene of St Paul's arraignment by the Jewish
community, who accused him, in the presence of the Roman
governor, of corrupting their faith. At first few Corinthians,
Greeks or Jews were impressed by the Apostle's preachings.

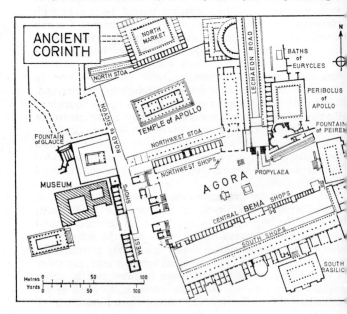

He was a disturbing element, and on one occasion his preaching in the synagogue provoked a riot in the course of which he was beaten up by Greek hooligans. On his own admission, he came to Corinth 'in fear, and in much trembling'.[1] He nevertheless spent eighteen months here, plying his craft of tentmaker and preaching the Gospel. He must have been an incongruous figure in this city of the most sophisticated carnal pleasures, picking his way among affluent merchants and flamboyant *hetairae*, bald and bow-legged (in Byzantine iconography he is generally represented with a square bullet-shaped head), and weak in 'bodily presence'.[2] In these times of political and spiritual upheaval, the pursuit of his missionary task was often put to the severest test. Yet his sojourn in Corinth was not in vain, for it inspired the two great Letters that proved to be among the most profoundly formative influences in the development of the Christian faith.

At the north end of the agora there is a very ruined propylaea, once surmounted by two gilded chariots in which Helios and Phaethon, the sun-god and his offspring, were depicted seated as they rode across the heavens. Through this Roman gateway, the Lechaeon, the road connecting Corinth with its port, was entered. Paved with limestone slabs in the first century A.D., the outline of the street is plainly visible and the paving in parts is well preserved. Almost a straight line, once flanked by shops behind colonnades (a few truncated columns survive), it cuts across fields of thistle and stubble. The number of shops underlines the commercial character of the city; wherever one turns there are more and more excavations of these little entrepots. Admittedly this was a market place, but not even in the Athenian agora, infinitely more spacious, is the emphasis on the purely mercantile aspect so pronounced.

East of the propylaea, on a lower level, lies the most attractive extant monument on the site: the **Fountain of Peirene**, a lady who was turned into a spring because of the unquenchable tears she shed for her son, accidentally killed by Artemis. Six rectangular chambers, each faced with an arch during the Roman period, contain basins connected with an underground reservoir fed by two different sources. Long before the Romans came, Pindar had admired the fountain

1. 1, Corinthians, 2, 3.   2. 2, Corinthians, 10, 10.

and described Corinth as 'the city of Peirene'. Situated in the centre of the agora, the spring was adorned with successive architectural embellishments from the sixth century B.C. to Byzantine times. In front of the middle arch stand two columns, one crowned by a Corinthian capital. In the second century A.D. Herodes Atticus had the entire front faced with marble. He also enlarged the court, adding apses with half vaults, thus giving a trefoil effect to the edifice. It is pleasant to sit in the shade of the arches and listen to the water trickling behind the dark chambers. Here the ancient archons of Corinth gathered on summer evenings to play at draughts and dice. At a later period the gardens of the Turkish governor extended around the fountain.

Another but less beautiful fountain – that of Glauce – is situated below the Temple of Apollo. Only a large block of natural rock, which contained four reservoirs, once preceded by a porch with three columns, remains to commemorate the end of the unfortunate Glauce, daughter of the King of Corinth. Courted by Jason, she was presented by Medea, his ageing mistress, with a magic robe smeared with a corrosive ointment as a bridal gift. Donning the fatal garment, the princess was instantly devoured by flames; but before her body could be entirely reduced to ashes, she flung herself into the fountain which henceforth bore her name. Having thus disposed of her rival, the Colchian sorceress slaughtered her own children by Jason and escaped in a chariot drawn by winged serpents to Athens.

The **museum,** notable for its wide range of terracotta vases, kraters, amphoras and other ceramics, lies immediately south of the Glauce 'fountain'. Of the famous Corinthian paintings only the lively bird and animal designs on the vases remain to remind us that Corinth, despite its lack of intellectual pretensions, was a centre of painters and craftsmen. Up to the sixth century B.C. large quantities of ceramics were exported to Italy; Corinthian potters, unlike those of Attica, were chiefly interested in the export trade. But in spite of mass production, the quality of their products remained high. In the so-called proto-Corinthian pottery (eighth–seventh century B.C.), which achieved great popularity in the ancient world, the linear precision of individual figures matches the impressive mass effect of collective groups. In the sixth century there is a predilection for the portrayal of birds, beasts and monsters. Then Attic influences creep in and the Athenian potter's desire to tell a story begins to influence Corinthian craftsmen. By the middle of the sixth century the Athenians had captured the principal markets, and Corinthian pottery declined in quality. The designs became larger and coarser, there is more lavish use of reddish-purple paint, and rosettes and other floral motifs are employed to fill in an already crowded background. A first class little guide-book, published by the American School of Classical Studies, is obtainable at the entrance. Among the more impressive ceramics are an eighth-century B.C. three-legged pitcher with elaborate geometric decoration and stylised deer on the upper band (case 11); a proto-Corinthian aryballos, or oil flask (used by athletes when anointing themselves after strenuous exercise), on the central zone of which warriors are depicted battling with each other (case 12); a beautiful amphora and oinoche (jug for pouring) of the early Corinthian period (seventh century), exquisite in shape, supremely elegant in floral and animal designs (case 15); and a late Corinthian aryballos (c. 580 B.C.) depicting a choragus leading a dance chorus of black male figures (case 15). Other exhibits include a mosaic of pebbles (one of the earliest in Greece, c. 400 B.C.) of griffons mauling a horse (vestibule, No. 5); votive offerings to Asclepius, god of healing, representing the afflicted limbs, breasts, genitals – even a hand with a cancerous growth – successfully treated by the god (west wall of Asclepion room). In the Roman and post-Classical hall there is a fine head of Nero Julius Caesar, son of Germanicus (No. 7), and another head (also Roman) of Tyche, or Fortune, wearing an elaborate crown in the form of battlements (No. 16).

It is pleasant to si↑in the village square, which is cool and shady, before ascending Acro-Corinth. There are some old-fashioned cafés, where men play *tric-trac*, a Greek version of backgammon, and the atmosphere is one of rusticity, in spite of the tourist shops and ubiquitous sellers of coloured slides. Apart from the usual ouzo, coffee and orangeade, one can also get *souvlakia* served on little wooden sticks.

Acro-Corinth has a splendid shape: dominant, aggressive, yet composing harmoniously into the complex configuration of land and sea. The view from the top is tremendous. In the immediate foreground the fertile strip extends to the wooded hills of Cyllene which rise to barren peaks, metal-coloured in a cloudless sky. The mountains of the Argolid, strangely eroded shapes, roll southwards; east and west lie the two seas, separated by the Isthmus, to the north, behind the tapering headland of Perachora, the placid expanse of the Halcyonic Gulf bounded by Helicon. To the north-west, the hazy massif of Parnassus exercises its eternal fascination.

During the Middle Ages the rock was a storm-centre of converging invasion routes. Geoffroy de Villehardouin, chronicler of the Latin carve-up of Greece, refers to it as 'among the strongest cities under heaven'. Its defence against the Franks fell to Leon Sgouros, Lord of Nauplia (see p. 155). When this fiery patriot realised that the fortress was doomed, he hurled himself on horseback over the 1500-foot-high cliff. Later, possession of the citadel passed from the seigniorial Villehardouins to the Florentine Acciajuoli, and, after them, to the Knights of St John, who in turn abandoned it to the Greeks. In 1458, five years after the fall of Constantinople, the 'star castle', as the Turks called it, was shattered by a massive bombardment of stone balls, one of which weighed nearly 900 lb., by the overwhelming forces of Sultan Mehmet II. From 1686 to 1717 it experienced a respite from Ottoman domination, being occupied by Venetian forces. A little more than a century later a wretched, cretinous and, by this time, disheartened Turkish garrison was finally ejected by the resurgent Greeks.

Although there are remains of Byzantine, Frankish and Turkish fortifications, it is the skill of Venetian military architects that is most striking in the watch-towers, the three imposing gateways connected by ramps and the crenellated ramparts. The route one follows from the entrance is very steep. You first cross the shallow moat, once spanned by a drawbridge, and pass through the outer gate to the second line of defence. The successive levels of formidable masonry, which seem to grow organically out of the increasingly precipitous incline, permitted the defenders to mow down all assailants with a devastating plunging fire. Another gate, square outside, with an arched passage within, leads to the west peak and the ruins of a Frankish dungeon. Descending (in a north-east direction) into a trough of ground overgrown

The temple of Apollo, ancient Corinth – one of the oldest in Greece built in the 'Golden Age' of Periander.

Fragments of the Temple of Zeus, Nemea (4th century B.C.), dominate the scene of one of the great panhellenic athletic festivals.

with spiky shrubs and long grass, one sees the shell of a ruined mosque (scattered all around here are vestiges of former chapels, minarets, barrack-rooms). Immediately north of the mosque is a postern, from which one climbs the east peak, once crowned by a temple of Aphrodite, where the goddess of love was worshipped in the most sumptuous eastern manner. Within the ring of fortifications there is not a single habitation; not a single living creature, except the odd sightseer, ants, bees and lizards. The enchantments of love seem rather unreal up here. Aphrodite no longer haunts the grandiose place.

West of Corinth the road runs through flowery villages among orchards and vineyards.[3] As the season advances, pale blue hydrangeas and climbing tea roses are succeeded by the scarlet refulgence of hibiscus, by the confetti-pink of oleander; in late summer multi-coloured dahlias replace the scorched sunflowers. There is an air of prosperity, very different from the rugged scrublands of Attica. Bicycles, geese, hens and carts clutter up the road. At Chiato, two roads climb up into the hills. The first ends (just beyond the village of Vasiliko) at the ruins of **Sicyon**, one of the most beautiful minor ancient sites in the Peloponnese.

The only building within sight is the museum, once the site of the Roman baths, which contains Corinthian pottery, figurines and Roman mosaics. The village is out of sight. The hill to the south rises to a triangular tableland on two levels, defended on both sides by shallow precipices. The curious shelving effect of the ground, so peculiar to the Corinthian scene, is again evident. The ancient city extended to the north along the ground descending towards the sea, the existing ruins being those of the Hellenistic town founded by Demetrius Poliorcetes in the course of his attempt to wrest most of Greece from all rival aspirants to the throne of Alexander the Great. He concentrated the city around its citadel and, in his usual extrovert way, gave it the name of Demetrias. In the Greek mind, however, it always remained Sicyon – 'the town of cucumbers'.

It was in the seventh century B.C. that the salubrious little cucumber-town, open to all the breezes of the Corinthian

3. The new west-bound highway from Corinth to Patras runs farther inland; it saves time, but is less interesting.

Gulf, began to acquire political prominence under the rule of Orthogoras, a former cook, who founded a Sicyonian dynasty which lasted over a hundred years and whose government was praised by Aristotle for its tolerance, by Plutarch for its harmony under a 'pure and Doric aristocracy'. But Sicyon's national hero did not emerge until the third century B.C. The city at the time was governed by a usurper-tyrant. Aratus, the exiled heir to the throne, was brought up in Argos. A resourceful youth, well informed of conditions within the city, he stole up on a moonless night with a handful of patriots and, despite the alarm sounded by a pack of howling dogs, scaled the walls. The *coup* came off, and it became Aratus' life-work to strengthen the Achaean League, assert Greek independence wherever he could and break the stranglehold of the warring Macedonian Diadochi. Poisoned by Philip V, the able if contemptible Macedonian king, he was buried in great pomp at Sicyon as the 'founder and saviour of his country'. In the first century A.D. the city was destroyed by a terrible earthquake, and when Wheler visited the site in the seventeenth century, he found it inhabited by only 'three Families of Turks, and about as many Christians'.

From the triangular shelf of ground, green fields descend to the coast; across the gulf, Parnassus and Helicon provide a dramatic backcloth, with the Perachora headland at the foot of the 'hill of cranes' and the hump of Acro-Corinth in the east. On the other side of the road, opposite the museum, lies the outline of the Bouleuterion. Following the path to the south (up the hill), you reach the gymnasium on a cool windy site. It was built on two levels, the lower surrounded by an Ionic, the upper by a Doric, colonnade. Unfortunately only one column remains. The restoration of others would give perspective to the ample and pleasing proportions of the two rectangular terraces. A stone fountain, a miniature Peirene, embellishes the south embankment of the lower gymnasium.

It is a pity there is not a single statue left to recall the fact that Sicyon was once an important artistic centre, the site of one of the earliest schools of statuary and painting in Greece; here Lysippus was born and Apelles, most celebrated of Greek painters, came to acquire a final polish to his style. Pliny says drawing in outline was invented by a native of

Sicyon, which he calls 'the home of painting'. At the time of
Aratus, himself an art critic of distinction, the paintings of
Sicyon were still famous throughout Greece, their colours,
according to Plutarch, being the only ones that proved
durable. The city was also a centre of sartorial fashion, famous
for the taste and skill shown by the weavers and cutters of the
flowing garments worn by its inhabitants.

Above the gymnasium is the theatre. The tiers, of which the
first two are more or less intact, were intersected by as many
as sixteen stairways – an unusually large number in relation
to the modest size of the auditorium. Apart from its position
and its solitude, there is the novelty of approaching the cavea
through one of two vaulted passages, so that one emerges
directly on to the diazôma, instead of approaching from the
orchestra. The cavity in the proscenium was intended for the
appearance of figures from the Underworld. Farther up the
hill (south-west), at its culminating point, is the outline of a
stadium, overgrown with corn. All over the hillside broken
slabs of limestone are concealed among thistles, mullein and
pungent-scented shrubs, but there is no sign of the *paideros*,
which Pausanias says grew only at Sicyon, one side of whose
oak-shaped leaves was dark, the other white, and which was
thrown in among the burning thighs of sacrificial animals at the
sanctuary of Artemis farther down the hill.

The other road from Chiato also leads southward, but
climbs much higher, winding through clefts and gulleys filled
with thickets of cypresses, towards the windy plateaux around
the base of Cyllene (modern Ziria). By the time the coast is out
of sight, a virtual boundary line has been crossed. We are no
longer in Corinthia, but on the northern fringe of Arcadia.
The narrow upland valleys converge on a six-mile-long plain.
Savage mountains crowd in on all sides. To the north rises the
formidable mass of Cyllene, slate-grey, breathtaking in its
cruel desolation. A projecting spur, called Mt Stymphalus,
rises sheer from the plain. At the southern end towers another
jagged peak, Mt Apelaurum, at whose foot the waters of the
Stymphalian Lake flow into a subterranean channel. Tall
reeds, some fields of maize, a few poplar trees border the
shallow lake, which shrinks considerably in summer, and is
full of weeds and patches of waterlilies. Nothing could be less
'Arcadian' than this forbidding place. The waters of the lake,

fed by mountain streams, are ice-cold, even at the height of summer.

Thousands of years ago the shores of the lake were thickly wooded, the haunt of the Stymphalian Birds, whom Heracles shot at the command of his master, Eurystheus. The demi-god shook a bronze rattle, fashioned by Hephaestus, which startled the birds so much that they flew out of their coverts, enabling him to aim his magic arrows at them. Diodorus, trying to rationalise mythology, says they were simply birds that fed on the crops. According to the legend, they were bred in the lake, had brazen beaks, claws and wings and, when they took flight in flocks, discharged showers of brazen feathers at men and beasts. The crops in the surrounding country-side were blighted by their excrement, and they emitted a nauseating stench (the marshy waters are still said to be very unhealthy). Pausanias says they were the size of cranes and 'like the ibis' and that no armour could pierce their dreaded beaks. Only lower kestrels now skim the unruffled waters of the lake.

The road skirts the western shore. To the left rises the shell of a Gothic church, a foundation of the Crusaders, with three naves and windows with pointed arches. A little farther on (left) are the negligible remains of an ancient acropolis on a rocky little promontory jutting out into the marsh. There are vestiges of a temple of Athena Polias, and to the south-west traces of foundations of public buildings, often submerged when the water level of the lake rises. The Temple of Stymphalian Artemis, in which Pausanias saw effigies of the Stymphalian birds carved in wood under the roof and, 'behind the temple', marble statues of maidens with birds' legs, has not been identified.

The road to the east crosses the saddle of a jagged mountain and descends into hilly vine country, the territory of the Phliasians, celebrated in antiquity for its wine (it is no longer): the native land of Pratinas, contemporary of Aeschylus and inventor of the Satyrical drama, in which the chorus, depicted as grotesque satyrs, introduced a bawdy slapstick element, intended to relieve the emotional strain of the main tragic theme. There are streams and poplars, and some cultivation, at the foot of white clayey mountains. Under shady plane trees women wash clothes in troughs, to the accompaniment of the furious chirping of cicadas in the scorched long grass. Opposite the village of Ayios Yiorghos (modern Nemea) a little monastery clings picturesquely to the side of a cliff. The road crosses another hill and enters a narrow vine-clad valley three miles long, less than a mile wide, where the village of Heracleion marks the site of ancient Nemea.

Never a township, Nemea was a sanctuary of Zeus where one of the four great panhellenic athletic festivals was held. The grove of cypresses that surrounded the sanctuary has disappeared, but dwarf cypresses, more elegant than the larger more common variety – the *Cupressus sempervirens*, the Gopherwood of the Bible – grow in alleys and thickets on the neighbouring hills. To the north-east flat-topped Mt Phuka, the ancient Apesas, looks as though its summit had been sliced off by a gigantic axe. Theocritus calls Nemea 'well-watered' and streams still flow down the seamed mountain sides.

The origin of the Nemean Games lies in a melancholy event. Ancient Greek athletics, like the games organised by Achilles round the funeral pyre of Patroclus, are often associated with ceremonies intended to speed the passage of souls to Elysium. One day Opheltes, a child of a priest of Zeus, was laid by his mother on a bed of wild celery in a meadow at Nemea while she fetched water from a spring for the seven Argive leaders bound for the investment of Thebes. On her return she found the child poisoned by a snake-bite. The Seven then founded the games to commemorate the child's death. Thereafter judges at the Nemean festival wore black in mourning for Opheltes. The victor's crown was of wild celery.

According to other legends, Heracles, after slaying the Nemean lion, instituted the games in honour of his father, Zeus. The lion was enormous, its hide impenetrable to iron, bronze or stone. When the monster was born, its mother, Selene, the Moon, gave such a terrible shudder that she dropped it beside a cave on Mt Tretus, whence it ravaged the countryside. When Heracles grew up, the lion was commissioned by Hera, in one of her uncontrollable fits of jealousy, to devour her erring husband's bastard son. But she did not reckon with the physical prowess of his semi-divine offspring. At first, Heracles was at a loss. Neither his arrows, sword nor

club made the least impression on the invulnerable hide. So
he finally came to grips with the monster, already bespattered
with the blood of numerous victims, and choked it to death
He then flayed the carcass with its own razor-sharp claws
girdled himself with the pelt (usually depicted by vase-painters
as part of his attire) and wore the head as a helmet. In this
apparel he presented himself to his master, Eurystheus, who
was so frightened by the horrific guises in which his protégé
had the habit of turning up after one of his triumphant
labours that he would scuttle into a bronze pot buried in the
earth.

The grove in which the games were held was crowded with
public buildings. Of these only the fourth-century B.C. Temple
of Zeus has survived. It marks the transitional period between
Classical and Hellenistic Doric, and the influence of Scopas
who designed the temple at Tegea (see p. 186) is evident. It had
twelve limestone columns at the sides, six at either front
Three, of which two support a fragment of architrave, still rise
from the stylobate – a pleasing landmark – among the vine
yards. The columns are unusually slender and their appearance
is thereby considerably heightened. To the south-east are the
sites of the theatre, stadium and hippodrome. The remains are
negligible. A hillock to the south is supposed to be the funeral
mound raised over the tomb of Opheltes.

The games, consisting of running in armour, discus
throwing, chariot-racing, throwing the javelin, shooting with
the bow, boxing and wrestling, were held every second year
By the sixth century B.C. the festival had acquired the status
of a panhellenic assembly, and the prize of wild celery was the
pride of every Greek athlete. Alcibiades won chariot races
here, and the most popular athletes in Greece competed. The
famous Andomedes of Phlius, who distinguished himself in
the pentathlon, is described by Bacchylides as shining 'among
the other pentathletes as the bright moon in the middle of the
month dims the radiance of the stars . . . as he . . . hurled the
shaft of black-leaved elder from his grasp to the steep height
of heaven.' There are also records of less agreeable incidents
Once a boxing match ended in tragedy. A blow delivered by
one of the antagonists below the ribs was of such violence
that his long sharp nails were buried in his opponent'

stomach. In extracting them, he unwittingly tore out the man's entrails. The victim died on the spot.

Five kilometres beyond the sanctuary the road joins the main highway into the Argolid.[4] In this undulating plain, surrounded by deeply eroded foothills, one of the decisive battles of the War of Independence was fought, when the northbound army of Dramali Pasha was ambushed by the Greeks as it emerged from a narrow gorge. The Church of Ayios Sostis (St Saviour), visible from the road, surrounded by cypresses on the side of a steep hill, commemorates the victory. A large Turkish army was wiped out by two thousand Greeks, aided by contingents of armed peasants from neighbouring villages. This small force was commanded by the intrepid Nicetas, known as the 'Turcophagos' (The Turk-Eater). The Greeks captured an immense booty and horses' skeletons littered the highway for years. The credit for this feat went to the Generalissimo, Kolokotronis, an arrogant and crafty soldier, as vain as he was brave. Finlay does not credit him with much military skill. His feats, he says, 'though celebrated in unpoetic verses and bombastical prose, were only the deeds of highwaymen and sheep-stealers'. Nevertheless, Kolokotronis' extrovert personality captured the popular imagination, and many of the most glorious exploits of the war of liberation are attributable to him.

From here one either returns to Corinth or enters the narrow pass of Dervenakia, the ancient Tretus, which follows the course of a dried-up torrent, its stony banks bordered with oleanders – in summer it is one of the hottest places in the Peloponnese – and crosses the watershed into Argolis.

4. A round trip (Corinth–Sicyon–Stymphalia–Nemea–Corinth) can easily be undertaken in one day. I have even done it from Athens in one day with comfort. With equal ease one can make the same trip, starting again from either Corinth or Athens, and spend the night at Mycenae or Nauplia (see Chapters 6, 7).

CHAPTER SIX

The Argolid: The Homeric Plain

❧

Mycenae: The Lion Gate; The Royal Grave Circle; The Palace; The Second Grave Circle; The Treasury of Atreus; The Tomb of Clytemnestra – The Argive Heraeum – Argos: The Larissa; The Roman Baths; The Theatre; TheMuseum – Tiryns

THE plain, roughly triangular in shape, is spacious, shut in on three sides by mountains, the highest range forming a natural wall guarding the Arcadian plateau.[1] If one takes the Tretus as the apex, the angles of the base would be the citadel of Nauplia squatting above its pellucid bay and the conical crag of the Larissa dominating the town of Argos. There is a warmth and radiance in the outlook, in the ample proportions of the Homeric plain, fringed by the Argolic Gulf, that heralds a new climate. The heat, the fields, the cultivation recall the epithets the poet applied to it: 'very thirsty' and 'horse-pasturing' – only flocks of sheep have now replaced the mares of Diomedes. In the evening, convoys of trucks roll northwards, loaded with fruit and vegetables for the Athenian market.

The first turning to the left (east) leads to the village of Mycenae and the Hotel de la Belle Hélène et de Ménélas. A line of low hills screens the prehistoric site. The road climbs between banks of luxuriant oleanders to the Tourist Pavilion which overlooks the shimmering plain. There is no shade, but breezes sometimes blow across the twin peaks above the citadel, and there is a pungent smell of herbs. Large slabs of Cyclopean masonry appear on the slopes of the chasm which begins to narrow. With one's back to the plain, the scene acquires a rugged denuded aspect. It is like a lofty recess

1. The ancient sites of the plain, Mycenae, the Heraeum, Argos and Tiryns can all be seen in one day.

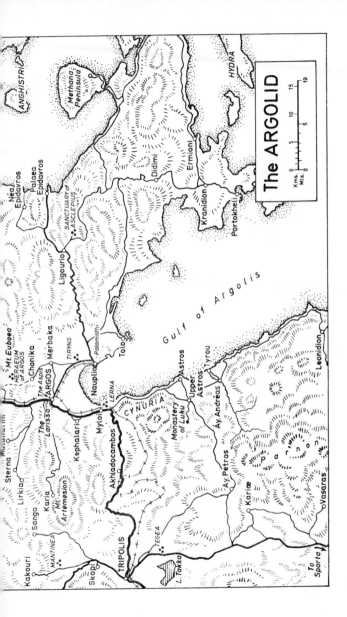

The ARGOLID

Kms. 0 — 5 — 10 — 15
Mls. 0 — 5 — 10

ANGHISTRI

Methana Peninsula

HYDRA

Nea Epidavros

Palaea Epidavros

SANCTUARY of ASCLEPIUS

Didimi

Ligourio

Ermioni

Kranidion

Portokheli

Mt. Euboea

HERAEUM of ARGOS

Chonika

The Aspis

Merbaka

Palamidhi

ARGOS

TIRYNS

The Larissa

Nauplio

Tolo

Gulf of Argolis

Sterna

Lirkia

LERNA

Astros

Tyrou

Karia

Kephalario

Mylisi

CYNURIA

Upper Astros

Kakouri

Sanga

Mt. Artemesion

MANTINEA

Akhladocambos

Monastery of Luku

Ay. Andreas

Parnon

Skopi

TRIPOLIS

TEGEA

Ay. Petros

Karia

Vasaras

L. Takka

To Sparta

Leonidion

commanding the upper part of the Argive plain, once a stronghold of immense strategic importance, with the citadel of **Mycenae**, girdled by formidable walls, crowning a rocky eminence above the confluence of two boulder-strewn ravines. In antiquity all the roads from the Corinthian Gulf united here and passed under the great natural bastion.

Whether Mycenae influenced Minoan civilisation or was dominated by it has remained a debatable point ever since Heinrich Schliemann, the indigo-merchant turned archaeologist, excavated the cities of Agamemnon and Priam, and Sir Arthur Evans, brought up in an environment of more conventional scholarship, revealed the sophisticated splendours of the Palace of Minos. What seems fairly certain is that, after the destruction of Knossos and the eclipse of Minoan supremacy, leadership of the Aegean basin passed into the hands of the Mycenaeans (c. 1400 B.C.). As sailors and colonists they surpassed the Minoans, whose trade they absorbed and developed, introducing their civilisation into islands as far away as Cyprus. About 1400 B.C. (Late Bronze Age), a period of great architectural, even artistic, activity seems to have set in. Grim barbaric edifices of sun-dried bricks were raised on bases of clay-set rubble. Lime plaster, sometimes decorated with frescoed designs or descriptive scenes, covered the floors and walls; the doors were wooden, the windows small, the roofs flat; baths consisted of pottery tubs. The poorer classes dwelt in huts with floors of beaten earth. But it is no exaggeration to say that Mycenaean palaces and some of the tholos tombs of their kings are the only buildings in Europe before the Hellenic period in which artistic as well as functional ends were aimed at by contemporary architects.

The view of the citadel is magnificently forbidding: a heap of prehistoric masonry, surrounded by huge polygonal walls consisting of limestone slabs skilfully hewn and fitted together and of an average weight of six tons, that ascends abruptly out of the gorge and follows the contours of the hill in straight and curved stretches and occasional sharp turns. The surface of the blocks reflects the fierce sunlight beating down on the scorched treeless terrain, once the nerve-centre of a maritime empire that dominated the Aegean and produced precious objects of the minor arts that have still to be surpassed for excellence of workmanship and elegance of design. No prehistoric tombs have yielded such varied and sumptuous treasure as those of Mycenae. Various fortified cities were scattered about the plain of Argolis, as well as elsewhere farther north, but they all had a common culture centred on Mycenae. Under Agamemnon (*c.* 1250 B.C.) the Myceanean kingdom, which included Corinth and Sicyon, and, at one time, the whole of Achaea (Homer calls all Greeks Achaeans), led a grand alliance of Greek states in a war against its commercial rival, Troy. Some time in the eleventh century the Dorian invasion swept in successive waves across Greece, and charred remains found at a level of stratification corresponding to the late twelfth century indicate that the great palaces of Mycenae, Tiryns, Argos and Pylos went up in flames. After that the Dark Ages descended on Greece. For a short period in Hellenistic times Mycenae revived, but not as a great power.

The road ends in an esplanade and car-park. In front (east) stands the **Lion Gate,** surmounted by the oldest piece of monumental statuary in Europe: a sculptured relief placed in the relieving triangle above the monolithic lintel. The two heraldic lions, whose heads are missing and were probably of steatite, are clumsily modelled, with hind legs more like an elephant's and thick bulging thighs. The detail is primitive, but there is a grandeur, even a dawning elegance in the turning movement of the body and shoulders, designed to enable the beasts' features to face those who approached the gate. Their paws rest on a plinth surmounted by a slender column crowned by a ponderous echinus and abacus. This column may have symbolised a household deity, the lions the attendants who guarded the royal citadel over which the deity presided. References in the *Agamemnon* of Aeschylus and the *Electra* of Sophocles suggest that the scene of both tragedies was probably set either just within or immediately outside the Lion Gate. In the *Agamemnon* Cassandra mentions 'this death-reeking porch', and again:

> 'A house whose stones
> Bear guilty witness to a bloody act;
> That hides within these gates
> Remnants of bodies hacked
> And murdered children's bones!'

In the *Electra* the protagonists – Electra, Orestes, Clytemnestra, Aegisthus – are constantly entering 'within' the gates.

Cassandra's allusion to 'remnants of bodies hacked and murdered children's bones' refers to the original myth, the curse of the Atridae, whose grisly consequences have haunted the imagination of writers from Homer to Eugene O'Neill. In the earliest times, Atreus and Thyestes, the sons of Pelops, divided the Peloponnese between them. But Thyestes seduced his brother's wife and stole the golden ram that symbolised the pledge of sovereignty over Mycenae. The injured Atreus then planned a gruesome revenge. Inviting Thyestes to dinner, he served up the latter's murdered children as the main course. On discovering that he had devoured his own flesh and blood – he had eaten heartily and with relish – Thyestes promptly vomited and invoked a curse on the house of Atreus. Later, while Agamemnon, son of Atreus and warlord of the Greeks, was campaigning in Troy, Aegisthus, offspring of an incestuous union between Thyestes and his own daughter, seduced Clytemnestra, wife of Agamemnon. When the war was over, Aegisthus, incited by Clytemnestra, the Lady Macbeth of Greek literature, killed Agamemnon and his Trojan mistress, the prophetess Cassandra, with an axe. Horrified by his mother's complicity in the assassination of his father, Orestes, in conformity with Cassandra's prophecy, 'set the apex on this tower of crime'[2] by murdering both Clytemnestra and Aegisthus, and was consequently hounded all over Greece by the loathsome Erinyes, until he received absolution from Athena on the Areopagus. It is an impressive catalogue of crime: assassination, adultery, theft, cannibalism, incest, regicide, matricide. 'A house of death if ever there was one,' says the tutor in the *Electra*. The prodigious blocks of Cyclopean masonry below Agamemnon's palace speak volumes – of hatred, vengeance and the shrieks of murdered victims. There can be few places where nature, architecture and literature have so successfully combined to make a story live with such palpitating intensity three thousand years after it was told.

Within the Lion Gate, through which men, horses and chariots passed, there was a sentry-box, largely hewn out of the cliff – the narrow niche, on the left as one enters, is still

2. Aeschylus, The *Agamemnon*.

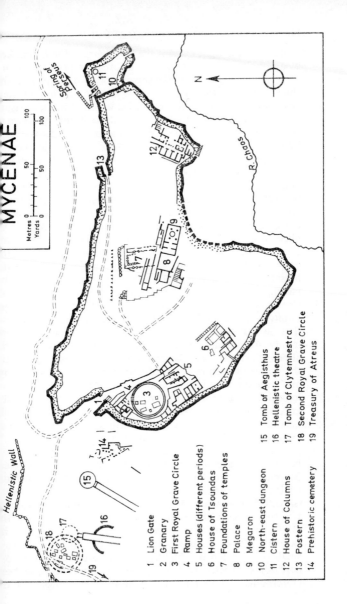

MYCENAE

Metres 0 — 50 — 100
Yards 0 — 50 — 100

1 Lion Gate
2 Granary
3 First Royal Grave Circle
4 Ramp
5 Houses (different periods)
6 House of Tsoundas
7 Foundations of temples
8 Palace
9 Megaron
10 North-east dungeon
11 Cistern
12 House of Columns
13 Postern
14 Prehistoric cemetery
15 Tomb of Aegisthus
16 Hellenistic theatre
17 Tomb of Clytemnestra
18 Second Royal Grave Circle
19 Treasury of Atreus

Spring of Perseus

R. Chaos

Hellenistic Wall

N

visible. On the right extends the **Royal Grave Circle**, marke
by a double row of erect stone slabs, the site of Schliemann
most famous discovery in the summer of 1876 (see p. 75). Th
chief interest of this circular graveyard (85 feet in diamete
lies not only in its age (c. 1600–1500 B.C.) but in the treasu
of gold and precious objects (now in the National Museum a
Athens) which it contained. When the great citadel wall wa
built at a later date the Cyclopean blocks were made to curv
round the bulge created by the grave circle so as to include
within the royal perimeter. Schliemann found six tombs con
taining sixteen skeletons, judged to be royal personage
because of the richness of the treasure interred with them
Gold masks, like the so-called 'Agamemnon death-mask' i
the National Museum, covered the faces of the men, gol
fillets decorated those of the women. Tombstones, som
carved, others plain (two of the latter are *in situ*), marked th
graves. The vast hoard of gold thus lay under the soil of th
hillside for two and a half thousand years, unsuspected b
passing brigands, plunderers and conquerors. It was th
wealth, too, that led Schliemann – a genius with a mor
intuitive than scientific approach to archaeology – to believ
that he had come upon the grave of Agamemnon and h
family. Admittedly Pausanias, visiting Mycenae when it wa
already in ruins, says 'There is the grave of Atreus, along wit
the graves of such as returned with Agamemnon from Tro
and were murdered by Aegisthus . . .' But modern archaeo
logical research precludes the royal shaft tombs from being th
graveyard of Homer's Atridae, if the Trojan War, as general
believed, took place in the twelfth century, some thre
hundred years later than the date assigned to the tombs.

South-east of the grave circle foundations of small house
believed to have been inhabited by well-to-do middle cla
Mycenaeans, are huddled together against the polygon
wall: the House of the Ramp, the House of the Warrior Va
(so-called because the Warrior Vase in the National Museu
was found here), the South House and a minor palace, th
House of Tsoundas (named after the archaeologist wh
excavated it) in the north-east corner of which there was
small court; from it a flight of thirteen steps led down to
corridor connected with what are presumed to have bee
storerooms. All that is known of the furnishings of the

houses – as, indeed, of all Mycenaean houses – is that low benches were ranged along the walls of the porches and that lamps and charcoal braziers stood in the main hall, in the centre of which there was a hearth.

Returning to the Lion Gate, one follows the course of the original zigzag ramp up which the chariots climbed to the western extremity of the hill crowned by the Palace buildings, home of the doomed Atridae. It is rough going, steep and shadeless, the rocky ground overgrown with prickly shrubs. In late spring clusters of scarlet anemones, the *Anemone hortensis fulgens*, with its green frill of lance-shaped bracts shelter in the scanty shade of projecting ledges. When their petals droop and wither they turn a faded purple and are blown across the hillside. The ramp was narrow and can never have been very imposing. In spite of the gigantic slabs of masonry employed by prehistoric architects, Mycenaean houses (as well as streets) were obviously very constricted, with none of the spaciousness associated with the chambers of Hellenic buildings.

The outline of the **Palace** indicates a complex of rather poky chambers. The royal esplanade commanded a dizzy view of the ravine below and the lovely patchwork plain beyond, at the end of which the fortified Larissa of Argos rises, a gaunt beige pyramid, out of the surrounding fields and orchards. The mountains of Arcadia, grim, slashed with tremendous precipices which retain deep shafts of light in the afternoon sun, form a seemingly impenetrable barrier in the west. There is an airy splendour about the impregnable position. One turns first into the Great Court, which had a cemented floor with painted squares and a dado in the form of a split-rosette frieze running along the base of painted walls. It was approached from the south by a flight of steps, of which one remains. The marks of burning on the floor are presumed to be traces of the great fire that destroyed Mycenae at the time of the Dorian invasion. West of the court is a small throne room (the throne was probably placed in a sunken part of the floor against the north wall). East of the court one passes through a porch and vestibule into the megaron, the largest chamber in the palace, half of which has now fallen into the ravine. Painted designs of circles, linear and other geometric patterns created a blaze of colour on the floor; the walls, judging from fragments in the National Museum, were daubed with frescoes depicting warriors, horses, chariots. This was where the court assembled, led by the barbaric monarch, surrounded by olive-skinned attendants armed with axes and Homer's 'lovely' Argive women in their 'long robes'. Three of the four column-bases surrounding the hearth, which was in the shape of a shallow circular trough, are preserved, as are many door-sills in the chambers. It is difficult, if not impossible, to identify the maze of small rooms north of the megaron. One is believed to have been a bathroom, because its sunken floor reveals signs of red plaster within a raised surround. Local (non-professional) guides like to say it is the bath in which Agamemnon was hacked to pieces. I remember a shepherd once pointing to a cluster of scarlet anemones. 'You see,' he said, 'they grow wherever the royal blood once flowed.' On that April day the whole citadel seemed to be aflame with their blood-red blooms.

East of the wind-swept summit one dips down to the so-called House of the Columns, near a tower (part of the whole system of fortifications, which was picketed with sentries) overhanging the desolate ravine. It must have been from here that the weary watchman, 'drenched with dew', gazed hopefully across the ravine for 'the fire to cheer this dark night with good news' – the long-awaited beacon that would signal the return of Agamemnon from Troy.[3] There are two interesting points about the foundations of this house. First, the design corresponds with Homeric descriptions of the palace of Odysseus in Ithaca. Secondly, it possessed a court surrounded by a colonnade aligned with the megaron walls: a feature that foreshadows houses and prostyle temples of the Classical period, with columns standing at each corner, forward of the side walls.

Following the line of walls, one reaches the **Secret Cistern,** an underground passage dated to the thirteenth century B.C., with a corbelled roof in the form of an inverted V. An initial sixteen steps is followed by a sharp turn and a claustrophobic descent down a flight of eighty-three steps into the limestone bowels of the citadel. At the bottom, where there is a square stone shaft brimming with water, a feeling of constriction grips at the throat. Death is omnipresent at Mycenae. In this

3. Aeschylus, The *Agamemnon*.

Head libation cup found in Royal
Circle at Mycenae by Schlieman
, now in the Nation Archaeologi-
seum, Athens. (p. 75).

Gold death mask of 15th century B.C.,
popularly believed to be Agamemnon's.
Also found in the Royal Grave Circle.
(p. 75).

Treasure of Atreus, Mycenae — one of the most astonishing monuments of the
prehistoric age in Greece dating from the 14th century, B.C.

View from Mycenae.

The Lion Gate, Mycenae —
surmounted by the oldest
piece of monumental
statuary in Europe.

etid chamber it makes an almost palpable impact. The cistern was connected by terracotta conduits with the Spring of Perseus, which lay outside the perimeter of the citadel. The water supply of the fortress was thus assured in times of siege. Back in the open, one welcomes the thyme-scented air and chirping of cicadas. Nothing seems to disturb the solitude of the bleak slopes of Mt Zara and the surrounding scrub-covered hills. Only once I saw a shepherd, followed by his flock of black mountain-goats, clambering up the rocky incline. Although the distance across the ravine was not great, the sound of goat-bells was remote, melancholy and infinitely nostalgic. A westerly course completes the circuit of the citadel, after passing the Postern Gate, a small but massive gateway with a double door, carrying an enormous lintel, through which Orestes fled, 'lashed and driven' by the Erinyes, their dreadful eyes dripping with bloody pus', after the murder of Clytemnestra.[4] The area between the postern and Lion Gate is littered with debris of the short-lived Hellenistic township.

The descent from the Lion Gate to the lower town is honeycombed with foundations of prehistoric dwellings and tholos tombs. Immediately across the road from the car-park lies the Second Royal Grave Circle, first excavated in 1952, and believed to be considerably older (c. 2000–1600 B.C.) than the one discovered by Schliemann – in other words, about half a millenium before the polygonal wall was built round the citadel. The epithet 'royal' is again inspired by the quantity of precious objects (jewellery, vases, swords and a lovely rock-crystal bowl in the shape of a duck, all now in the National Museum) discovered in the graves. In one, the skeleton of a young woman, a 'Mycenaean princess', was found richly bedecked in gold and silver clasps and necklaces; a crystal-headed bronze pin attached to each of her shoulders was obviously intended to hold up a garment, the fabric of which had perished. In another grave two male skeletons were buried with their weapons: a lance, knife and ivory-pommelled sword, all of bronze. In yet another a little girl of about ten was adorned with miniature ornaments. Beside the tiny skeleton lay a baby's rattle of gold.

Left of the road are the foundations of the House of the

4. Aeschylus, The *Choephoroi*.

Oil Merchant, a once largish construction containing a store room with oil-jars ranged in a row against the wall (as ofte described by Homer) and clay tablets inscribed with Linear I script (see p. 263). Daggers, shields and bronze implement were also dug up. In the adjacent House of the Sphinxes wer found ivory figurines, including a plaque with two heraldi sphinxes facing each other, and a large number of ivor columns representing the columnar deity depicted on th Lion Gate. We thus have visual evidence of the weapons use by Homer's heroes, of the ornaments worn by their women an of the layout of the houses in which they dwelt. But apar from establishing a method of dating prehistory by th comparison of potsherds at different levels of stratificatior archaeologists like Schliemann, Tsoundas, Papadimitriou an Wace have performed a notable service to literature b raising Homer above the level of a mere mythographer wit an incomparable talent for story-telling. After visitin Mycenae, one returns to the *Iliad* and the *Odyssey* with sense of increased intimacy.

The **tholos tombs** come next. They are unquestionably th most astonishing monuments of the prehistoric age in Greec Believed to be an entirely Mycenaean invention, they com bined different characteristics of Aegean prehistoric arch tecture in a symbolic representation of man's eternal awe c death. The circular chambers were subterranean, preceded b a *dromos*, or paved way, cut out of the rock. Earth covere the apex of the conical chamber so that it created the effec (from without) of a tumulus. The most impressive – right c the descending road – is the so-called **Tomb of Agamemnon** c **Treasury of Atreus,** a huge sepulchre, dated by means c pottery fragments to the fourteenth century B.C. Th cemented *dromos* is bordered by well-shaped blocks of dar grey conglomerate set in more or less regular courses. At th end of this 120-foot passage stands the doorway, its side slanting inwards as they ascend, originally flanked by tw half-columns of green breccia with zigzag and spiral design of which the bases remain, and covered by a relieving triangl which probably contained a sculptured plaque similar to th one above the Lion Gate. The door-sill of reddish conglome ate is perfectly preserved. Passing under the eighteen-foot-lon slab of limestone, one enters the dark empty beehive, whose diameter is nearly fifty feet and height only slightly less. A few bronze nails in the upper of the thirty-three courses indicate the original existence of some form of decoration, probably metal rosettes. To the right is a small rock-hewn chamber, where the corpse of the royal personage, encased in gold leaf, lay. But it cannot have been that of Agamemnon, since the edifice precedes the Trojan War by about two centuries.

Some visitors tend to poke their nose in, sniff the fetid air, think it all looks rather gloomy and regain the shade of the *dromos* with a sigh of relief. But it is wise to stay a little longer, to get used to the dark and run your eye up slowly, course after contracting course, to the towering cone. It is not difficult then to realise that this primitive monument must have been designed by an architect who not only knew how to deal with the technicalities of thrusts, weights and stresses, but was also inspired by creative imagination. A. J. B. Wace – no twentieth century archaeologist was more familiar with the site of Mycenae – goes so far as to say that 'the unknown master of the Bronze Age who designed and built the Treasury of Atreus deserves to rank with the greatest architects of the world.'

There are eight more tholos tombs, far less well preserved, scattered about the surrounding countryside. One, the so-called Tomb of Clytemnestra, just below the citadel, next to the Second Royal Grave Circle, is interesting in so far as the beehive chamber is taller and slightly narrower and the upper courses ascend more sharply; the design thereby gains in refinement. Beside it is the less well preserved resting-place of the Queen's paramour, Aegisthus. All these names are, of course, designed purely for classification; they possess no historical significance.

Mycenae is a haunted place, peopled by figures whom legend and literature have inflated into creatures of demonic stature, as sinister as the natural boulders and slabs of Cyclopean masonry raised to protect them from the hatreds which their own tragic destinies engendered. But the treasure of gold and silver and ivory and alabaster which the Mycenaeans knew how to work with such unerring skill and taste remains a priceless testimony of the degree of civilisation achieved by such a cruel people.

From Mycenae a rough road skirts the base of Mt Euboea to the **Heraeum of Argos**. One can also approach it from Argos itself, passing through Chonika, where there is a restored twelfth century Church of the Koimesis (Dormition of the Virgin). The Heraeum is situated on a shelf overlooking the plain, at whose western end the wall of Arcadian mountains is gashed by a broad winding gorge that penetrates into the heart of the massif. The immediate vicinity is uninhabited, the ground stony, once covered with the plant *asterion*, from whose leaves priestesses wove garlands for the goddess. Here was the centre of the worship of Hera, the national deity of the Argives. Throughout the Argolid the myths are dominated by the commanding figure of the 'Ox-eyed' Queen of the Heavens. Twin sister of Zeus, she was born either at Argos or Samos, and courted by her brother in the form of a cuckoo. They spent their wedding night at Samos and it lasted three hundred years. After this prolonged ecstasy, Zeus, surfeited with his sister's charms, began to look elsewhere for amorous distraction, and his infidelities drove Hera insane with jealousy. She became the most vindictive of deceived wives, bickering in a strident peahen screech and was always devising petty schoolgirl tricks in order to catch out Zeus and humiliate him.

The ruins are not very impressive, but the prospect is spacious, and the loneliness of the site unique in the populated plain. It was, for all its religious importance, a small, as usual compact, sanctuary, to which pilgrims flocked on foot and in chariots along dusty paths from the various citadels in the plain. A stepped wall (south) leads to the remains of the mid-fifth century B.C. south stoa, of which the interior colonnade is well preserved. From this level a monumental stairway climbs to a higher terrace across which spreads the stylobate of square blocks of tufa of the Doric Temple of Hera, also fifth century. Although built of limestone, it had marble decoration and within the cella stood the great statue in gold and ivory of the goddess by Polycleitus, depicted in the full panoply of her rank, carrying a pomegranate in one hand, her royal sceptre in the other. In Roman times Nero offered the goddess a golden crown and purple robe, Hadrian precious stones and a gold-wrought peacock, her sacred bird, whose vanity and gorgeous plumage aptly symbolise the goddess's personal attributes. One then climbs to the third terrace, not only to look at the scanty vestiges of the stylobate of the old seventh century B.C. temple, destroyed by fire, but also to stand on the deserted ledge where the Achaean leaders swore allegiance to Agamemnon before embarking for Troy. South-west of the terrace are remains of a Roman bath with an atrium and mosaic-floored rooms, under which there were hollow spaces heated by a furnace – one of the earliest recorded forms of central heating. South of the baths is a very ruined L-shaped stoa of an ancient gymnasium or palaestra.

Argos itself (in summer the Mycenae–Argos road is lined with children selling melons) is a busy little market town devoid of distinction, straggling round its picturesque acropolis. But few Greek towns have such a rich legendary and historical past. Here Danaus, father of fifty daughters, took refuge, after quarrelling with his brother, Aegyptus, father of fifty lusty sons, who pursued their uncle from Egypt in order to marry their cousins and fulfil an obligation incumbent on all bachelors with unmarried female relations. Girls in ancient Greece were considered a liability (at a later date Attic law defined them as 'an encumbrance on the estate') and they had to be married off to their closest relations if other suitors were not forthcoming. (Even today in conventional working class circles no bachelor may contemplate marriage until husbands have been provided for his sisters). Danaus, who had a vindictive nature, seized the opportunity presented by the family loyalty shown by his nephews to revenge himself against his brother and the latter's progeny. He consented to the multiple marriage, but secretly instructed his daughters to kill their husbands on the wedding night by stabbing them in the heart with long pins. The girls, inventors of the art of sinking wells, dutifully obeyed and, as a punishment for their crime, were condemned to pour water eternally into a bottomless well from perforated jars.

In Argos was organised the expedition of the Seven against Thebes, led by Adrastus and Amphiaraus, a war of aggression that haunts the legends of both states. At the time of the Trojan War Argos was governed by Diomedes, the famous horse-tamer, and Hera, worshipped as the goddess of fecundity and symbolised as a cow, was revered above all other deities.[5] After the Dark Ages the city reached the height of it power under Pheidon, who introduced coinage and a ne scale of weights and measures. The rise of Sparta eclipse Argive ascendancy in the Peloponnese. Nevertheless i classical times Argos was a commercial and artistic centre situated at an important junction of roads, three miles from the sea. Although generally joining coalitions against th hated Spartan juggernaut, Argive diplomacy during th Peloponnesian War tended to play off one side against th other.

The modern town spreads across the ancient site, dominate by the Larissa (named after the daughter of Pelasgus), 900-foot-high conical rock rising sheer out of the plain. It take just under an hour to climb to the castle and its double circu of medieval ramparts, studded with ruined towers, built b Byzantines and Franks, with Turkish additions: a mor enduring piece of masonry than the roofless temple of Zeu which once stood open to the cool breezes above the stiflin town. From the summit, or even from the whitewashed chap in a cypress grove less than halfway up, one looks down on th 'horse-pasturing' plain from a new angle. Cornfields sprea northward beyond the gravelly oleander-bordered bed of th Charadrus which flows (when it has any water) into th Inachus. To the east orchards fringe the coastal strip as far a Nauplia. The lower hill (east) is the Aspis, so-called becaus its shape resembles that of a shield. There are some Bronz Age remains and shaft tombs, and a rectangular terrace on th south-west slope is believed to be the sanctuary of Athen Oxyderces (The Sharp-Sighted), consecrated to the goddes by Diomedes as a token of gratitude to her for removing mist before his eyes in the course of a battle during the Troja War.

South of the centre of the town, left of the road to Tripoli are some fragmentary remains of the Agora. A great schoo of sculpture flourished here in the fifth century B.C. unde Ageladas, teacher of Phidias, Myron and Polycleitus, an ancient writers repeatedly refer to the quantity of statues tha embellished the city. It was also a musical centre and Herodo tus calls the Argives the best musicians in Greece. But Argo

5. Homer applies the name Argos indiscriminately to the city, t Agamemnon's kingdom and to his capital at Mycenae.

produced none of the immortal names in Greek literature.

Opposite the Agora are more important ruins: first the red brick shell of part of the complex of the Roman baths, whose *calderia* (drying-rooms) were heated by means of small brick piers connected with subterranean pipes which circulated warm air under the floor; then the crypt of an apsidal hall containing three sarcophagi, fragments of mosaic floors and marble polychrome paving-stones. Behind the hall (right) rise the tiers of the theatre, more impressive for its size and unusually steep cavea than its state of preservation. Dated to the late fourth century B.C., it had eighty-one tiers and could seat twenty thousand spectators. Above the theatre stood a statue of Telesilla, the lyric poetess, depicted with her books lying at her feet. This literary lady persuaded the women of Argos to defend the ramparts when the city was invested by Cleomenes, the Spartan king, who had just defeated the Argive army near Tiryns (*c.* 500 B.C.). The spectacle of the female warriors manning the ramparts so astounded the Spartan helots that they turned and went home. Herodotus, on the other hand, maintains that Cleomenes refrained from attacking Argos because, when sacrificing at the temple of Hera, he saw a flame issue from the breast (instead of the head) of the goddess's statue: an omen that he was not destined to become master of the city. The Argives subsequently claimed that Cleomenes' failure to capture the city so preyed on his mind that he went mad. The Spartans found this interpretation humiliating. The King's illness, it was officially stated, was the result of a pernicious habit, learnt from the Scythians, of mixing wine with water. South of the theatre, an aqueduct leads to a first century A.D. Roman odeum, a small concert hall, of whose cavea fourteen tiers survive.

The museum in Vasilissis Sophias Street possesses Proto-Geometric and Geometric vases and Neolithic finds from neighbouring Lerna which include a gruesome terracotta female statuette with sharply pointed breasts, stunted childish arms and a mouth in the shape of a bird. From these primitive objects one turns to the sumptuous elegance of the large fifth century A.D. mosaic floors, depicting hunting scenes with startlingly life-like portraits, removed from the Roman baths. There is also a head, allegedly of Sophocles, fished up from a nearby stream. Fifth century B.C. writers describe the dramatist as one of the most handsome young men of his generation. The head in the Argos museum does little to indicate that he retained his looks in maturity.

East of Argos the low oblong hump of 'wall-girt' **Tiryns** rises above the alluvial plain, beside the trimly-kept garden of a local prison. At first sight unimpressive, it soon makes an impact, for the entire circumference is encased by massive walls (20–25 feet thick), the oldest of which date from the fourteenth century B.C., composed of huge limestone blocks, grey or reddish in colour, eight feet long and four wide. Strabo says the walls were built by the Cyclops, imported from Lycia and called 'bellyhands' because they obtained their food from wages earned by manual labour. Here dwelt Heracles, generally represented in mythology as a good-natured chivalrous lecher and glutton prone to fly into violent rages. In one of his tempers he flung Iole's brother (who disapproved of the demi-god's proposed marriage to his sister) from the highest tower of Tiryns. But unlike Mycenae, to which it was probably subject, Tiryns had no Homer, no Aeschylus, Sophocles or Euripides to recount the bloody deeds of its ruling house. No royal tombs have revealed the treasure that astounded the eyes of Schliemann at Mycenae. Owing to its position close to the sea, it was obviously more open to plunder than the Mycenaean citadel. But like Mycenae, it suffered a violent end and the palace was gutted by fire long before the Classical era.

To view this pile of monstrous stones strung out on three levels, it is best to take the path east of the knoll up to the site of a ramp, which was wide enough to hold chariots and led to the main east gate; then turn left to the upper terrace, where the palace was encircled by an inner rampart until another gate is reached. Judging from its dimensions, it may have resembled the Lion Gate at Mycenae. Cuttings for pivots and jambs, where an enormous bar was drawn back into the wall, are still identifiable. Beyond the gate (following a southerly course) is a **stone gallery** (thirteenth century B.C.) in a remarkable state of preservation and of a singular vaulted construction, with doorways overlooking the lemon groves and fields of tobacco and maize. The endless rubbing of sheep against the walls of the gallery, for centuries a sheep-pen, has given he huge stones an extraordinarily smooth shining patina. One then turns right (west) to enter the larger of two propylaea (the sill of which consists of an enormous monolithic blue-coloured slab), the formal entrance to the palace (thirteenth century B.C.) whose interior was built of sun-dried bricks. Only the foundations exist. Below them fragmentary remains of a circular building (*c*. 2000 B.C.) have been excavated. In the construction of this edifice burnt bricks, it is believed, were used for the first time in Europe. The propylaea leads into the great court, at whose southern end there is another covered stone gallery with five doorways, approached by a flight of steps. To visit a confusing labyrinth of foundations of small chambers one turns right from the large court, passes through a smaller propylaea and enters the megaron, preceded, as at Mycenae, by a porch and vestibule. In the centre there was a hearth surrounded by four wooden columns which had stone bases and supported the roof. The floors were stuccoed and painted with designs of sea monsters. Adjoining the megaron were the royal private apartments. West of the palace, a secret passage, consisting of a well preserved irregular flight of steps, tunnels through the west rampart to a postern, whence one descends to the main road.

Tiryns has little to offer in the way of architectural refinements – nothing but the sheer bulk of its stone masonry. The size of the stones, hewn by men of whom we know next to nothing, haunts the imagination. The architecture was purely military in conception, execution and function. According to the findings of archaeologists, Tiryns was inhabited in the third millenium B.C. – say, a thousand years before these stupendous walls were raised. At such a distance in time, it is not difficult to imagine the Argive women, driven mad by Dionysus, roaming the plain in search of their children whom they devoured raw. Hotels, petrol stations and the suburbs of Nauplia now encroach on the barbaric site.

CHAPTER SEVEN

The Argolid: The Periphery

✆

Nauplia – Tolo – Epidaurus – Kephalari: The Erasinus – Th
Lernean Marsh – Astros – The Convent of Luku – Leonidio

AFTER the prehistoric nightmare of Tiryns it is a relief to
enter **Nauplia,** a charming little port sheltering in the right
angle formed by a rocky headland and a large natural fortress
crowned by a Venetian castle. Some people find a hint of
Italian architectural distinction in the town. It would be a
mistake to expect palazzi, loggias, Renaissance order or
Baroque extravagance. There are, however, some tall derelict
colour-washed houses with corbelled balconies, Turkish
fountains embedded in blind arches and walled gardens filled
with hibiscus and bougainvillaea, mandarin and rubber trees;
there is a Cathedral, originally Roman Catholic, containing
some indifferent seventeenth century Italian paintings, and
escutcheon of the Lion of St Mark on the north-east gate
(there are more within the fortress); there is also the typically
Greek provincial wispy public garden (next to the railway
station) with an equestrian statue of the ubiquitous Koloko
tronis, the familiar dusty wasteland of a main square, an old
upper town with winding stairways and paved alleys undefiled
by any mid-twentieth century excrescences and a waterfront
looking out across a pellucid bay towards the purple-shadowed
Arcadian mountains. The situation is perhaps unrivalled
even in the Peloponnese.

Nauplia is an obvious centre from which to visit the sites
on the periphery of the Argive plain.[1] There are plenty of
hotels (at all prices). The more expensive ones are strikingly
situated: the Xenias on a saddle, beside the seventeenth
century Venetian Grimani bastion, between the two fortresses
of the Venetian Palamidhi and the Turkish Itch-Kaleh, over

1. A minimum of two days is required to visit all the sites describe
in this chapter.

looking the two bays and a beach on the southern one; the Amphitryon, beside the West Mole, whence a road follows the Pendadelphia (Bastion of the Five Brothers) which forms part of the sixteenth century circuit wall; the Bourdzi, on a fortified islet, a miniature Château d'If, 500 yards offshore, designed by a fifteenth century Venetian architect and subsequently embellished with Turkish crenellations and a pretty octagonal tower. For years it was the home of retired executioners who were so cruelly ostracised by the inhabitants that they had to take refuge on this pile of sea-girt rocks. At the beginning of the War of Independence, Captain Hastings, commanding a force of Greek patriots, besieged Nauplia by firing combustible cannon balls, invented by a French colonel also in the service of the Greeks, into the town from the Bourdzi. The cannonade, Finlay says, was very noisy but only succeeded in making a great deal of smoke. The dank cells of the Bourdzi have now been converted into comfortable bedrooms. The deep water bathing is superb. At night it is not difficult to imagine the ghost of Hamlet's father roaming the battlements.

Travellers, haunted by the grim prehistorical sites of Mycenae and Tiryns should not miss the **museum,** housed in a former 18th century Venetian barracks (Syntagma Square). Here are displayed prehistoric pottery, Mycenaean stelae, and, more important, an almost complete and indeed unique suit of Mycenaean armour, as well as the only inscription from Tiryns, some fragments of frescoes also from Tiryns, a mould for gold jewellery found at Mycenae, seventh century B.C. votive discs, figurines and amphorae.

In itself, Nauplia has no ancient history to speak of. The days of affluence and heroic sieges belong to the Venetian era. It first emerges from obscurity in the early thirteenth century as the domain of Leon Sgouros, a venal, violent and bloodthirsty tyrant who went so far as to murder a page, the nephew of the Bishop of Athens, for breaking a glass in his presence. On another occasion, he invited the Bishop of Corinth, with whom he was on bad terms, to dinner. After feasting the prelate, he gouged out his eyes and cast his body over the cliff. The French Crusaders made Nauplia the capital of a duchy; later they sold it to Venice, and the whole area of the kingdom of the Atridae passed under the rule of a Venetian *podestà*. In the prolonged struggle between Venice and Turkey for possession of the maritime stations of the Morea,[2] Nauplia underwent some great sieges, and its inhabitants suffered terrible privations, while the peasants in the surrounding countryside were almost exterminated and had to be replaced by Albanian settlers. The most heroic siege was withstood by the Venetians, aided by Greek civilians and *stradioti* (light horsemen recruited by the Venetians from among the local population), for fourteen months (1537–8), in the course of which Kassim, the Turkish commander, succeeded in capturing the fortress of Palamidhi and firing heavy missiles into the town from a large gun which the inhabitants ruefully christened 'the bone-breaker'. The siege of 1715 was more tragic. A bold attack by the Janissaries secured for the besiegers a lodgement on the covered way leading to the summit of the rock. The next day the Ottoman fleet opened a devastating bombardment, and the Venetians were routed. Finlay records a casualty list of 25,000. Another thousand Italian soldiers were beheaded, to the accompaniment of wailing fifes and beating drums, outside the Grand Vizier's tent, which was bedecked with Damascus silks and Bokhara rugs and surrounded by fluttering pennons. For the next hundred years the Crescent flew unchallenged on the highest battery of the fortress.

Nauplia was wrested from the Turks early in the War of Independence and from 1829 to 1834 was the official capital of the country. But political machinations and personal rivalries sabotaged all attempts at a proper administration of the liberated areas. Finlay, who suffered from the familiar love-hate complex of the philhellene (his quarrels with the Greeks are lovers' quarrels) puts it strongly, but justly, when he says, 'Greece at this juncture was saved by the constancy and patriotism of the people, not by the energy of the government or the valour of the captains.' Ten years of bitter campaigns against the Turks had brought out most of the qualities and shortcomings of the Greek character: the stubborn bravery and unquenchable patriotism, the passion for political intrigue and incurable envy of the man at the top. Administra-

2. In medieval times and during the Venetian and Turkish occupations the Peloponnese was known as the Morea. I refer to it as such within its historical context.

ve anarchy and exaggerated reports of burning villages and
massacres of civilians by self-styled patriots (in other words,
rigands) heightened the tension in the overcrowded little
apital and culminated in the assassination of Count Capo-
istria, a Corfiot aristocrat formerly in the service of the Czar,
lected President of Greece by the National Assembly in 1827.
He was shot and stabbed outside the early eighteenth-century
hurch of Ayios Spyridon (Ioannis Capodistrias Street)
hich has a pretty Venetian portal, by the brothers Mavro-
ichalis, members of a fierce Maniot clan, who represented
ist that kind of lawlessness that Capodistrias, a sophisticated
autocratic statesman of international stature, was trying to
amp out. In 1834 King Otho arrived at Nauplia, the first
apital of his tiny turbulent kingdom. The nineteen-year-old
avarian boy landed from an English frigate, escorted into the
rgolic Gulf by the fleets of the three Protecting Powers, and
de between ranks of English, French and Russian sailors,
llowed by a train of Bavarian officers in plumed hats and
right-coloured uniforms, while massed bands played martial
ines which must have rung strangely in the ears of Greek
easants accustomed to 'klephtic' ballads: dirges in the minor
ey extolling the exploits of roving warrior-robbers whose
epredations had been as much the bane of the Christian
easantry as of their Moslem overlords. The ballads – the
lephtika' – have now passed, heavily coated with romantic
hitewash, into the repertory of Greek national folksongs.

Sightseeing in Nauplia is limited. The lower fortress, Itch-
Kaleh, is reached through an arched gateway surmounted by
Venetian lion: a welcome reminder of the advantages
njoyed by maritime Greece under the colonial administration
f the Serene Republic at a time when the rest of the country
as being reduced to an 'abomination of desolation' by
orrupt and rapacious pashas. The enclosure of the flattish
ummit, the Castel del Toro, has a bleak desolate air. There
re ruined bastions, a jungle of prickly pears (called 'Frankish
gs' in Greece), some straggling passion flowers and a grim
nced-in prison and barracks.

On the other hand, the **Palamidhi,** a gleaming pile of rock
wering above the town is one of the finest fortresses in the
Morea. Its name is derived from the mythological Palamedes,
eputed inventor of dice, scales and lighthouses. To reach the

summit by car one follows 25 Martiou (25th March) Avenu
in an easterly direction. The Church of the Evanghelistria (th
Annunciation), surrounded by cypresses, crowns a rock in th
suburb of Pronea. This is where the National Assembly me
in 1832 and ratified the election of Prince Otho as King o
Greece. The citadel is entered through a gateway consisting c
a five-sided fort. Within the enclosure, which is on an incline
five distinct forts are discernible (there were seven originally)
built by the Venetians at the beginning of the eighteent
century. Each fort had its cistern, which enabled the garriso
to withstand a long siege, and the highest battery, dominatin
the entire defence system, was furnished with shell-proo
shelters. At the southern end of the summit there is a shee
drop of over 700 feet to the base of the cliffs which run eas
ward in an unbroken line. Westward, across the crescent
shaped bay, fringed with mud-flats, the mass of Mt Artemisio
rises above the Lernean marsh.

At the west end of the fortress a stairway (857 step
zigzags down the perpendicular face of the cliff, passing unde
four arched gateways. It was down this dizzy flight of hairpi
bends that the Janissaries poured into the town in pursuit c
the routed Venetians in 1715. The stairway leads into a wid
road (near the Xenias Hotel) which winds round the grea
cliff to the south.

From Nauplia one can visit Merbaka in the plain and i
twelfth-century **Church of the Panayia** (the Virgin). Cruciforn
with a single dome, its combination of brickwork and faienc
decoration on the exterior walls creates a charming poly
chrome effect. The village is named after William of Meerbek
a Flemish hellenist and Latin prelate of Corinth, who settle
in Greece during the Frankish occupation. At the beginnir
of the road to Epidaurus (east) a turning to the right (di
road) leads to another pretty twelfth century church, that c
Zoodochos Pighi (The Source of Life), a dependency of tl
Monastery of Ayia Moni, situated near a spring common
identified as the Canathus, in which Hera bathed once a yea
in order to renew her virginity. Remains of an ancient wa
and aqueduct add charm to the rustic setting.

Another turning to the right off the Epidaurus road leads t
Tolo, a fishing village strung out along a strip of sandy beac
in a shut-in bay filled with caïques. Boys stand on woode

jetties casting fishing lines. Occasionally a caïque chugs in, and nets full of slithering silver-grey *maridhes* (the nearest Greek equivalent to whitebait) are unloaded. There is a modern hotel and several open-air tavernas, where the freshly caught fish is apt to be expensive (you pay by the weight, and the scales are brought to your table under the vine trellis so that you can check the actual weighing). At week-ends, Tolo is crowded with Nauplians and Argives anxious to escape from the oppressive heat of the plain. At the beginning of the Morosini campaign (1686) the placid little bay was the scene of the landing of Count Koenigsmark, a field-marshal in the service of the Doge and connected, through a labyrinth of amorous intrigues, to George I and the Elector of Saxony and King of Poland. At the head of an advance-guard of red-coated Hanoverians, Koenigsmark proceeded from Tolo to occupy the Palamidhi and seize Nauplia from the Turks. At the eastern end of the bay a little promontory crowned by a prehistoric acropolis, with vestiges of polygonal walls, has been identified as Asine, mentioned by Homer in the Iliad. East of Asine, extends a long stretch of sandy beach, finer in quality than that of Tolo. The hinterland, however, is flat and featureless.

The road to **Epidaurus** passes through a lonely stretch of the Argolic peninsula. Scrub-covered hills and rocky valleys replace the shimmering plain. It was from the summit above the village of Ligourio that the signal was flashed to the palace at Mycenae to announce the fall of Troy. A turning to the right leads to the **Sanctuary of Asclepius** which spreads across a narrow plain studded with pine trees and surrounded by grey barren mountains. The highest, Mt Tithius (which means nipple) dominates the scene and has a forbidding aspect. On its slopes Asclepius, child of Apollo and Coronis, was suckled by a goat, while lightning flashed from his head to proclaim his semi-divine nature. Asclepius studied medicine under Cheiron, the old Centaur, on Mt Pelion in Thessaly and then travelled about Greece, healing the sick, inventing new prescriptions from herbs and plants, and even raising the dead. About this last activity there was some unpleasantness. Zeus was so angry with Asclepius for restoring Hippolytus to life and thus reversing the laws of nature, with which he alone had the right to tamper, that he cast a thunderbolt at him and sent him to dwell in the Underworld. Nevertheless the cult of the god of healing flourished and had its centre of worship at Epidaurus, in the shadow of the 'nipple-mountain', famous for the growth of plants with medicinal properties.

The sacred enclosure was called the Alsos, which means grove, and must have been thickly wooded with tall pine trees. A few still cast their shade over foundations of temples, hostels and dormitories. The Lourdes of antiquity, Epidaurus was equipped with all the amenities of a spa; and invalids flocked to it from the farthest corners of the Hellenic world. So great was the fame of the sanctuary that when Rome was ravaged by a terrible epidemic in 293 B.C. ambassadors arrived at Epidaurus to inquire what treatment should be prescribed. Diagnosis of the patient's malady seems to have been made by priests, impersonating Asclepius, in a vision – probably while the patient was asleep. Miraculous cures were effected by the ministrations of tame yellow serpents, peculiar to Epidaurus and symbolical of the act of renovation (because they slough their skin every year), which licked the patients in their sleep until recovery was complete. The last person reputed to have seen one of these well-intentioned reptiles was an early nineteenth century English traveller. The curative rites were a closely guarded secret, to which only priests had access. In the tricky matter of the restoration of life, mythographers say this was effected by the administration of Medusa's blood stored in a holy phial. The miraculous cures did not preclude the application of conventional remedies, such as baths, poultices and therapeutic unguents. In some cases the god recommended exercise and strict diet. The place swarmed with persons afflicted with paralytic, dropsical and renal ailments. Convalescents were able to applaud the most popular athletes of the day on the race-track or find distraction at the theatre. The whole place was fragrant with resinous pines, surrounded by shrub-covered hills, from whose slopes the breeze still carries the scent of thyme and sage; and it is nice to feel that nobody has ever died here, for no deaths were allowed to occur within the sacred enclosure.

The ruins, apart from the astonishing theatre, the greatest single classical ruin in Greece outside Athens, are little more than foundations. But it is agreeable to wander under the pines, among the marble slabs and limestone bases, to breathe

Tolo — a small fishing village near Nauplia.

The Palamidhi — the Venetian fortress which towers above Nauplia.

The Theatre, Epidaurus, built by Polycleitus, the Younger (mid-4th century)
The acoustics are so perfect that a whisper uttered in the centre of the
orchestra can be heard from the highest tier.

the purity of the air and yield to the serenity of the place. The outline of the stadium lies on the right of the road, as one drives in from Nauplia. Unlike the course at Delphi, perched on a high ledge, it is hollowed out of a depression, so that one climbs down, not up, to it. On the grassy south embankment there are a few well preserved tiers, which once accommodated querulous patients exchanging news about their latest symptoms, while burly wrestlers and swift-footed runners performed spectacular feats on the track. The sphendoneis at right angles (not curved as elsewhere) and broken pillars beside the starting-point (east end) probably formed part of a formal gateway. Athletes entered the stadium through the passage between the rubble of tiers on the north embankment.

Across the road extend the debris of temples, baths, stoas, houses and fountains. First come the foundations of the circular tholos (round temple): an unimpressive ruin, but once a very holy building and the show-piece of the sanctuary. An idea of its opulent decoration is obtained from the sculptured

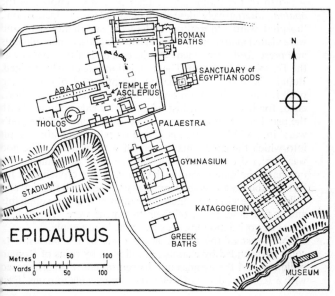

fragments in the museum. It was designed in the mid-fourth century B.C. by Polycleitus the Younger and, judging from the donations recorded on an inscription, the cost must have been enormous. Surrounded by a base of three steps, the exterior colonnade of twenty-six Doric columns screened the cella, paved with a chequer-board of coloured marbles and surrounded by fourteen Corinthian columns. The roof was conical, the stuccoed walls of the cella painted with frescoes; the marble gutter was lavishly sculptured with acanthus leaf designs and the frieze decorated with metopes with large rosettes in the centre. The foundations consist of three concentric inner walls. Originally there were six and the architectural design so labyrinthine that in order to approach the centre of the building one had to proceed in serpentine windings round each of the six rings. At the centre was the altar, where sacrifices and offerings were made to Asclepius' yellow snakes which dwelt in a subterranean pit. The curiously serpentine approach was deliberately devised to create a symbolical illusion of the sacred reptiles' movements.

North of the tholos are vestiges of a stoa, known as the *abaton*, alternatively described as a 'place of incubation', 'hospital ward', 'dormitory'. Here the suppliants slept and were visited in dreams by the god who diagnosed their ailments and prescribed a treatment. At the east end of the *abaton* was the Temple of Asclepius. The foundations are clearly outlined. Built in the second half of the fourth century B.C. of Corinthian tufa, it was of the Doric order, though somewhat foreshortened, for it had eleven instead of twelve side columns (with the usual six at either front). This was the centre of the god's worship, and his effigy in gold and ivory towered above a pit into which the suppliants descended with offerings. The god was depicted enthroned, touching the head of a snake with one hand, holding a staff in the other. A dog crouched at his feet. Strabo describes the temple as crowded with the sick and full of votive gifts on which the names of grateful suppliants and a full description of their treatment were recorded. A forest of votive monuments surrounded the temple.

South-east of the temple lies the site of the palaestra (a court surrounded by chambers), followed by ruins of Roman buildings and the gymnasium, its central court superimposed with a Roman odeum of which there are visible remains. East (left) of the gymnasium is the outline of a large structure, the *katagogeion*, which served as a hostel for visitors, built of mud bricks on a stone foundation, and consisting of four equal parts, each with a central court, separated from the adjoining rooms by Doric colonnades. In spite of its size, the *katagogeion* cannot have accommodated all the patients who crowded the sanctuary. More modest hostels were probably scattered about the periphery of the sanctuary.

Next comes the **museum.** First there are the inscriptions from the Temple of Asclepius, recording recoveries from diseases ranging from tapeworm to sterility; then statues (some are casts) of Asclepius and Hygeia, goddess of health; followed by sculptural pieces from, and reconstructions of sections of, the temple and a fragment of the tholos pavement. Beside this is an elaborate Corinthian capital, also from the tholos, said to have been carved by Polycleitus the Younger. Finally, there are some lovely architectural fragments from the tholos, including part of the circular wall and its deeply coffered ceiling lavishly ornamented with rosettes in the centre of open petalled flowers and turned in acanthus leaves at each corner within a beaded frame. A section of the external entablature consists of metopes ornamented with rosettes between triglyphs and an elaborate and extremely elegant cornice of tendril patterns interspersed with palmettes and lions' heads with open mouths and strikingly human expressions.

South of the museum are a tourist pavilion and little motel on different levels. In summer it is enchanting to dine under the great pines, the silence of the deserted place broken only by the hum of an electric generator and the chirping of a few indefatigable cicadas. From the tourist pavilion one climbs a pine-clad slope to the **theatre.** One can see it from a distance, as one approaches the sanctuary, its grey stone tiers, framed by dark green shrubs, on a slope of Mt Cynortium. At close quarters its completeness and the beauty of its proportions are more impressive. It was built by Polycleitus the Younger about the middle of the fourth century B.C. in the hollow of a hillside so naturally amphitheatrical that every spectator, wherever seated, had an excellent view of the orchestra and stage. The forty-one semi-circular tiers of stone, accommodating up to fourteen thousand spectators, are separated by eleven stairways below, by twenty-one above, the wide diazôma. They are in an admirable state of preservation. The seats are plain, except for the first two rows and those immediately above and below the diazôma whose backs are carved and were reserved for officials. The tiers above the diazôma rise more steeply in conformity with the natural declivity and are symmetrically shaped in their entirety; something that was not possible in the Theatre of Dionysus at Athens, which is overtopped by a cliff and had adjacent buildings at the sides. The acoustics are so perfect that a whisper uttered in the centre of the orchestra, a large circle of white stone, can be heard from the highest tier.

Of the proscenium and skene only the foundations exist, superimposed by a modern construction used as a stage and backcloth for present-day performances. The skene consisted of two stories crowned by battlements and adorned with columns and divided by a continuous balcony called a *pluteum*, along which the *theologeion*, a platform surrounded by clouds intended for the appearance of the gods would be moved backwards and forwards. From this Olympian perch divine personages conversed with mortals on the stage or with the chorus in the orchestra. The cast was thus ranged on three levels: gods, protagonists and chorus (who represented the people). Sometimes mortals would be snatched up from the stage by a crane-like contrivance called the *gheranos* and raised to the godly level. From behind the skene movable chambers were rolled out on wheels to indicate a change of scene, as when Clytemnestra suddenly appeared standing beside the corpse of Agamemnon lying in a purple shroud in a silver bath. Then there were devices such as the rolling of bladders filled with pebbles on copper sheets to simulate thunder and a triangular prism of mirrors to represent lightning. Scenery consisted of painted canvases on a wooden frame placed in front of the skene. Tragic actors wore high-soled leather boots, of which the upper part was elaborately ornamented, so as to increase their stature; their heads were crowned with large masks with wide open mouths. Comedians, on the other hand, were shod in light-soled buskins. Slaves were distinguished by masks with deformed mouths. In the *Birds* of Aristophanes the chorus's masks projected into huge beaks, in the *Wasps* into long stings. Actors were paid by the

State and received a high salary. They underwent rigorous training and a strict diet. On the stage their movements were confined by the narrow space and their gestures were probably abrupt and angular. Their lines, it is believed, were delivered in a sing-song stentorian chant which penetrated every cranny of the immense theatre.

On either side of the stage were the *paradoi*, through which the chorus entered the orchestra, whereas actors passed through five doors on to the stage. One of the paradoi at Epidaurus has been restored: an elegant Hellenistic structure consisting of a double gateway between pilasters supporting a decorated cornice.

A festival of ancient drama, organised by the National Theatre of Athens, is held in the theatre every summer. Motor coaches carry passengers from Athens and other provincial towns. There is a charming alternative route by sea. The steamer sails from the Piraeus in the morning, cruises across the Saronic Gulf past the islands of Aegina and Anghistri, reaching the port of Palaea Epidavros at noon. This ancient little town was situated on a headland, dividing the bay in two. The sea has encroached on the coast and there are thought to be underwater ruins of classical buildings. The maritime strip is dotted with lemon groves and surrounded by high mountains; to the south, the volcanic mass of the Methana peninsula is very imposing. There is time to have lunch and bathe off pine-fringed rocks. The short drive by bus to the sanctuary is through a wooded ravine, with streams running through orchards between banks of agnus castus, ivy, laurel and oleander. On arrival at the sanctuary one wanders among the ruins under the great pines (the scent of resin is particularly pungent in the evening), where the crowds from Athens and neighbouring towns and villages eat ices and drink orangeade.

At the play, if you choose a seat on one of the highest tiers, you can lean back against the sun-warmed stone, without being jabbed in the back by the feet of some restless neighbour. When the sun sets, a brief twilight hangs over the valley and Mt Tithius assumes a less forbidding aspect. Down below in the orchestra the chorus weave stylised choreographic designs as they invoke the gods and lament the hero's tragic fate. In the brushwood glow-worms send out luminous signals to their mates. A few cicadas drone on, but never loud enough to prevent a single word uttered on the stage, 193 feet below, from being heard. The plays are performed in modern Greek. Buses then drive one back to the little port (alternatively to Nauplia or Athens), where the steamer's lights are reflected in the glassy water. There is a snack-bar on board. Some passengers start up a melancholy 'klephtic' dirge; others fiddle with their transistors. At first everybody is noisy and restless; but sleepiness gradually overcomes the majority, and soon there is no sound except the swish of phosphorescent wash brushing off the ship's sides. Land is never out of sight. Shapes of rocky islets and barren headlands emerge suddenly out of the dark and disappear. One is back in Athens at about two o'clock in the morning.

*

Travellers bound for the southern Peloponnese should now take the road back to Nauplia and Argos. Five kilometres south of Argos a side road (right) leads to Kephalari, where the waters of the Erasinus, after a long underground journey from the Stymphalian Lake, gush out of the rock at the foot of a steep cliff. The smaller of two caves contains a chapel dedicated to the Virgin, painted a garish yellow, with a rock-hewn narthex. Pausanias believes that Pan, always an enthusiastic speleologist, was worshipped here. Water plants grow in the pool below the cave; the stream divides into willow-lined rivulets which water the fields, uniting again into a single stream that flows into the sea through the Lernean marsh. It is a shady place, and the Erasinus is the only Argive stream that is not dry in summer. One can stop here for a coffee or an ouzo. There is nothing much else to do.

Beyond the fork to Kephalari the road continues between the mountains and the sea. The village of Myloi is the site of ancient Lerna, where Heracles slew the Hydra, which had a dog-like body, a breath so venomous that one exhalation was enough to destroy life and, according to different myths, anything between ten and ten thousand heads, one of which was immortal. It dwelt below a plane tree beside a bottomless lake. In its struggle with Heracles it was aided by a huge crab (subsequently placed by Hera among the signs of the Zodiac) that nibbled at the hero's feet. The titanic grapple ended when

Heracles seized the Hydra's immortal head, chopped it off and quickly buried it, still hissing and foaming, under a boulder. The myth probably symbolises the achievement of some prehistoric Argive king who drained the swampy fields and brought the land under cultivation. Close to the legendary tree – the shore nearby is still shaded by the gnarled branches of ancient planes – extended the Alcyonian pool, in whose placid waters swimmers would be sucked down by unsuspected whirlpools. Nero is said to have tried to fathom its depths by tying stones to ropes, but failed to find one long enough. Dionysiac nocturnal revels were performed annually on its banks. Between the sea and the road, amid the rushes and long grass, a prehistoric site (probably *c.* 2000 B.C.) has been excavated by the American School of Classical Studies. It includes the foundations of a once two-storied palace called the House of Tiles, because of the large number of roof tiles found here. Above the swampy ground rises Mt Pontinus, crowned by the ruins of a Frankish castle.

Just beyond Myloi there is a fork. The main road climbs west into Arcadia. The traveller who opts for the south-bound road (as far as Leonidion) – the deviation takes the better part of a day – passes through the deserted splendour of Cynuria, where the mountains rise sheer from the sea, broken occasionally by narrow strips of fertility. The ancient tribes, descendants of Perseus, that inhabited this country were savage and predatory. Patches of water dyed a turbid shade of red suggest the outflow of *katavothras*, subterranean streams which pour out the silt and sludge accumulated in the course of their underground meanderings into the sea.

The first fertile strip is the Thyreatic plain. Here there is a fork. The left prong leads to Astros, situated on the neck of a spit of land crowned by the insignificant ruins of a Frankish fortress. On the north side of the headland are fragments of ancient walls, composed of unhewn blocks. The site has not been identified. Astros only came into the limelight in 1823 when the Second Assembly of Greek revolutionary leaders met here in preference to Nauplia because the temperamental but influential Kolokotronis, at loggerheads with the Central Government which he refused to recognise, was himself in occupation of Nauplia, where he had established his personal wayward rule. In terms of the prosecution of the war the

Assembly was a striking manifestation of dissension and disunity.

The right prong leads to Upper Astros, whence a rough road climbs to the whitewashed buildings of the **Monastery of Luku** (from the Latin *lucus*, a sacred grove) spreading across a wooded hill surrounded by cypress thickets.[3] Left of the entrance to the monastery the ruined arch of a Roman aqueduct, strung with stalactites, spans a brook. About half a kilometre to the north-east five granite columns lie in a field. The ancient site may be the Eua mentioned by Pausanias. Herodes Atticus, the second century B.C. public benefactor, is thought to have had a country villa here.

Entering the court of the monastery on an autumn morning, we saw walls ablaze with morning glory, well-tended flower-beds filled with salvias, chrysanthemums and multi-coloured dahlias. Slabs of sculptured marble, including a headless statue of Athena were ranged round the court. Benches were placed in shady corners. Out of the middle of this charming garden rises a sturdy yet elegant little twelfth century Byzantine Church of the Metamorphosis (Transfiguration), with a tall octagonal drum and three-sided apses, founded, it is said, by neighbouring 'holy people'. Faience plates are inlaid in the exterior walls and plaques of ancient sculpture have been built into the south wall, at the east end of which there is a fragment of mosaic paving. Two fine Corinthian capitals flank the west doorway. This lavish use of materials from ancient pagan edifices is a fairly common feature of rural churches in Greece. It creates an agreeable sense of continuity. Within the church, which is in basilica form, four old marble columns form miniature aisles, and there is a fine historiated pavement with marble slabs, dark green, reddish ochre, buff and pale grey in colour, arranged in geometric designs of cubes, diamonds and rectangles, with a double-headed eagle in the central medallion. The post-Byzantine frescoes are not outstanding, but some of the icons of the same period

3. At present Luku is actually a convent. The terms *monastiri* and *moni*, however, are applied loosely to religious communities of both sexes in Greece. One reason for this may be that tenure of minor religious communities does not appear to be fixed. Within a period of a few decades a religious house may be occupied successively by monks and nuns.

on the carved walnut-wood iconostasis are worth looking at.

An ascetic-looking Abbess led us to the guest-house overlooking the Thyreatic plain. An aeroplane with yellow wings was flying low in circles, like a huge toy moth, spraying the olive groves with insecticide. In the garden below nuns in black habits went about their daily chores. The order and serenity of the place compared to the picturesque untidiness and slapdash friendliness typical of most male monastic establishments was striking. The Abbess offered us ouzo with an unusually fragrant flavour, coffee and *loucoumi* (Turkish Delight). She told us that the monastery had squandered its treasure during the War of Independence, that it had provided the rough chieftains with money and shelter, and that most of its relics had been sold in order to contribute to the war effort.

Returning to Upper Astros, one follows the dirt-road to the south, climbing into the folds of Mt Parnon which overlook a succession of deserted creeks shut in by crags and cliffs seamed with bright red mineral deposits. In autumn the hills are covered with heather. It is a strangely silent coastline, sparsely inhabited; occasionally a peasant riding a donkey waves in the usual friendly Peloponnesian way.

Beyond Tyrou, a little harbour strung out across a crescent-shaped plain of olive trees below great cliffs, a row of windmills spans the spine of a hill. Strands of untrodden shingle fringe the coves, and cypress groves increase in number. Soon the mountains withdraw sufficiently to make room for another crescent-shaped enclave, filled with olive and fruit trees, shut in, except at the seaward end, by conical peaks and rugged cliffs of tremendous height. **Leonidion,** one of the most beautiful villages in the Peloponnese, is splayed out across the mouth of a dramatic gorge which recedes in a succession of curiously stepped cliffs of a fantastic flame-like colour into the heart of the wild Tsakonian country (see p. 220), the habitat of wolves, where the inhabitants, never tamed by the Turks or other conquerors, are said to speak a dialect of Dorian origin. The whitewashed houses of Leonidion are square and low; streets, alleys and little squares, built on different levels, compose into a charming architectural pile within the great arena of refulgent cliffs. Here the coastal road comes to an end. A track, passable only when the ground is dry, climbs over the Parnon massif to Sparta.

It is wiser (at the time of writing) to return to the fork just beyond Myloi and rejoin the main road into Arcadia which ascends a series of hairpin bends between fierce escarpments. There are entrancing backward views of the bay of Nauplia and the Palamidhi. Beyond the pretty village of Akhladocambos (The Plain of Pears), terraced on the side of a cup-shaped valley, the road mounts between slate-grey mountains until it reaches the Arcadian plateau, scattered with little oases of poplars and morello cherry trees. One senses a highland climate: barely forty miles from the stifling heat of the Argolid. The road cuts across the plain to Tripolis, the modern capital of Arcadia.

CHAPTER EIGHT

The Arcadian Scene

❧

Tripolis – Mantinea – Orchomenus – Dimitsana – The Ladon – Megalopolis – Karytaena – Andritsaena – Bassae: The Temple of Epicurian Apollo – Tegea

IN a famous picture in the Louvre, Poussin depicts a group of shepherds reading an inscription – '*Et in Arcadia ego*' – on a Roman tomb. In the background extends a leafy landscape with wooded mountains. Pink fleecy clouds sail across an indigo blue sky. The atmosphere is elegiac. Nothing could be more different from the Arcadian scene today – or from the one described by ancient Greek writers. 'Leafy' is the last adjective one would associate with it, although the highland valleys are sometimes dotted with stunted oaks and the mountain slopes, the colour of gun-metal, with spruce and other conifers.

A scrub-covered massif, dominating the centre of the Peloponnese, from which the sea is seldom visible, it was famous in antiquity for its asses. The inhabitants, reputed to be the rudest people in Greece, tended flocks of sheep and goats and hunted bears and wild boar. For all their boorishness, they were said to be a musical people, and Hermes, an Arcadian deity, born in a cave on Mt Cyllene, made the first pipes from reeds and the first lyre from cow-gut and tortoiseshell on the banks of the Ladon torrent. Here, too, Pan, tutelary god of this land of shepherds, a good-natured easygoing creature, who liked nothing better than his afternoon siesta (he only lost his temper when he was disturbed in the middle of it), invented the syrinx.

Why then has the adjective 'Arcadian' been so long associated with a pastoral landscape traversed by limpid streams, inhabited by rosy-cheeked shepherds and shepherdesses basking in an eternal summer? 'Shepherds' is the operative word. These bare shut-in valleys were, and still are, inhabited

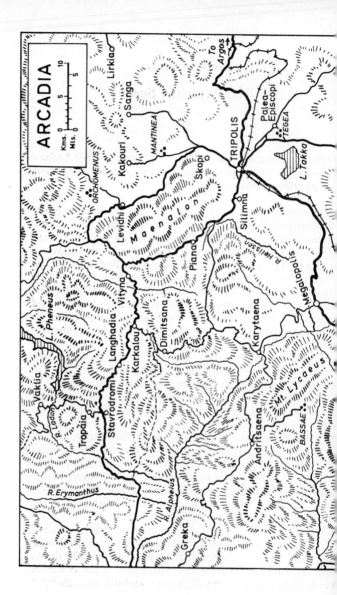

y shepherds – solitary figures, clad in heavy sheepskin cloaks, perched on dizzy ledges surrounded by mountain-goats scrabbling among prickly shrubs between jagged boulders. Apparently Roman poets, particularly Virgil, taking the word shepherds' as a cue (probably from Pindar's reference to Arcadia as 'a land of flocks'), and ignoring other Greek writers' descriptions of the severity of the long winters, of snowfalls so heavy that snakes were frozen to death in their holes, imagined a rural landscape inhabited by flock-tenders who had nothing better to do than recline in flowery meadows and play their reed pipes under the dappled shade of elms and planes. The legacy was handed down through the centuries, and great works of art were inspired by a wholly false image of Arcadia which reached its apotheosis in the paintings of Poussin and the poetry of Milton.

The local myths go a long way back. Pelasgus, whom Hesiod describes as a Chthonian creature born of the Earth, was the first king of Arcadia. He invented huts and sheepskin coats to protect his subjects from the inclemencies of the weather and replaced their diet of roots and leaves with nuts and acorns. His granddaughter, Callisto, was the object of Zeus' affections. When Hera learnt of the amorous intrigue, she turned Callisto into a bear and, in her usual vindictive way, asked Artemis to shoot her. Zeus, heartbroken, honoured the memory of Callisto by placing her in the heavens as the constellation known as the Great Bear. The Arcadians took part in the Trojan War; but, being a mountain people, without ships or sailors, they embarked for Troy in Agamemnon's vessels. In the Peloponnesian War they were allied, under duress, to Sparta, but after the Theban victory over Sparta at Leuctra, they became enthusiastic members of the Arcadian Confederacy, the brain-child of Epaminondas, which aimed at breaking Sparta's stranglehold over the Peloponnese. They were equally enthusiastic members of the Achaean League, one of the many abortive Greek attempts at political unity, designed to resist the tyrannical encroachments of the Macedonian Diadochi. No Arcadian state ever became a great power; but the rugged inhabitants seem, on the whole, to have been on the side of democracy against autocracy, except when under pressure exercised by their formidable Spartan neighbour.

Tripolis, first heard of during the Turkish occupation, when it was the residence of the pasha of the Morea, lies near the site of Pallantium, an ancient Arcadian city, of which nothing remains. There is little to recommend the modern town except a couple of passable hotels and a large arcaded public square with cafés. But it is a pivot of Peloponnesian travel. From it roads branch out to Laconia and Messenia in the south, to Olympia in the west, and to the Arcadian sites, ancient and medieval, in the north and west, which can be comfortably visited in two days.

*

In the mountainous north the first objective is **Mantinea**, where Spartan militarism repeatedly pitted its strength and near-invincibility against the democratic city states of Greece. The narrow plain, north of Tripolis, is flat and treeless. The sky, except at the height of summer, is often overcast, and drifting clouds are reflected on the dun-grey mountains whose conical peaks surround the elliptical-shaped plateau like the rim of a vast crater. At Skopi a line of rocky hills projects into the plain which contracts to about a mile in width. In 418 B.C. one of the decisive engagements of the Peloponnesian War was fought here, when the Spartans, ten thousand strong, led by King Agis, inflicted a major defeat on the allied armies of Athens, Argos, Elis and Mantinea. The victory was a classic example of the triumph of Spartan discipline and its 'chain of command' system, unknown in other Greek armies whose generals relied on impassioned rhetoric to exhort their troops to rush at the enemy in impulsive and sometimes foolhardy charges. The Spartan method was more expert. Grote describes the opening of the battle in the Mantinean bottleneck as the Spartan pipers, a hereditary caste, 'began to play, while the slow solemn and equable march of the troops adjusted itself to the time given by these instruments without any break or wavering of the line'. No other Greek army had thought of indulging in the luxury of pipers or musicians.

But if the field of Mantinea, in the shadow of its amphitheatre of grey mountains, witnessed the prelude to Spartan supremacy, it was also the setting, eighty years later, of one of the most violent convulsions in the long-drawn-out death agony of Spartan militarism. From this rocky projection

dominating the fateful bottleneck, once so auspicious to
Spartan arms, Epaminondas, most brilliant of Theban
statesmen and generals, watched the second battle of Mantinea
(362 B.C.). Only when the irresistible charge of the Theban
Sacred Band, clad in shining helmets and armed with burnish-
ed shields and spears, had broken the ranks of the brute mass
of Spartan helots did the wounded Epaminondas remove his
hand from his breast, pierced by an enemy arrow, and let the
blood drain from his body. But the loss of this noble man
robbed the Thebans of the fruits of victory. The army,
horror-struck by his death, remained as though paralysed,
with arms suspended in the hour of triumph, and allowed the
defeated Spartans to stream southward unmolested.

North of Skopi a fork to the right leads to the site of the
city, built, contrary to the general rule, on level ground,
without an acropolis. Although forced by their geographical
position to acknowledge Spartan supremacy, the Mantineans
were no lovers of their powerful neighbour and they possessed
a constitution much praised by Polybius. In Hadrian's time,
Antinoos, a native of Bithynia, more famous for the extravagant passion he inspired in the Emperor than for his abilities
or accomplishments, was worshipped here, for the Mantineans
claimed to be of Bithynian descent. Pausanias refers to statues
and pictures of Hadrian's favourite in the gymnasium, to
games celebrated in his honour at the hippodrome 'beside the
walls'. The city was surrounded by walls with ten gates and
many watchtowers, of which there is no visible evidence. The
outline of the theatre, however, is easily identified on a low
knoll. Two tiers are preserved and some slabs of the proscenium litter the marshy field. The stage was placed at a slightly
oblique angle to the orchestra, and the cavea was greater than
the usual semi-circle. All this part of the plain is swampy
ground, crossed by unsuspected streams, one of which
enabled the Spartan King Agesipolis to crush Mantinea in
385 B.C. Raising an embankment across the Ophris which
flowed through the town, he blocked its efflux. The stream
overflowed, the low walls made of sun-dried brick collapsed
and the town was inundated. The inhabitants were obliged to
disperse to neighbouring villages. The reduction of Mantinea
into scattered settlements is a typical example of Spartan
policy, aimed at breaking up those civilised city states on

which Hellenism – 'all that there was of refined and rational sociality', says Grote – was founded. But with the ascendancy of Thebes and consequent decline of Spartan power Mantinea was rebuilt on a plan that excluded the streams from its midst. The problem raised by the constant flooding of this level ground, however, remained unsolved, for in spring the water of the swollen streams was unable to run off at a slope into the *katavothras*, the subterranean channels with which the Arcadian massif is riddled. Polybius says the Mantineans finally took to cutting trenches through which the waters were directed into the *katavothras* and thence flowed underground to the coast where they emerged from caverns into the sea. Inundation played an important and costly role in Mantinean history and there are repeated references by historians to provocative attempts by Mantineans and Tegeans (who dwelt at the southern end of the plain) to flood each other's territory. There is a melancholy beauty about Mantinea. In summer the mountains have a forbidding metallic quality, with billowing clouds reflected in dark patches that expand and contract on the barren slopes; kestrels fly overhead, and frogs plop in the adjacent pools. No village has grown up on the site, and the marshy ground extends untilled over the bones of generations of soldiers: of Arcadian patriots and Peloponnesian mercenaries, of Spartan helots in striped woollen garments and caps of dog's skin and flashily armed Theban youths bound to each other by solemn ties of eternal friendship.

Beyond the turning to Mantinea the main road runs through a wide pass between arid hills that divide the Mantinean from the Orchomenian plain. At the village of Levidhi a rough road to the right descends into a bowl-shaped valley, once 'abounding in flocks', says Apollodorus, surrounded by craggy peaks. The village of Kalpaki on a hillside facing the summit of Mt Maenalon is the site of the ancient acropolis of **Orchomenus** at an altitude of 3000 feet. From here Orchomenian kings ruled over Arcadia in the earliest times. Beside the chapel of Ayios Ioannis and a circular threshing-floor there are three well preserved column bases of a temple of Artemis, overlooking the sparsely cultivated plain. A steep climb to the summit, sown with corn, brings one to the fragmentary ruins of a little temple of Athena and some ancient foundations. To the right, the terrace of the Bouleuter-

The Temple of Apollo, Bassae, designed by Ictinus (5th century B.C.) is one of the best preserved temples in Greece.

The village of Langhadia — a strikingly situated village on the Tripolis - Olympia road.

Mosaic of Europa and the Bull, Sparta. It once decorated the floor of a Roman villa.

Sparta – looking across the valley of the river Eurotas towards the Taygetus mountain range.

on overlooks the valley between the acropolis and the peaks
to the east. The hollow of the theatre, its tiers buried in the
soil, is discernible. The place has a wintry air: bleak, desolate
and grand.

From Levidhi the road skirts the northern slopes of Mt
Maenalon and passes through the alpine village of Vityna,
where there are fir forests, sanitoriums and a motel. At
Karkalou a branch road leads to abandoned half-ruined
Dimitsana, crowning a terrace above a deep chasm through
which the stream of the Lousios flows in a wide loop. The
mountains slope gradually down to the upper valley of the
Alpheius and plain of Megalopolis, bounded in the west by
Mt Lycaeus, in the south by the Laconian ranges. During the
Turkish occupation Dimitsana was a centre of learning and
possessed a school and famous library. Today it is only
visited for its lovely view. Down below, in the gorge, the
Monastery of Ayios Ioannis Prodromos (St John the Baptist),
originally an imperial Comnene foundation of the twelfth
century, is tucked away in a shady ravine. Most of Dimitsana's
inhabitants have now emigrated to Athens or America.
Abandoned villages, inhabited by half a dozen families, a few
sheepdogs and some scraggy hens, clinging to the mountain
sides like petrified sentinels with nothing left to guard, are a
melancholy feature of the Arcadian scene. From Dimitsana
a bad road descends into the plain of Megalopolis (see pp. 178-
79), past Ipsous, where there is a simple but good hotel.

West of Karkalou begins the long winding descent, one of
the loveliest in the Peloponnese, to Olympia. A bend in the
road soon affords an astonishing view of the large village of
Langhadia, its red-roofed houses climbing a steep mountain-
side. Here one can stop for lunch on a terrace overlooking the
gorge. There are tourist shops, filled with sheepskin rugs,
woollen bags with crude designs in garish colours, modern
imitations of peasant embroideries, striped bedspreads, sheep
bells – and the inevitable Venus de Milo in bronze and plaster
casts. Nowhere does the sophistication of the Hellenistic age,
personified in this majestic incarnation of feminine beauty,
seem so out of place as in this isolated mountain village –
almost as alien as the streamlined motor coaches, filled with
Nordic tourists, trundling up the endless hairpin bends.

Farther down the descent, at Stavrodromi, a turning to the

right leads to Tropaia, another strikingly situated village
beyond it a rough and dangerous boulder-strewn dirt road
winds between slopes dyed crimson by manganese deposits
Soon a vertiginous precipice falls sheer into a deserted valley
streaked by the Ladon, which flows through a *katavothra*
from its source in Lake Pheneus. It is a savage setting
beetling crags towering above the gorge at the bottom of
which lies a pool of pale green crystal-clear water – the lake
formed by a recently constructed dam.

Beyond Stavrodromi the main road descends into more
pastoral country as it follows the course of the Ladon, its
banks lush with planes and poplars, the rolling foothills
thickly wooded with tall feathery pines, the gullies bright with
gorse and broom in late spring. On these banks Demeter was
found by her brother, Poseidon, who was suddenly seized by
an uncontrollable passion to possess her. In order to escape
his attentions, she changed herself into a mare, whereupon
Poseidon promptly transformed himself into a stallion and
ravished her on the spot. Demeter then bathed in the waters
of the Ladon, which, according to Pausanias, contained
'dappled fish' that twittered like thrushes. In the late nineteenth century a violent earthquake blocked its flow and dead
fish littered the dry river-bed. But they were not dappled. A
bridge across the Erymanthus, flowing in a swift torrent
through the gorges of the Erymanthine range, marks the
boundary between Arcadia and Elis. Green rolling hills
enclose the lower valley of the Alpheius, as it winds serenely
between sand-banks towards Olympia.

*

Travellers taking the south-west route from Tripolis follow a
road which zigzags across a spine of featureless hills separating
the eastern plateau from the western Arcadian plain. In a fold
of one of these hills a large stone cross marks the spot where
three hundred Resistance fighters were made to dig their
graves before they were shot by the Germans in 1944. Ten of
them refused. The Nazi commander was so impressed that he
commuted their sentence to life imprisonment. The descent
into the plain, which is studded with copses, hillocks and little
oases of vegetation and traversed by the upper Alpheius
reveals a new aspect of Arcadia. The altitude is lower, the

atmosphere warmer, more humid, the vistas wider, the mountains less austere. The range of Mt Lycaeus, a series of broken ridges running north to south, forms a barrier in the west. In the disastrous earthquake of 1965 the whole mountain is said to have shifted slightly and the villages on its slopes were reduced to heaps of rubble. The modern town of Megalopolis, whence the main road continues to Kalamata and the Messenian plains in the south, is without character, but the site of the ancient city is worth visiting.

Megalopolis, the 'Great City', founded by Epaminondas during the heyday of Theban supremacy, was the head-quarters of the Arcadian Confederacy which aimed to contain Sparta and prevent her from repeating her hitherto all too successful attempts to divide the Peloponnese into small units under her subservience. Politically, Epaminondas' idea was a good one. But somehow Megalopolis did not quite come off. The 'Great City', meeting place of the Council of the Ten Thousand (composed of representatives of all the federated states), was 'great' only in name. Laid out on either side of a double circuit of walls, five and a half miles in circumference, its size was out of proportion to its population. Polybius, who was a native of the city, says its power quickly declined, and in the late Hellenistic age a comic poet facetiously described the 'great city' as a 'great desert'. When visited by Pausanias it was abandoned and largely in ruins. Apart from Polybius, Megalopolis produced no outstanding man except Philopoemen, a tough soldier, who rallied the Arcadians to the cause of Antigonus, the Macedonian king, against Nabis, the Spartan tyrant, and was renowned for his ugliness, his military postures and lack of social graces. Pausanias, rather exaggeratedly, compares him to Miltiades. Plutarch adds that 'one of the Romans' described him as 'the last of the Greeks'. But there is little of the Greek of the Classical age about Philopoemen. Alcibiades, too, liked posturing, but he was neither ugly nor did he lack social graces.

Yet the 'youngest city' in Greece possessed the largest **theatre,** capable of accommodating twenty thousand spectators. Hollowed out of a hillock shaded by large pines, its beautifully proportioned cavea is turned towards the west and the wide bed of the Helisson, with the earthquake-

shattered foothills of Mt Lycaeus in the background. To the
north-west the undulating plain is dominated by the flat-
topped crown of the fortress of Karytaena. Only the front
row of seats is more or less intact, with considerable fragments
of another six visible. I was alone there once, on a summer
afternoon. The drone of cicadas was accompanied by the
croaking of frogs on the sandy banks of the Helisson. A herd
of sheep passed under the arch of a stone bridge. Tethered to
a slab, once part of the proscenium, a couple of goats munched
scorched herbs. Amid the long grass, on the higher courses of
the cavea, fleshy bulbous heads of the parasitic *Cytinus
hypocistis*, their yellow flowers encircled by bright orange
scales, clung to the roots of bushes of cistus. Monarch
butterflies, their wings speckled black and orange, flitted
among these extraordinary plants.

Beyond the proscenium are some bases of the numerous
columns of the Thersilium, a great assembly hall, which
seated six thousand people – a kind of ancient prototype of
the Palais des Nations at Geneva: equally fleeting, equally
ineffectual. The historical stage was now set on infinitely
wider dimensions, and the endemic rivalries of the Greek city
states, often little more than border quarrels, were destined to
pale before the imperial ambitions of Macedonia and Rome.
In the centre of the hall a space between four columns was
reserved for the orator (both Demosthenes and Aeschines
spoke here). Other columns, Doric and fluted, sprouted from
bases along equidistant rectangular colonnades. The site of
the agora, which was built on a magnificent scale, has been
identified on the north-west bank of the Helisson.

North-west of Megalopolis rises the formidable pile of
Karytaena, most splendidly situated of Frankish castles. The
deeper one penetrates into the Peloponnese, the more one is
impressed by this succession of ruined medieval castles.
Compared to Venetian military architects, the Franks were
amateurs, but the sites on which they raised their strategic
redoubts cannot be matched for wild and romantic beauty.
Disputes over dowries and legacies increased the market value
of these castellated strongholds which were repeatedly
changing hands between predatory barons. Great feudal
names were inscribed on the escutcheons above the gateways:
Villehardouin, Bruyères, Champlitte, Neuilly, Tournay

Nivelet, St Omer, la Trémouille. But the sojourn of the northern knights in this sun-drenched land of dusty olive groves and vine-clad valleys was not a long one. Internecine strife and sporadic wars with the conquered Greeks took their toll. Perhaps Divine Providence, appalled by the iniquity of the Fourth Crusade, intervened on behalf of the Greeks, for only two generations after the Crusaders had overrun the Morea many of the illustrious names were extinct. But not all the Latin rulers were the boorish knights one associates with the Fourth Crusade. Some were cultured men, like Leonardo of Veroli, Chancellor of the Principality of Achaea, who was a bookworm, catalogued a library and had a predilection for romantic fiction and medical works. William de Villehardouin, though bellicose, was chivalrous, and he genuinely loved Greece.

Karytaena is built on twin peaks dominating the passes leading into the heart of the Morea. The eastern summit is crowned by the village, the western, which is higher and has a singularly flat top, by the castle. Village houses straggle across the saddle between the two. A sloping ledge, at the foot of the castle, suddenly falls away sheer. Hundreds of feet below, the green streak of the Alpheius winds through a narrow chasm between russet-coloured cliffs. Seen from the other side of the gorge – from the road to Andritsaena – Karytaena composes into a strikingly beautiful and perfectly proportioned pile. On the left of the road up to the village, a little Church of the Panayia (originally of the eleventh century) clings to the side of the steep declivity beside a pretty brickwork Frankish belfry. It possesses an elaborate iconostasis brightly painted with birds and other ornamental patterns. A maze of increasingly narrow alleys between dilapidated, often uninhabited houses, some with projecting balconies, ascends towards the saddle. Huge slabs of masonry which have fallen from the medieval keep lie choked in brambles and spurge. There is an air of melancholy abandonment about the village. The younger generation has packed up and gone to Athens, America, Australia. Sometimes one cannot help wondering what this mountain province will look like, say, in ten or twenty years, if the exodus continues at the present rate. It is a frightening vision – the rubble of deserted villages littering the scrub-covered slopes below the restored

bastions of Frankish keeps, the exiguous ruins of classica
sites neatly fenced in with wire netting, and the inhabitants o
Arcadia reduced to the staff of motels, tourist pavilions and
petrol stations. Then Milton's words will have proved
prophetic.

> 'Nymphs and shepherds dance no more
> By sandy *Ladons* Lillied banks.
> On old *Lycaeus* or *Cyllene* hoar,
> Trip no more in twilight ranks,
> Though *Erymanth* your loss deplore,
> A better soyl shall give ye thanks.'

North of the saddle, the Byzantine Church of Ayio
Nikolaos (St Nicholas) overlooks a cemetery and grove o
cypresses. Cruciform, with four small domes at the extremitie
of the arms of the cross, and a larger one on a squat drum i
the centre, its gabled roofs compose into an agreeable inter
section of planes. The proportions of the interior are strictl
classical and give an impression of loftiness in spite of th
church's relatively small size. The frescoes (probably post
Byzantine) are too damaged to give one a chance to judg
their quality, although the general effect is one of a lovel
roseate glow.

To visit the **castle** it is wise to ask a villager to show you th
way, for the going is steep and confusing. In spring the pat
is bordered with bee-orchids and long-stalked mauvy-pin
Anemone hortensis with elliptical-shaped petals and thre
bracts well below the flower. Two thirds of the way up,
chapel of curious structural design clings to the rock, it
west end in the form of a basilica, the east in that of half
Greek cross. The little ruined house beside it is called th
house of Kolokotronis, who probably stayed here during th
campaigns of 1821. On one occasion the flamboyant genera
issimo was thoroughly routed in the plain below by a Turkis
cavalry detachment. In the general confusion, he lost his rif
and beat a hasty retreat, unarmed but unabashed. Years later
he declared that he had offered the fortress of Karytaena t
the King of Greece as a personal gift, since he himself ha
built it.

The castle is entered through the barbican. Although th
seat of one of the great baronies of the Morea, it is dis

appointing within – very ruined and with little of the splendid
military architecture evident in the Venetian fortifications of
Acro-Corinth and Nauplia. Founded in the thirteenth century
by Hughes de Bruyères, father of Geoffroy, most famous
representative of French chivalry in the Morea, it conveys a
greater impression of impregnability than any other medieval
castle in Southern Greece, with the exception of Monemvasia.
It was clearly chosen by the de Bruyères for its spectacular
position, commanding the valley of the upper Alpheius and
its tributaries and the routes through the Arcadian mountains
into the Messenian plains and the coast of Elis. Purely
strategic in purpose, its history is uneventful. With the decline
of Frankish ascendancy in the Morea, it was sold to the
Greeks in 1320 and became a dependency of one of the
monasteries of Mistra. In 1460 it was captured by the Turks.
It served a final military purpose in the Second World War,
when the German army of occupation, constantly harassed by
guerillas, installed fire positions on the summit. From the
barbican the path turns left to the main arched gate, which is
set in the curtain wall, flanked by a square tower to the north.
The gate leads through a vaulted passage into the triangular
keep, with a square tower at its apex (north) and a ruined hall
at the base (south). Hundreds of feet below lies a circular
threshing-floor, with the foothills of Mt Lycaeus rising
abruptly on the other side of the gorge. In the foreground, to
the north, the Church of St Nicholas hangs precipitously
above the chasm. To the south-east, the river winds across the
undulations of the plain towards its source in the distant
massif of Taygetus.

Following the road to the west, one crosses a modern
bridge superimposed on an old Frankish construction with six
arches, of which four remain. A somewhat dotty effect is
created by a tiny chapel, connected with the bed of the
Alpheius by a stone stairway, crowning the middle pier. The
road climbs the foothills of Mt Lycaeus, and the lovely chasm
is lost to sight. At the end of a highland stretch, one reaches
Andritsaena, its houses banked up on an abrupt slope amid
gnarled shady planes some of whose trunks are so large that
they have been hollowed out in order to form reservoirs from
which water flows through metal pipes. To the north roll the
spurs of Erymanthus. I was recently at Andritsaena on a

market day. There was much animation. Brightly coloured clothes (latest models from Athenian department stores) were displayed on wooden stalls and roofs of motor-vans. Our car, driving at a snail's pace, occupied most of the available space in the narrow main street and the inhabitants, distracted from the fascinating ritual of bargaining, were literally pinioned to the walls of their houses. They nevertheless showed great good nature, and the boys shouted at us in their few words of German. In remoter parts of Greece all travellers are expected to be German tourists. 1941–44 is forgotten – or ignored. Andritsaena possesses a Xenias Hotel and a library, vast in relation to its ever-decreasing population, donated by a native of the village who had literary interests ranging from the ancient writers to the masterpieces of nineteenth century French fiction.

From Andritsaena one road descends into the lower valley of the Alpheius and the coast. Another climbs up to **Bassae** through a scene of utter desolation. Not a dwelling, barely a tree, none of the usual wild flowers relieve the austerity of the denuded landscape. Only scrub, and range upon range of mountains. One passes several circular stone threshing-floors – sole evidence that men and animals still inhabit, or once inhabited, these friendless uplands. Suddenly the road comes to an end, and the columns of the **Temple of Epicurian Apollo,** grey as the stones from which they sprout, raise their fluted shafts, crowned by pieces of architrave, on a ledge at the foot of Mt Cortylium. It seems extraordinary that a major temple, designed by Ictinus, the leading architect of the fifth century B.C., should have been erected on one of the loneliest sites in the Peloponnese, at an altitude of nearly 4000 feet. Pausanias says it was built at the expense of the people of Phigalia, a neighbouring city, as a token of gratitude for the succour granted by Apollo to victims of the great plague during the Peloponnesian War. The temple was certainly dedicated to Apollo 'Epicurius' (The Saviour). On the other hand, Thucydides, a contemporary, says the plague was confined to Athens.

Except for the keeper's hut, there is no house, hamlet or village within sight. And yet outside Athens there is no better preserved temple in Greece. The architectural arrangement is unconventional. It has six columns, front and back, and fifteen, instead of the usual twelve, on either side. The building thus acquires an air of unusual elongation. The adytum, the secret chamber, from which the public was generally excluded, is not separated from the cella by a wall. Since the temple was dedicated to Apollo, the front faces north, towards Delphi, the god's holiest shrine. The stylobate, unlike the Parthenon, is level, but the columns possess a marked *entasis*. It would be too much to expect all the subtle curves and refinements of the Parthenon which Ictinus, no longer working in marble as he did on the Acropolis, could not apply to the hard local limestone. Only part of the architrave remains, but thirty-seven Doric columns of the peristyle are still standing. Twenty-three panels of the frieze, depicting battles between Centaurs and Lapiths and Athenians and Amazons, were removed to Corfu in the nineteenth century and bought by the British Government for £15,000. They are now in the British Museum. The cella is almost complete, and seven of the ten engaged pillars, with beautiful bases and a smooth grey patina, are well preserved. They were once crowned with Ionic capitals which must have given an air of greater variety to the chamber which also contained the large bronze cult statue of Apollo. At the south end the base of the first known Corinthian column is discernible. This, too, by combining the use of all three orders of Greek architecture, Doric, Ionic and Corinthian, must have added further diversity to the building, without destroying its essential harmony. The proportions of the temple are best seen from the slope of Mt Cortylium, the rocky hill behind the north entrance. The air is cool and wonderfully bracing, although the sun burns in summer. There is no shade, and the solitude is immense; but the cluster of slender columns, worn and rutted by time and weather, still dominates the arena of arid mountain peaks. If ever a place of worship was in harmony with its setting, this was surely it. Like the Acropolis at Athens and the site of Delphi, it makes the same tremendous impact of timelessness.

After Bassae, Western Arcadia contains little of major interest.

*

From Tripolis a road runs south to Sparta. At the eighth kilometre a dirt road (left) ends at the site of **Tegea**. Once the

most powerful city state in Arcadia, Tegea put up a prolonged
resistance against Sparta; but in the Peloponnesian War its
position on the Lacedaemonian border obliged its rulers to
ally themselves with the hated neighbour. Of the Temple of
Athena Alea, burned in 395 B.C. and rebuilt by Scopas, little
remains above the level of the second drum of the columns
(town and temple alike were razed to the ground by Alaric).
Contemporary writers describe the temple as superior in size
and quality to any other in the Peloponnese. It was distinguished for its fine proportions, for the slender Doric columns
of its outer colonnades, for its pedimental sculptures and the
introduction of Corinthian half-columns engaged in the sides
of the interior walls of the splendidly ornamented cella. The
famous cult image of Athena Alea by Scopas was carried off
by Augustus after the battle of Actium. The stylobate of the
temple, overgrown with grass, is now hemmed in by village
houses, one of which has a charming Turkish-style glass
frontage projecting from the first story. Some of the great
grey drums, each about four feet high, lie on their side, others
are ranged in rows so that the spacious proportions of the
temple are easily perceived. The museum possesses copies of
several Scopaic works, including the lovely head of the
goddess of health in the National Museum at Athens (see
p. 80), some slabs of the architectural decoration of the
temple and a fragment of cornice with a course of acanthus
leaf design below and egg and dart moulding.

The neighbouring village of Palaea-Episcopi is the site of
medieval Nicli, a well-walled stronghold commanding all the
lines of communication across the Morea. Here William de
Villehardouin held court in the thirteenth century and presided over jousts, archery contests and tilting at the ring.
There seems to have been some intermarriage – a rare
occurrence – between Franks and Greeks at Nicli, and the
hybrid inhabitants, some of whom spoke French and em-
braced the Catholic faith, emigrated, after the sack of the city
by the Byzantine Emperor, to the southern tip of the Peloponnese, where they afterwards formed one of the most warlike
communities in the whole of Greece (see p. 235).

After the fork to Tegea, the main road skirts the marshy
waters, mud-brown, of Lake Takka, whose southern end,
abounding in wild fowl, is bordered by a range of grim-

looking hills, followed by a bleak featureless mountain stretch. Gradually the hairpin bends grow narrower, more frequent. Then the slow winding descent begins. The air loses some of its highland quality; vestiges of vegetation, heralds of the aloes and cactuses of the Eurotas valley, appear in the gullies. Rounding the bend of a hogsback, the road suddenly emerges out of a trough of hills, and a view of immeasurable grandeur opens up. The range of Taygetus, highest of Peloponnesian mountains, cut by huge crevices, raises its famous five fingers, the Pendodactyla, snow-capped for more than half the year, above the plain of olives. At its foot extends 'hollow Lacedaemon': a wide and fertile valley traversed by the oleander-bordered stream of the Eurotas. In the middle of it lies the modern town of Sparta.

CHAPTER NINE

'Hollow Lacedaemon'

❦

*Modern Sparta – The Ancient Site – The Sanctuary of Artemis
Orthia – The Museum – The Roman Mosaics – Amyclae –
Therapne – The Langhada Pass*

THE name alone – Sparta – recalls the fear and hatred it once
inspired in those Greek city states, whose relatively enlightened
civilisation was arrested, often extinguished, by the will of this
single 'master race'. Yet the Lacedaemonian landscape has a
radiance and fertility that make an instant appeal to the
senses. The red earth of the shut-in valley is covered with olive
groves, broken up by escarpments and gullies – Homer says
Laconia was 'full of hollows' – thick with evergreens and
aromatic shrubs. Streams, bordered by plane trees, flow down
from Taygetus through groves of oranges and mulberries into
the swift muddy currents of the Eurotas, where frogs croak
in sudden explosive choruses. The river banks are bordered
with luxuriant oleanders, precious antidote to snake-bite;
orchards are studded with dwarf palms, from whose branches
rope was made in the Bronze Age. Over it all looms Taygetus,
omnipresent: the result of some prodigious primeval convulsion, crowned by a series of jagged summits, on the highest
of which horses were sacrificed to the sun, its spurs rent with
chasms and precipices, infinite in their variety of forms. From
certain angles the range has a savage, even cruel, aspect;
then it is not difficult to associate it with the austere militaristic
community that dwelt in its shadow.

Laconia, with 'hollow Lacedaemon' at its heart, is a
traveller's paradise. Landscape, mythology, history, primitive
sculpture, Byzantine churches, medieval castles – it has them
all.[1] The obvious route runs north to south, with deviations

1. Based on Sparta, the traveller requires a minimum of four days to
sightsee comfortably: one day for the site of ancient Sparta, the
museum, Amyclae and Therapne; one for Mistra; one for Monemvasia;

st and west. One begins, actually, at the end of the story, at point where a turning to the right (before the final descent to the plain) leads to the battlefield of Sellasia. Here, in 22 B.C., the prolonged struggle which the Spartans had waged stubbornly and courageously against the overwhelming rces of the Macedonian king, now allied to the Peloponsian states, came to a calamitous end when repeated charges f Macedonian heavy cavalry (one of Alexander the Great's novations in the art of warfare) broke the Spartan line and ut their king to flight. For the first time in history a hostile my entered Sparta.

The modern town of Sparta was built in the nineteenth ntury on the site of the sprawling communes of antiquity. tersecting parallel streets are surrounded by gardens filled ith magnolia trees and semi-tropical plants. The people are iendly, industrious and devoted to agricultural pursuits. partan highhandedness is a thing of the past. Possessing a ch soil, they tend to emigrate less than their neighbours, the rcadians. Traditionally right-wing and 'Royalist' – so is ost of the Peloponnese – they have inherited their ancestors' ve of order. The incidence of crime in Laconia is lower than ywhere else in the Peloponnese. C. Palaeologou Avenue, e main street, has little to recommend it except some different restaurants. More palatable meals (grilled meats) n be had at the Tourist Pavilion at nearby Mistra. There are veral hotels, most of them modern. The Xenias is pleasantly tuated on a pine-clad hill behind the museum. Served only y buses – no train comes here, no aeroplane touches down s yet) – Sparta, or rather its memory, is still capable, wever, of stirring the national conscience. In a state in hich the constitution recognises no titles, the heir to the reek throne alone bears the honorific one of Duke of parta.

It is less than half an hour's walk from C. Palaeologou venue to the ancient site, situated on a low eminence, xcavated by the British School of Archaeology at Athens. n the edge of the urban periphery, a rectangular substructure ith two or three well preserved courses of square stone slabs

nd another for the churches at Chrysapha and Yeraki (the least nportant).

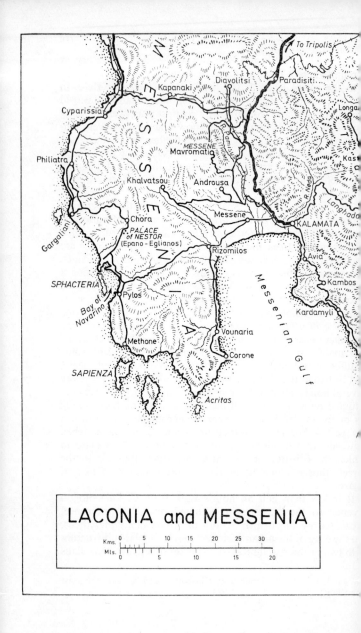

LACONIA and MESSENIA

is commonly but incorrectly referred to as the tomb of
Leonidas – in actual fact, it is the remains of a small Hellenistic
temple. Next comes a low Roman wall, and, beyond it, the
centre of ancient Sparta, undefended by walls until the second
century B.C. The ruins are not impressive, but the setting is
bucolic, the hilly ground, shaded by olive trees, covered with
vetch and mullein. The relative insignificance of the site
compared with the brilliance of the Athenian Acropolis
underlines the difference of outlook, character and way of life
between the two states. The Spartans, confident in their
military pre-eminence and the ring of mountains that defended
their hollow land from invaders, did not feel the need to
huddle round a fortified citadel. The temples and public
buildings were few and, though scattered amid gardens and
orchards, remarkable neither for beauty of form nor sculptural
embellishment. Thucydides, in a famous passage, was forced
to conclude: 'For I suppose if Lacedaemon were to become
desolate, and the temples and the foundations of the public
buildings were left, that as time went on there would be a
strong disposition with posterity to refuse to accept her fame
as a true exponent of her power.' Prophetic words. Even at
the magical moment when the late afternoon sun turns the
snow-capped fingers of Taygetus into a range of flame
coloured peaks and the sound of sheep-bells echoes from one
bushy hummock to another, the most romantic of travellers,
scrabbling among the weeds and dog-roses for the odd piece
of ancient masonry, is unlikely to find the verdict of Thucy
dides exaggerated.

Not only was architectural distinction lacking. Rare among
ancient Greeks, the Spartans were indifferent to the arts and
literature. Music and verse served only as a means of extolling
the martial virtues. One can imagine the jingoist claptrap.
Ignorant of international commerce, unmoved by social
graces, they were also devoid of any talent for philosophy,
rhetoric or dialectics. Conquest, regimentation and observance
of the law were deemed worthier goals. Simonides compared
these charmless though courageous people to 'horses that are
broken in while colts' and equally 'tractable and patient of
subjection'. Citizens were divided into three classes: Spartans
proper, of unmixed Dorian descent, who dwelt in the city and
constituted the ruling class; Perioeci, freedmen, who lived in

neighbouring townships but were not allowed any share in government; and helots, who were bound in serfdom to the soil, performed military service and farmed the king's estates. Plutarch, in his life of Lycurgus, whose laws established the social pattern for centuries to come, has more than a sneaking admiration for so much efficiency, discipline and single-mindedness – qualities rare in the most deservedly celebrated Greeks of any age. The spirit of heredity was ingrained, and it applied, says Herodotus, to all professions – even cooks, flute-players and town-criers. A man with a fine loud voice, eager to prove his talent as a herald, could not do so unless his father had been one before him. At the summit of the oligarchical chain were the two kings, that curious dual monarchy, peculiar to Sparta, which Herodotus believes had its origins in the birth of male twins to the reigning monarch – an event that placed the Spartans in a dilemma and even perplexed the Delphic oracle. As there was no way of telling which was the elder, both sons ascended the throne and the dual monarchy became a permanent institution. The system prevented either monarch from gaining preponderant power. The kings led the army into battle, says Plutarch, 'to the accompaniment of flutes, and the march of well-drilled feet'. In the eyes of the people, the kings were thus more closely identified with the army than with the government. When they died, women ran round the town, banging on cauldrons, and one man and woman in every family was obliged to go into mourning, Administration and policy-making were in the hands of a body of ephors (literally 'overseers'), who were elected annually and protected the people from royal abuse. This election, democratic in essence, is paradoxical in an otherwise wholly dictatorial system. The ephors wielded immense power and had the authority to recall a monarch from the wars, even to try him and punish him if his conduct of a campaign was questionable. Behind the ephors lurked the Crypteia, an unsavoury secret service, as all-pervading as any modern totalitarian institution of its kind. Its agents consisted largely of young thugs, fully armed, who roamed the country-side terrorising insubordinate helots.

The position of women was curiously anomalous. Spartan maidens did not lead as joyless or secluded an existence as their sisters in other Greek city states. Clad in short tunics and those famous slit skirts that scandalised the rest of Greece, where prudes referred to them in shocked tones as 'thigh-showers', they underwent as rigorous a physical training as the youths, taking part in foot races, wrestling and boxing matches. A Spartan princess, who kept a stud farm, was the first woman to gain a victory at the Olympic Games. In order to harden the women, Lycurgus ordered them to go naked in processions and, Plutarch adds, to 'dance too, in that condition, at certain solemn feasts, while the young men stood around, seeing and hearing them'. These exhibitions were intended as incitements to matrimony, i.e. procreation, sole Spartan object of union between man and woman. Homosexuality between men was not only condoned but encouraged, particularly in the army, where high-ranking paederasts trained their protégés in the science of war and principles of Spartan discipline. Bachelors, however, were so heartily despised for failing to produce male children that they were disenfranchised and obliged to march naked round the market place on the coldest winter day as a mark of their disgrace. Married youths only approached their wives at night and, after spending an hour with them in total darkness and silence, returned to the men's quarters. Often a man did not see his wife's face by daylight until after the birth of their first child. From the age of seven, all healthy male children led a barrack-like life. If they showed any physical disability they were left to die of exposure on Mt Taygetus. A mother's final exhortation to her son going to the wars was a blunt command to return alive if victorious, dead if defeated. Everything – education, diet, love and recreation – was geared to the single aim of military efficiency. Plutarch, in a passage which rings with depressing familiarity in twentieth century ears, says Lycurgus forbade Spartans 'to travel abroad and go about acquainting themselves with foreign rules of morality . . . and different views of government'.

That the ideals of regimentation and militarism alone should have sustained a whole people and made them a great power which dominated the civilised Hellenic world for nearly half a millenium remains a tribute to their staying power, selflessness – and stupidity. To realise that such a 'civilisation' was possible, one has only to glance at the map. With the Arcadian massif to the north, the sprawling bulk of

Parnon in the east, the sea (and its paucity of anchorages) in the south, and the impassable barrier of Taygetus in the west, the iron curtain was complete. There was hardly a chink through which the new currents of thought that were galvanising the rest of Greece could penetrate. Moreover, all the records indicate that Sparta's attitude to her victims was one of arrogance and high-handedness. She was, in fact, thoroughly hated by everyone.

Silence now reigns over the exiguous ruins of the 'hated' city. Beyond a late Roman wall there is evidence of some stone-built 'ovens' or 'bakeries', also Roman. To the left (west) is the cavea, overgrown with thistles and wild olive, of the Hellenistic theatre which was among the largest in Greece. A few tiers are preserved. According to Colonel Leake, the nineteenth century scholar and topographer, the theatre had no skene until Roman times, dramatic representations being prohibited on the grounds that they were effete and frivolous. The edifice was therefore reserved for public assemblies. Nearby was a spacious agora, of which nothing remains. Its most striking monument was the Persian portico, composed of spoils from the Persian wars, with statues of the 'barbarian' leaders, including Mardonius, crowning the columns. The agora also contained the famous 'choros', embellished with statues of Apollo, Artemis and Leto, around which naked boys danced, drilled and performed mock wrestling matches at the annual festival of the Gymnopaedia, an athletic-cum-religious ceremony intended to glorify the ideal of masculine toughness. Xenophon, who had a pro-Spartan bias, says the Gymnopaedia was an occasion for rejoicing and merriment and that strangers came from afar to attend the festival. No Spartan of the upper classes would dream of missing it. Bachelors, being socially ostracised, were forbidden to attend.

Above the theatre is a thicket of eucalyptus and pine trees, and some fragmentary foundations of the most famous building in Sparta, the Temple of Athena Chalcioecus (The Brazen House of Athena), so-called because its walls were entirely covered with bronze shields depicting the exploits of the Dioscuri and the labours of Heracles. It stood in a sacred enclosure surrounded by colonnades, with the tomb of the Homeric king, Tyndareus, at the southern end. Laconian

mythographers say the Brazen House was begun by Tyndareus'
children, Castor and Polydeuces, Helen and Clytemnestra. It
was completed, according to Pausanias, by Gitiadas, a com-
poser of Dorian lyrics and a sculptor of some distinction, in
the early sixth century B.C. Sculpture, of a sturdy virile
character, certainly existed in Sparta during the Archaic
period. Important fragments are now displayed in the museum
(see pp. 197-99). It was outside the Brazen House that
Lycurgus, fleeing one day from his enemies, was attacked by a
hot-headed youth, who blinded him in one eye. He took the
disfigurement very philosophically and promptly ordered a
temple of Ophthalmitis to be raised within the enclosure to
commemorate the event. For all the severity of his laws,
Lycurgus was not without humanity, and Plutarch says that,
instead of punishing his assailant, he summoned him to his
house and 'bade him wait upon him at table'. The boy
became one of his most devoted admirers.

At the east end of the plateau is the outline, with column
bases and traces of an apse, of the tenth-century basilica of
St Nicon Metanoitis ('Repent'), a nomadic anti-Semitic
missionary with thaumaturgical powers. Implored by the
Spartans to deliver them from a devastating plague, he
refused to enter the city until all the Jewish inhabitants were
driven out. The moment his ultimatum was accepted, the
plague ceased. As a reward for his services, he was accorded
the honour of patron saint of Sparta. From here the undulating red earth ascends gradually towards the foothills of
Parnon which lies farther back from Sparta than Taygetus,
giving a feeling of spaciousness which is absent in the west,
where the immense range rises like a wall, with the rocky hill
of Mistra projecting slightly into the plain, its near-vertical
slopes littered with ruins of Byzantine churches, towers and
walls. A path to the east leads round another hummock to the
Sanctuary of Artemis Orthia ('Upright') on the west bank of
the Eurotas, among the reeds and croaking frogs. This was the
religious centre of the sprawling city, where ferocious fecundity
rites were performed, including the flagellation ordeal, in
which boys were whipped on an altar in front of the temple
until their flesh was torn to bleeding ribbons. Those who
endured the ordeal without crying out were awarded the title
of altar-winner and a prize of a sickle blade. The excavations

– a muddle to the unprofessional eye – have revealed a series of substructures of altars one below the other, dating from the eighth century B.C. to the third A.D., the earlier ones consisting of unworked stones and rough slabs. The walls were of unbaked bricks. The site has little to offer, except gruesome memories, the sound of running water and the sight of peasants pruning fruit trees. The way back from the acropolis is through the olive groves – perhaps along that Aphetais, the main thoroughfare of ancient Sparta, which ran between rows of statues from the agora to the communes beyond the 'cenotaph of Leonidas'. It was somewhere along here that Chateaubriand, appalled by the scene of devastation, cried out despairingly 'Léonidas!' and, hearing nothing but the thrumming of cicadas in reply, wept with disappointment.

The **museum** in Lycourgou Street should not be missed. The exhibits, found mostly around the acropolis and the sanctuary of Artemis, are the only existing relics of creative art in ancient Sparta. Laconian Archaic sculpture is crude but arresting. It would be manifestly absurd to expect anything like the Athenian kouroi and korai, members of a sophisticated upper class, aristocratic by birth, breeding, education and outlook. Spartan models were obedient subjects trained for nothing but war. The best fragments – more vigorous than elegant, symbolical than idealistic – belong to the sixth and early fifth centuries B.C. After that the curtain comes down and all art withers and dies. In the fourth century, when Scopas, Lysippus and Praxiteles were producing a succession of bronze and marble masterpieces, nothing of any merit seems to have emerged from a Laconian sculptor's workshop.

The entrance hall contains pedestals of statues of victors in the flogging ordeal. Some are inscribed with the names of youths, trained to bear the most atrocious physical pain in the service of a puritanical goddess, whose career, in spite of its associations with such homely pursuits as midwifery, hunting and a healthy out-of-door life, is punctuated with the killings of innocent young people – the seven sons and seven daughters of Niobe out of wounded pride, Orion out of jealousy and Actaeon for the transgression of her rigid rules of propriety. Some of the plaques bear marks of sickles, the winners' prize (Nos. 218, 1505).

Taking the right wing first, one enters Room 1, the hall of

the Chthonian deities. No. 1 is a **pyramidal stele** (*c.* 600 B.C.)
sculptured on all four sides, with effigies of the most important
persons in Laconian mythology. Two sides are devoted to
snakes, symbols of the Dioscuri, which occur repeatedly in
Laconian art. On the third side we see a helmeted Agamemnon
beseeching Clytemnestra, a Spartan princess, to marry him.
Both figures are very squat. Clytemnestra's hair hangs in
tight curls down her shoulders and she holds the mysterious
sickle in her left hand. On the fourth side (less well preserved)
Menelaus is followed by an affectionate Helen, who, before
her Trojan escapade, was presumably in love with him.
Stele No. 505 (early fifth century B.C.) depicts an unknown
bearded man in profile in the very flat relief typical of Laconian
sculpture, seated on a throne, the legs of which terminate in
lions' feet. In his right hand he holds a large cantharus, in his
left a pomegranate. A dog is about to place its front paws on
his knee. Above the cantharus, a symbol of idolatry, is the
effigy of a horse. The elegant throne, the self-assured pose of
the seated figure, the details of dog, cantharus and horse on
successive levels, combine to produce a minor masterpiece.
Stele No. 3 is an earlier work (beginning sixth century), in the
same flat relief, of a seated man and woman. The man's face
is missing, but the woman's, with large almond-shaped eyes
and firm chin, has an Egyptian impassivity. At the couple's
feet two minuscule figures are seen approaching. They carry a
pomegranate and cock (also a symbol of idolatry) and an
object which may be an egg, symbol of afterlife. In another
stele (unnumbered) a seated male figure holds a cantharus out
of which wriggles a snake.

   Room 2 is filled with stelae of the Dioscuri, Helen's
brothers, the most ubiquitous characters in Spartan mythology. **Stele No. 575** (early sixth century B.C.) depicts the
immortal twins armed with spears, facing each other on either
side of two large amphorae with slender necks (another of their
symbols). Above them, two snakes flank the egg of Leda,
from which their lovely sister was hatched. Executed in grey
marble and the shallowest possible relief (only the outlines of
the faces are carved), crude and primitive in technique, it
nevertheless possesses remarkable symmetry and formality.
Two other stelae (both unnumbered) are worth looking at:
one of Pentelic marble representing the brothers frontally,

their spears resting on their horses' manes; and a smaller one of red Taygetus marble, in which they are depicted mounted, facing each other.

In Room 3 we move into a more classical atmosphere. An unusual and very fine (unnumbered) capital from the throne of Apollo at Amyclae (see p. 201) is a good example of the polished workmanship of Ionian sculpture of the late sixth century B.C., with its felicitous blending of Doric vigour and Ionic grace. No. 468 is a fifth century stele of the Attic school – consequently more evolved in style and technique – of Artemis pouring a libation into a vase extended by Apollo, who holds a lyre, with the omphalos of Delphi between the two eagles which Zeus sent forth to find the centre of the world. The richness of the drapery, the flowing line and graceful design seem extraordinarily effortless after the harsh austerity of the stylised Laconian reliefs. The same room contains a bust of a **helmeted warrior** (unnumbered) in Parian marble, found on the site of the Brazen House and immediately called 'Leonidas' by the workmen on the dig. Although an early fifth century work, it was probably executed some years after the death of the hero of Thermopylae. The warrior is depicted at the age of maturity, the half-smiling mouth is full-lipped, the neck short and thickset. A row of curls peeps under the huge Attic-style helmet. Stylistically related to the great Aeginatan marbles in Munich, it is obviously the work, powerful though singularly unmoving, of an accomplished artist. More beautiful is the headless **torso of an athlete** (No. 94) of the mid-fifth century B.C., legless, without fore-arms, sometimes ascribed to Polycleitus. In its economy and perfection of modelling, with the torso growing organically out of the slender waist, it recalls an earlier and greater masterpiece, the Kritios Boy of the Acropolis Museum (see p. 41).

The left wing of the museum is less interesting. Room 1 possesses a collection of tiny metal figurines in very flat relief of warriors, animals and winged creatures, and two beautifully shaped funerary kraters of terracotta with representations of men and horses. In Room 2 there are torsos of headless youths, mostly smaller than life-size – eternal glorification of the self-centred Spartan male. One tends to leave the museum with mixed feelings: admiration for the

vigour of execution of the totem-like stelae; nostalgia for the
purity and perfection of Attic sculpture; and a sense of relief
that a tiny chink of light has at last illumined the strange
sullen character of Xenophon's 'master race'. The Spartans
may have been militaristic bullies, but they were not unmoved
by the desire to create an aesthetic image, crude but sincere,
of their religious aspirations. In the final analysis, however,
Laconian sculpture is a blind alley. Like its citizens, it was
incapable of evolution.

From the museum it is five minutes' walk to the corner of
C. Palaeologou Avenue and Dioscuri Street, where two fine
mosaic pavements, which once adorned the floors of a
sumptuous Roman villa, are preserved.[2] Gone are the aus-
terities of the stelae in the museum. Idolatry and superstition
have been replaced by an intense pleasure in colour and
sensuousness. Thousands of little painted pebbles form
glittering compositions of set-piece mythological scenes. They
are evocative of wealth and a patrician way of life – Roman,
spacious, luxurious. Life in Roman Sparta was uneventful,
and probably very agreeable, for the conquest of Flaminius
had banished all thoughts of further military aggression from
the minds of its inhabitants.

The first mosaic tells the story of **Europa and the Bull,** in
which the pretty daughter of the King of Tyre is borne away
on the back of Zeus, transformed into a bull maddened with
lust. The princess has a thin waist and wide hips; on her face
is an expression of mixed beatitude and pertness, with just a
hint of pleasurable alarm at the prospect in store for her. Two
chubby little Erotes unfurl a swirling piece of drapery round
her head. The second mosaic represents **Orpheus playing to
the animals.** The figure with the lyre is conventional and the
poet-musician's features lack the spirited expression of the
flirtatious Europa. He is surrounded by the usual animals –
lion, boar, panther, dog, rabbit, duck, peacock, turtle and
snakes. Across the road, in another court, there is a third
mosaic (of inferior quality) of Achilles dressed as a girl
among the daughters of Lycomedes.

Just south of Sparta, along the highway to Gytheion, a dirt
road to the left runs through orange groves to a hillock with a

2. An attendant at the museum shows one the way. He also has the
key of the house in which the mosaics are displayed.

chapel of Ayia Kyriaki, the site of flowery **Amyclae,** where, in pre-Hellenic times, the cult of a bearded man representing a 'vegetation deity' was practised under the patronage of Apollo, god of agriculture. Later Amyclae was linked with Sparta by a sacred way, and the Hyacinthia, a national festival with melancholy associations, was celebrated at the height of summer, season of torrid heat and wilting flowers, in commemoration of one of the god's ill-starred love affairs. Practising quoit-throwing at Amyclae one day, Apollo inadvertently killed his favourite, Hyacinthus, when Zephyrus, the jealous West Wind, who was also enamoured of the youth, deliberately blew Apollo's quoit in the wrong direction so that it struck Hyacinthus on the head and killed him. The flower that grew from the soil watered by his blood was the first hyacinth, emblem of death. Now, in early spring, purplish-blue grape-hyacinths grow in clusters among the asphodel at Amyclae. A colossal Archaic statue of Apollo, seated on an ornate throne, the foundations of which lie under the present chapel, was famous throughout Greece. All that remains now is a Roman inscription, part of a votive gift offered by the Emperor Tiberius to the memory of Hyacinthus, and a semi-circle of supporting wall running in an arc round the north-east side of the hill. When the sun sets at Amyclae, there is a sudden chill in the air, in spite of the haze hanging over the orchards, and the snow on the five peaks of Taygetus turns an ice-cold grey as the radiance fades behind their dentilated ridges.

Amyclae has another less romantic association – with the sadistic contemptible Abbé Fourmont, most eccentric of eighteenth century travellers in Greece, who derived a ghoulish pleasure from the desecration of ancient inscriptions. In his malevolent imagination, the whole of Graeco-Roman antiquity awaited the fire and brimstone of his avenging wrath. At Amyclae he claimed to have pulverised important inscriptions with his own hands. Manic in his frustrated urge for mutilation – a phenomenon in an age of tolerance – the schizophrenic priest regrets, in one of his astonishing letters, that he has not yet had the opportunity to hack all the ancient sites in Greece to pieces. '. . . *Mantinée, Stymphalie, Tegée et surtout Olympie et Nemée meritoient bien que je les renversasse de fond en comble . . .*' adding with superlative insolence,

'*J'en ai l'autorité*.' The destruction of Sparta, he vaunts, took him six whole weeks.

Therapne, probably of equal antiquity, is even more evocative in its commanding position. At the beginning of the road to Yeraki, a footpath to the left mounts an escarpment covered with tall grass, brushwood and fruit trees, past a giant eucalyptus, and then climbs between hedgerows of gorse and broom interlaced with honeysuckle. The so-called **Menelaeum** is perched on a precipitous bluff above the orange groves bordering the gravelly bed of the Eurotas. To the north extends the upper valley of the river, powdery blue in the afternoon sun, its main stream of ice-coloured water winding towards the saddle between Taygetus and the Arcadian massif where it has its source. In the east roll the bleak Tsakonian hills, seamed with shallow ravines. The Dioscuri are supposed to have slept in the woods around here, and snakes, their holy emblem, slither about in the prickly undergrowth. The stylobate of the Menelaeum, probably the mausoleum of some ancient king, is a stepped rectangular structure, with three courses of enormous blocks of conglomerate and porous stone. Tradition – confirmed by Pausanias – holds that it is the site of a temple of Menelaus which contained both his and Helen's tombs. Suppliants used to flock here: the men to implore Menelaus to grant them victory in battle, the women to beseech Helen to endow them with beauty. Herodotus tells the story of a beautiful queen of Sparta who had the misfortune to give birth to a hideous baby. A nurse took it repeatedly to the shrine at Therapne and placed it before the statue of Helen. One day a strange woman of incomparable beauty appeared and stroked the infant's face. From then on its features daily grew less ugly. It is nice to think of Helen as such a beneficent ghost.

Close by lay the Phoebaeum (the site has not been identified), which contained a temple of the Dioscuri. Sacrifices were offered here before the ceremonial fights, designed by Lycurgus to harden the young men of Sparta. Slain puppies, symbolical of the tamest of domestic animals, were laid on the sacrificial altar of Enyalius, a minor but bloodthirsty god of war. The ceremony, a nocturnal one, was accompanied by the croaking of frogs plopping in the streams. The subsequent boy-fights were an all-in wrestling affair, with the contestants kicking, biting and gouging each other's eyes out. When the ceremony was over, they hurled the bruised and battered bodies of their opponents into the river. There were no half-measures in Lycurgus' toughening programme.

West of Sparta, the village of Trypi overhangs the plain on a buttress of Taygetus. On all sides the mountain is slashed by profound chasms strewn with spiky rocks. Into one of these the Spartans used to hurl criminals and political prisoners. Only Aristomenes, the Messenian national hero, had a miraculous escape. His fall was probably broken by a projecting ledge, for he reached the bottom unhurt, and, clinging to the tail of a fox, found his way out of the gloomy canyon and rejoined the Messenian patriots.

Trypi already has a mountain air. Here begins the **Langhada Pass,** which crosses the spine of Taygetus at a tremendous altitude and descends towards Kalamata through the most splendid mountain scenery in the Peloponnese, the route presumably followed by Telemachus on his way from the capital of Nestor to the court of Menelaus. The road is winding, precipitous, even dangerous. Beyond Trypi it is extremely narrow, the mountain sides vertical and bare of vegetation. In antiquity, Pausanias says all this country was 'well stocked' with deer, boar and wild goats – the black mountain-goat is still there, hopping from one dizzily perched ledge to another. Passing through a tunnel of rock, the road weaves round towering bluffs and along narrow platforms blasted out of the limestone. Rocks spiral up in contorted formations, like petrified ganglions – pyramidal, nodular, rhomboid. Landslides and avalanches are common. After reaching the conifer belt and crossing the frontier between Laconia and Messenia, the road enters a densely wooded valley, bowl-shaped, majestic in its proportions. The ground is covered with thick bracken, and the air, even at the height of summer, cool and bracing. On one occasion, I remember storm-clouds suddenly blotted out the peaks, the rain pelted down and the thunder ricocheted across the crater-shaped arena (the heart and centre of the Taygetus range). Equally suddenly it was all over. The brick roofs of two hamlets flashed like garnets; a pale rainbow in the west formed a tenuous arc from one pinnacled summit to the other; and the chestnut forests turned gold as shafts of sunlight pierced the scudding clouds. The road then funnels into another narrow gorge and the descent begins, winding interminably between imprisoning heights. Slowly the walls of rock yawn open, the horizon widens and there are glimpses of green lowlands and a distant range of mountains crowned by a Fuji Yama-like peak. The descent becomes more abrupt; hundreds of feet below, the town of Kalamata, dominated by the ruins of William de Villehardouin's castle, sprawls across the edge of the shimmering plain.

Medieval Cities

❧

IN the thirteenth century William de Villehardouin, most
sympathetic and philhellenic of Frankish Princes of Achaea,
built a strong fortress on a spur of Mt Taygetus called **Mistra**,
originally known as Myzethra because its shape resembled the
cone-like mould of a *myzethra*, a popular Greek cheese.
Although not his capital, it was William's favourite residence,
from which he could dominate the Sclavonian settlers dwelling
in the valley of the Eurotas and the tribesmen of the Taygetus
range.[1] Looking down from the summit of the keep on these
fertile domains enclosed by ranges of purple mountains, one
understands why he felt so deeply about it and was heartbroken when, after his capture at the battle of Pelagonia by
the forces of a renascent Byzantium, he was obliged to
surrender Mistra as part of his ransom. From that moment
begins the hill-town's brief but glorious history. Steep narrow
stairways climb between ruined chapels and roofless houses.
'A Byzantine Pompei', some guide-books call it. But unlike
Pompeii, Mistra is not surrounded by industrial suburbs; and
Taygetus is a more beautiful mountain than Vesuvius. An
entire medieval city, enclosed within walls, with the layout not
only evident in ground plans but clear to the naked eye, it is
unlike any other Byzantine site.

1. After the Slav invasions of the 7th century Laconia was largely
peopled by Sclavonians. The descendants of Lycurgus fled southwards
into the Mani or up into the Taygetus highlands. Slav blood is therefore
assumed to run in the veins of most present-day Spartans (as indeed of
most Peloponnesians).

After William de Villehardouin's cession of the castle to the Greek Emperor Michael VIII, Mistra increased in importance as a haven of Byzantine civilisation in a rapidly dwindling empire. High-ranking officers came from the capital to command its garrison, and by the early fourteenth century eminent architects were building lavishly decorated churches In 1348 the Emperor John VI Cantacuzenus appointed his second son, Manuel, governor of Mistra, with the title of Despot. During the thirty years of his Despotate, Manuel not only improved the living conditions of the Laconian population but also encouraged church-building, engaged book illuminators to copy valuable manuscripts, promoted the collection and study of books and created facilities for scholars. When his father, the erudite John Cantacuzenus, abdicated the throne he had usurped and donned the habit of a monk, it was to Mistra that he retired. By the first half of the fifteenth century the city was a recognised seat of learning frequented by scholars, sophists and courtiers. The analogy with an Italian city of the Renaissance is not too far-fetched. Here came the distinguished Western-minded prelate Bessarion; here dwelt Gemistus Plethon, the celebrated neo-Platonist philosopher, and Hieronymus Charitonomos, one of the earliest Greek scholars to obtain a chair at a Western university – that of Paris. Politically, too, as the Turks drew the ring tighter round Constantinople, Mistra's ascendancy rose. Moreover, never, in its short heyday of fame, was Mistra's history debased by the catalogue of political crime and assassination which punctuated that of Constantinople with such depressing regularity. In 1449, when the end was near, Constantine XI Dragases, last and most heroic of Byzantine emperors, was crowned at Mistra. It was the final coronation and the first at which the Patriarch of Constantinople did not officiate. Constantine then sailed in a Catalan vessel to his doomed capital. It was all over by 1459 – six years after the fall of Constantinople. Under Turkish rule, the town was inhabited, and, at one time, local pashas resided in the Palace of the Despots. They do not, however, appear to have turned any of the arcaded churches or princely mansions into harems or hammams.

Here Goethe, who never visited Greece but had probably

ead the medieval chronicles, set the scene for his love story of
Faust and Helena.

'Thus stood for many years the forlorn ridge
That northwards to the height rises in Sparta's rear,
Behind Taygetus . . .'[2]

Mistra is a brief but brilliant flowering of the best qualities in
Byzantine civilisation, a last refuge of sanity and scholarship
in a dying world. Today its fame rests mainly on its church-
frescoes, some of which are among the finest examples of late
Byzantine painting. Subject of a long controversy between
pro-East and pro-West factions, the Mistra frescoes are
claimed by enthusiastic connoisseurs to be the purest reflection
of the Hellenistic tradition continued in terms of Christian art
(not without an admixture of Eastern mysticism and Oriental
splendour) and to have directly influenced Giotto. Other
critics, more cautious, point out that the Mistra cycles were
executed between 1330 and 1430 – that is to say, in the century
following Giotto's death – and that they possess undeniable
evidence of Western styles. Greek iconographers had certainly
begun to emigrate to Italy by the fourteenth century, and
Giotto may well have been influenced by Byzantine models;
but he never saw the Mistra frescoes. Moreover, since
Byzantine scholars were visiting Italy in increasing numbers, it
is unlikely that, on returning to Constantinople and Mistra,
they did not communicate some of the lessons they had learnt
in the West to local artists and architects. It was probably,
therefore, a case of two-way traffic.

At its worst, late Byzantine (or Palaeologue) painting is
illustrative and fussy; at its best, as at Mistra, it reveals a
considerable development of the twelfth century tendency to
introduce a more human element into the representation of
the Divine. Occidental influences have tempered the rigid
rules laid down in the *Painter's Guide*, compiled by Dionysius
of Phourna, an eremetic but scholarly monk, from earlier
manuals. Poses, gestures and attitudes are more relaxed, the
manipulation of colours (fresher and livelier than anything
seen before) is more subtle, attention to detail greater and the
treatment of crowd scenes more dramatic. But what Palaeo-

2. The poet's topography is slightly confused. 'Westward' would have
been more accurate than 'northwards'.

logue painting gains in richness and variety, it loses in economy and sturdiness. The inspiration is no longer on the grand scale and insipidity is sometimes peeping round the corner. The new trends, for all their exhilarating effects, sap the monumental vigour which is the glory of the mosaics at Daphni and Hosios Loukas. The theme is played out. It did, after all, last a thousand years. After Mistra, Byzantine painting dies. Post Byzantine art continues the tradition in other parts of the country: notably on Mt Athos, in Crete and the Italianised Ionian Islands. But it is always a requiem – splendid, solemn and rather redundant.

There is only one way to begin – at the main entrance, through the outer walls. The lower city is a warren of dereliction: empty shells of churches, houses, shops. A steep north-bound path leads to the **Metropolis**, dedicated to St Demetrius, first in rank though not in artistic quality among the churches of Mistra. A three-aisled basilica, it is surmounted by a cruciform upper story with a gallery and five cupolas. This conflation of the two main architectural plans in Byzantine church-building – the Roman-inspired basilica and the Greek Cross plan – is repeated again and again at Mistra. Although small, the churches have an air of complexity and over-crowding. The upper register, the Greek Cross, where the celestial hierarchy is depicted in frescoes set out in strict conformity with liturgical canons, crowned by the central cupola whence Christ reigns over the world, creates an impression of loftiness from within which is absent from without. The lower register consists of aisles, side chapels, porches, arches and screens, all possessing a symbolical significance, which break up the main body of the church into different compartments and heighten the impression of complexity. This is deliberate, for Byzantine church-builders sought thereby to create an air of mystery and religious awe. The whole of Heaven and Earth is represented within the holy edifice. It is both a vision and a pocket edition of the universe. The Metropolis was built in the early fourteenth century, restored in the fifteenth. The damaged frescoes are rather stereotyped in style. In the apse, the Virgin, an elongated, severe, almost monkish figure in a brick-red mantle, holds the Child. Recent cleaning, however, has disclosed the brilliance of the colours, as well as fresh details formerly overlaid by

Palace of the Despots, Mistra, dates from mid-13th to late 14th century. It is rare in Greece to find such a finely preserved piece of Byzantine lay architecture.

Roof of the Aphendiko, Mistra. (14th century) — ornate, redolent of wealth. The number of churches alone suggests a prosperous city.

14th century fresco of St John Chrysostom in the Church of the Peribleptos, Mistra. (p. 218).

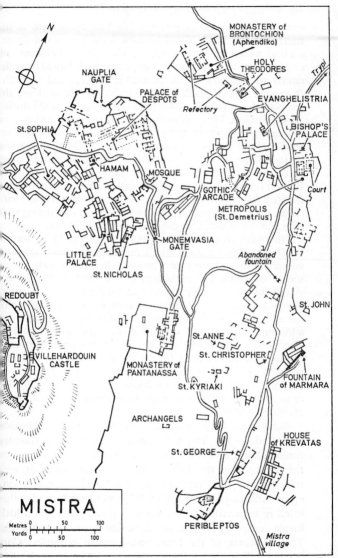

MISTRA

Metres 0 — 50 — 100
Yards 0 — 50 — 100

S.G.—O

inferior works of later periods. The Last Judgement in th
narthex is full of the usual horrors, including naked figure
around which snakes are coiled. The marble columns, o
either side of the central aisle, support capitals looted from th
debris of ancient Sparta. A marble slab, carved with th
Byzantine double-headed eagle, indicates the spot on th
the historiated pavement where the last emperor stood durin
his coronation. The sculptures (some are stored in the adjacen
museum), a jumble of styles and periods, many of them re
worked, have been collected from other ruined churches an
houses. The courtyard, surrounded by arcades, is a lovely quie
place overlooking the plain, with the billowing foothills c
Parnon forming a bluish barrier, full of shadows, in the east
Beside a tall cypress tree is a Roman sarcophagus, carved wit
reliefs depicting a Bacchic procession (figures alternating wit
vine shoots), which also came from ancient Sparta.

The next two churches, dependencies of the **Monastery o
the Brontochion** are small. The Evanghelistria's high apse an
octagonal drum with four windows alternating with arche
niches overlook the outhouses of the Metropolis. In th
simplicity of its single dome and inclined roofs, it seem
almost out of place at Mistra, where the number of archi
tectural variants is constantly increasing, especially i
additional porches and arcades. Ayioi Theodoroi (the Hol
Theodores), the oldest church in Mistra (end thirteent
century), is conspicuous for its large squat dome (recentl
restored), perched like a vast tea-cosy above a confusion c
planes created by three roof-levels and a triple three-side
apse with elaborate brickwork decoration around multipl
arched windows. The frescoes are very damaged.

North of the Holy Theodores is the rather showy **Aphendik
dedicated to the Virgin Hodghetria: a mass of rounde
forms, almost concentric in effect. Once the main church c
the Brontochion, the Aphendiko is a sumptuous affair, wit
tall supporting buttresses, toy cupolas, barrel vaults, billowin
apses (with two rows of arched blind windows framed withi
brick revetments), a succession of inclined roofs and a littl
loggia composed of three slender columns on the north side
This is Mistra of the fourteenth–fifteenth centuries: Con
stantinopolitan, Palaeologue, ornate, redolent of wealth an

a cosmopolitan way of life. The number of churches alone
suggests a populous city.

The interior plan is similar to that of the Metropolis –
basilica below, cruciform with gallery above – but grander.
The **frescoes** are of better quality and represent the current
taste for movement, narration and dramatic incident. In the
narthex, generally reserved for the miracles, the Woman of
Samaria stands between two groups on either side of the well,
where she is drawing water. The figures are relaxed and
naturalistic, the drapery of their garments subtly shaded. In
the north chapel of the narthex nine martyrs of varying ages,
bearded and beardless, their expressions devoid of the usual
rigid tension, screen a host of other martyrs, three deep,
whose haloes recede into an opaque haze. The chapel contains
the tombs of the Despot Theodore II Palaeologus and the
Abbot Pachomius, founder of the church, who is portrayed
in a fresco as a humble diminutive monk offering his foundation to a tall upright Virgin. The walls of the sombre south
chapel, the so-called Chamber of the Chrysobulls, are lined
with copies of imperial charters listing the monastery's assets
which included entire villages and tracts of the Peloponnese.
Four angels, with overlapping outstretched wings, swirl
among wine-dark shadows below the bust of Christ, of which
only the mandorla remains.

In the main nave a beautiful ancient capital crowns the
first column of the south colonnade. In the fragmentary
Nativity on the upper register an emerald-green ox browses
below the crib. In a diminutive south cupola a portrait of the
Prophet Melchizedek is framed within rolled leaves: a venerable head with an expression of fierce intensity, the flesh
standing out ivory smooth against green and brown shadings,
his beard opaque, with pink tints. He holds a golden scroll,
and the drapery of his garment is the colour of faded rose. A
new and subtle use of colour is apparent in this portrait. One
of the objects of the use of a wider range of colours was to
heighten the human quality of the faces, and the head of
Melchizedek is a landmark in this process.

In the Heaven of the Greek Cross Christ reigns in glory,
worshipped by apostles with conventional expressions of
awe. Below the celestial plane figures of saints and prophets
in garments of brown and old gold are scattered across vaults

and outer aisles (mortal creatures who inhabit the Earth).
The frescoes of the Aphendiko, dated to the first half of the
fourteenth century, are an important manifestation of the
new tendencies: of restlessness and curiosity, of increased
sensitivity to a more varied use of colour and the introduction
of objects and persons actually seen – not just copied.

Leaving the lower town, you now take the painfully steep
path which winds up through the double-arched Monemvasia
Gate to the aristocratic quarter, where the Despot dwelt. The
size alone of the shell of the **Palace of the Despots** is proof of
the splendour and solemnity with which the Emperor's son
surrounded himself. The palace faces north-east, towards the
valley through which the Eurotas flows between ranges of
foothills from its torrent origins. The great shell occupies a
wide ledge of the mountain-side. A mass of ruined chambers
dating from the mid-thirteenth century to the late fourteenth
(therefore partly Frankish) are ranged along the east wing of
the L-shaped court, where the remains of a little Turkish
mosque strike a somewhat incongruous note in a setting
which could not be less Oriental. Here were held large public
gatherings, attended by the social and intellectual élite of
Mistra. The dominant figure in this society was the eccentric
humanistic philosopher Gemistus Plethon, who derived his
name, Gemistus ('Replete') from the extent of his erudition,
and whose advanced views on the abolition of private
property alarmed many wealthy Byzantine landowners. As a
humanist he demanded a reform of the penal code which
would include the end of capital punishment; and he never
stopped inveighing against the accumulated wealth of the
monks, whom he called 'a swarm of drones'. An avowed and
romantic Hellenist, he helped to make Plato fashionable in the
Western world (he visited Florence and greatly impressed
Cosimo de' Medici).

The west wing of the palace is more imposing, with its
superimposed stories: first a vaulted ground floor now half-
buried, then a low-ceilinged first floor with eight chambers
which were not intercommunicating, and finally a long
rectangular story consisting of a throne-room with shallow
apses in the walls and stone seats for dignitaries under arched
windows; higher up are successive rows of square and round
windows through which diagonal shafts of light fell on the

assembled court. On the north façade of the east wing, a narrow projecting balcony, supported by six great arches, overlooks the flanks of Taygetus rolling northwards. It is rare in Greece to find such a finely preserved piece of Byzantine lay architecture.

Due west of the palace, near the small Church of Ayios Nikolaos (St Nicholas) is the shell of a large mansion known as the Palataki (The Little Palace), residence of one of the leading local families, once full of arcades and balconies and interior stairways. The tower on the south side, which is dated to the second half of the thirteenth century (the three-storied north façade is a fourteenth century addition) is rich in brickwork decoration. Even in its present jumble of tottering masonry the Palataki succeeds in conveying an impression of a great town residence, where the good life was led, where rich men and women dwelt in cultivated ease, waited on by well-trained attendants.

North of the Palataki the coquettish little Church of Ayia Sophia (St Sophia), recently restored, crowns a ledge below the castle. Dedicated to the Holy Wisdom, it was a palace chapel built in the mid-fourteenth century by the first Despot, Manuel Cantacuzenus, whose coat-of-arms is carved on a marble slab. It is entered through an unusually large domed narthex and the historiated pavement is the most lavish in Mistra. The architectural arrangement is the usual maze of naves, chapels and galleries; the frescoes are negligible. The charming belfry above the north gallery was transformed into a minaret during the Turkish occupation.

A steep twisting path leads up to the keep. The **castle** was built by William de Villehardouin in the mid-thirteenth century. Born in Greece, he loved the country and governed it better than any other Frankish prince. But his education, outlook and way of life were French. At Mistra, where he established a school of chivalry famous throughout Europe, he was protected by a bodyguard of a thousand horsemen, who must have offered a strange spectacle to the inhabitants of the plain when they rode out with the Prince to visit some neighbouring vassal, their lances crowned with pennons fluttering above the dusty olive branches.

The outer gate is on the north-west side. A vaulted passage leads through the curtain wall into the outer bailey. The path ascends again to the inner bailey. To the left is a vaulted cistern; used in times of siege, it still contains a pool of slimy water. Beyond it a round tower commands an immense prospect of the plain. Still higher up – we have now reached the peak of the cheese-like cone – extends the rubble of the irregular oval-shaped keep. Its rounded bastions are all Frankish, with a few Byzantine and Turkish additions. On the wind-swept summit wild flowers grow among crannies between stone slabs eroded into strange pock-marked forms. On the Taygetus side (west) the rock falls away sheer into a deep and wild ravine.

The descent is identical to the ascent as far as the Monemvasia Gate. Only at one point, just above St Sophia, a footpath leads to the main road running round the city and hill in an arc. At the Monemvasia Gate, another path slants to the right (south) towards the **Monastery of the Pantanassa,** its pretty bell-tower flanked by cypresses, clamped on to a narrow ledge. The Pantanassa is the most homely place in Mistra, and it is still inhabited – by nuns. Visitors are offered an ouzo or spoonful of jam. Films, coloured slides, post-cards and pocket guidebooks are on sale in the guest-house. The courtyard is full of flowering pots.

The Pantanassa may be small, but there is a great deal to see. An hour is well spent. Take the exterior first. Founded in 1428 by the Despot's first minister, the church is architecturally a replica of the Aphendiko on a smaller scale, with very high apses decorated with arched windows. The two apsidal stories are separated by a frieze in the shape of a garland painted blue and red. All these broken ellipses (the garland too, is in the form of reversed arches) compose into a multiplication of convexities which provide a striking contrast to the classical severity of earlier Byzantine churches. Within the built-in arches, too, there are more blind arches – a central one flanked by two broken ones. Even the belfry at the extremity of the east façade has arched porticoes on its two upper stories and is crowned by an elliptical dome. The whole thing is a riot of warm red-brick curvatures.

Passing through a doorway ornamented with Cufic designs, one enters the usual Mistra-type basilica with a cruciform upper story. The six marble columns, three on each side, which divide the aisles are crowned by capitals with floral designs combining the Ionic and Corinthian orders. The light is dim, the space confined; consequently the anonymous master of the Pantanassa must have had an agonising task trying to condense the whole of Heaven and Earth into this maze of little cupolas, shallow pendentives and narrow barrel vaults. The most important compositions are high up on the cruciform level and it is not always easy to view them from a satisfactory angle (examining them in reproductions afterwards, one is struck by the amount of detail one has missed).

The frescoes are roughly contemporary with the foundation. In the variety of costumes, the lavish architectural backgrounds, the treatment of draperies, the picturesqueness of facial expressions, above all, the startling range of colour (there is a novel introduction of lemon yellow and pea green), the artists of these crowded compositions seem to have turned their back on the majestic severity of the eleventh–twelfth centuries. The perspective is still halting, the drawing often awkward, the inspiration liturgical, but the artist or artists of the Cretan School who worked here were clearly trying to achieve a new liveliness and animation. In doing so, they were in a sense precursors of the religious art destined to flourish on Mt Athos, in Serbia and Russia in the sixteenth century. So that if the frescoes of the Pantanassa are the swan song of Byzantine fresco-work they are also an important stage in the evolution of religious painting in Eastern Europe.

The greatest compositions are those from the Dodecaorton. Take the **Ascension** first, in the arch above the altar. Two groups of apostles, centred round the figures of the Virgin and the Archangel respectively, gaze upwards in awe. The unaffected grace of the articulation of the apostles' limbs, the luxuriance of the trees, less stylised than usual, have a Botticelli-like quality. The head of the Archangel, one of the most idealised portraits in Byzantine painting, might almost be a forerunner of the celestial beings that swirl across the roof of the Sistine Chapel.

The acknowledged masterpiece is the **Raising of Lazarus,** in the vault overlooking the nave (left of the altar). The scene is dominated by the tragic mummy, flanked by a weeping figure, at once moving and naturalistic, and by a man vigorously unwinding the mouldering opaque-coloured shroud which matches both the little white flowers with brown

leaves sprouting from the ground and the pink and buff lid of
the marble coffin borne away hurriedly by two men. Within
the limits imposed on him by tradition and convention, the
artist has succeeded in conveying the dramatic anticipation
inherent in the situation. The **Entry into Jerusalem,** on a
curved vault above the nave, is another favourite. Although
the composition loses in quality from excessive overcrowding
(some art critics have compared it to a Breughel), its colour
range is incomparable. Towers, walls and roofs are strawberry-
coloured with mauve shadows, encircled by a bright yellow
rampart below amber-hued rocks. Amid this riot of colour
(the background is a pea-soup green) Christ rides into the city
on a snow-white donkey, while the children play along the
path before him and the elders of the city, one of whom wears
a zebra-striped cloak, advance to meet him. With the increase
in crowd effects, Byzantine painters intended the onlooker's
eye to travel swiftly but penetratingly from one sequence to
another, each within its own boxed-in perspective, so that the
tension and dramatic unity at which they aimed could be
immediately grasped and their virtuosity in experimenting
with colour combinations quickly appreciated. But it is not
always easy to take in such a multiplicity of detail in these
small dimly-lit interiors. Some of the compositions are best
seen from the gallery (when there is one) reached from the
narthex.

The very damaged Nativity in the south transept recalls, in
its detail, more than one Giottesque representation of the
same scene: the crib, the animals, the dashing yet stylised
horses – pale grey and terracotta-coloured – on which the
Magi, in green and pale yellow cloaks, are mounted. As a
composition, it is more 'quaint' than moving; but the figure
pouring water from the pitcher is very compelling. In the
Annunciation the beautifully propelled angel (its face is
damaged beyond repair) is borne by outstretched wings of
metallic greens and yellows tinged with a softening grey,
against an opulent palatial background broken up by porphyry
columns. The marble floor is deep pink, and at the angel's feet
a striped quail drinks from a pool into which water flows
from a pineapple-shaped fountain. Elsewhere on the walls
and vaults there are monks, prophets and Fathers of the
Church – some of them monumental in their intensity of

expression. The **head of a bishop** in a little north-west cupola is particularly impressive: a dark mass painted entirely in green and purple, with light provided, according to Byzantine methods, by a series of white brush-strokes which follow the wrinkles of the brow and matted strands of the beard.

From the Pantanassa the path zigzags down the hill. This must have been a populous residential quarter, now scattered with ruins of private houses, including that of John Phrangopoulos, the founder of the Pantanassa, which has a balcony supported by arches, a vaulted basement and water cistern.

At the end of the incline the small early fourteenth century **Church of the Peribleptos** (The Resplendent One), a plain cruciform edifice with architectural adaptations necessitated by the sharp declivity of the ground, shelters in a pine-wood. Like the Pantanassa, it too once formed part of a monastic establishment. Two heraldic lions are carved on either side of the monogram lying on a bed of fleur-de-lys – a Frankish legacy – above the main doorway. There is none of the coquettishness of the Pantanassa, and more Byzantine austerity. The apses are three-sided, not arched, and they have no brickwork decoration. The frescoes are the work of two artists – those of the inferior one are easily distinguished by their oleograph-like quality. But the good frescoes are very good indeed, the most important in Mistra. They radiate sobriety and dignity in the best tradition of Constantinopolitan taste. At the Pantanassa the artist's joy of life, his desire to express the beauty of the physical world was uppermost; at the Peribleptos his colleague (and predecessor) blurred his colour tones, making his transitions less clearly defined, thus achieving a greater idealism. The artist's predilection for a luminous dark blue sets the tone immediately – a cool solemn grandeur. The best preserved frescoes are in the aisles and apses. In the sanctuary apse a tight-lipped shrewish Virgin Orans stands between two archangels with tender expressions, while the apostles in bold contorted attitudes gaze up at the wonder of the **Ascension,** and four angels in flowing drapery support the mandorla of Christ. In the central apse the Virgin, in red-brick garments and a more tender mood, sits on a throne holding the Child, painted in gold, her feet on a dais, flanked again by archangels. In the north apse, unfortunately very badly lit, unfolds the superb **Divine Liturgy,** a masterpiece of hieraticism, in which russet-haired angels with green wings (blue inside) clad in long white dalmatics of a pearl-grey opacity, carry the bread and wine for the Eucharist against a background of intense dark blue. In spite of the solemnity of the procession, the attitudes of the angels are natural and relaxed, and the drapery of their stiff linear garments has a strangely living immobility. Equally impressive is the figure of **St John Chrysostom,** author of the famous 'golden-mouthed' homilies, with a gentle sensitive expression, wearing ceremonial vestments and unfolding a scroll.

Next come the scenes from the *Dodecaorton*: the **Transfiguration** (west nave), with its red-headed Christ in a white robe with orange tints; the Crucifixion (south transept), with its variety of costumes; the tragic Virgin in the **Descent from the Cross,** which betrays Siennese influences; the Virgin again, this time a reclining figure, in the **Nativity** (south transept), brooding, sullen, as though stunned by the momentous event that has just befallen her, watched by angels with expressions of wonderment, their faces lit by brushes of sky-blue, all framed within a sombre rocky background. In the south aisle the scenes from the Virgin's childhood are of varying quality – the hand of more than one artist is apparent – but the dancing figures holding hands in one of the episodes are charmingly conceived and executed. The Peribleptos frescoes remain among the last great masterpieces of Byzantine art. Henceforward, a feeling for elegance and elaboration, so prounounced at the Pantanassa, increases; but in the process the inspiration becomes blurred.

Descending from the Peribleptos to the main road, one passes the ruined mansion of Krevatas, a local dignitary of the eighteenth century. Thus Mistra, or at least the lower city, was still inhabited by people of consequence two centuries ago. Below it, as the hill slopes more gently into the plain, extended the Turkish quarter of Mufteika ('of the Mufti'), where Ottoman officials dwelt in shady boscages. From there it is only a few minutes' walk to the village, where there is an hotel, the Mistra, in the main square.

*

After Mistra the churches at Chrysapha and Yeraki are an anticlimax. But the setting, among the scrub-covered foothills of Parnon, presents a new aspect of Laconia, more rugged and remote. The churches, sturdy country chapels with interior walls once covered with frescoes painted by peasant iconographers, seem to sprout, as though by some natural process, out of the stones of the Parnon country. Like Taygetus, Parnon is a range rather than a mountain, running parallel to it, but unlike Taygetus, composed of a number of detached amorphous masses. Stony, covered with brushwood and sparsely populated, much of it is dotted with wild almond trees twisted into contorted shapes by the north wind that blows across the plateaux in winter.

A dirt road on the east bank of the Eurotas mounts slowly between escarpments of red Laconian earth to the village of **Chrysapha.** It is essential to have a guide (ask for one at the café in the main square) who will know where to find the keys of the churches. The straggling village, and the fields below it, are dotted with churches dating from the fourteenth century onwards. In late medieval times Chrysapha must have been a prosperous community. The four main churches are typical of Laconian provincial art of the late Byzantine period. The first two are in the village itself: Ayios Demetrios (St Demetrius), cruciform, with a seventeenth-century narthex, its charred walls creating a sombre but well-matched effect of puce, grey and brown, possessing a good post-Byzantine icon of Christ 'Elkomenos' ('Christ being dragged'), presented to the church by the inhabitants of Monemvasia in exchange for the one they were accused of stealing from Chrysapha (see pp. 225-26); the fourteenth century Koimesis (Dormition), smaller and less elegant than Ayios Demetrios, with a hideous new iconostasis and some frescoes in a fair state of preservation in the north transept. The most important outlying churches – half an hour's walk across the undulating upland – are Ayios Ioannis Prodromos (St John the Baptist), in the south transept of which there is a fine Transfiguration, with Christ clad in dull yellow garments ascending to Heaven in a pink cloud, and the Chrysaphiotissa, once a small monastery with foundations of cells and a square tower, probably of a later date, into which the dome of the church is now embedded. The frescoes are very damaged.

*

The road to Yeraki crosses the rugged high-lying plateaux of Tsakonia. Taygetus recedes, until the whole splendour of the range, as it tapers southward into its final extremity, the Mani, is seen in proper perspective – a great bluish snow-capped spine severing the Southern Peloponnese. In front, the folds of Parnon run in irregular seams towards the Laconian Gulf. Between Sparta and Yeraki there is hardly a village worthy of the name. The few inhabitants are called Tsákones (corruption of Lákones, i.e. Laconians), a race of which little is known, probably Slav in origin, wild and independent, speaking a dialect of their own, which a sixteenth-century Byzantine satirist called a 'barbarian' (i.e. foreign) tongue.

Yeraki lies at the foot of a bare hill, near the site of ancient Geronthrae, a Spartan township, where an annual festival was held in honour of the god of war. Its Frankish castle, built by Guy de Nivelet, formed part of the string of fortresses running in a rough horseshoe (west-north-east) that protected the fertile Lacedaemonian valley. Yeraki in Greek means a falcon: a legacy of the days when French knights, hawks perched on their gloved hands, cantered across the bleak countryside to hunt woodcock and wild pigeons. Having only been at Yeraki in the middle of the day, in the great heat of August, I have not had the opportunity to see the male inhabitants dance the famous *tsakonikos*, a traditional folk-dance distinguished by wild war-cries and acrobatic leaps. As at Chrysapha, it is essential to have a guide, for the churches are scattered among almond orchards around the village. When the castle passed from the Franks to the Byzantines after the battle of Pelagonia it obviously remained a strategic stronghold; a small town grew up around it and a number of churches were built. But unlike Mistra, Yeraki was no cosmopolitan centre, no seat of learning. The churches are very small, their architecture and faded wall-paintings wholly provincial. First (I follow the route taken by my local guide) is Ayios Ioannis Chrysostomos (St John Chrysostom), a barrel vault edifice with a single nave and apse. The south exterior has some haphazardly arranged decoration – bricks mixed with inlaid stone slabs, which create a quaint but not unattractive effect. More slabs round the main doorway (an inscribed one serves as lintel) form an impressive frame for this modest entrance to an even more modest interior. The

exterior walls of Ayios Sostis (The Saviour) are decorated
with the same inlaid slabs. In the fields below the village lies
Ayioi Theodoroi (The Holy Theodores) – its walls again inlaid
with inscribed plaques – and Ayios Nikolaos (St Nicholas),
now inhabited by bats, with faint traces of painting (probably
rather good late thirteenth century work).

Returning to the village along paths between stone walls,
we looked at the Evanghelistria, a little cruciform church in a
cypress grove. Although the cylindrical drum is disproportionately tall, it is balanced by taller cypresses. Some of the
frescoes are in a fair state of preservation: a Pantocrator with
glowing eyes in the cupola; a Transfiguration in the barrel
vault above the sanctuary.

From the Evanghelistria it is at least an hour's climb up the
steep hill covered with prickly holm-oaks to the castle, one of
the hundred and twenty-two that crowned the strategic heights
of the Morea. A whole side of the hill is scattered with remains
of Byzantine buildings, but, unlike those at Mistra, they are
utterly ruined and were never the dwellings of an aristocracy,
either of class or wealth. The ramparts are also poorly
preserved, except on the south side. The thyme-scented keep
is entered from the south-west through an arch. At the north
end of the enceinte is a postern. More interesting is the Church
of Ayios Yiorghos (St George), near the main gateway.
Frankish in origin – one of the few that remain in Greece – it
bears a coat-of-arms, probably of the de Nivelets, in the form
of a shield, decorated with chequers, over the arched entrance.
Within the church (left) there is a little stone shrine framing a
modern icon, with two knotted columns supporting a Gothic
arch carved with stars, fleur-de-lys and a coat-of-arms of
serried lozenges. Nothing could seem more incongruous than
this crude piece of Gothic sculpture in the ruined chapel
overlooking the sun-scorched Tsakonian wilderness.

*

The road from Sparta to Monemvasia runs through flat, then
undulating country; crosses the rush-bordered Eurotas and
the plain of Sykia, covered with dense orchards of fig trees;
climbs a range of lonely hills and descends abruptly to the
barren east coast of Laconia, with the rock of **Monemvasia**
squatting elephantine at the southern extremity of a crescent-

shaped bay, where Pausanias found the prettiest pebbles of a
colours he had ever seen.

The first, the inevitable, association is with the butt c
Malmsey wine (the produce of vines around Monemvasia) i
which the Duke of Clarence was drowned in 1478. There is n
sign today of the grapes from which the most highly-prize
wine in medieval Europe was pressed. When, in 1540, th
Venetians surrendered the keys of Monemvasia, the las
Christian fortress to hold out against the Turks, they nc
only removed their garrison and artillery, but many of th
inhabitants who wished to settle in other Venetian colonies
in Crete, Santorin, Corfu and Dalmatia. As they left, th
Monemvasians tore up the vines, which they replanted i
their new homes. A sweet amber-coloured wine, now produce
on the volcanic island of Santorin, is said to be the neares
thing to medieval Malmsey.

The situation is remarkable, with the walled town lying a
the foot of a formidable reddish-coloured rock, which turn
violet in the late afternoon sun, joined to the mainland by
narrow causeway – *i moni emvasis* ('the only entrance')
hence its name, Monemvasia. Lying on the main trade route
between Italy and the Levant, its strategic value was onc
considerable. Wisely governed, under Comnene rule enjoyin
liberties and privileges unknown elsewhere in Greece, th
inhabitants were renowned for their sense of civic respons
bility, and nobody complained when the estates of those wh
died without close relatives were confiscated in the form c
death duties, the proceeds of which went towards the upkee
of the castle. Its trading vessels ranged all over the Easter
Mediterranean and its sailors were among the most experienc
ed in the imperial fleet. Finlay goes so far as to say that fror
the tenth century to 1204 Monemvasia was 'What Venic
became at a later period'.

As the Frankish conquest swept over Greece Monemvasi
became a last refuge of Hellenism and a formidable obstacl
in the way of William de Villehardouin's domination of th
Morea. The siege lasted three years, the fortress holding out
as a medieval chronicler picturesquely puts it, 'like a night
ingale in its cage,' and the garrison was reduced to a diet o
cats and mice. To effect the final reduction, William had t
invoke the aid of the Dukes of Athens and Naxos, the Baro

of Euboea and Count Orsini of Cephalonia, as well as the
Venetian fleet – an impressive force. But the French did not
stay long. Eleven years after its capture, William suffered his
humiliating defeat at Pelagonia and was forced to cede
Monemvasia as part of his ransom to the Byzantine emperor.
Henceforward the history of the Morea becomes more
turbulent, with Greeks and Franks contending for supremacy.
From the north-west at Andravidha to the south-east at
Monemvasia, it was subjected to invasion and counter-
invasion, to plunder, anarchy and bloodshed.

Once more under Byzantine rule, Monemvasia became an
important bishopric and a flourishing commercial centre. The
Emperor Michael VIII was so impressed that he granted the
merchants fiscal exemptions. The great squat rock, with its
impregnable fortress, towered above a port filled with vessels
flying the flags of Byzantium, Venice, Genoa and Amalfi.
After the fall of Constantinople, when Sultan Mehmet II was
overrunning the Morea, his greatest ambition was to reduce
the 'violet rock', as the Turks called Monemvasia; yet even
he, brilliant tactician that he was, refrained from attacking it,
having a profound respect for the tradition of courage and
endurance established by its inhabitants. While he was
hesitating, the Monemvasians sought the protection of the
Pope, whose local representative was a Catalan corsair. But
they soon grew resentful of Pius II's attempts to extend his
spiritual sway over this stronghold of Orthodoxy, turned out
the papal agents, including the Spanish corsair, and placed
their fate in the hands of a less bigoted Catholic power, the
Serene Republic. The Venetian condottieri who took over
ruled wisely and tolerantly. Affluence returned and the
podestà confirmed the special privileges enjoyed by th
merchants under Byzantine rule. But most of the vineyards on
the mainland slopes were now in Turkish-held territory, and
little Malmsey wine found its way to the dining tables of
Western Europe. The rock, isolated, remained a bastion of
Christianity on a Moslem shore. By 1540, with Ottoman
power reaching its zenith, Venice was no longer able to supply
and maintain its maritime stations, and Monemvasia, like
Nauplia, surrendered to the army of Suleiman the Magnificent.
The loss of the two fortresses marked the end of Venetian
colonial expansion in Greece, and the banner of the Lion of

St Mark disappeared from the mainland. There was a brief respite in 1690–1715, when, following Morosini's expedition, the Venetians recaptured Monemvasia, to the joy of the inhabitants. But in 1715 the Turks returned and the curtain came down on Monemvasia for ever. The buildings fell into ruins, the inhabitants lapsed into illiteracy, the birth-rate dropped and commerce languished. In the records of the Turkish occupation, Monemvasia is mentioned once. From its now dismantled harbour the Turks exported a red dye called 'primokokki', extracted from a parasitic insect that infests the holm-oak of the Morea and used for dyeing the fezes worn throughout the Moslem world. Otherwise there is silence – except for a fitting tailpiece. When the War of Independence broke out in 1821, Monemvasia was the first fortress in the Morea to be liberated by the Greeks.

The remains of the once flourishing port are strung out along a narrow ledge between the 'violet rock' and the sea. A modern village, with a cinema, hotel and petrol station, has grown up on the mainland, where the vineyards once extended. Across the causeway, under the perpendicular cliff, one has the feeling of entering a stage-set. Inhabited by no more than about half a dozen families, it faces seaward and is approached through a vaulted passage forming part of a triangular bastion. Left of the passage a stairway leads up to the parapet. Two parallel walls run down to the sea, thus enclosing the town from the west and east. The rectangle is completed by the vertical cliff to the north and by a sea-wall along which one can stroll, to the south. The silence is broken only by the squawking of gulls and the waves breaking on the rocks. There are not even any fishing caïques in the harbour. A steamer, bound for Cythera from the Piraeus, puts in twice a week. Within the walled enclosure there is no wheeled traffic.

A narrow paved alley is lined with hovels, including (on the right) a primitive taverna where one can get eggs, wine and, with luck, fish fried on a primus stove. The alley, which is the main street, ends in a little esplanade. A Turkish cannon points out to sea. To the south, the last spurs of Parnon run into Cape Malea, whose wild and rocky coast was the terror of ancient sailors. On the east side of the esplanade is the seventeenth century Church of Christ 'Elkomenos', restored

Church of Ayia Sophia, Monemvasia, founded at the end of the 13th century by Emperor Andronicus II, crowns one of the last Christian fortresses to hold out against the Turks.

A typical tower house in the Mani. For centuries the fierce inhabitants of this wild peninsula would ride out of their towers to make war on their neighbours in the next village.

and whitewashed, built on the site of a more ancient foundation, once the home of a famous icon of 'Christ being dragged', which was considered so holy and beautiful that the Emperor Isaac II Angelus removed it to Constantinople. Today the church's only artistic treasure is a fine icon of the Crucifixion. Two pilasters with Corinthian-style capitals frame the main doorway, and above the lintel there is a cornice with a decorative design in which two peacocks, facing outwards, perform an awkward but animated dance. Above the 'Elkomenos' is the more severe pile of the fourteenth century Church of the Myrtiotissa, with its shapely dome. The interior (with slightly pointed arches) is as bare as the exterior, whose stone-work presents a greyish chocolate-coloured surface – very forbidding after the extravagance of Mistra.

East of the 'Elkomenos' extends a shambles of abandoned dwellings, three-storied windowless shells, tiled roofs caving in, gables falling apart, doorways bricked in. Occasionally a cat or hen scuttles down a rock-hewn stairway. Low battlements overhang the sea. At the eastern extremity there is another esplanade, larger than the first. Here are two more churches. Ayios Nikolaos (St Nicholas) is structurally almost identical to the Myrtiotissa, mud-grey in colour, and with the same sturdy architectural lines. There is an economy and austerity about these churches which harmonises with the desolate scene. The Chrysaphiotissa ('The Virgin of Chrysapha') is more modern (early seventeenth century), ugly and whitewashed, with a huge tea-cosy dome. But in the minds of Laconian peasants, to whom the dividing line between religion, superstition and folklore is often somewhat tenuous, the church holds a special place, for it contains a chapel in which the famous flying icon of Chrysapha was found. The Virgin herself indicated the spot – a water well, which still exists – in a dream to an old woman. The icon, it was said, had flown of its own volition from Chrysapha to Monemvasia at the Virgin's command. But the inhabitants of Chrysapha had doubts about the mechanics of the miraculous flight. Suspecting foul play, they came to Monemvasia on some specious pretext and stole the icon. Again it flew, like a homing pigeon, across the Tsakonian mountains to its new abode. In the end the people of Chrysapha accepted a substitute icon, presented by the triumphant Monemvasians who kept the disputed one. The holy image's nocturnal flights ceased forth-with.

At this point the south rampart is well preserved, and it is possible to walk along the entire length of the sea-wall, which is slit with gun embrasures. Equally well preserved is the long descending line of the east wall (from the cliff face to the sea). Beyond it there is nothing but rocks, waves and a lighthouse, with the crenellated fortress towering a thousand feet above.

The **fortress** or upper town is approached by a path zigzagging up the cliff, passing (halfway up) under a low arch, with a sentry post (on the left) commanding an aerial view of the domed churches and roofless houses below. At intervals the parapet is cut with arrow slits. It is difficult to imagine how an invader could have contemplated scaling the perpendicular rock. William de Villehardouin, the only con-queror, forced the surrender of the garrison by blockade. One passes through a second archway to enter the upper town. Above the main arch is a plaque inscribed with the words 'Christ reigns here' (a militant Christ who grants his blessing to Byzantine arms which protect and glorify his Church). The iron-plated doors are studded with nails, and prison cells line one side of the vaulted passage. Emerging into the open, you face a slope covered with the debris of barracks, posterns, cisterns, guardrooms. A crenellated wall encircles the summit, except on the north side where the cliff is sheer. The bastions and a square fort are Byzantine structures. The shell of one house bears a Venetian coat-of-arms, and the Lion of St Mark is carved on a well-head. The rest of the fortifications, choked in spurge, thistles and thyme, are Turkish. In summer the scent of scorched herbs is over-powering. A wild fig tree points the way up to the **Church of Ayia Sophia** (St Sophia) on a last crowning terrace. Founded at the end of the thirteenth century by the Emperor Andronicus II, an untiring patron of religious art, it was built on the same plan as that of Daphni – lofty in conception, cruciform in plan, majestic in proportions. Above the entrance a marble slab depicts two lambs and two doves. The interior is very bare: some fragmentary frescoes in the pendentives and narthex; a rather better preserved Christ holding an open Book of Gospels above the main apse; a cornice with carvings along the divisions separating the narthex and nave. In its adornment St Sophia is negligible, in its proportions it is in the best tradition of Byzantine architecture. To the north, the crescent-shaped bay, with its mile-long strand of sand, is dominated by the heights on which the Argives founded the colony of Epidaurus Limera. Immediately below, the cliff is fringed by black spiky rocks flecked with the spray of breaking waves.

Each time one goes to Monemvasia the decay seems greater than before. But the woman who fried our fish at the taverna informed us that 'many foreigners, many, many . . .' – she bunched up her fingers to convey an idea of the multitude they represented in her imagination – were buying up old houses. Dirt cheap, too. Soon, perhaps, Monemvasia will become another magnet for enterprising expatriates. It has an excellent anchorage for yachts. The mainland beach is superb. And there is nothing to prevent the abandoned towers, open to the stars, from being transformed into cosy little bars with juke-boxes, their Venetian stone-work festooned with fish-nets and strung with conches. One can see it all happening.

CHAPTER ELEVEN

The Mani

❧

Gytheion – Cranae – Passava – Areopolis – The Evil Mountains –
Pyrgos – The Niclian Country – Kitta – Yerolimena – Cape
Taenerum – Oitylo – Kelepha – Nomitsi; The Byzantine
Chapels – Kardamyli

THE Mani, or Maina, offers no antiquities and little mythology. Pausanias scrabbled among some ruined shrines which
failed to arouse his enthusiasm. The peninsula, the southernmost point of mainland Europe after the Spanish Tarifa,
projects like a misshapen fang, flanked by two others, into the
Eastern Mediterranean. Its history is that of a small but
important section of the Greek people, descendants of the
ancient Spartans with a strong mixture of Slav blood, fiercely
independent, indifferent to every new current of thought
outside their own stony wilderness. Their warlike virtues
inspired sufficient dread in the Sultan's armies to persuade the
Sublime Porte to let them indulge their passion for fratricidal
strife rather than subdue them by means of costly operations.
In the eighteenth century they were granted official autonomy,
thus securing a privileged status in the Ottoman Empire. For
centuries the treeless plateaux and boulder-strewn ravines
echoed with the crack of pistol shots fired by feuding families.
Armed with yataghans, axes and muskets, sheathed in
bandoliers, they rode out of their towers (no house worthy of
the name did not possess its protective tower) – not to till the
fields or tend the vines, but to kill their neighbours in the
next village. The great Maniot families, the Mavromichalis,
Stephanopoloi, Mourtzonoi, lived by the rule of blood and
iron. The Mani may not be in the main stream of Greek
history, but for anyone anxious to open a little chink into the
fascinating enigma of the Greek character, it is immensely

rewarding. For the lover of landscape it is one of the most exciting experiences in Southern Greece.[1]

Technically the Mani begins at Gytheion, once the naval base of Sparta, terraced on a hill overlooking a sickle-shaped bay. The houses on the waterfront are colour-washed, cream, pink and lemon yellow. South of the caïque-filled harbour a causeway joins the waterfront to a flattish islet, now called Marathonisi (fennel island), planted with pine trees and crowned by a chapel built on the foundations of an ancient temple. It is not in the least striking. Yet this is Homer's Cranae, where Helen and Paris spent the first night of their journey from Sparta to Troy. Everything else about Gytheion pales before the thought of that delirious night under the stars at Cranae – its molluscs fished by Phoenician sailors for the purple dye they yielded, its roadstead filled with Lacedaemonian triremes, its cheeses, which Lucian says were celebrated throughout the Graeco-Roman world, its twilight years under the Roman administration, evidence of which still exists in the ruins of a marble theatre built on an olive-clad declivity north-east of the town.

Geographically, the Mani divides into two distinct regions: the Outer Mani, its deep, fertile, even wooded, gullies overhung by precipitous crags, running approximately east to west from Gytheion to Kardamyli and from the bay of Ayeranos to that of Oitylo; and the Deep Mani, its southern extension, which is a scorched land of rocky plateaux, shaded only by ferocious barren slopes which reproduce, right down to the tip of Cape Taenarum, the special character of the Taygetus range – bold, angular, and always in the grand style.

From Gytheion the road winds inland through vineyards, olive groves and fields of maize bordered by aloes and cypresses. The sea disappears behind a screen of hills. The spine of Taygetus draws nearer, and the road enters a canyon of reddish rock. Vestiges of crenellations line the east ridge. At the exit of the canyon, the scene comes into focus: the crenellated ridge forms part of a hill, fringed by vineyards within a wooden enclave, commanding the Laconian Gulf in

1. Starting from Sparta early in the morning, one can drive to the tip of the Mani across the central spine and back along the spectacular west coast, reaching Kalamata in the evening. One can alternatively spend the night at Yerolimena, where there is simple but decent accommodation.

the east, the passes across Taygetus in the west. Leake believed this to be the site of ancient Las, mentioned by Homer in the *Iliad*, and, according to a Laconian myth, destroyed by the Dioscuri. The hill is crowned by the remains of the Frankish castle of **Passava** (so-called from the French war-cry '*passe avant*'), stronghold of Jean de Neuilly, hereditary marshal of the principality of Achaea. It takes half an hour to climb up to the castle (there is no path) through dense bushes of arbutus and brushwood often higher than one's angle of vision. The centre of the enceinte is empty, except for the roofless shell of a chapel choked in prickly shrubs. But there is a spectacular walk along the west battlements, with arrow slits in alternate embrasures, overlooking the chasm which the fortress was intended to defend against unruly Maniots who broke out of their mountain redoubts.

When captured by the Emperor Michael VIII at Pelagonia, William de Villehardouin was obliged to surrender hostages as well as castles as part of his ransom. Among the hostages he picked on (not without calculation, perhaps) was Marguerite, daughter of the Baron of Passava, last in the line of the de Neuillys. At Constantinople the French lady, although a captive, was well treated. When released, she married Jean de St Omer, whose influential family lost no time in espousing her cause, for, during her captivity, William de Villehardouin had seized her other inheritance, the barony of Akova. His subsequent quarrel with the haughty St Omers, Marguerite's champions, led to prolonged litigation, and two assemblies of the court of the principality were summoned to deal with the case. William, more astute, got the better of his opponents; but in the end he made a gesture and presented Marguerite with one third of her inheritance, reserving the other two for his own daughter. The case is typical of the double-crossing that characterised relations between Frankish barons in thirteenth century Greece.

In the mid-fourteenth century Passava fell to the Byzantines; then to the Turks and Venetians. The latter dismantled the castle, believing they could guard the passes equally well from Gytheion. Passava is one of the few strictly historical sites in the Mani. Seen in the afternoon light, with the woods and vineyards reflecting a lambent serenity, it is an idyllic place. Ahead lies little that can be so described.

The road now follows a narrow valley. In summer feathery branches of agnus castus, flecked with pale blue blooms, straggle among bright pink oleanders along banks of dried-up torrent beds, where the heat seems to be trapped in an almost palpable stillness. The valley alternately widens and narrows. Beyond the village of Vachos the aridity becomes more pronounced. The saddle has been crossed. The Messenian Gulf opens up in the west. A chain of slate-grey mountains, each one more angular, geometric and desiccated than the other, extends southward. The road dips and bends between low stone walls enclosing plots of red earth from which stunted olive trees sprout in twisted dwarf-like shapes, until it reaches the village of **Areopolis** spreading across a wide ledge.

Originally called Tsimova, it was renamed Areopolis (the city of the god of war) in the early nineteenth century by the head of the most bellicose clan in the Mani, the Mavromichalis (the 'Black Michaels'), later destined to provide Greek cabinets with eminent ministers. The Mavromichalis and their exploits have virtually passed into Greek folklore. On their maternal side they claim descent from a mermaid. The men, armed to the teeth with scimitars, yataghans and embossed carbines, were said to possess a virile god-like beauty with bushy eyebrows and huge black moustaches. The war waged by one of them against the Turks in the eighteenth century was so fierce that he earned the *nom de guerre* of Skyloyannis ('Dog-John'). But it was his son, Petrobey, established in the stronghold of Areopolis, who brought the greatest lustre to the name of Black Michael. In the national interest, he even effected a truce between the warring clans and, when the War of Independence broke out, led three thousand Maniots to enforce the surrender of the Turkish camp at Kalamata. During the war he fought in forty-nine battles and was regarded as a reincarnation of Ares. But when peace came, he succumbed to the heady delights of political intrigue, fell out with Capodistria, whose rank of head of state he coveted, and was thrown into prison. For this intolerable insult to Maniot honour his nephews assassinated Capodistria at Nauplia and the entire population of the Mani rose in revolt against the first government of the new Greek state.

The thing that strikes one about Areopolis is its lazy sun-drenched air. With the removal of the Mavromichalis to luxury penthouses in Athenian blocks of flats, the spirit of Ares no longer haunts their little capital. The alleys are empty, and a hush has fallen on the place. The hoarse shouts, the orders and blasphemies, the neighing of prancing horses and shots fired in the air echo only in the imagination. The men have lean brown faces, their skin desiccated by long shadeless summers; their small bodies are lithe and sinewy, like a spring wound up, their movements quick and nervous-fingers on the trigger, one feels. The women are kept well out of sight. Occasionally a bent figure draped in black from head to foot, a little brown face peeping out of the funereal garments suitable to her sex, scurries along the side of a whitewashed wall. The Mani is definitely a man's country.

The centre of Areopolis is a minute square distinguished by the **Church of the Taxiarchoi** (The Archangels), a domed single nave basilica with a tall tapering belfry of dazzling white and an exterior decoration which is a masterpiece of folklore fantasy. The general effect of whiteness is heightened by the lime-washed trunks of acacia trees on the raised platform of the church. First look at the apse: a course of pink rosettes from which rise five pilasters, their capitals joined by arches in shallow relief. Above these runs a bossed fairy-tale frieze of seraphim and grinning beady-eyed round-faced Suns, surrounded by spikes like a hedgehog's, within a border of triangular petals; the signs of the zodiac are represented by prancing animals.

The colour scheme of the bas-relief above the main doorway is yellow, black and green. In the centre, a shield rests on the breast of a Byzantine double-headed eagle with rich plumage and outstretched claws, flanked by two lions rampant. Below the eagle, a scroll between two large rosettes bears the date 1798. Patrick Leigh-Fermor, intrigued by the bird's heraldic origins, wonders whether it could be a crude copy of a Maria Theresa thaler or 'remotely inspired by the arms of Russia'.[2] Above the bird two sun-disks stare with enormous round eyes. On either side stand the Archangels, one holding a

2. Patrick Leigh-Fermor, *Mani, Travels in the Southern Peloponnese*, John Murray, London, 1958.

sword, the other a cross. The frieze of rosettes is crowned by a sphinx-like face emerging out of a crescent-moon between two perky birds, flanked by two staring faces, almost Archaic in their tense immobility of expression. Peasant art, applied to church architecture, is sometimes monotonous, even boring. Not so at Areopolis. The mind that conceived the exterior church decoration had a sense of both humour and fantasy. The whole composition is an extraordinary example of crude vigour, imagination and expressive force. But what does it all mean?

No less striking is the bas-relief above the south doorway. Again we have the Archangels: clad in dove-grey garments, with cream-coloured faces. On either side of them the military saints, George and Theodore, ride puce-coloured horses. Above the frieze of rosettes the Dove and the Hand of God are framed within more rosettes. Throughout, the emphasis is on the warlike character of the Archangels, patrons of the main church of an arsenal dedicated to the god of war. The interior of the church is without special interest.

A few minutes' walk from the Archangels lies the more conventional Church of Ayios Ioannis Prodromos (St John the Baptist). The interior walls of this minute barrel-vaulted single nave chapel are covered with monkish peasant-art frescoes. The figures have enormous faces with bulging eyes, out of all proportion to their puny bodies. There is no lack of animation in the scenes of miracles and martyrdoms (St Peter crucified upside down against a pink background is worth noticing) and a charming effect is created by the decorative stars and rosettes on the dark blue robes of a rather plebeian-looking Christ on the iconostasis.

South of Areopolis begins the Deep Mani. The last spurs of Taygetus, still formidable, though diminished in altitude, plunge through a series of savage ravines into the sea. These are the Kakovounia (The Evil Mountains) or alternatively Kakovoulia (The Land of Evil Counsel). Dramatic in their forms, stark in their aridity, their pyramidal peaks, sudden vertical declivities and huge sheets of limestone belong to a nightmare world. Yet there is order and composition in their arrangement. In the middle of the day their colour is that of molten lead; in the afternoon they turn beige, in the evening mauve. The Evil Mountains is no misnomer.

At the village of Pyrgos the tiny Basilica of Ayios Ioannis (St John) is dated to the early twelfth century, a period associated with the widespread diffusion of the domed church. Nearby is Ayios Petros (St Peter), of an earlier date. Maniot church-builders, though working far from the centres of culture, were quick at picking up the latest trends. In the wasteland between Pyrgos and Yerolimena there are a number of Byzantine chapels dating from the eleventh to the thirteenth century decorated with exterior brick revetments (step-pattern frieze, diaper work) then coming into fashion. Of greater interest to the Byzantine specialist than to the average traveller, these chapels (they are more than just wayside shrines) emphasise the power exercised by the Church over the remotest regions of the Empire.[3] They also indicate that the country must have been relatively thickly populated before the great vendettas of the Turkish occupation.

A winding descent leads to the bay of Dyrou, once the port of Pyrgos. The beach is strewn with enormous pebbles covered with pitch. Little caves honeycomb the cliffs. There are a couple of cafés. It is hot, humid and, at the weekends, crowded with trippers visiting the large caves discovered in 1958. The entrance to the first is just above the cafés. There are spacious chambers with galleries and annexes. The second (south of the cafés) is more spectacular. Two kilometres long, it consists of a winding channel of water which visitors navigate in a rowing-boat. Narrow in parts, it occasionally widens out into large expanses of water, locally called 'lakes'. The water is fresh on the surface, brackish below, and salt at the bottom. The stalactites vary in colour, and there are some very striking ones seamed with veins of red Taygetus subsoil.

The caves are a dead end. One has to return to the village of Pyrgos, where one gets a first glimpse of a tower-house – a tall rectangular obelisk of grey stone. From here on the towers become more frequent. This is the country of the

3. Outstanding among these churches are Ayia Varvara (12th century) at Eremos, architecturally the finest in the Mani, Ayios Theodoros (11th century) at Vamvaka, which has a fine sculptured lintel above the west door, and Episkopi, near Stavri, with wall-paintings in a good state of preservation. To visit these churches (on foot or mule-back) it is absolutely essential to find a peasant who will serve as a guide (ask at the police station at Kitta). It would mean spending an extra day in the Mani (accommodation at Yerolimena).

iclians. These were originally refugees from Arcadia, a
ybrid Franco-Greek people with Slav blood who fled
outhwards after the defeat of Frankish arms at Nicli in the
irteenth century. They populated the villages of the barren
lateau between the Evil Mountains and the sea. Referred to
s Niclianoi (Niclians), they soon acquired the reputation of
eing the fiercest and most warlike community in the Mani.
he derelict region in which they settled became the heart of
ie Deep Mani, the symbol of every association that the word
Mani' conjures up – vendettas, killings and death-laments.
During the period of the vendettas the ritual wail of the
eath-lament – the haunting, sometimes beautiful *myroloyoi*,
irges often sung to the accompaniment of a lute or clarinet –
choed from one warring village to another.

As time passed, the Niclians developed into an aristocracy
f power. They possessed arms, owned land and towers, and
ere skilled in the arts of piracy and pillage. Their tower-
ouses dominated the villages, their minions, subservient
milies of non-Niclian origin, inhabiting the lower levels.
o the west extends the crescent-shaped bay of Tigani, with a
ong southern arm ending in a rocky hump, where the villagers
ome to gather salt. The shadeless plateau at the foot of the
vil Mountains has an infernal quality. Boulders are strewn
cross walled-in fields in frantic confusion. There are still
ome stunted olive trees, and occasionally a couple of needle-
ke cypresses flanking a crumbling tower. The hill-tops are
rowned with piles of rubble. One is struck by what must once
ave been the density of population. Sometimes less than a
ile separated one warring village from another.

If the Niclian country was the heart of the Deep Mani, the
llage of **Kitta** (corruption of *città*) was the brain-centre.
oday Kitta is a shattered monument to this shut-in self-
ontained community, whose habits and pursuits had the
rimitive quality of the granite rock across which their
nbattled dwellings spread. It is a maze of ruined towers,
eir surface broken by no visible doorway, portcullis or first-
ory window – thus creating an optical illusion of exaggerated
eight – and only four windows (one on each side) on the
ighest level. The roofs are flat, with occasional gun-slits.
'ithin the towers dwelt the men, fully armed, while the
omen worked in the fields. Niclian wars were generally

provoked by some infringement of property rights, often ov
the right of quail-shooting (in late summer the count
around here abounds in these migratory birds, which a
pickled in vinegar and form one of the staple diets of t
population). To trespass on one's neighbour's property mea
war, formally declared by a family council and proclaime
throughout the village by a herald and the ringing of chur
bells. As with the Montagues and the Capulets, the servan
also took part and picked violent quarrels with the riv
household. Victory was only complete when the enemy
tower was captured and destroyed – very often by a bombar
ment of boulders directed from a higher tower. Runni
battles were a routine occupation. Maniot children grew
to the accompaniment of day-long fusillades and the spirit
vendetta was so widespread that even the clergy, so far fro
frowning on it, participated in the murderous quarrels. In or
instance a monk entered a church and shot the officiati
priest because their respective relations were at war. Truc
were proclaimed on important occasions, and a feudir
warrior was allowed to cross no man's land to attend
christening or a funeral of a near relation. The Niclian wa
only came to an end after the War of Independence, when th
inhabitants of Kitta and neighbouring villages were enrolle
in a Maniot phalanx and dispatched to quell disorders in oth
parts of the Morea.

In summer the sun burns with a North African intensi
and the heat is thrown back in refractory waves from th
scorched boulders. To the west, two miles away, lies Nom
(with which Kitta was always at war) in a shallow troug
chequered with labyrinthine stone walls bordered by prickl
pears, its towers ranged like ninepins across a ridge behin
the village. Kitta is now almost wholly deserted. Occasional
an old woman in black scuttles across an alley and disappea
behind a pile of stones. I noticed the police station situated c
the upper story of one of the tallest towers. A wrought-irc
balcony had been added to it, and a policeman, his fac
shaded by a plastic straw hat, sat there reading a newspape
There was little else for him to do. In the walled lan
goats munched dried-up weeds. The jagged wilderness of gre
rock was only relieved by the dust-coated branches of son

withered almond tree trailing over a wall, and a couple of red blankets hanging from a battered tower.

Twenty minutes' walk from Kitta (you must have a guide and it is not always easy to find one) is the twelfth-century Church of Ayios Yiorghos (St George): cruciform and three-naved. The exterior, three-sided apse has some brickwork decoration, and a step-pattern frieze, an obvious importation from the north, surrounds the little edifice. The wall-paintings of the interior are hopelessly damaged, but the acanthus-leaf capitals are in the best tradition.

After Kitta the road descends from the plateau to Yeroli-mena, a handful of whitewashed houses strung out along a semi-circular harbour. The bay is small and the water pellucid (when the sirocco is not blowing). To the west a rocky bluff, Cape Grosso, juts out into the sea, terraced into strips of stubble by low parallel walls. For centuries Yerolimena, the most southerly inhabited point on the Greek mainland, was a notorious pirate's lair, and its inhabitants, like those of other maritime villages of the Mani, had a bad reputation. Gibbon thunders '. . . they dishonour the claim of liberty by the inhuman pillage of all that is shipwrecked on their rocky shores'. A French traveller describes priests and children joining gleefully in shipwrecking forays. Today the fishermen and their families are a friendly peaceable people. The harbour, with the caïques rocking in the underground swell, is littered with coils of twine. Men and boys busy themselves net-making. There is a feeling of relaxation after the tension and ferocity of the plateau and its clusters of grey obelisks thrusting skywards out of the 'abomination of desolation'. At the café-restaurant on the waterfront (rooms to let on the first floor) one can get fried fish, good *retsina* and freshly baked bread: also eggs, tomatoes and *feta* cheese. As yet Yerolimena is untouched by tourism. In the evening there is nothing but the sound of rowing-boats bumping against the sides of the mole, where the corsairs used to moor their galleys when they returned from their buccaneering expeditions to the accompaniment of beating drums and blood-curdling yells.

Yerolimena is virtually land's end. The last of Taygetus' terrible spurs vanishes eastward in the final convulsion of Cape Taenarum, one of the several gates of Hell, through which Heracles descended into the Underworld and seized the three-headed dog Cerberus by the throat. Protected by his lion pelt from the furious lashings of the hound's barbed tail, he brought it back to the light of day. The sea is generally rough round the cape, whose only historical association is of more recent date, for it was in these waters that the Battle of Cape Matapan (otherwise Taenerum) was fought between the British and Italian fleets in the Second World War. Somewhere along the east coast of the cape is thought to be the site, as yet unidentified, of the castle of Maina, William de Villehardouin's Le Grant-Maigne, which, with Mistra and Monemvasia, composed the strategic triangle guarding the Southern Morea.

From Yerolimena there is only one way back to Areopolis – across the Niclian country again. Beyond Areopolis the road winds along the shore of the Messenian Gulf, climbs and descends in hairpin bends, crosses whale-back humps and skirts pebbly bays bordered with rushes and agnus castus. The first of these is the deep bay of Oitylo. At the southern end a few dilapidated houses mark the site of Limeni, where the Mavromichalis dwelt in state and Petrobey entertained foreign travellers in oriental style. The little anchorage is protected by a headland rising sheer from the sea, like a huge drop-curtain of grey stone.

In 1770 a Russian expeditionary force under Feodor Orloff, commanded by Catherine the Great to liberate the Greeks, landed in the bay of Oitylo. The Maniots received the Russians with open arms. But the first tumultuous acclamations had barely subsided when distrust of the liberators' intentions began to poison relations. First, the expeditionary force was too small to be effective. Secondly, the Greeks were expected to become loyal citizens of the Empress. It was soon manifest that the expedition was no more than a diversion, though led by a sincere philhellene, in the course of Russia's long struggle with the Ottoman Empire. At first, the Turkish first line of defence was overrun. But as the shock wore off, the Turks threw into battle increasing numbers of Albanian troops, who behaved with their usual atrocious brutality. Invaders and native patriots alike were thrown back and the Russian fleet sailed ignominiously out of the bay of Oitylo, not to reappear in Greek waters for over half a century. For the

reeks the 'diversion' brought nothing but disillusionment
nd cruel reprisals.

The coastal strip is fringed with olive trees; beyond the
nchorage of Nea Vitylo the road climbs up to the prosperous
llage of **Oitylo** (or Vitylo), its castellated houses overlooking
e calm unruffled bay. The contrast between Oitylo and
itta is striking. Here are pergolas of climbing roses and
ack-plots filled with hibiscus and pomegranate trees. Canna
lies grow out of petrol tins on the balconies. Domed chapels
estle amid terraced groves of cypresses. Women wearing
normous umbrella-like straw hats (a feature of the Mani)
ander along serpentine paths between low walls. Oitylo was
nce the most important place in the Mani, the centre of a
ave market, crowded with corsairs from North Africa, not
 mention local pirates from the Deep Mani. In 1675 one of
e leading Oitylian families, the Stephanopoloi, crippled by
urkish exactions, invoked the aid of the Republic of Genoa.
he Genoese duly came and removed nearly a thousand
embers of the clan to Corsica. There they remained,
roudly speaking Greek, preserving Maniot customs. One of
eir descendants, the Duchesse d'Abrantès, wife of Napoleon's
arshal, Junot, declared that Napoleon himself was of
Maniot origin, Buonaparte being a literal translation of the
reek name Calomeris ('the good part', i.e. *buona parte*).
nother important Oitylian family were the Iatranoi, who
aimed to be scions of the Medici, descendants of a Floren-
ne gentleman of that name who had emigrated to the
Mani. Why a rich and civilised Florentine should have
hosen to exchange the sophisticated charms of Renaissance
uscany for the remote wilderness of the Mani remains a
ystery.[4]

South of Oitylo, across the ravine, a series of escarpments
se to a natural platform surrounded by a low wall: the vast
nceinte of the Turkish fort of Kelepha. This boulder-strewn
nclosure (some 15,000 square yards), treeless and beige-
oloured, represents the limit of Turkish penetration in the
Mani. From its commanding position, the inhabitants of
Vitylo could be carefully watched and the exaction of tribute
acked up by force, with guns trained on the bay and its good

4. Iatranos is admittedly a translation of Medico, a name which the
itylian family did not hesitate to append to their signatures.

anchorage. It also served as a defensive bastion agai
violent eruptions of Niclians from the south.

After Oitylo the landscape is much less fierce, and co
graze in green fields shelving down to the sea. Just befo
entering the hamlet of Nomitsi, a little group of minusc
churches appear on either side of the road. They are of t
middle Byzantine period, charming in their bucolic settir
Right of the road is the Ayioi Anarghyroi (SS. Cosmas a
Damian), with a little squat dome. The iconostasis is bu
into the main structure and there is a well preserved fres
(left on entering) of the two philanthropic doctors (sometim
regarded as a Christian reincarnation of the Dioscu
depicted as venerable bearded gentlemen. Ayios Sos
(farther along the road – also right) contains vestiges
frescoes and four marble columns, two of which are engag
in the iconostasis. Left of the road, where the orchards d
down towards the sea, is the tiny domed Hypapanti (Present
tion at the Temple).

Beyond Nomitsi the road winds through olive grov
spliced with cypress alleys, scales brush-covered saddle-bacl
and descends into deserted coves. It is a Mediterranean lan
scape *par excellence*. Its exploitation as a tourist attraction ca
only be a matter of time. The show-place is **Kardamyli,** whe
a dramatic gorge opens out into a wide gravelly river-bed.
the little port there is a rocky islet, on which Neoptolemus
supposed to have landed on his way to the court of Menela
to woo Hermione. Farther south another islet is referred to
Spartan mythology as the birthplace of the Dioscuri.
bridge spans the river-bed, and the upper village ascen
through orchards towards a wooded flat-topped hill crowne
by the remains of a Venetian castle. An eighteenth centu
church with a tall pointed campanile adds an Italiana
touch. Eastward the valley contracts into a rugged defile
Taygetus with the familiar jagged peaks towering above a be
of black spruce.

After Kardamyli the scenery remains grand and woode
with thickets of cypresses concealed in gullies of red Tayget
rock, but the spirit of the Mani, of its towers, vendettas an
lunar wastelands recedes until it loses all sense of reality. Th
little valley of Varosia is dominated by a cone-shaped hil
littered with fragments (curtain wall) of the seventeent

century Turkish fort of Zarnata. Sometimes a tower, shorter
and squatter than the grim obelisks of the Deep Mani, is
silhouetted against the skyline. The coastline is very steep, as
the road descends in hairpin bends towards Kalamata. The
first building of any consequence is the Xenias Hotel, a
modern structure on a wide beach. Its bar, its showers, its
well-sprung beds have a charmed quality after the rigours of
Niclian travel.

CHAPTER TWELVE

Messenia

❧

Kalamata – Messene – Corone – Pylos – The Bay of Navarino –
Neocastro – Sphacteria – Coryphasium – Palaeocastro –
Methone – The Palace of Nestor – Cyparissia

THE numerous sites scattered across the Messenian plain
cover the whole range of Greek history. There is a great deal
to see, and the general configuration does not help. A circular
tour is impossible. Two hotels at Kalamata and one at Pylos
are good. There are admirable beaches everywhere. The
following itinerary would take in all the important sites.

First day – Kalamata – Messene – Mt Ithome – Corone.
Second day – Pylos (Museum, Neocastro) – Methone.
Third day – Tour of Sphacteria (by boat) – Coryphasium –
  Palaeocastro.
Fourth day – Epano Englianos – Cyparissia – Olympia
  (in Elis).[1]

In a clockwise tour of the Peloponnese, one would reach
Kalamata from the Mani. It can also be approached from
Sparta through the Langhada Pass (see pp. 203-04), and
from Tripolis and Megalopolis – the direct route from Athens.
Beyond Megalopolis the road crosses the upper course of the
Alpheius and descends in hairpin bends into the Messenian
lowlands: a shimmering canopy of olive trees, streaked with
cypresses. Vineyards are hedged round with spiky cactuses
and waving plantains. Date-palms shade whitewashed farm-
houses. The groves are succeeded by cotton and wheat fields
and orchards of mulberries; in winter there is the fluff of
mimosa, in summer the blaze of sunflowers. North to south

1. The first night could be spent at Corone, the second and third at
Pylos (or Methone), the fourth at Olympia. Alternatively, the first
night could be spent at Pylos, allowing for a brief visit to Corone.
Hurried travellers may confine themselves to visiting Corone and
Methone and the prehistoric Palace of Nestor.

flows the stream of the Pamisus, in whose curative waters ailing children were brought to bathe in antiquity. No wonder the Greeks called these plains the Macaria ('The Blessed Land'), that Tyrtaeus, the seventh century B.C. poet, rhapsodised about their 'wide dancing-grounds' and Euripides extolled their 'flowing waters, pastures for cattle and flocks'. In summer the sun burns so fiercely on this dazzling expanse of fertility that it acquires an almost sub-tropical quality.

Kalamata, linked by rail and air with Athens, is undistinguished and prosperous, famous for its purple oblong olives, its olive oil, the best in Greece, its pimps (local inhabitants swear this is a slander) and the *kalamatianos*, a national dance, performed in chain formation by men and women, while the leader (a man) waves a handkerchief and, at intervals, detaches himself from the shuffling chain to execute a great turning leap in the air.[2] A straight road joins the town, which lies at the foot of a spur of Taygetus, to its port. There is a good beach, with fish restaurants, the Xenias Hotel and a fine view of the coastline of the Outer Mani.

There is little to see in Kalamata except the Villehardouin castle overlooking a bend in the stream of the Neda which issues out of a gorge of Taygetus, flows past two sides of the fortified hill and then through the town. Kalamata was the hereditary fief of the Villehardouins for a hundred years. Geoffroy de Villehardouin, in his chronicle of the Fourth Crusade, an ingenuous attempt to whitewash some of the major infamies committed by the Latin knights, calls the castle 'Chalemate, which was very strong and fair'. Here William, Prince of Achaea, was born and died, although he had his official residence at Andravidha (see pp. 288-90) and loved Mistra more.[3] After William's death the castle passed to his daughter, Isabella, who was a widow. Cheated of her legacies by the intrigues of her Angevin in-laws, she died in the Low Countries, a wistful disappointed creature, far from sunny Messenia, her birthplace. The castle was then bandied about

2. The *kalamatianos* is danced in many Athenian tavernas, at weddings and other festive occasions throughout the country.
3. Although Achaea was in antiquity, as it is today, the name applied to the coastal province of the Northern Peloponnese, the Franks extended it to include the whole of the Morea, i.e. the Principality of Achaea.

between Burgundian dukes and Florentine bankers until 1387, when it was acquired by Marie de Bourbon, titular Empress at Constantinople, who had a mania for collecting baronies for her son, the Prince of Galilee. At one time she was mistress of sixteen castles in the Principality of Achaea alone. Throughout the Frankish chronicles of Greece, the figures of proud strong-minded women, ancestors of future crowned heads of Europe, stand out as large, ambitious and power-hungry as any of the grasping barons. In the fifteenth century, the Venetians, trying to hold up the Ottoman invasion, set fire to the castle rather than let it fall intact into Turkish hands.

Little is left of the vaulted chambers in which Villehardouins, Anjous, Savoys and Bourbons hatched plots, drew up marriage settlements and drafted acts of restitution. Two oval enclosures can be discerned, the inner one on the higher level. The outer gate, overgrown with moss, is the best preserved: a square tower with an arched entrance. The keep is a muddle of incomprehensible ruins.

The road to the west runs along the seaward end of the plain – once a malarial marsh, now a chequer-board of rice-paddies – and crosses the Pamisus, up which deep-water fish, says Pausanias, used to swim'. . . especially in the spring, as they do up the Rhine and the Meander'. At the village of Messene (not to be confused with ancient Messene) a dirt road winds up into the hills, skirting the walls and ruined towers of the Frankish castle of Androusa, seat of the High Court of Justice of the principality, as far as Mavromati, a village among mulberry trees, on a slope of Mt Ithome. The palmate-lobed leaves of a large plane tree form a cool arbour above the café beside an ancient spring from which women in large Maniot straw hats fill petrol tins with water gushing out of an aperture in the rock. It is the sole water supply of the village.[4]

There are three things to do at Mavromati: climb up to the summit of Mt Ithome; walk along the line of fourth century B.C. fortifications; visit the ruins of the ancient city. Chronologically, the ascent of Mt Ithome (one hour; mules can be hired at the village) comes first. There are no ruins. But it is, in a sense, a pilgrimage. The mountain, its flat top rising like

4. The owner of the café beside the spring provides fried eggs, bread and *feta* cheese. There is as yet no restaurant at Mavromati.

a lofty watchtower above the Macaria, is profoundly associated with the long and tragic wars waged by the Messenians in defence of their country against the Spartans. The Messenians claim that the First Messenian War (eighth century B.C.) was provoked by the Spartans who introduced a group of armed youths dressed as girls into a chamber where some eminent Messenian men were resting. Ostensibly provided for the pleasure of the Messenians, the Spartan 'maidens' promptly whipped out daggers and swords. In the ensuing scuffle, the 'maidens' were killed and Sparta was provided with a pretext for a punitive expedition. Actually the *casus belli* was irrelevant. Sparta was determined to conquer the fertile lands of Messenia by force.

The Messenians performed prodigious deeds of valour. But exhaustion and pestilence finally drove them to abandon their unfortified towns and settle on Mt Ithome. Moreover, the portents were consistently unfavourable. When their king was about to sacrifice to Zeus, the sacrificial rams broke loose and dashed their horns against the altar with such violence that they were instantly killed. At night dogs howled around the stronghold and fled to the Spartan camp. A shield fell from a statue of Artemis. And the Delphic oracle predicted a harsh fate for 'the dwellers in the circle of the dancing-ground'. After the suicide of their king, the last defenders surrendered. But in the seventh century the oppressed Messenians revolted, thus provoking the Second Messenian War, celebrated for the exploits of Aristomenes, an intrepid leader who carried out daring raids in Spartan territory, even penetrating the Brazen House of Athena, where he left a shield inscribed with the words, 'The Gift of Aristomenes to the Goddess, taken from Spartans'. On another nocturnal foray he was repulsed by apparitions of Helen and the Dioscuri, who were outraged by the Messenian leader's impudence. In this second war the Messenians chose Mt Eira, north of Ithome, as their stronghold, and it only fell when the Spartans, well informed by spies, scaled the walls during a torrential rainstorm and surprised the defenders. The country was reduced to serfdom and a large number of Messenians emigrated to Sicily, where they founded Messina. A final revolt broke out in 464 B.C. (Third Messenian War) and Ithome was again the last stronghold to surrender.

Nothing is left on the summit (2600 feet) of the sanctuary of Zeus or the citadel which held out so long and courageously. There are only tortoises and lizards. The view of the 'blessed land' is prodigious, with the Arcadian highlands rising abruptly to the north, Taygetus, gashed by the Langhada Pass, tapering off eastward into the Mani, a chain of low mountains capped by a Fuji Yama-like peak separating the plain from the bay of Navarino in the west. The zigzag path is steep, bordered by vetch and spiky thistles, but not as painful as Homer implies when he calls it 'ladder-like'. The Messenians claim that Zeus was born beside a spring below the summit, where he was nursed by two nymphs, Ithome and Neda, who gave their names to the mountain and the river. A festival in honour of Zeus, called the Ithomaea, which included musical competitions, was held here annually. A more remote and lofty setting for a musical festival can hardly be imagined. On the east slope of the mountain, below the saddle between Mt Ithome and Mt Eva (so-called because the Bacchic cry 'Evoe!' was first heard here from the lips of Dionysus and his ferocious Maenads), the monastery buildings of Vourcano form a quadrangle round a church among cypresses and oaks. Apart from its airy position the monastery has little to offer.

The descent to Mavromati is relatively easy. West of the village begin the **fourth century B.C. fortifications,** the best preserved and most extensive in Greece, which guarded the city of Messene from Spartan and later Macedonian aggression. Like Megalopolis, Messene was born of the defeat of Sparta at Leuctra and the fear of a possible Spartan recovery. Epaminondas' choice of this well defended site was deeply resented by the Spartans, who, alone among Greek states, abstained from guaranteeing the autonomy of the new city. In Athens Demosthenes defended Messenian independence in a majestic oration.

A six-mile circumference of walls, broken at intervals by watchtowers, can still be traced, almost in its entirety, straggling across the scrub-land around Mt Ithome. The enceinte is best preserved in the north, where the road from Mavromati ends at the **Arcadian Gate,** a round court with niches for statues and double gates facing each other. Nine courses of stone-work are preserved, and the blocks are so admirably fitted that each course diminishes in height as the masonry rises. The gateway's massive lintel is propped up against the inner walls of the court. A considerable garrison was probably stationed here, and the towers must have commanded such a wide prospect of the hilly countryside that a hostile army marching from the north would have been quickly spotted by sentinels. One can stroll in either direction along the sentry-walk. To the east, the chain of redoubts climbs the slope of Ithome; to the south the fortified line vanishes into a more domesticated landscape. Clusters of cyclamen, whose stalks were said to be the favourite food of wild boars, sprout from crannies in walls which once enclosed a vast area of cornfields intended to save the Messenians, when besieged, from starvation. The finish and workmanship of the stone courses, entirely of ashlar, make the rough masonry of the Crusader castles, built a thousand years later, look a very shoddy affair. The fortifications underwent their severest test when the Messenians withstood a massive siege by a Macedonian army under the young Demetrius, son of Philip V, whose phalanx was so fiercely bombarded with boulders – and tiles hurled by female warriors – that it was almost entirely wiped out.

Halfway back to the village a path to the right plunges down between borders of agnus castus to the site of ancient **Messene,** lying in a conch-shaped fold of the mountain. Leading architects of the day were commissioned to design the monuments, and Epaminondas, mindful of a Boeotian nymph-oracle predicting that 'the bright bloom of Sparta [shall] perish and Messene again shall be inhabited for all time', attended the foundation ceremony and offered the first sacrifices, to the accompaniment of Boeotian flutes. Less pretentious than Megalopolis, Messene seems to have been more durable. Statues by Damophon, the only Messenian artist of note, who repaired Phidias' great statue of Zeus at Olympia, adorned the temples and courts. The memorial to Aristomenes, the national hero, was one of the principal sights. The ruins are not extensive. At the bottom of the shell-like depression, on the right, are four chambers (ruins at knee level) with truncated columns which probably formed part of the agora; on the left two columns flank a stairway; east of it is the well preserved **Council Chamber,** in the form of a little

theatre – an extremely elegant ruin. At least ten tiers of grey
limestone, which repeat the amphitheatrical configuration, are
intact, and the floor of the orchestra is composed of red,
white and blue paving-stones. Adjoining it (south) are
foundations of two buildings, one in the shape of a large
square hall with a stone settee running round the four walls.
West of the agora extends the rubble of what is thought to
have been a temple dedicated to all the gods. A few slabs of
the tiers of the stadium lie among the olive groves to the
south.

That ends the Ithome deviation. From modern Messene, the
road follows a south-west course, as far as Rizomilos, a well-
watered village, where there is a fork. The turning to the left
(south) leads to the third prong of the Peloponnese which has
an essentially mellow character, with none of the ferocity of
the Mani or the ruggedness of Cape Malea. At Vounaria, oil
and wine jars, with a capacity of seven hundred quarts, are still
made by methods handed down from antiquity. In medieval
times these were filled with oil and loaded on Venetian
merchantmen bound for the Levant. Farther south **Corone**
climbs up the side of a headland crowned by one of the finest
Venetian castles in the country. Below the bastions fishing
caïques chug across the pellucid water, where the galleys
anchored.

Corone and its twin castle at Methone (see pp. 257-60),
the medieval Coron and Modon, 'the chief eyes of the Republic' – *Oculi capitalis communis*, in the official Venetian docu-
ment – were the Doge's first colonies on the Greek mainland.
A provisioning station for merchantmen, Corone was celebrated for its export of cochineal, its manufacture of siege-
engines and its olive oil, of which there was supposed to be
more than anywhere in the world, the saying being that 'it even
rains oil in Coron'. With their usual religious tolerance, the
Venetians allowed Greek bishops complete spiritual authority
over their Orthodox flock, and prosperity grew as increasingly
large numbers of pilgrims broke the journey to the Holy Land
at one or other of the two stations. The Venetians fraternised
with the natives, and only insisted on one mark of distinction:
they forbade their troops to grow beards, which the Greeks,
like good Byzantines, favoured. In 1500 Corone fell to the
Sultan's army and Bayazit II, called the Mystic, made a

spectacular entry into the port, to the accompaniment of thunderous drum-beats and wailing fifes. During the reign of Suleiman II the Magnificent, the Genoese admiral, Andrea Doria, hoisting the imperial colours of Charles V who was at war with the Sultan, temporarily wrested Corone from the Turks; but he was unable to hold it, and the inhabitants, who had received him with open arms, suffered appalling reprisals when he sailed away.

There is not much of a waterfront at Corone, but the houses on the cliff-side are washed with bright colours. Massive walls and bastions defend the eastern projection of the headland. The **castle** is in the shape of a quadrangle divided by a north–south wall into two separate enclosures of unequal size. One approaches the main entrance (north) from a cobbled ramp-like street. The gate, a beautifully shaped Gothic arch, framing an entrancing prospect of the port and the mountains beyond, forms part of a tower-like structure leading into the vaulted passage. It is one of the most impressive castle gates in Greece. It was from a village house hereabouts that Chateaubriand watched the Turkish fleet sail up the coast of the Mani in 1806 and bombard the forces of Petrobey. The enclosure consists of a rectangular plateau dotted with almond trees; there is a cemetery and some small churches, of which the most important is the Convent of Ayios Ioannis (St John) – right of the Gothic gateway – with black-painted gates, five domes on slender but awkward-looking cylindrical drums and a crypt. It is inhabited by nuns. The whole plateau, surrounded by crumbling Venetian masonry, with its wispy vegetation and hump-backed, black-draped crones scuttling along paths bordered by lop-sided tombstones, has a sinister haunted air.

East of the entrance to the enclosure two gigantic round bastions, one higher than the other, rise perpendicularly from the rock-fringed shore. A soaring expanse of smooth perfectly wrought stone-work, like a natural wall of cliff that turns gold in the afternoon light, the double bastion is most impressive when seen from the harbour – one can sail all round the battlemented promontory in a caïque. Beyond the double bastion there is a large outwork of later date (Turkish, sixteenth century), followed by plots of cornland enclosed within stone walls; then another fortification wall, lower than the curtain; below it a moat. The bastion at the south-east end has a domed roof supported by embrasures, and the gun platform is reached by a spiral stairway. On all sides, except the west, the vista is one of open sea. At right angles to the south curtain wall, which is less impressive, stretches a long sandy beach. A modern stairway descends from the plateau to a shaded terrace with a church and a small museum which contains little of interest.

Corone is virtually a dead end.[5] One returns to Rizomilos. The highway from Kalamata to Pylos affords splendid backward views of the Messenian gulf and plains, with Taygetus vanishing southward in the metal-coloured haze of the Evil Mountains. The road descends towards the west coast and the Ionian Sea: a new climate, much softer. Below lies the oval landlocked bay of Navarino, with the cream-coloured houses of **Pylos** at its southern end. To understand all that has happened here, it is essential to grasp the configuration of land and sea, which is very complex, with a crescent-shaped bay (three miles long and two wide), the island of Sphacteria running like a huge reef from one mainland promontory to the other, the two narrow channels, the islets, the reed-fringed lagoon and the elegant peak above the town.

The bay is, of course, best known for the battle of 1827. But the port, the island and the two castles have a much earlier history. The medieval town gravitated round the castle hill at the southern end of the bay. Originally it was called Avarino, after the tribes of Avars who overran the country in the sixth century. With the present Greek passion for reviving classical names, it has become Pylos, although the ancient city of the same name and Nestor's palace lie farther north.

Here the insatiable Marie de Bourbon took refuge in the fourteenth century from her rival in castle-collecting, the Venetian Carlo Zeno, who was Canon of Patras but had more taste for soldiering than theology. When the Emperor John VIII, in the tragic twilight years of Byzantium, travelled to Florence in a vain attempt to enlist Western aid against the Turks, it was from Navarino, then a flourishing maritime station, that he sailed in one of the Doge's vessels. During the War of Independence Greek patriots seized Navarino, but

5. A dirt road links Corone with Methone, crossing the olive groves of Cape Acritas, skirting sandy coves and passing through a pretty fishing hamlet, the ancient Phoenicus.

when Ibrahim Pasha, the scourge of the Morea, laid siege to the castle in 1825, it was found that the untrained Greek irregulars, bedecked in embroidered jackets glittering with gold obtained from English loans, were no match for the more simply clad but better equipped 'Arab boys', as Finlay calls them, of Ibrahim's army.

It is pleasant to sit in an open-air café in the arcaded square, opposite the monument to the three Allied admirals. Here one can pore over maps and try to work out the different moves in the battle of 1827. It seems incredible that four major fleets should not only have been able to penetrate this landlocked body of water, but also actually found room to engage in combat. In a sense, the battle was a mistake. In 1827 the Greek effort against the Turks was waning and, six years after it had begun, the crusade for liberation had degenerated into a squalid civil war between self-styled generals. On the international level Russia alone championed Greek independence. Austria and Prussia were openly inimical to Greek aspirations, and England and France, while sympathising with the Greeks, had no wish to be involved in a war with the Porte.

The brief of Admiral Codrington, Commander-in-Chief of the Allied fleets of Britain, France and Russia, was to ensure that the Turks did not commit any more atrocities, like the wholesale deportation of the inhabitants of the Morea which had so shocked Western public opinion. In October 1827 the entire Turco-Egyptian fleet was concentrated in the bay of Navarino. Fearing it was about to break out in order to perpetrate some further enormity on the island population, Codrington, encouraged by de Rigny and Count Heiden, his French and Russian colleagues, sailed into the bay to stage a warning demonstration. The Turco-Egyptian Fleet, disposed in a wide semi-circle, consisted of eighty-two sail, the Allied of twenty-seven, but the preponderance of line of battle vessels lay with the Allies. Codrington, on his flagship *Asia*, was the first to pass between the southern tip of Sphacteria and the Turkish castle. His squadron was followed by the French. The Russians came last. Twenty thousand Turkish troops encamped on the slope below the castle watched breathlessly as ship after ship nosed its way through the narrow channel. It was just past noon. The first shot was fired by the Turks – probably in panic; certainly without their commanders' orders. *Dartmouth* and *Sirène*, the French flagship, replied. In a few minutes the action was general. The vessels were stationary – for there was no room to manœuvre – and the range point-blank. Skilfully avoiding the Turkish fire-ships, Codrington and de Rigny concentrated their fire on the enemy's line of battle, while Count Heiden's squadron destroyed the rest of the enemy's

rigates and sloops. The conflagration, judging from eye-
witness accounts and contemporary prints, must have been
appalling. By the evening the whole bay seemed to be ablaze,
as one Ottoman ship after another exploded, sending myriads
of sparks flying through the smoke-laden sky. The rocks of
Sphacteria reflected the fiery lights, and the heat was intolerable. Wreckage of masts, poops, yards floated in the lurid sea
and sank under the weight of Turkish sailors clinging to them.
Allied crews had to fight all night to prevent their own vessels
from catching fire. By morning only twenty-nine of the eighty-
two enemy ships remained afloat.

After Navarino the Turks lost the command of the sea.
Never again would the Sultan or his Egyptian vassal, the
hideous pock-marked Ibrahim Pasha, be able to supply and
reinforce their mainland troops. The Greeks had virtually
gained their independence. But no Greek fought in the battle.
It was won by British, French and Russian sailors in a
remarkable demonstration of international co-operation. In
London, however, there was consternation. In the Speech
from the Throne the battle was referred to as an 'untoward
event', and the Sovereign, George IV, deplored that a 'conflict
should have occurred with the naval force of an ancient ally'.
Codrington was recalled from his command in the Mediterranean. Nevertheless Navarino, the last major engagement
to be fought before the steamship revolutionised naval warfare,
was one of the decisive battles of the nineteenth century. By
making Greek independence possible, it altered the map of
Eastern Europe and ushered in the long period of sickness
from which the Ottoman Empire was ultimately to perish. It is
also ironical that exactly twenty-two years after Trafalgar, a
British and French admiral should have been able to operate
in such perfect accord and with so fortunate an outcome.
Their memory, together with that of their Russian colleague,
is enshrined in the street-names of towns and villages throughout the country.

The admirals' portraits hang in the little museum on the
way up to the Turkish castle. There are also some charming
coloured prints of oriental figures in billowing robes against
backgrounds of bright blue sky drawn by Dupré, a pupil of
David, who furnished a fascinating pictorial commentary on
nineteenth-century Greece in his *Voyage à Athènes et Con-*

stantinople. Among other exhibits are ceramics, jewellery daggers, amphorae, a terracotta tub from a local Mycenaea tomb and some Hellenistic fragments dug up in a field nea the town.

From the museum it is a few minutes' walk to Neocastro the sixteenth century Turkish castle guarding the entrance to the bay. The hexagonal fortress is entered through the wes gate. Bastions protect the angles of the hexagon (the north east one was destroyed by Morosini in the seventeenth century). From the wall-walk, which overlooks barrel-vaulted prison cells, a French nineteenth century traveller watched verminous prisoners in chains perform national dances i the court below and witnessed an execution preceded by prolonged argument, accompanied by blows, between the executioner and his victim. A curtain wall, supported b recessed arches, descends towards the shore where tw quadrangular bastions command the channel. A post-Byzantin church, Ayia Sotira, lies within the enclosure where th Turkish population once dwelt in pestilential conditions. Th capture of the fortress in 1821 by Greek peasant patriots wa followed by a fearful blood-bath. Phrantzes, a Greek cleri has left a lurid eye-witness account of Turkish women their flesh hanging in ribbons from sabre-cuts, felled b potshots as they ran dementedly towards the sea, of babie torn from screaming mothers' arms and hurled against wall bespattered with human brains, of children thrown into th sea where they were left to drown, of piles of hacked corpse littering the blood-soaked shore. Six years later, after th battle of Navarino, the French garrison, commanded b General Maison, demolished all the squalid Moslem hovel and built the modern town below. The whole of this onc putrefying slum is now a thyme-scented scrub-land.

Motorboats (for hire) are moored alongside the jetty a Pylos. In one of these you can make a round trip of the bay a more than worthwhile experience. It is wise to start early, i you want to see the hulks of the Turkish vessels lying at th bottom of the sea, before the water is ruffled by mid-mornin breezes. The minimum time for the trip is a long half-day The boat bears south-west towards an islet, on either side o which Codrington's squadrons entered the bay. A rock-hew stairway leads to its summit, crowned by a lighthouse and

monument to the French sailors who fell in the battle. The
channel is dotted with curious flat-topped rocks, one of which
is pierced by a natural arch through which the water swirls
into the strait. You then chug northward under the lee of the
rugged coast of **Sphacteria**, three miles long and sometimes
no more than five hundred yards wide. Cliffs, speckled with
evergreens, rise sheer from the water, like an immense break-
water protecting the bay. After passing a memorial, its marble
base lapped by the sea, to Count Santarosa, a Piedmontese
philhellene, the boat puts in at the little cove of **Panagoula.**
It was around here that the fiercest fighting took place and
that the wrecks of the Ottoman vessels sunk by the Russians
can be seen through the translucent water. It is the only
anchorage on the island. There is a white chapel and a cypress-
shaded memorial to the Russian sailors, lately refurbished by
the Soviet Embassy in Athens.

Panagoula is also the site of the Spartan encampment
described by Thucydides. It was the seventh year of the
Peloponnesian War (425 B.C.). The Athenians, with great
audacity, had entrenched themselves on enemy territory on
the mainland of Coryphasium, guarding the northern entrance
to the bay. The Spartans retaliated by landing on Sphacteria.
But the Athenian triremes, entering the bay from both
channels, inflicted a severe defeat on the Spartan fleet and the
garrison on Sphacteria was cut off. The Spartan ephors sent
envoys to Athens to sue for peace, but the Athenians refused
to parley. Quick to react to adversity, the Spartans made
every effort to break the blockade. Helots were promised
freedom and large sums of money in return for landing
provisions secretly on the island. 'Divers also,' adds Thucydides, 'swam in underwater from the harbour, dragging by a
cord in skins poppy-seed mixed with honey, and bruised
linseed.'

The island was uninhabited – Grote describes it as 'untrodden, untenanted and full of wood': much as it is today.
As winter approached, the Athenians, controlling all sea communications, decided to risk an all-out assault. The attack seems
to have taken the Spartans by surprise. The Athenians, according to Thucydides, 'could see with their own eyes that they
were many times more numerous than the enemy . . . and
accordingly their fear changing to disdain, they now rushed

all together with loud shouts upon them, and pelted then
with stones, darts and arrows . . .' The deafening battle-cries of
the Athenians prevented the Spartans from hearing their
commanders' orders; blinded by dust and a hail of arrows
which pierced their dog-skin caps, they retreated up the cliff
where they were taken in the rear by another enemy detachment. A brief parley was followed by total surrender. The
Athenians set up a trophy and triumphantly carried off the
prisoners, the *corps d'élite* of the Spartan army, to Athens.
The siege had lasted seventy-two days. The blow to Sparta's
prestige was enormous, and the victorious Athenians became
even more intractable. So the long and tragic war went on.

The line of cliffs, their bases eroded with caves and fissures
by the endless lapping of waves, continues northwards; then
suddenly Sphacteria ends in one of its familiar soaring humps.
The Sykia channel between the tip of the island and the
mainland promontory of Coryphasium is a hundred yards
wide and too shallow to afford a passage for vessels other
than caïques. The width and depth of the channel must have
altered since the time of Thucydides, who talks of several
triremes sailing abreast through it. Vestiges of a fourth-century
B.C. mole are visible beside the landing stage at Coryphasium,
site of the Athenian camp and probably of the classical city
of Pylos. Otherwise there are no traces of the 'fortress situated
on the sea', mentioned by Strabo, who suggests it was founded
by the inhabitants of Nestor's city when they fled from their
burning citadel at the time of the Dorian invasion. Here in the
Middle Ages was the Port Junch of the Franks. A sandy reed-
fringed beach borders the shallow sea.

It is a good half-hour's climb to the castle of **Palaeocastro**
on the summit of the hump. Outgrowths of rock thrust jagged
edges through a mist of blue-grey thistles. Lizards and snakes
keep up a continuous rustling in the brushwood. The *Chastel
de Port de Junch* was built on this imposing site by Nichola
de St Omer, a thirteenth-century baron of Flemish origin who
married into wealth and was renowned for his arrogance but
respected for his expenditure of money on the erection and
preservation of fortifications. The quadrangular castle spread
across the crest. Right of the arched entrance a passage leads
into the enceinte. There are round bastions at either end of the
south wall, and the battlements and part of the wall-walk are

well preserved. The redoubt at the north end of the plateau identified by remains of four towers, may be the site of the clasical acropolis. The ruins of the inner enceinte are Frankish, those of the outer Venetian or Turkish. St Omer's castle went through all the usual vicissitudes, and was occupied, after the decline of Frankish power, by Venetians, Turks, Morosini (who found it garrisoned chiefly by Negroes, and Turks again. There is probably no walk-walk in the Morea along which it is more fascinating to stroll. Looking round clockwise, you see: to the east, the rush-bordered lagoon of Osman-Aga; the crescent-shaped bay sweeping southward towards Pylos; Port Junch at the foot of the south-west slope, with the cliffs of Sphacteria behind it; westward the expanse of the Ionian Sea, with an almost circular bay, not inaptly called Voido-Koilia ('Ox-belly') biting deep into the north coast. To complete the circle, green hills, rather hazy, ascend to the north-east and the strangely articulated forms of Mt Aegaleion vanish into the horizon.

On the north slope of the hill, concealed among rocks and brushwood, is the entrance to Nestor's cave (the descent from the keep is frighteningly steep). Pausanias calls it 'the stables of the oxen of Neleus and Nestor'. According to another myth, the cave served as a cow-shed for the oxen stolen by the infant Hermes from his half-brother Apollo, and the animal skins which he hung from its roof were petrified into stalactites.

On the return journey, the motorboat gives a wide berth to Sphacteria, skirting the islet of Chelonaki ('Little Tortoise') in the middle of the bay. A low flat rock, it bears an unassuming monument to the British sailors who fell at Navarino. Deprived of the more dramatic setting of the French and Russian memorials, it has the air of an almost deliberate understatement of the British contribution to the victory. For it was around here that Codrington's squadron destroyed the Turkish line of battle.

In the opposite direction, south of Pylos, lies **Methone**, or Modon, the second 'eye of the republic'. A semi-circular beach of fine sand fringes the battlements of a Venetian fortress sprawling across a land's end that faces the island of Sapienza. The beach is bordered with tavernas. At night fishermen dance the *zeibékiko*, solitary whirling figures on the moonlit sands.

Its origins are more ancient than Corone's. Homer calls it Pedasus, 'rich in vines' (the low hills to the east still are) and it was one of the seven cities offered by Agamemnon as a bribe to induce Achilles to stop sulking and resume the fight against the Trojans. In the Roman era it was strongly fortified by Antony, who placed his ally, King Bogus of Mauretania, in command of the garrison. In the early Middle Ages it was a nest of corsairs who preyed on merchantmen returning from the east. After the Latin sack of Constantinople, Geoffroy, the first Villehardouin, hurrying from Syria to Constantinople to secure his share of the spoils, was carried, he writes, 'by wind and chance . . . to the port of Modon'. The origins of future Villehardouin supremacy in the Morea stem from this fortuitous visit, for, while he was at Methone, waiting for the storm to abate, a Greek traitor approached him, suggesting that they join forces and occupy the neighbouring country. Realising with what ease a relatively small number of knights could overcome the ill-equipped Greeks, Geoffroy enlisted the aid of his Champenois compatriot, William de Champlitte. Together they conquered the Morea. A few years later the French sold Methone to Dandolo, the blind doge, whose first station on the Greek mainland it became. Noted for its wine and cochineal, its port was filled with vessels of so many nations that one historian calls it 'the Port-Said of Frankish Greece'.[6] On the landward side the citadel was surrounded by orange groves, and a fifteenth century friar, enthusing over its grapes, writes 'the mere thought of the muscat of Modon delights me'. There was also a busy market, where the Turks sold pigs to the Venetians. Another fifteenth-century pilgrim says all the bacon sold in Venice came from Methone, where sausages were also made.

The village lies about half a mile inland. Just before the shore, a turning to the right leads to the **castle,** which possesses some of the finest Venetian military architecture in Southern Greece. A bridge, supported by a succession of arches, built by the French after Navarino, spans a wide moat crossing the promontory from sea to sea. Walls and bastions are well preserved and their unbroken line gives an air of impressive

6. William Miller, *The Latins in the Levant*, John Murray, London, 1908.

impregnability to the land approach. The arched entrance, flanked by pilasters with capitals and carved designs of Venetian trophies, is placed between the Bembo (right) and Loredan (left) bastions. The Bembo, fifteenth century, is fan-shaped, crowned by a tower. The entry is succeeded by a second and third gateway. Entering the huge enclosure, one is faced with a squat granite pillar crowned by a carved capital, known as the Morosini capital. In the seventeenth century Turco-Venetian war, Morosini himself commanded the besieging army. While he was inspecting an advanced position, accompanied by a retinue of ostentatiously dressed Venetian dignitaries, the Turks spotted them and opened fire. The noblemen ran in all directions; only Morosini stood immobile, unflinching, the embodiment of a Venetian *bella figura*. His behaviour greatly impressed the Turks, who then surrendered. The two bastions at either end of the moat and the one in the centre, next to the Bembo, are also the work of seventeenth-century Venetian architects.

The entire enclosure, surrounded by a parapet and dotted with ruined towers, was once a congested urban quarter, first Venetian, then Turkish. The only surviving edifice is a little domed hammam. The east walls, with Venetian and Turkish gun emplacements, overhang the beach. The west side, facing the open sea, is the oldest part of the castle, perhaps thirteenth century, its ruined ramparts overlooking savage rocks against which the waves break in showers of spray. The paths are choked with thistles, and it is wise to stick to the wall-walks, although these are often on different levels and involve a great deal of scrambling up and down. On this plateau a Venetian garrison of seven thousand defenders withstood a terrible siege by a hundred thousand Turks under Sultan Bayazit II, pounded throughout a sweltering August in 1500 by five hundred cannon. When the Janissaries finally scaled the walls, the buildings were set on fire, the Latin bishop was immolated while preaching to his flock and every male over twelve years old decapitated. In Venice the fall of Methone was regarded as a national disaster and the members of the Council of Ten burst into tears on hearing the news.

At the southern end of the enclosure rise the ruins of the Sea Gate, flanked by two towers, which leads to a landing-

stage protected by a parapet with battlements. Only sea and
sky are visible through the arch. A causeway connects the
Sea Gate, the tip of the headland, with a **Turkish fort** on a
rocky shoal. It is the most picturesque ruin at Methone – an
octagonal double tower in two sections, the higher one smaller
and domed, both surrounded by a crenellated parapet. On
this shoal the Venetian garrison made its last heroic stand
against Bayazit's Janissaries. From the fort one can row (even
swim, for the distance is short) under the lee of another
square-towered sea gate bearing the heraldic arms of Venetian
governors, to the western end of the beach, where the medieval
galleys anchored and Ibrahim Pasha landed in 1825 with his
horde of Arabs and Negroes. In this bay, too, Miaoulis, one
of the most intrepid leaders of the War of Independence, sent
six fire-ships among the Egyptian armada, causing such
destruction that the explosions of the powder magazines were
heard all over Southern Messenia.

Littered with ruins of artillery bastions, look-out posts,
ravelins, Methone is one of the most evocative Venetian sites
in Greece. The Lion of St Mark smirks down from pointed
arches and sweeping curtain walls, and escutcheons of famous
Venetian families choked in weeds crown blocked-up gateways. But neither the arts nor literature flourished here. Only
Jewish silk-workers plied their trade. Visiting the citadel early
in the nineteenth century, Chateaubriand found '*partout le
silence, l'abandon et l'oubli*', and nothing but Tartars sitting
cross-legged in front of evil-smelling hovels, puffing at
hookahs.

Methone is one of the southernmost tips of the Greek
mainland. Forcibly the traveller now turns northward –
through Pylos again. All the way up the west coast the
country has a mellow domesticated quality. But the softness
never degenerates into formlessness. The chain of Mt
Aegaleion, running south to north in a line of rocky saddle-
backs, repeats the humps of Sphacteria on a larger scale.
North of Pylos the road skirts the bay and winds up into
wooded hills. Lush ravines are spiked with rows of dwarf
cypresses which serve as wind-breaks – in summer they are so
heavily coated with dust that they look like miniature petrified
forests, beige-coloured. At the eighteenth kilometre from
Pylos the signpost Epano-Englianos marks the site of the so-

called **Palace of Nestor** and the Mycenaean city of Pylos
which extended across a wide ledge against a background of
rugged hills.

Ancient writers do not agree about the locality of Nestor's
capital. Some imply it was in Elis, others in Messenia. Homer
is rather contradictory. In the *Iliad* he says the palace crowns
a 'steep hill overlooking the Alpheius, on the borders of sandy
Pylos' (the bay of Pylos is certainly sandy, but at no point
does the winding Alpheius flow through Messenian territory),
and in the *Odyssey* he says Telemachus found the inhabitants
of Pylos 'on the foreshore . . . doing sacrifice to the earth-
shaker' (Epano-Englianos is situated well inland). But when
Telemachus mounted his chariot and drove through 'the
echoing porch', the horses 'glad to be loosed, flew down from
the steep crag of the citadel of Pylos out on to the plain'.
Here the relation between citadel and plain fits the Epano-
Englianos site, although 'crag' is an overstatement.

The excavations conducted at Epano-Englianos by Professor
Blegen, at the head of an American-Greek team, have cast
fresh light on Homeric topography. This palace (1300–1200
B.C.) is, in size and arrangement, comparable to that of
Mycenae and must therefore have been the residence of a
great king. As Professor Blegen says, 'The only royal dynasty
strong enough and rich enough in the thirteenth century B.C.
in western Messenia to build and maintain such a palace is
that of the Neleids.'[7] Nestor was the son of Neleus, founder
of the dynasty, and his contribution in ships in the Trojan
expedition was second only to that of Agamemnon.

Where all ancient writers and poets are in agreement is on
the bucolic character of the land over which Nestor ruled.
Homer calls it 'sheep-breeding Pylos' and 'rich in horses',
Pindar 'hallowed'. Strabo mentions herds of sheep browsing
in olive groves and describes the cattle raids carried out by
Nestor, in one of which he made off with 'fifty herds of cattle,
and as many flocks of sheep, and as many droves of swine,
and also as many herds of goats, and one hundred and fifty
sorrel mares, most of them with foals beneath them'. The

7. Carl M. Blegen and Marion Rawson, *A Guide to the Palace of
Nestor*, University of Cincinnati, 1962, to which I am deeply indebted
for its detailed description of the architectural complexities of the
palace.

poets also agree on the character of the king. Although a confirmed cattle-thief, he was wise, just, cautious, a generous host and a bore without much sense of humour. More fortunate than Agamemnon or Odysseus, he returned from Troy to enjoy a happy old age in the bosom of his family.

It is fascinating how quickly one is able to form an idea of how this man and his court lived over three thousand years ago. There is, admittedly, none of the drama of the citadel of the Atridae, in spite of architectural features in common and the fact that both palaces were gutted by fire at the time of the Dorian conquest. There are no encircling Cyclopean walls, no gateways supporting huge lintels, no circular royal graveyards. This, so far as we know, was no blood-drenched palace. Nothing standing is more than waist-high, but being built on a level hill-top, without the declivities of ground that add such complexity to the layout of Mycenae, its architectural disposition and domestic arrangements are more quickly grasped than those of Agamemnon's palace. The metal roof, put up in 1961, does not improve the general effect, but it protects the prehistoric foundations and walls of clay from drenching rain and scorching sun.

The main unit is the royal residence, with apartments of state, storerooms and wine magazines grouped round it. The king and his household lived well. The residential section was two-storied, with flat roofs on different levels. In the centre of the outer and inner porticoes are two stone bases which supported fluted wooden columns; left of the doorway was a sentry stand, where a guard checked the identity of visitors entering two small chambers believed to have been the tax-collector's office in which the palace accounts, recorded on tablets, were kept. Right of the portico, a stairway (three steps are preserved) mounted to a tower, thought to have been a look-out post; from here sentinels commanded a view of the rolling wooded hills and shallow gullies with evergreens.

The portico led into an interior court open to the sky; left was a pantry and waiting-room with a stucco-coated bench where visitors sat and were offered wine by servant-boys. Cups, vitrified by time, still lie scattered about the floor. In the 1939 excavations a large quantity of clay tablets, inscribed with the signs of a hitherto undeciphered language, were found in these chambers. More were excavated in 1952. At this

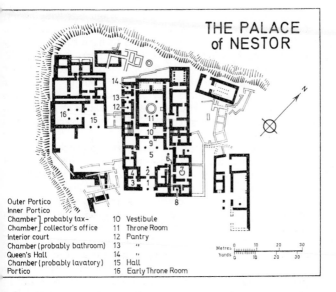

THE PALACE of NESTOR

Outer Portico
Inner Portico
Chamber ⎤ probably tax-
Chamber ⎦ collector's office
Interior court
Chamber (probably bathroom)
Queen's Hall
Chamber (probably lavatory)
Portico

10 Vestibule
11 Throne Room
12 Pantry
13 "
14 "
15 Hall
16 Early Throne Room

Metres 0 ... 10 ... 20 ... 30
Yards 0 ... 10 ... 20 ... 30

point, Michael Ventris, an R.A.F. officer turned architect, began the decipherment of a script which had hitherto baffled Greek scholars, and, it was thought, might even be unrelated to any known Greek dialect. Ventris soon recognised an interrelationship of phonetic values that corresponded with the Archaic declensions used by Homer.[8] The grammatical structure of the language gradually emerged, and Linear B, the script used by the Minoans and Mycenaeans of the Bronze Age, was revealed to be a form of Archaic Greek. The only disappointment was that the Pylos tablets were inscribed with nothing more than household inventories and accounts.

A long narrow chamber (right of the interior court) contains a terracotta tub painted with stuccoed patterns set on a clay base against the south-east wall. A clay step facilitated the royal bather's entry into the tub. Vessels found nearby were probably used for pouring water into the tub. South-east of the bathroom lies the so-called Queen's Hall, with a hearth

8. Michael Ventris, 'Greek Records in the Minoan Script', *Antiquity*, Vol. XXVII, December, 1953.

in the centre, its walls, judging from fragments lying about, decorated with stucco and frescoes of griffons and wild beasts. The hall and bathroom are believed to have been gutted by flames from burning oil which fell from jars stored on the upper floor when the great fire swept the palace. Another chamber, separated from the Queen's Hall by a corridor (south-west), is thought to have been a lavatory, for there are indications that water could be flushed through an aperture in a stone slab at the east corner and thence flow into a subterranean drain.

It is now best to return to the court and proceed through another portico into what must have been a brightly frescoed vestibule, from which a stairway to the right (eight steps are preserved) led to the upper story where the royal ladies probably dwelt. The vestibule served as an entrance hall, which might have been the place where Telemachus slept 'on an inlaid bedstead in the coved entry of the house, under its reverberant roof'. Nestor was famous for his hospitality and he liked to boast that 'there was a great deal of bedding' in the palace. The vestibule leads directly into the large Throne Room, a hall of state, and the most sumptuous apartment in the palace. In the centre is the great ceremonial hearth of clay, once surrounded by four wooden columns supporting a broad gallery. Impressions of the columns' shallow flutes can be discerned on the floor. The smoke from the hearth, which was the holiest place in the palace, is believed to have escaped through a terracotta chimney in the roof. The throne of wood, decorated with ivory and other inlays, was placed against the right wall. The shallow hollow, probably a basin, to the right of the seated king, may have been a contrivance to enable Neleus, Nestor and their royal descendants to pour out libations, without descending from the throne, as when Nestor, anxious to honour Telemachus, ordered the sacrifice of a heifer, and 'the dark blood gushed forth', while the King's sons 'crowding about their father with the five-pronged roasting fork in their hands . . . chopped up the rest of the flesh into morsels which they impaled on their points and broiled . . .'

The grooves in the walls of the Throne Room were intended to receive the ends of vertical and horizontal beams, which Professor Blegen thinks may have been left exposed, as in the

English half-timbered style. The whole room was bright with dazzling decoration: frescoes of leopards, lions and other wild beasts covered the walls; linear designs within squares adorned the floor; and a representation of the familiar octopus served as a doormat at the foot of the throne. The colours used were red, blue, yellow, black and white, all of the gaudiest hues, and it seems clear from the fragments assembled in the neighbouring museum at Chora (see below) and the National Museum in Athens that the scene must have been one of barbaric splendour.

Two corridors separate either side of the Throne Room from a maze of little storerooms. The ones on the south-west side are believed to have been the main pantries, because of the mass of crushed pottery (over six thousand pieces) found here. Tablets stacked in two large storerooms directly behind (north-west of) the Throne Room bore inscriptions describing the different qualities and flavours of olive oil.

South-west of the palace another complex of buildings, more devastated and more methodically plundered (two Frankish coins were found here), rises above the sloping olive grove, where the lower town descended in terraces. The walls of the large entrance hall, preceded by two stone bases for wooden columns, were decorated with an elegant frieze of pink griffons, fragments of which were found scattered about the floor. The hall led into a large reception chamber of an earlier period than the Throne Room. Right of the palace (north-east) is another complex of storerooms, where raw materials were kept. Tablets referring to repairs in leather and bronze materials indicate that this may have been the main workshop of the city. To the north are wine magazines, where many of the jars, cracked, broken and of different sizes, still stand as they were found.

Tholos tombs, possibly burial places of kings, have been excavated in the vicinity. The most important is in an olive grove about a hundred yards north-east of the palace. Its contents included gold, jewellery, amethysts, amber necklaces, rings, effigies of little owls and a royal seal on which the image of a winged griffon was stamped. The other tombs lie south of the palace hill.

Beyond Epano-Englianos, past Chora, where the museum possesses fragments of pottery, frescoes and stucco flooring from the palace, the road continues northward between the sea and the range of Agaleion whose rocky fingers thrust upwards in a succession of strange nodular peaks. At Cyparissia, founded by Epaminondas in the fourth century B.C. at the same time as Messene and Megalopolis, and later a flourishing Byzantine port, one can drive up to the upper town, Ano-Cyparissia: a maze of rock-hewn stairways and village houses, with ruins of a medieval castle (there is little to see except an oubliette and a large metal basin, possibly Turkish), built on the site of an Hellenic tower, so ancient that it was supposed to have been raised by the giants when they were at war with the gods.

An inland road joins Cyparissia with the Tripolis–Kalamata highway. After crossing the densely olive-clad Triphylian plain, the main coastal road to the north enters the territory of Elis.

Olympia

❧

OLYMPIA lies in Elis, which Homer calls 'goodly' – not without reason. When the traitor Oxylus, an outlawed Calydonian prince, led the Dorian invaders across the Peloponnese in search of rich pasture lands, he deliberately conducted them through the rugged Arcadian defiles so that they should not observe the fertility of Elis, which he coveted for himself. As a reward for his services, the Dorians made him king of the country they had never seen. According to a local legend, Oxylus then founded the Olympic Games.

The lower valley of the Alpheius, which flows past Olympia and irrigates the ancient country of Pisatis, is one of the most gracious landscapes in Greece. Pine-clad hills overlook gullies filled with ilex and arbutus; streams bordered by oleanders and agnus castus wind through humid shut-in valleys; the walls of village houses are bright with flowering creepers; in spring the hills are covered with wild flowers; but in antiquity the lagoons were infested with mosquitoes and the inhabitants had to appeal to Zeus and Heracles, two very Elean deities, to rid them of these pests.

Olympia can be approached direct from Athens via Corinth and Patras; from Tripolis (see pp. 177-78); and from the south – the route normally taken by travellers making a circular tour of the Peloponnese.[1]

North of the coastal belt of Triphylia the Arcadian foothills push out new spurs towards the sea. Below Mt Minthe, named after a girl loved by Hades whom Koré, in a fit of

1. The first route, Corinth–Patras–Olympia, is described in reverse in Chapter 14.

jealousy, trampled underfoot and transformed into garden
mint, lies the pine-fringed lagoon of Caiapha with a spa
situated on a wooded islet. As the road ascends gently, the
pine trees grow larger, more luxuriant. Beyond Caiapha a
track to the east leads to the fine fourth century B.C. walls o
Samikon, which commanded one of the passes into Arcadia
built by the Eleans as a bulwark against Spartan aggression
The highway skirts another lagoon, north of which a rough
road climbs up to Andritsaena and Bassae. Along the coas
stretch miles of sandy beaches, with no coves and few harbours
After crossing the Alpheius the road enters a flat alluvia
plain, passes through Pyrgos, notorious for its earthquake
and sexual crimes, and turns east into an undulating woodland
country. The whole way, bordered by evergreens and hedge
rows, was once sacred to men in search of peace and pleasure
On foot and in chariots they converged by the thousands or
the sanctuary. Today the road climbs, dips, swerves; then
suddenly one is in the middle of the village, shut in by low
hills. A feeling of anti-climax is inevitable. Tourist shops line
the main street, and the stone bridge across the stream of the
Cladeus is hideous. Not a gleam of marble meets the eye.

There are plenty of hotels. The SPAP is expensive and
beautifully situated on an eminence commanding a view of the
Altis (the sacred enclosure) and the valley of the Alpheius
The Xenias, in a hollow below the museum, is modern and
less expensive. Small hotels in the main street, or just off it
are cheap and clean. The inhabitants are quick-witted
acquisitive and friendly. After Athens and Delphi this is the
most important classical site in the country. In one day (two
nights) one can visit the Altis and the museum in relative
leisure. But it requires a rather longer stay to experience tha
charmed moment when the astonishing harmony between the
ruins and their setting suddenly comes into focus and the
historical associations can be revived in the perspective of land
scape and topography.

Every fourth year during the full moon period following the
summer solstice, for century after century, men flocked to the
sanctuary to praise the benefits of peace and watch Greek
youth display its prowess in the stadium. Primarily, the
festival was an occasion for athletic contests, and the winning
of the cherished olive crown considered the greatest honour to

which a young man could aspire – far more highly prized
than the Pythian laurel, the Isthmian pine branch or the
Nemean wild celery. The sanctuary, scene of the most dazzling
assembly of celebrities in the ancient world, was sacred to
Zeus. Mythographers say the first games were instituted by
Heracles and that Apollo vanquished his half-brothers,
Hermes and Ares, in a foot race and boxing match. The
first recorded festival is dated to the year 776 B.C. and henceforward Greek chronology is based on Olympiads, the periods
of four years between festivals. The Games began as a series
of foot races, to which more elaborate events were soon added,
organised by a confederacy of Western Greek states gradually
acquiring panhellenic proportions, but always under the aegis
of the Eleans. Throughout the country heralds would announce
a Sacred Truce between all warring states for the month of the
celebrations. On one occasion, Elis, a comparatively weak
state, had the audacity, in the capacity of chairman, to impose
a fine on Sparta, the mightiest power in Greece, for violating
the truce and even to exclude Spartan athletes from participa-
tion. Thus Peace became the symbol and keynote of the
Games, and Hellenic unity, if only for a few days every four
years, a reality.

Other meetings of less importance proliferated throughout
the country, but from Thrace to Sparta, from Ionia to Sicily,
the programme remained the one established by the Hellenodicae of Olympia, an executive committee chosen by lot. The
actual rules were never, according to Aristotle, codified; athletes
knew them by tradition and instinct. The sacred element
attached to athletics was illustrated in the sacrifices preceding
the events and the quantity of altars raised in the precinct.
Physical exercise ranked so high in the curriculum that the
fitness and worship of the human body acquired a religious
significance, and the principal male deities were often represented as participating in titanic contests or championing one
competitor against another. At Olympia, the festival was,
from beginning to end, a paean of worship of the father of the
gods. Every athlete offered a solemn sacrifice to Olympian
Zeus, Lord of the Lightning, before entering a competition,
and the Eleans sacrificed once a month at his altar, burning
incense mixed with olive twigs and wheat kneaded with
honey, accompanied by copious libations of wine.

The sanctuary was not only the haunt of priests and sports
fans, but the resort of men of fashion and eminent politicians.
The latter went to the Games as diplomats go to cocktail
parties, hoping to make new contacts and pick up useful
information, Discreet *pourparlers*, held in the shady recesses
of the Echo Colonnade, paved the way for new alliances, new
alignments, new betrayals. In 420 B.C. Alcibiades, in one of his
most extravagant displays, deeply impressed his allies with the
power and prestige of Athens. He not only participated in the
races, but personally led seven chariots, each with four horses,
and won the first and second prizes. His solemn sacrifices, his
elaborate banquets, his lavishly adorned tents were the talk of
Olympia.

The place swarmed with temperamental athletes, surrounded by trainers, admirers and publicity agents; and a vast fly-
infested encampment, teeming with beggars and pedlars,
spread across fields and vineyards. Roofed accommodation
was reserved for athletes, while the crowds slept under canvas
or in the open. Plato, already famous, shared a tent with total
strangers. About five centuries later, Lucian complains of the
lack of transport, of the paths leading out of Olympia jammed
with pedestrian traffic.[2] At night, after the victorious athletes
had marched in procession in the light of the full moon,
chanting praises of Zeus the All-Seeing, the great concourse
was transformed into a vast sexual playground. Although
women were not allowed to attend the Games, they could
approach the periphery of the sanctuary. During Roman
times, Olympia did not decline in importance, but the ideal was
tarnished, the standards lowered. Hadrian, as might be
expected, did much for the embellishment of the sanctuary,
but in 392 Theodosius the Great, anxious to extirpate every
trace of paganism in the empire, decreed a series of proscrip-
tions which temporarily banished all light and gaiety from the
civilised world. Thus the Olympic Games came to an end.
With them perished a great Hellenic ideal.

The main street of the village descends, beyond the Xenias

2. The scene, although on a much larger scale, probably resembled
some modern *paneghyri*, an open-air religious feast, attended by crowds
of villagers shuffling between ranks of ice-cream stalls and pedlars of
'sacred objects', while fire-works crackle overhead. For a list of the
more important *paneghyria*, and where and when they occur, see
Appendices, pp. 378-85.

Hotel, to the bridge across the Cladeus, a tributary of the
Alpheius. The prospect is one of immense serenity, with the
Alpheius flowing through the wide valley, its shingly bed
streaked with winding streams. Across the bridge is the
entrance to the Altis. At first it seems difficult to associate all
this rubble of grey limestone with the brilliant panhellenic
sanctuary where sport was born, and statesmen and philosophers assembled to preach political unity. The setting,
however, is idyllic. Tall dark pines have replaced the plane
trees of antiquity; in spring the paths between the ruins are
bordered with irises and gladioli and the furry scalloped
leaves of golden henbane peep out of cracks in shell-pocked
slabs of masonry; in summer the bitter-sweet fragrance of
agnus castus is overpowering; in autumn the air is balmy with
the scent of resin from the pines and deep pink cyclamen cover
the sides of the hill of Cronus overlooking the sanctuary. The
sinuous contours of the parkland landscape cry out for their
Poussin. There is a feeling of sensuousness about the place.
Gradually the spaciousness of the grove and the sheer volume
of the rubble – the huge drums, the imposing stylobate of the
Temple of Zeus, the ample proportions of the administrative
buildings, where the athletes trained and ate and slept – begin
to make an impact. One is conscious of a sense of grandeur,
of immeasurable peace.

The devastation is not wholly the work of Alaric. The
Alpheius is a capricious river. Constantly changing its course
and flooding its banks, it has buried many monuments under
the porous soil of the Altis. Earthquakes, to which Elis is very
prone, have also taken their toll. It required the patient work
of a team of nineteenth century German archaeologists to
bring the foundations to light and reveal the ground plan of
the various edifices which grew up without any architectural
or chronological relation to each other. Visitors can choose
their own course. One of the most practical is to follow a more
or less straight line from the gymnasium to the Bouleuterion
(properly speaking, these two buildings lay outside the
enclosure wall of the Altis), turn north to the Prytaneum and
then east to the stadium. With minor deviations right and left,
the ground is then covered.

The gymnasium, its walls once inscribed with the names of
victors of the olive branch, was famous for the excellence of

its running tracks. It is identified by a double row of truncated columns. The excavation of a row of hip-baths has revealed earthenware vessels embedded in hollows in which the athlete placed their feet while warm water was poured over them The **palaestra,** beside the Gymnasium, is a more attractive ruin, a forest of short slender Doric columns with plain capitals, with two pine trees growing out of the central court Seen from the south, with the colonnade silhouetted against a line of cypress-clad hills, the scene is one of extraordinary harmony. The building was quadrilateral, with chamber opening on to the colonnaded courts: a club room, a hall where ephebes were anointed with oil, tanks for bathers and drying rooms. There were also exedrae where retired athlete lectured, and seats where spectators sat and gossiped, while wrestlers trained and practised, their torsos caked with the yellow powder they sprinkled over their bodies so that their flesh, says Philostratus the Sophist, shone with 'the bloom of ripe peaches'. The athletes were generally of the upper classes but working class boys with a talent for sport were not debarred from participating. Professionalism was unknown until Hellenistic times, when the festival became a spectacle provided for a noisy rabble by highly paid competitors. Athletes considered themselves a race apart and were generally very conceited. One competitor in the foot race went so far as to commission and bring his own statue to Olympia – all the way from Cyrene – before the event. Sometimes they were strait-laced as well as arrogant, and a Theban winner of three awards is reported to have left the room ostentatiously whenever an obscenity was uttered in his presence. The palaestra was also crowded with trainers, who lived in a special enclosure and were very important people. They were fussy about the athletes' diet, forbidding them starch, but no cheese, and debated the merits of deep sea versus inshore fish as a suitable diet for muscle-building. Plutarch says they would not even let the young men talk at dinner lest conversation should give them a headache.

After the palaestra comes the Theocoleion – only the outline is traceable – built around two courts, headquarters of the priests in charge of sacrificial rites, followed by the shell of an Early Christian basilica – the site of an ancient workshop greatly venerated by the Eleans because Phidias and his

The Turkish fort at Methone where the Venetian garrison made its last
heroic stand against Bayazit's Janissaries.

General view of Olympia showing the fertile valley of the river Alpheius.

The Palaestra, Olympia. Here spectators sat and gossiped, retired athletes lectured and wrestlers trained and practised.

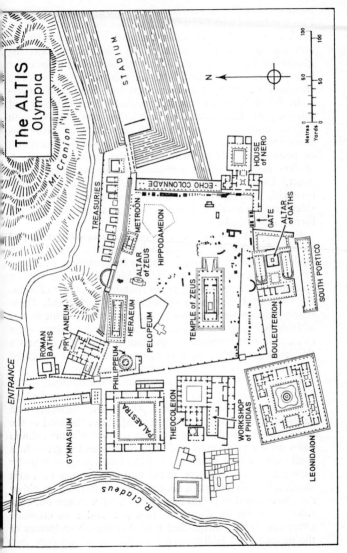

The ALTIS
Olympia

STADIUM

Mt. Cronion

TREASURIES

HOUSE of NERO

ECHO COLONNADE

METROON

HIPPODAMEION

ALTAR of ZEUS

GATE

ALTAR of OATHS

PRYTANEUM

HERAEUM

PELOPEUM

TEMPLE of ZEUS

BOULEUTERION

SOUTH PORTICO

ROMAN BATHS

PHILIPPEUM

ENTRANCE

PALAESTRA

THEOCOLEION

WORKSHOP of PHIDIAS

LEONIDAION

GYMNASIUM

R. Cladeus

N

Metres 0   50   100
Yards 0   50   100

pupils worked there on the huge ivory and gold statue of Zeus. Fluted columns with foliate designs frame the ruined Christian altar. South of the basilica the foundations of a large square building have been identified as the **Leonidaeion,** near the processional entrance to the Altis, which served as a hostel for high-ranking officials and later for Roman governors. The chambers were ranged round a court with ponds and flower-beds. The exterior colonnade consisted of one hundred and thirty-eight columns. Most of their bases, now crowned with Ionic capitals, survive on the north and east sides. From this shaded stoa visitors obtained a close-up view of the procession of priests and athletes with which the festival opened. A shallow moat surrounds a circular area in the centre of the court. Large rectangular and smaller square chambers (probably bedrooms) are outlined on the west and south sides. In spring wild larkspur grows among the debris in the former flower-beds.

East of the Leonidaeion, across a waste of Greek and Roman foundations, two apsidal halls, later joined by an Hellenistic edifice, formed part of the Bouleuterion, where the officials responsible for the administration of the festival assembled. The committee room contained a statue of Zeus, the Oath-God, holding a thunderbolt in each hand. These deadly missiles were intended to strike terror into the hearts of athletes who swore on pieces of boar's flesh to observe the rules. All that remains of the fourth century B.C. South Portico – probably a market place – is a row of truncated column bases crowned with Corinthian columns.

To the north-east a ramp mounts up to the stylobate of the **Temple of Zeus,** at once the heart of the sanctuary and its holiest edifice. Between them, Alaric, the Alpheius and earthquakes have left nothing standing above the level of the lowest drum, but the huge platform with formidable column bases on the north colonnade still dominates the grove in a most majestic way. It was built of local shell conglomerate by Libon, an Elean architect, in the mid-fifth century B.C., and the fluted Doric columns, six at each end, thirteen on either side, were equal in height to those of the Parthenon but considerably wider in diameter. Two gilt cauldrons crowned either end of the marble-tiled roof. The superb sculptures of the metopes and pediments are happily in the museum, and ew have found their way to foreign collections. Hidden from sight for hundreds of years under a protective layer of loam and clay mixed with pine needles, the marbles were at least preserved from the attentions of Western antiquarian-plunderers. The general effect made by the temple, peripheral and hexastyle, is thought to have been massive and uninspiring – probably not unlike the Theseum in Athens. As a ruin, however, it could not be more imposing. All around the high stylobate lie gigantic drums speckled with fossilised shells: some neatly sliced in rows, others in a mass of contorted rubble as though blown sky-high by some demonic force before crashing down in a pile of shattered masonry.

The mass and weight of the exterior colonnade were only a foretaste of what awaited the spectator in the cella, which was entered through bronze doors. Here the base of Phidias' Zeus, most celebrated of ancient statues, occupied a third of the nave. Thanks to Pausanias, we have a minute description of his mammoth effigy (it stood 40 feet high). The result must have been like some fifth century B.C. version of the Albert Memorial. The god was depicted seated on a throne, his head, almost touching the ceiling, crowned with a garland of olive branches. In his right hand he held a victory, in his left an ornamented sceptre on which an eagle was perched. The flesh was of ivory, the drapery of gold worked with designs of animals and lilies. Strabo says Phidias' intention was to interpret Homer's famous description: 'Cronion spake, and nodded assent with his dark brows, and then the ambrosial locks flowed streaming from the lord's immortal head . . .' But the greatest sculptor of his age must have been suffering from a temporary delusion if he imagined that this outsize monstrosity bore any relation to the poet's noble evocation of the son of Cronus. Nevertheless, Dio Chrysostom, Livy, Pliny and Lucian all refer to the awe the statue aroused in the beholder. Arrian considered it a calamity for a man to die without having seen it. The finished product probably owed much to the popular notion of God as a kind of implacable Nemesis. Zeus' thunderbolts and Poseidon's trident are instruments intended to strike terror into men's hearts. In Byzantine times the Daphni Pantocrator scowls threateningly down at the faithful from his celestial cupola. The continuity is obvious.

The decoration of the bejewelled throne and footstool sound more what one would expect from Phidias' chisel. His genius for creating poetic images out of human and animal processionals was revealed in figures of athletes and striplings of sphinxes ravishing children, of Apollo and Artemis aiming arrows at the children of Niobe, of Theseus' combat with the Amazons. Screens, intended to keep curious spectators at a respectful distance, were decorated with panels painted by Panaenus, the sculptor's nephew. In front of the statue the floor was paved with black tiles within a circular marble ring intended for the retention of the olive oil which, says Pausanias, was 'beneficial to the image', and prevented the statue 'from being harmed by the marshiness of the Altis'. One day Caligula decided to take the head of the statue to Rome and substitute the 'ambrosial locks' with his own. But each time the imperial executioners approached the statue with the intention of decapitating it, the image roared with laughter and frightened them away. In the fifth century the statue was removed *in toto* by the Emperor Theodosius II to Constantinople, where it perished in a fire.

Around the temple extended a forest of votive statues mostly of Zeus, but also of distinguished athletes. Paeonius' great Niké, now in the museum, stood near the east façade of the temple. Pliny estimates the number of statues at three thousand. Many, probably the best, were removed to Rome and Constantinople. In Pausanias' catalogue of the sculptures the names of Phidias, Myron, Polycleitus and Lysippus constantly recur. There were also effigies of the 'tallest of all men' who slew a lion without a weapon, of Herodotus who won a foot-race, of a lively mare that threw its rider but went on to win the race, of the Rhodian brothers who, after defeating their father in a boxing match, carried him shoulder high, pelted with flowers, through the cheering crowd.

There were also over fifty altars scattered about the Altis, including one of Zeus: a huge mound of ashes piled up with innumerable sacrifices. Around the statues and altars well known actors declaimed to groups of theatrical students, and great public figures were surrounded by admirers: Themistocles, at the height of his fame; Herodotus, followed by the boy Thucydides who burst into tears from emotion when listening to a public reading of the Histories; the ranting boastful Sophists; Xeuxis, the fashionable painter, his name embroidered in gold thread on his purple robe; the dazzling Alcibiades.

North-west of the temple is a grass-grown mound surrounded by stone slabs: the only surviving trace of the pentagonal enclosure of Pelops, Poseidon's cup-bearer, who gave his name to the peninsula and to whom the Eleans annually sacrificed a black ram on a fire piled with white poplar-wood. Pelops was the son of the notorious Tantalus, who stole nectar, ambrosia and a stew, intended for divine consumption, from the larders of Mt Olympus. The theft was detected and Tantalus condemned to hang eternally from a luxuriant fruit tree beside a burbling stream in the Underworld, tortured by an unquenchable thirst and insatiable hunger. To the west (left) of the Pelopeum lies the stylobate of the pine-shaded Philippeum, a circular edifice with an external colonnade and Corinthian half-columns engaged in the inner wall of the cella, commissioned by Philip of Macedon after his victory over the united Greeks at Chaeroneia and later adorned with statues of the Macedonian dynasty, from which Nicanor proclaimed Alexander the Great's divinity in 324 B.C. The beams of its bronze roof were bound together by a sculptured poppy. All that remains now are the inner and outer circular walls (at knee level), two courses of stepped wall and a ring of column bases over which chameleons glide.

West of the shattered Prytaneum, where the magistrates resided, and the Philippeum, extends the impressive stylobate of the seventh century B.C. **Heraeum** (sufficiently well preserved for the outlines of the cella to emerge clearly), the oldest extant temple in the country, Doric and peripteral, dedicated to the worship of the Queen of the Heavens. Originally built of limestone and sun-dried bricks, with wooden columns and a tiled roof, it ranked second to the shrine of Zeus in religious importance and contained the ivory and gold table, carved by a pupil of Phidias, on which the victors' olive crowns rested. Squat and bulky, but with all the dignified self-assurance of Archaic art, the Heraeum is a perfect place in which to sit on a stone slab and pore over plans and guide-books. The edifice, although the most ancient, is the best preserved in Olympia. The stone-work of the truncated columns of the north colonnade has acquired a light almost honey-coloured hue, and in spring the shady paths around the stylobate are speckled with cistus – pink, white and mauve. Two short columns, complete with flat Archaic capitals, rise intact at the west end of the stylobate – the capitals were originally of different designs, according to their age: Archaic (flat) or classical (with echinus and abacus). An elongated base, which once supported a statue of Hera enthroned with a helmeted Zeus beside her, is still visible. Pausanias found the statues 'crude works of art', but he admired the Hermes of Praxiteles which was found lying across the floor of the cella at the time of the excavations.

On a bank to the east rises the second century A.D. Exedra of Herodes Atticus, with two broken unfluted columns and a circular basin, its cornice decorated with lions' heads. The little semi-circular enclosure is followed by a row of ruined treasuries belonging to the principal states ranged along a narrow ledge supported by a stepped base. The first of these, the treasury of Sicyon, is the best preserved (indeed better than its more famous namesake at Delphi) and easily identified by a single short Doric column, with a complete capital, raised on a stone parapet. Opposite the ledge are three courses of the stone wall of the Metroön, a little Doric temple dedicated to the Mother of the Gods. Fragments of broken columns lie lop-sided among the pine needles and volutes of Ionic columns are framed in straggling weeds.

Beyond the treasuries is the tunnel of the Krypte, 'The Hidden Entrance', a vaulted passage-way of Roman construction leading to the Stadium. Beside it stood two of the numerous Zanes which dotted the Altis. The cost of these statues, mostly of Zeus, was defrayed from fines imposed on athletes who broke the rules. There is no evidence of large-scale cheating at Olympia, and there is only one recorded instance of cowardice, when an Alexandrian athlete, entered for the pancration, lost his nerve and fled before the event. But after the Hellenistic period, when professionalism vitiated the religious nature of the festival, bribery was not unknown. The two Zanes, strategically placed at the entrance to the stadium, were probably meant to serve as a warning. From the Krypte the Echo Colonnade, one of the finest in Greece, ran along the east wall of the Altis. It is unfortunately completely destroyed. Built in the mid-fourth century B.C., and famous for its sevenfold echo, it was designed to offer shade to spectators waiting to enter the stadium. Here, during Roman times, were held musical competitions, in which Nero, with his passion for singing (he would chant for hours on end, while his hired audience beat their hands in dutiful applause), frequently participated.

At the southern extremity of the one-time colonnade there is another group of foundations and ruins which are believed to have been the residence of the judges and umpires. To the east, where the main stream of the Alpheius used to flow below the Altis, are the excavations, still in progress, of the villa where Nero dwelt during the summer of A.D. 67, when, hoping to impress his Greek subjects with his magnanimity, he declared all northern Peloponnesians free men. But the expense involved in surrounding the licentious emperor with the trappings of a divine personage caused prices to rise astronomically, and the Greeks had to pay dearly for the imperial condescension.

One returns to the Krypte, through which athletes entered the **stadium.** Ahead extends a large rectangular race-track between earth embankments sown with grass. Unlike other Greek stadia, it never possessed marble, stone or even wooden seats. The spectators, some forty thousand, sat or stood on the ground, which was probably covered with dry grass at the time of the festival. The simplest, most unadorned Greek stadium, it still ranked first. Assured of attracting the largest assembly, the Hellenodicae preferred to spend money on the architectural and sculptural embellishment of the sanctuary. Strabo says the stadium was situated in an olive grove. The olive trees have gone. But the surroundings – the exquisite contours of the wooded hills, the streams flowing through the valley – cannot have altered much.

Here then, at the height of summer, athletes assembled from all over the Greek and Roman worlds to take part in an unchanging programme of events which lasted for a thousand years and whose ideals were handed down to posterity like an unwritten Magna Carta of sport. The festival lasted five days, beginning with a procession and sacrificial rites and ending with feasts. The track accommodated twenty runners and Lucian speaks of sprinters running in deep fine sand. Dio Chrysostom says the foot races began at dawn, so that the runner could benefit from the cool air of early morning. All athletes, runners, boxers, wrestlers, discus-throwers, were naked. There is a story that nudity came into fashion after an incident in 720 B.C. when a sprinter's shorts accidentally slipped off during a race, whereupon the Hellenodicae decided that even the skimpiest garment hindered the athlete's movements and forbade the wearing of any clothing whatsoever. To the Greeks, seldom if ever prudes, there was nothing immodest in nakedness, and the worship of the human body was strongly ingrained in their aesthetic traditions. It is unlikely that the presence of the naked athlete in the Olympic stadium was the cause of the exclusion of women from the Games. In Greek society women held a subservient position; they stayed at home and did not aspire to the pleasures and entertainments provided for men. At Olympia, women who tried to enter the stadium were cast off the neighbouring Typaean rock. One women, however, succeeded in slipping through the Krypte. Disguised as a trainer, she accompanied her son, a competitor, to the Games. But she was found out and consequently all trainers were also obliged to enter the Stadium naked. On the other hand, women were not prevented from owning horses entered for races in the hippodrome.

Other events were held in the middle of the day. Wrestling and boxing matches (boxers wore thongs instead of gloves) were followed by the pentathlon, introduced in 708 B.C., a composite event – long jump, discus-throwing, javelin throwing, foot race and wrestling match. Finally, most popular of all, came the pancration, a form of all-in wrestling with boxing thrown in to make it an even severer test of physical endurance. In the blinding August sunshine, the audience excitedly followed the punching, kicking and throttling, as the tanned muscular bodies, anointed with fine sand, grappled amid clouds of dust raised by their straining feet.

The initial feeling of anti-climax at the absence of any major visible ruin wears off. At the west and east ends respectively are the *aphesis* and *terma*, the starting line and finishing post, consisting of narrow rectangular slabs, with grooves for the starters' toes in the slabs of the *aphesis*. The water conduits are preserved, and halfway along the south embankment there are vestiges of a tribune for the judges.

opposite, on the north embankment, are remains of an altar of white marble, over which presided a priestess of Demeter, the only woman permitted to enter the arena.

The length of the track, from start to finish, is 630 feet. Along it once paraded Milo, the notorious wrestler, who was so strong that he would cover the distance carrying a full-grown bull, which he subsequently ate at a single meal. On other occasions, he would stand in the middle of the course, tie a ribbon round his forehead and, amid frantic applause, snap it by simply swelling his veins. Victorious athletes, clad in purple garments, returned to their native cities at the head of enormous processions – in one case, three hundred chariots drawn by white horses – and laid their olive crowns on temple altars. Sometimes city walls were torn down to make the victor's entry more spectacular. Poets and writers of all ages, with the exception of Plato and Euripides, who doubted the wisdom of such extravagant hero-worship, never ceased to laud the athletes. 'Welcome the Olympian victor,' cries Pindar, 'welcome for the Graces' sake, this minstrel-band, this long enduring light of widely potent prowess.'[3] Cicero claims that no victorious general entering Rome was received with such manifestations of homage. Thus the memory of the Greek athlete remained enshrined in the minds of European poets, and even Milton's fallen angels indulge in epic contests 'as at th' Olympian Games and Pythian fields'.

After the stadium there are no more ruins. No vestige remains of the theatre mentioned by Xenophon, who lived in retirement at neighbouring Scillus, where he owned a large estate, complete with woods, orchards and grazing-grounds, and spent his time hunting, riding and writing his reminiscences of the March of the Ten Thousand. Near the entrance to the Altis a path winds up the slope of the Cronion, a conical hill, thickly wooded with the tallest, most luxuriant pine trees in Greece. The scent of resin is intoxicating. The summit, where sacrifices were held at the spring equinox in honour of Cronus, father of Zeus, overlooks the Altis and stadium. From there, on summer evenings, you may see village boys running races in the stadium. Beyond it, where the hippodrome is supposed to lie under its age-old layers of silt, the streams of the Alpheius

3. The 'minstrel-band' was composed of musicians, who accompanied the returning hero, playing on flutes.

wind between sandbanks. The air is loud with the croaking of frogs. Although a heat-haze extends across the rapidly darkening vista of vineyards and cornfields, a breeze sometimes blows through the branches of the pines, and suddenly the victorious shout of one of the boys, who has reached the *terma* first, rings out.

The neo-classical building of the **museum** is shaded by pine trees below the SPAP Hotel.[4] It possesses one of the finest collections of ancient sculpture (Archaic to Roman) in the country. The vestibule is crammed with outsize statues of Roman emperors: a giant Augustus, a Claudius with an eagle perched on his feet, a martial Hadrian, Trajan, Poppaea. The arrangement disregards chronology. Room A (east aisle) possesses more Roman statues, including the Bull of Regilla from the Exedra of Herodes Atticus, an Elean votive offering to the worthy wife of the public benefactor, and a good **head of Antinoos** – contemplative, wistful as usual, but with a more appealing quality than most of the well-known effigies of Hadrian's favourite. In Room B there is a striking fifth century B.C. **bronze statuette of a horse**: taut, alert, even fiery, in spite of the heavy cylindrical little body. The halter, snaffle, thongs and knots on the girth are beautifully executed. The fragment of a shield of Miltiades dedicated to Zeus, assumed to be that of the victor of Marathon (the name is clearly legible), is of purely historical interest.

One returns to the vestibule and enters the west aisle. In Room A the most striking exhibit is a late sixth century B.C. tufa **head of Hera,** probably part of the cult statue in the Heraeum. The effigy has an air of authority and majesty proper to the Queen of the Heavens, and the half-smiling autocratic mouth gives remarkable distinction to the broad flat face, with its expression of concentrated intensity, under the stylised head-dress. The grooved incisions of the eyebrows represent a halting attempt to produce a lifelike rendering of human features. No. 677 is a stone, weighing 316 pounds, belonging to the famous weight-lifter Bybon, with the inscription 'Bybon, son of Phola, has lifted me over his head with

4. It is soon to be replaced by a modern building on the east bank of the Cladeus, large enough to accommodate the numerous sculptural fragments and vases now stored in cellars. Only a few exhibits in the present museum are numbered.

ne hand.' Besides the usual figurines there are numerous
riffon heads. These marvellously chiselled protomes, mostly
f the seventh century B.C., with arched beaks and open jaws
bout to snap, sabre-like ears thrusting outward vertically,
nd an air of thorough malevolence, first appeared in the
ighth century B.C. and served as adornments, stylised but
reathtakingly alive, to bronze cauldrons. In Rooms B and C
here are numerous bronze figurines and fragments of weapons
shields, breastplates, arrow-points, greaves).

One has to pass through the vestibule again to reach the
entral hall, where the remains of the **pediments and metopes
f the Temple of Zeus** – huge figures, some headless or limbless,
nonumental in simplicity of conception and execution – are
anged majestically along the walls. It is that exciting transi-
ional period when Archaic rigidity and tension have relaxed,
nd the liberating breath of classical art has galvanised the
tatic figures, rendering them mobile and articulate, without
lepriving them of the poise and grandeur of the earlier
nodels.

On either side of the entrance are four metopes, depicting
he labours of Heracles. Left to right: Heracles bringing the
tymphalian Birds (the birds and their poisonous feathers are
nissing) to Athena – it is a relief to find her in a relaxed
nood, and without her usual ungainly helmet; Heracles,
esting his head on his right hand, reflecting for a moment in
he midst of his grapple with the Nemean Lion, encouraged
y Athena above; Heracles, a lithe vigorous figure cleansing
he Augeian Stables, assisted by Athena – now martial and
nelmeted – who has lost her chin and consequently acquired
. rather fatuous expression; Heracles dragging the dog
Cerberus, its open jaws ready to snap, from the Underworld.
There are two more metopes at the north end of the hall. On
he right, Heracles captures the Bull of Knossos (the greater
art of this metope is now in the Louvre). The powerful
ackward sweep of the hero's sinewy torso emphasises the
iolence of the combat. The last extant metope (left) is the
cknowledged masterpiece. Heracles, a monolithic figure of
mmense power, supports the heavens, with the aid of Athena,
vhile Atlas brings him the Golden Apples of the Hesperides,
ruits of the Tree of Life. The vertical symmetry of the com-
osition – the strictly linear folds of Athena's garment and

the erect postures of the male figures – is only broken by the horizontal projection of Heracles' forearms. The head of Heracles is identical throughout the series – an indication that the metopes were executed by a single artist.

From end to end of the east and west walls, which correspond exactly to the width of the Temple of Zeus, tower the fragments of the temple's pediments, slightly later in date than the metopes and executed in the finest Parian marble by an anonymous Elean sculptor. The east pediment depicts the last minute preparations for the fateful chariot race between Oenomaus, the Pisatan king, and Pelops, no longer cup bearer to Poseidon but suitor of the king's daughter, Hippodameia, who reciprocates his love. The king's assent to their union is dependent on his own defeat in the chariot race with Pelops, a matter which the infatuated Hippodameia, in collusion with Pelops, has already settled by bribing her father's charioteer to remove the nails from the hubs of the royal chariot wheels. The race is run, the accident occurs according to plan and the king meets with his death. Some mythographers say it was Pelops – not Heracles nor Oxylus – who held the first Games in commemoration of his basely won victory. In the centre of the composition is a colossal headless Zeus, umpire of the race, holding a thunderbolt, flanked by the two contestants. Other figures represent members of the household of Oenomaus, including his famous winged mare and Myrtilus, the treacherous charioteer. The figure of the aged seer is a masterpiece. He has already divined the king's fate, and his expression is one of anguished consternation. The flabby folds of flesh indicate his advanced age. Equally impressive is the head and figure of a reclining groom in the right corner. The consummate modelling of the anatomy is only matched by the beauty of the head, with its expression of tension and excitement. All the figures, whether erect crouching or reclining, seem to be filled with a sense of awareness of impending disaster, which heightens the unity and dramatic quality of the composition.

The west pediment, a group of twenty-one statues, is even more exciting. Here the feeling of expectancy is replaced by the confusion of battle. It depicts the climax of the combat between the Centaurs and Lapiths at the wedding of King Pirithoos and the Lapith Deidameia, celebrated in a cave on

Mt Pelion in Thessaly. The Centaurs, who were among the guests, got so flushed with wine and desire that they sought tc rape the Lapith women, until the Lapith men, led by Theseus, came to the rescue. Stylistically, the west pediment is more evolved than the east. In both, however, the respective moods, tension and conflict, are conveyed by a surprising economy of effects. There is no over-emphasis, no elaboration of detail; a logical and utterly felicitous feeling for space governs the groups of figures locked in ferocious grapple. Over it all broods the figure of Apollo. For sheer style – the curve of the neck, the powerful but graceful modelling of the arms, and the expression on the imperious mouth with the full slightly parted lips – there is no finer statue in early classical sculpture. The personification of order and spirit over lust and chaos, austere yet serene, the perfect combination of god and man, he dominates the conflict. The figures of the combatants flanking him are no less striking. Among the finest (right of Apollo) are the beautiful Lapith bride, submitting (very unwillingly) to the violent attentions of the Centaur leader, another Lapith maiden trying to free herself from a bestial embrace, (left) an enraged Centaur preparing to kick a Lapith woman whose nails are dug deep into his cheek, a Lapith youth, his features alight with exultation, strangling a Centaur who bites his arm viciously.

A modern author, whose admiration for the west pediment is unquestioned, sensibly suggests that enthusiasm for this astonishing assembly of primitive creatures depicted in a frenzy of unbridled passion is not without certain blemishes.[5] The modelling of some of the figures is rough, there is an awkward disproportion between the human and equine parts of the Centaurs' bodies, and the drapery of the Lapith women's chitons is heavy and tubular. Although the pediment was meant to be viewed by an onlooker fifty feet below, no Athenian sculptor of the fifth century would have tolerated such imperfections.

Paeonius' **Niké**, at the north end of the hall, offers a contrast and an antidote, as she floats down to earth from Olympus in an ecstasy of sheer movement, her wings (now gone) outstretched, her gossamer garments, fastened to her right shoulder with a clasp, clinging to her rounded form as

5. Robert Liddell *The Morea*, Jonathan Cape, London, 1958.

they are blown back by the wind. The statue, raised during the Peloponnesian War to commemorate the abortive Peace of Nicias, the second clause of which granted autonomy to the shrines at Delphi and Olympia, stood on a pillar in front of the east entrance of the Temple of Zeus.

Left of the Niké there is a headless terracotta of a nude warrior with a painted cloak draped over his left shoulder. Better preserved and more lively is the **painted terracotta** (in front of the Niké) – one of the few extant large-size terracottas of the fifth century B.C. – depicting an exultant Zeus abducting a pert little Ganymede, who bears a cock as a love-gift, to the marble halls of Olympus, where he will serve as cup-bearer, pouring out nectar (fermented honey and melted snow brewed into a mead) for his divine master. Several show-cases are scattered about the hall. One near the first four metopes contains a lovely Archaic head of Athena: eyes protruding, expression concentrated yet detached. Only the enigmatic smile has become more faint (the head is dated to the early fifth century B.C.).

Behind the Niké a doorway leads into the museum's holy of holies. Here the famous **Hermes,** supposedly one of the few extant statues of Praxiteles,[6] the most distinguished sculptor of the late Attic school, stands proudly, rather coldly, alone on his pedestal against a sky blue apsidal background. Chiselled out of Parian marble, which has acquired an astonishingly white, almost soapy, patina, the Messenger of the Gods carries his baby brother, Dionysus, in one arm. The infant god of wine, who has a very knowing look, stretches out a hand to grasp what is believed to have been a bunch of grapes, teasingly held at a distance by his elder brother. The modelling of the god's figure is masterly, neck, diaphragm, buttocks, thighs, calves forming a unity of separated but interrelated volumes. His expression is calm and aloof; some critics have described it as 'icy'. But this distant, if slightly vacant, expression of the eyes, fixed on something far beyond the child, adds to the effect of aloofness. The god is leaning on a tree-trunk, draped with his cloak, which forms

6 Modern scholars believe that if the Hermes at Olympia, the one described by Pausanias as standing at the west end of the Heraeum, is not the Praxitelean original, it must at least be a masterly copy by a Graeco-Roman sculptor of a work by Praxiteles.

n integral part of the composition. But the grace is rather
elf-conscious, and the small mouth almost mean; the skilfully
rranged locks suggest curling-tongs. The work is an out-
tanding example of the consummate technique of the late
ourth century B.C., of that smooth perfectionism that pro-
uced a series of polished masterpieces whose insipidity often
natches their spiritual emptiness. In the fourth century B.C.
he sculptural scene was dominated by Scopas and Praxiteles.
'emperamentally Scopas was attracted by the harsher, more
iolent aspects of beauty, Praxiteles by the gentler tenderer
entiments that it inspired. In the Hermes at Olympia his
chievement does not fall short of his inspiration.

CHAPTER FOURTEEN

Frankish Elis and the Achaean Coast

❧

Andravidha – The Cyllene Headland – Castel Tornese -
Glarentza – Patras – Rhion and Antirrhion – Aeghion – The
Buraicos Gorge – Megaspileon – Kalavryta – Xylocastro

THE highway from Olympia to Athens runs north, then east.
The traveller has just enough time to see all the places mentioned in this chapter in one day (only the deviation to
Megaspileon and Kalavryta entails spending the night at one
or the other). The most important sites, both medieval, are
Castel Tornese (Frankish) and Megaspileon (Byzantine); the
others lie mostly along the level road or just off it. The walk to
Glarentza can be omitted by the hurried traveller. The high-
light of the journey is the lovely Achaean coast, steep, wooded,
washed by the inland sea of the Corinthian Gulf.

North-west of Pyrgos, the road enters a flat plain. The
mountains recede in the east and the prospect is less shut-in
than elsewhere in the Peloponnese. Treeless, it is still rich
agricultural country. Elis remains 'goodly' – though far less
beautiful – and the Venetians were sufficiently impressed by
its fertility to call it 'the milk-cow of the Morea'. The landscape, it has been said, recalls Champagne and Flanders.
Perhaps that is why the French knights felt so strongly about
it. At Gastouni, the Frankish Gastogne, a track to the east
leads to the village of Bouchioti, near the site of the ancient
city of Elis (not to be confused with the state or province)
where Heracles cleansed the stables of King Augeias by
diverting the course of the Peneius into the royal yards. In
antiquity the quantity of sheep that roamed the river bank
accounted for the monstrous accumulations of cattle-dung
whose stench threatened to pollute the countryside. The ruins,
mostly Roman, are negligible.

North of Gastouni the road passes through Andravidha,
the Andreville of the Franks. It is difficult to associate this

Apollo, from the West Pediment of the Temple of Zeus at Olympia.

The monastery of Hosios Loukas, the south wall. Arches, sculptures in bas-relief, brick and marble revetments add to the splendour of this masterpiece of 11th-century Byzantine architecture. (p. 340).

Araxos

Kato Achaea

To Patras

Lapa

Nea Manolas

Spata

GLARENTZA
(ancient Cyllene)

Lechaina

Andravidha

R. Penelus

CASTEL TORNESE

ELIS (ancient)

Simopoulon

Cyllene Headland

Loutra Cyllene

Gastouni

Chavari

Amalias

Mouzaki

Marathias

Karatoula

Mirtia

Katakolon

PYRGOS

R. Alpheius

OLYMPIA

Epitalion

SAMIKON

Caiapha

ELIS

Kms. 0   5   10   15
Mls. 0   5   10

Kakavotos

unprepossessing village, once a Turkish market town, with the
flourishing medieval city, seat of successive princes – Champlitte, Villehardouin, Anjou, Savoy, Valois, Bourbon – who
ruled from here over the whole principality through an
administrative council composed of Latin lay and ecclesiastical
figures. Its historical buildings are gone: the palace in which
the Villehardouins dwelt in princely state and the chapel in
which they were buried; the hostelries of the religious orders –
Teutonic, Carmelite, Knights Templar. There is just one
Gothic ruin – not without charm. North of the main square,
the third turning to the left leads to the shell of the Latin
Church of St Sophia, built of honey-coloured stone in an
enclosure full of rose bushes and broods of ducklings. After
Olympia, with its glut of classical associations, this diffident
little medieval relic with pointed arches – choir, apse and rib-
vaulted side chapels – fascinates by sheer contrast. The church
was the scene of more than one political assembly; and it was
here that Geoffroy de Bruyères, the quixotic but much loved
Lord of Karytaena, came with a noose round his neck,
accused by the outraged barons of running off to Apulia with
a new mistress when he should have been crushing a Sclavonian revolt in the Southern Morea.

Crossing the railway line, the road enters the village of
Lechaina, distinguished only for being the birthplace of
Carcavitsas, a popular novelist and caustic commentator on
Greek society a t the turn of the century. A track to the left
(west) leads to a low sandstone table mountain crowned by
the keep of Castel Tornese, one of the grandest medieval
castles in the Morea, a landmark for miles around, overlooking the little port of Cyllene (not to be confused with the
Arcadian mountain). At this point, the traveller should
beware of being misdirected – either by guide-book, road
map or well-meaning local inhabitant. It is useful to bear in
mind that the name Cyllene (in Elis) can be applied to:

(a) The whole headland, which is also called Chelonatas,
'the turtle', because of its tortoise-like shape.

(b) The long stretch of sand-dunes south of the headland,
washed by the rollers of the Ionian Sea, site of the Olympic
Holiday Beach (bungalows to let).

(c) The village, thermal establishment (also called Loutra)
and little port (whence a ferry boat sails to the island of

Zante) at the foot of the castle on the south tip of the tortoise-shaped headland.

(d) The site of the ancient port of Cyllene to the north.

Castel Tornese is very impressive seen from the wheat fields surrounding it on the landward side. Built by the Franks, it was known as Clermont. Later the Venetians called it Castel Tornese, and as such most English writers refer to it. The Greeks call it Chlemoutsi. The castle's history begins with a quarrel between the Pope and the Achaean Prince, for Geoffroy II Villehardouin had no qualms about financing the construction of his new citadel out of revenues from sequestered ecclesiastical fiefs. Honorius II, amid all the flurry of crowning Frederick II Hohenstaufen emperor in Rome, found time to argue that church property – in this instance rich in oil, figs, raisins, honey and cochineal destined for lucrative Italian markets – could not be arbitrarily disposed of by a lay prince. Geoffroy refused to abandon his project, and the Pope excommunicated him. More interested in military defence than holy communion, the Prince of Achaea paid little attention to the fulminations of Rome and completed the castle, whose strategic position made the Morea safe against any possible Greek resurgence.

Geoffroy's brother and successor, William, increased the importance of the castle by establishing a mint. The coins, known as *tournois* (originally minted at Tours), were stamped with the prince's title, an effigy of the Church of St Martin de Tours and the inscription *De Clarencia*. From these *tournois* the castle afterwards acquired the Italianised name of Tornese. Here Marguerite, William's daughter and heir, was caught up in a web of intrigue spun by false claimants. A typically strong-minded Frankish princess, she refused to surrender her hereditary rights and, seeking support from a foreign power, arranged a marriage between her fourteen-year-old daughter and the Infante Ferdinand of Majorca. The Burgundian barons, fearing that the principality might pass into Spanish hands, seized Marguerite and cast her into a dungeon of the castle, where she died, the last of the Villehardouins, proud and courageous to the end, in 1315.

In the fifteenth century, Constantine Dragases, soon to become the last Byzantine emperor, resided here while conducting a brilliant campaign against the Italian buccaneer-overlords of the Morea – Tocco, Malatesta, Centurione – heirs to the old Frankish principality. In 1825, when Ibrahim's Egyptian army swept across the Morea, leaving nothing but an uninhabited wasteland in its wake, the castle was blown up.

You drive through the village of Cyllene in order to reach the castle entrance. A hexagonal court within a bailey is encircled by great walls, whose original height is defined by crenellations. Most of the ruins date from the original thirteenth century construction. The outer curtain wall sweeps majestically round the north, north-west and west sides. The outer gate at the north-west angle of the curtain penetrates a mass of masonry nearly 50 feet high. Two domed archways lead into an open space, followed by a vaulted passage and an enclosure with vestiges of houses. The inner gate of the keep is at the north angle of the hexagon, flanked to the right by a round tower. A vaulted passage opens into the north gallery – the best preserved of six halls strung round the keep like a chaplet. In this enceinte of spacious galleries, the nomadic Villehardouins often took up their official residence. Now empty except for nesting swallows, its barrel-vaulted roof partly open to the sky, the north gallery has seven arched windows on the south side. Although the other five galleries are not so well preserved, they contain traces of fireplaces which must have required enormous logs to heat the lofty stone halls when winter gales blew across the Ionian Sea. From all the galleries doors opened on to balconies, supported by arches, commanding a wide prospect of the dunes and surf-fringed beaches of the Zante channel.

It is an hour's walk along the stubble fields fringing the coast to the site of Glarentza, once the busiest medieval port in the Morea. The country is flat or faintly rolling, green but never wooded. Along the shore, white-crested waves break on alternating stretches of spiked boulders and seaweed-covered sands. Gulls squawk overhead. North, across the sea, loom island shapes, earthquake-shattered – mountainous Cephalonia and Homeric Ithaca; to the west the low outline of Zante crowned by its pyramidal peak. Here, too, was the ancient port of Cyllene, with its sanctuaries of Aphrodite and Asclepius, and a famous statue of Heracles in the shape of a monolithic phallus thrusting skywards, which Pausanias says was 'most devoutly worshipped by the inhabitants'.

Glarentza has no history before the Fourth Crusade, none after its destruction in the fifteenth century. Tufts of arbutus and heather cover the sandstone undulations of the deserted site, once so thriving a trading centre that the Glarentza branch of the Florentine banking firm of Acciajuoli equalled that of London in importance. Its harbour, with artificial defences, was full of Italian trading galleys, and among its buildings was a great Franciscan monastery. The weights and measures used for corn and wine at Glarentza became the standard form of notation throughout Latin Greece. Outside the city gates was paraded the Infante Ferdinand's head on a lance after his defeat by the Burgundian barons on the neighbouring field of Manolada (1315). His headless body was dispatched to Perpignan.

The only traces of Glarentza's medieval architecture are some fragments of moles and ramparts scattered about the shingly beach. The few blocks of heavy masonry, considerably older than any of the Burgundian or Angevin harbour works, are substructures of edifices dating back to the ancient Hellenic Cyllene. There is nothing else. For the city's total destruction – more complete than any caused by Goths or earthquakes – Constantine Dragases was responsible. Afraid of Glarentza falling into hands that might use it as a strategic linchpin for a Latin reconquest of the Morea, he ordered it to be razed to the ground. Its banks, trading houses, shops and churches were flattened, its bankers, merchants and seamen sent into exile. The Byzantine destruction of Glarentza – ironically enough on the eve of the Turkish conquest – marks the end of the Latin period, that strange elusive interlude in the history of Greece, when its sunny plains and rocky defiles became the hunting-ground of successive generations of uncouth Western adventurers. Of the Latin colonisers in Greece, only the Venetians now remained in their maritime strongholds.

Beyond Glarentza there is nothing but the flat dreary outline of Cape Araxos, an important Greek Air Force base. One walks back to Castel Tornese and regains the highway at Lechaina. To the north-west an extensive vine country, where some of the best wines in the country are produced, is succeeded by orchards of oranges, lemons and other citrus, which George Wheler, three hundred years ago, found 'much esteemed for their Taste'.

Patras, a town of over a hundred thousand inhabitants and terminus of the car ferry from Brindisi (travellers taking this route may have to spend a couple of hours here) has a number of arcaded streets and an air of having known better days (when it was the chief port for the export of currants). It only seems to liven up during Carnival, when its inhabitants stage spectacular processions and pelt masqueraders and decorated cars with chocolates wrapped in silver paper. Its position, however, is impressive. Immediately above the harbour, the town is strung out along a spur of Mt Panachaicus; higher up are wooded foothills with curiously convulsed shapes. To the north, across the gulf, two huge perfectly proportioned pyramids of limestone rise vertically from the mainland shore.

Patras played no important role in ancient history. Devastated during the wars between Rome and the Achaean League, it was repopulated by Augustus, who raised it to the rank of *Colonia Augusta Aroe Patrae*. Pausanias found the women, who outnumbered the men, of exceptional charm. Today the men of Patras, still in a minority, suffer from a reputation for effeminacy – probably no more justified than that of the men of Kalamata for their alleged predilection for pimping.

After Augustus, Patras' most distinguished visitor was St Andrew, who became its patron saint, converted the Roman governor and, it is believed, suffered his martyrdom here, when he was crucified on an X-shaped cross of olive wood, the *crux decussata* or St Andrew's Cross. No saint's relics seem to have undergone so wide a dispersal. Some went to Amalfi, a tooth, knee-bone and three fingers to St Andrews, and the head, after being bandied back and forth between Patras and Constantinople, was carried by the Despot of the Morea, fleeing from the advancing Turks, to Rome, where the Pope organised a great ceremony for its reception on the Mulvian bridge.[1] In spite of the farflung dispersal of his mortal remains, the first-called of Christ's disciples did not forget his flock at

1. The head is now back in Patras – in the Church of Ayios Andreas (Ayiou Andrea Street), on the site of a pagan oracle. Foundations of Roman ruins are visible to the right of the church. The skull will soon be removed to the adjacent Cathedral, now nearing completion: a wedding-cake affair built in a mixture of styles as grotesque as they are tasteless.

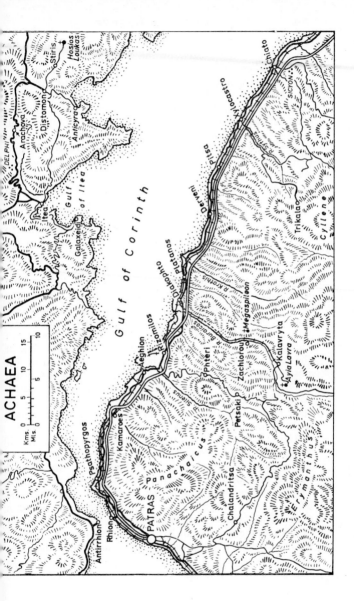

Patras. His intervention, relate the chronicles, saved the town from being sacked by the Sclavonians in the ninth century, when, in the form of a shining apparition, he personally hurled the invaders back from the battlements. After the Frankish conquest Patras became a strategically important barony, guarding the Corinthian Gulf from invasion from the west. It fell to the lot of Guillaume Aleman, a rough Provençal, who shocked the clergy by amputating the nose of the Latin archbishop's steward and converting his house of worship into a military redoubt. But the Church was ultimately avenged when another Latin archbishop became governor of Patras and declared the city a dependency of the papacy which subsequently rented it to the Serene Republic.

Patras re-enters the limelight in 1821 when it was a hot bed of intriguing Greek patriots. Whether the summons to hostilities against the Turks, leading to the outbreak of the War of Independence, was made at Patras or Kalavryta (see pp. 302-02) remains debatable. What seems fairly certain, as Finlay says, is 'that the people . . . took up arms boldly while their superiors were temporising'. Makriyannis, one of the most colourful leaders of the insurrection – a brave, honest and foul-mouthed soldier – has left, in his picturesquely written memoirs, a vivid account of the first days of the war in Patras. Pursued by Turkish secret agents, he sought refuge in the Russian Consul's house, where he was upbraided for his unsanitary personal habits. Venturing out with his sword drawn, he then witnessed the fighting which was very fierce, with the Turks holding the castle, while the Greeks drew up their ranks along the shore, 'and the sea was full of women and children up to the neck'.[2]

The **castle,** site of the ancient acropolis, is worth visiting if only for the magnificent view of the screen of mountains rising abruptly from the Locrian shore, with the channel fanning out into the Corinthian Gulf which cuts deep into a mass of mountain ranges for another hundred miles to the east. To the west spreads the town and the fertile Achaean plain. Ayios Nikolaos Street leads uphill. In adjacent Sotiriadou Street there is the shell of a Roman odeum, recently restored with red brick walls, white marble tiers and frag-

2. *The Memoirs of General Makriyannis,* 1779–1864, edited and translated by H. A. Lidderdale, Oxford University Press, 1966.

ments of mosaic paving. A charming but unimportant ruin. One climbs nearly a hundred steps to reach the summit of the acropolis, scene of a savage annual festival of Artemis Laphria. The method of sacrifice to the goddess of the chase, who seems to have possessed an even stronger streak of cruelty than her sister deities, was unusual in Pausanias' view. The festival opened with a procession in honour of the goddess winding up the hill, with the officiating maiden-priestesses (originally nine-year-old nymphs) riding in a chariot drawn by deer. Logs of fresh wood were then placed in a circle round the altar. The next day the logs were ignited and the worshippers cast live 'edible birds' into the flames and 'every kind of victim as well . . . boars, deer and gazelles; some being wolf-cubs, others the full-grown beasts . . .' together with the choicest fruit (always plentiful in Achaea).

The ruins of the castle are a hotchpotch of Byzantine, Frankish, Venetian and Turkish work. The approach by car is from the south side (Papadiamandopoulou Street) and then through a Frankish arch within a Byzantine structure. On the left (south-west angle) rises a well preserved Turkish octagonal bastion. The north curtain is ninth century Byzantine – one of the points from which the Greeks (with St Andrew's aid) threw back the Sclavonians. The enclosure is in the form of a triangle, with the quadrangular keep at the north-east base, with a tower at each end, reached along a causeway over a shallow moat and then through a ruined archway on which the effigy of a heraldic lion is carved. A walk along alleys of oleanders, bordered with arbours of honeysuckle and flower-beds shaded by cypresses and quince trees, brings one to a round Venetian bastion which marks the apex of the triangle.

Eight kilometres east of Patras a turning off the main road to Athens (left) branches off to Rhion, whence a car-ferry sails every twenty minutes to Antirrhion on the opposite coast. The narrow channel, called 'the little Dardanelles', between the Peloponnese and continental Greece, is one of the most important crossroads of sea and land communications in the country. East and west of the mile-wide waterway extend the two deep gulfs – of Corinth and Patras. Two low circular forts with outworks, built by Sultan Bayazit II on the site of two ancient shrines of Poseidon, face each other across the narrows. Known as the castles of the Morea and Roumeli,

they look oddly toy-like sprawling across the flat shore. At the
end of the War of Independence the castle of the Morea was
the last Turkish fortress to hold out – against the French. For,
after the battle of Navarino, the mutual rivalries of Britain and
Russia had delayed the pacification of the Morea, now
reduced to a desert by Ibrahim, while its remaining inhabitants
were terrorised and plundered by so-called Greek patriots,
whose conduct was often no better than that of common
brigands. So the French Government sent an army of fourteen
thousand men under General Maison which swept across the
Morea, clearing up pockets of Turkish resistance. Maison
was accompanied by a mission of engineers and welfare
officers who built roads and cleared up the shambles left by
the Turks. The only serious opposition he encountered was at
Rhion. If Greek independence owed its inspiration to the
people of the country, who endured and suffered and fought
for it, and Navarino made this independence a reality, it was
the French army that delivered the *coup de grâce*.

Beyond Rhion wooded coves, with rowing-boats moored to
jetties, alternate with reed-fringed strands and bushy promontories, but the beaches of this inland sea are not among
the best in Greece (there is a useful motel at Psathopyrgos).
Everywhere there are vineyards – this is the currant-producing
country – and flowering hedgerows. The mountains to the
south are still relatively withdrawn, but the convulsed nature
of their earthquake-rent forms is already apparent. In
antiquity the inhabitants were called 'coast-men' – for Achaea
was all coastline and little else. Aeghion, built on three levels,
is backed by terraced cliffs. Cafés spread across a square
shaded by plane trees, overlooking the railway station and
harbour, whence a car-ferry sails for Itea, the port of Delphi.
In the local sanctuary there was once a statue of Zeus in the
unusual guise of a boy. A prize for beauty was an indispensable qualification for the boy-priest chosen to look after
the image of the Father of the Gods. But as soon as his beard
began to grow he was dismissed and replaced by another
handsome stripling.

There is not much to do at Aeghion except to have a drink
(or indifferent meal) in the shady square and gaze across the
gulf at the Locrian mountains. Gone is every trace of the
sanctuary of Eileithyia, goddess of childbirth, and of the

headquarters of the Achaean League, whose federal assembly, one of the few serious attempts to achieve Hellenic unity, met twice a year at Aeghion to establish a common policy in resisting Macedonian and later Roman aggression. As though haunted by the ghost of the League, Greek patriots and priests from all over the Morea assembled here in February 1821 to fix the date for the decisive rising against the Turks.

East of Aeghion the village of Rizomilos marks the site of ancient Helice, an important Achaean city – said to have been founded by Ion, a temple-servant at Delphi and father of the first colonisers of Ionia – which sank into the sea one night during the fourth century B.C., drowning the entire population, as a result of a violent earthquake. The accompanying tidal wave so completely inundated the grove of Poseidon that only the tree-tops remained visible. In antiquity, the Achaean coast – a mountainous land mass rising precipitously from the Corinthian Gulf – was, as it still is, a country of earthquakes, which were regarded as manifestations of the anger of the gods, especially of Poseidon, always a truculent deity (in the case of Helice, he was incensed by the inhabitants' refusal to present a statue of himself to the Ionian colonists who were his protégés). The ever-present menace of earthquakes is always on the surface of the Greek consciousness. The inhabitants have had to come to terms with it and a whole lore of superstition has grown up around the manner and place in which the Earth-shaker will strike next. In ancient times earthquakes were said to be preceded by portents. The sun would be screened by a red or black haze and trees up-rooted by whirlwinds, springs would dry up, flames dart across the sky and stars change their shapes. These would be followed by the roar of winds below the earth's crust – the Earth-shaker working himself up into one of his tantrums. This ominous premonitory rumbling is as familiar to the present inhabitants of Achaea as it was to those of antiquity.

Around Rizomilos the coastal strip is at its widest, but soon the last spurs of the Arcadian limestone mass advance dramatically towards the sea, the chalky soil of their scarred and ravaged precipices sprinkled with pines, the lower ledges with spiky cypresses. South of Diakophto, which lies slightly inland, a huge wooded cleft cuts the mountain wall in two. This is the opening of the Buraicos gorge, so narrow and steep that no road penetrates it. The way up the beautiful defile, which leads to Megaspileon and Kalavryta, is by a miniature railway, partly rack and pinion (departures connect with arrivals of trains from Athens and Patras). The toy carriages sway and clatter as the wheels grind up the narrow track at an alarmingly steep gradient between walls of rock, then descend into little verdant glens, where pools of ice-green water surrounded by large smooth boulders are shaded by stunted plane trees. In autumn the imprisoning cliffs blaze with the orange, amber and coral of autumn leaves. Luxuriant ferns and sheets of maidenhair fringe the turbulent stream, and bright pink cyclamen grow beside the rail-track. There are no dwellings, and the sun only lights up the chasm with the briefest of shafts at noon. Somewhere along here was a cave sacred to Heracles, visited by pilgrims for purposes of divination. The suppliant, after offering a prayer before the demi-god's image, would throw dice on a table. The design they made was then interpreted through a set of explanations inscribed on a tablet.

As the altitude increases, the gorge widens out and the train stops at Zachlorou (the station for **Megaspileon**), a mountain hamlet, full of farmyard animals, where there is a modest little hotel. It takes three-quarters of an hour to walk to the monastery. The path mounts the maquis-covered hillside, above a mountain valley traversed by the Buraicos. The orchards and kitchen-gardens of the monks are terraced on the slope below the monastery. Along this path once came two Early Christian fathers from Jerusalem, to whom the Virgin had appeared in a vision, accompanied by SS. Andrew, Paul and Luke, and ordered them to travel to Achaea, where they would find her image in a cave in a mountain recess. When they reached the Achaean coast, the Virgin appeared before them again and directed their steps up the gorge to the foot of a great cliff, where St Euphrosyne, a shepherdess of royal blood, stood perched on a rock and hailed them. Imperiously striking the ground with her crook, she caused a spring to gush forth and commanded them to proceed to a cave where a dragon had its lair. A sudden flash of lightning caused the monster to drop dead and the pilgrims then found not only the holy icon of the Virgin but also the table on which St Luke had copied out his Gospel.

The cave subsequently became a place of pilgrimage and a monastery grew up around it – the *Mega Spileon*, the great cave. The present monastic buildings (they date from 1934, when fire destroyed the older edifice and its fine library) could not be more ugly. But their position, clinging, story upon story, to the surface of a vertical cliff whose flat summit is crowned by a cross, is very striking. In the fissures of the rock the shapes of three crosses are said to be discernible – to devout Orthodox eyes only. In Byzantine times the monastery was one of the most prosperous in Greece, and Pouqueville, historian, traveller and French Consul at the court of Ali Pasha in Yannina, relates how monks, fleeing southward after the fall of Constantinople, enriched the library with valuable manuscripts, including a copy of the lost comedies of Menander. When attacked by Ibrahim's 'Arab boys' in 1826, the monks saw a wall of rock suddenly rise up in front of the infidels, preventing them from advancing. Undeterred by this supernatural intervention, the Egyptian commander ordered a second detachment to climb to the summit of the cliff and roll down large boulders which crashed harmlessly into the valley below, just missing the monastery which is tucked away in a concavity of the mountainside.

In spite of the ugliness of the modern restoration, the interior of the monastery is worth visiting, if only to stroll along the gallery overlooking the mountain-girt valley. The church is dedicated to the Panayia Chrysopiliotissa ('The Virgin of the Golden Cave') and its most revered object is the icon discovered by St Euphrosyne and the two holy fathers which miraculously escaped destruction in successive fires. It is a primitive image of wax, attributed to the hand of that most prolific of iconographers, St Luke. During the War of Independence the icon talked frequently and wept when things went badly with the Greeks. The historiated pavement (imperial double-headed eagle, designs of the sun, moon and stars) is of the seventeenth century. Among the relics, now in the treasure, that survived the 1934 conflagration are St Euphrosyne's skull in a silver reliquary with trap-doors and one of her hands in a silver sheath, as well as the skulls of the two military saints, Theodore the Tyro and Theodore Stratelates – noticeably larger than St Euphrosyne's – and a fine twelfth-century cloisonné Gospel book cover.

Visitors may spend the night here – accommodation bein
provided in a guest-house – in return for a gratuity. The air
wonderfully salubrious, and there are beautiful walks alon
paths bordered by cyclamen in autumn, by primroses an
wild violets in spring.

From Zachlorou the little railway continues through mor
open country to **Kalavryta,** which is both a mountain reso
on the rugged Chelmos range and a national shrine. Stream
course through the village, and the waters of one, the Alyssu
were supposed to cure men and dogs of rabies. In the thirteent
century the great French family of La Trémouille dwelt in
castle on the table mountain that towers a thousand fee
above the village, guarding the Frankish-held coastline c
Achaea against incursions by Arcadian mountaineers. Th
ruins of the castle, known as Tremolo, are hardly worth th
climb. Although no more than a barony of strategic signif
cance, Kalavryta, in its alpine wilderness, could not hav
been a place devoid of all importance in subsequent centurie
for in the fifteenth Cyriac of Ancona came here and met
scholarly Greek gentleman who possessed a large library an
lent him a copy of Herodotus. Hardy mountaineers, th
Kalavrytans no longer show any indications of that boorish
ness and brutality for which their ancestors were so notoriou
that when their city, the ancient Cynaethra, was razed to th
ground by the Aetolians in the third century B.C., Polybiu
says other Greeks hailed the event as an act of god.

Above the town, on the north slope of Tremolo, stands
large cross commemorating a wholesale massacre of the mal
population by the Germans in 1943 as a reprisal against loca
guerilla activity. It was December and freezing. Men and boy
were led up the snow-covered slope and machine-gunned; th
principal buildings were gutted by fire. The hands of th
clock on the main church, the Metropolis, still stand at th
hour, 2.34, at which the massacre took place. That is wha
Kalavryta means to many Greeks.

Most of them, however, come, like good patriots, to visi
the **Monastery of Ayia Lavra,** situated seven kilometre
south-west of the village among ilex woods and cypres
alleys. Here Germanos, Metropolitan Bishop of Patras, a
intriguing prelate inspired by the most patriotic motives, i
supposed to have raised the standard of revolt against th

Turks beside the large plane tree in front of the main church on 25th March, 1821. That is the story – taught in schoolbooks, sung in verse and painted on canvas by countless Greek poets and artists. History only records that Moslem men were killed in Kalavryta by Greeks on or about 25th March, that Bishop Germanos was probably staying at Ayia Lavra on his way to Tripolis and that the monastery was one of the many places where the signal for the uprising was given.

The monastery, burnt by Ibrahim Pasha in 1826, rebuilt and burnt again by the Germans in 1943, has, in its post-war transformation, the air of a Western Roman Catholic convent, neat, well-ordered and colonnaded. The adjacent seventeenth-century cross-inscribed Church of the Dormition, more evocative of the Byzantine heritage, escaped both fires; in it was held the service which preceded the raising of the standard of revolt. The treasure contains sacerdotal vestments worn by local prelates at the historic service and the banner representing the Dormition of the Virgin – the hole in the face of the angel on the top left corner was made by a bullet – unfurled by the martial bishop. There are also manuscripts dating from the eleventh to the fourteenth centuries and a hideous Gospel book cover presented by Catherine the Great.

Apart from the railway there are three ways of regaining the coast by road from Kalavryta. The motorist will, of course, have travelled to Kalavryta along one of them. I describe them here in reverse, i.e. from Kalavryta to the coast.

(i) A dirt road climbs up into the mountains, passes through the bleak village of Phteri, crosses a watershed, descends through oak forests and enters the majestic Selinus gorge, with towering buttresses of rock overhanging a winding torrent bed which runs parallel to the Buraicos and is of equal natural beauty. The road reaches the coast at Aeghion (see pp. 298-99).

(ii) An asphalt road crosses a deserted plain streaked with poplars, ringed round to the south by a half-moon of Erymanthine crags pointing skywards in a series of ever-changing forms of naked limestone, their bases thickly wooded with spruce. Here Heracles stalked the Erymanthine Boar through snowdrifts until he netted the beast and carried it off, slung across his shoulders. Ancient vase-painters never tired of depicting the poltroon Eurystheus peeping out of his bronze jar at the terrifying creature with the monstrous tusks which Heracles brought back in chains to Mycenae. Beyond Chalandritsa, once a Frankish barony, forming part of the ring of strongholds encircling the Arcadian plateau, the road descends into the olive-covered plain of Achaea, bounded to the east by Erymanthus, whose weird crags are now replaced by a misty summit crowning a succession of alternating rounded and precipitous forms, breathtaking in the perfection of their composition. Below the slopes of Mt Panathaicus – a relatively featureless mountain compared with the splendours of Erymanthus – a path to the right leads through fields of pink garlic, blood-red adonis, funnel-shaped arums and Serapias orchids, to the little Church of the Panayia. This minor deviation is not recommended for the architectural beauty of the church – it has none. The dilapidated little chapel lies half-buried in a flowery field (you have to descend steps to enter it), but it is the oldest extant, now roofless, Byzantine church in the Peloponnese (possibly ninth century). Two marble columns with sculptured capitals, preserved intact, separate each of the tiny naves.

The rest of the way is through flat agricultural country to Patras (see pp. 294-97).

(iii) A dirt road (passable only in dry weather) runs more or less parallel to the Buraicos from Kalavryta to Diakophto.

East of Diakophto the coastline is very splendid and the Corinthian Gulf widens to its greatest extent. Across the water towers Parnassus, its bluish summit often wreathed in cloud, with the landlocked Gulf of Itea in the foreground. Somewhere on the stupendous mountainside is Delphi. The gorge of the Pleistos, which the sanctuary overlooks, is just visible in clear weather. On the Peloponnesian shore the Achaean mountains approach so close to the sea that they leave nothing but the narrowest coastal strip along which road and railway wind below pine forests. Along this road[3] – jammed with buses, ice-vans and fruit-carrying trucks – once rode from Corinth to Patras the first Crusaders, Champlitte and Villehardouin, to found the Principality of Achaea, which was to include the whole of the Morea and last over two hundred years. The chalky surface of the crags and escarpments is scarred with ravines and precipices. There are

3. The new highway follows a less interesting route farther inland.

two more great gorges, the Krathis (into which flows the trickle of the Styx) and the Sythas, which opens out fanwise to reveal terraces of the same whitish soil thick with dwarf cypresses. The inlets are bordered by vines, myrtles, orange trees and willows. It is as though the main characteristics of the Peloponnesian landscape – bare jagged mountain ridges, wooded gullies and pockets of shimmering fertility – had reached their apotheosis on this confined coastline.

At Xylocastro, probably the port of ancient Pellene, one of the twelve Achaean cities, which was said to have been founded by a giant, there are hotels, restaurants, rooms to let, a camping-ground reserved for the Club Mediterranée, a shingly beach bordered by a dark forest of tall umbrella pines – also a branch road to Trikala on the slopes of Cyllene, where there are skiing fields. One is soon at Chiato, below the terraced plateau of Sicyon, with the familiar hump of Acro-Corinth, key to all the treasures of the Peloponnese, squatting above the vineyards.[4]

4. The circular tour of the Peloponnese can be done in reverse. But most travellers generally like to begin with the Argolid, and I think the clockwise tour the most satisfactory from every point of view – geographically, chronologically, scenically. It builds up to the climax of Olympia, and the Achaean coast is a lovely tailpiece.

CHAPTER FIFTEEN

The Way to Delphi: Boeotia

❧

Thebes – Plataea – Leuctra – Thespiae – Haliartus – The Copaïc Basin – The Sanctuary of Apollo Ptoion – The Lakes – Gla – Orchomenus – Skripou: The Church of the Dormition – Levadeia – Chaeroneia – Daulis

BACK in Athens the traveller looks to the north-west: towards Delphi. The approach, through what are virtually the southern confines of Central Greece, is very rewarding. The landscape, particularly in the mountains, is superb; there are fragmentary ancient sites and Byzantine churches; mythology and history vie for supremacy; and the name of one famous battlefield succeeds another.

Beginning at Athens, road and rail follow a roughly parallel course along the east coast. After making a wide loop round a wooded spur of Parnes, they descend into the first and least interesting of the Boeotian plains, watered by the Asopus, the only local stream to flow straight into the sea without first forcing a way through an underground channel. A round trip is not practicable in Boeotia, which is virtually a large hollow isthmus enclosed between coastal ranges. Strabo calls it 'ribbon-like'. Most travellers cross it in a day, with deviations to the more important sites – Plataea, Orchomenus, Ptoion. Two days would allow time for a more roundabout itinerary. The best place to spend the night is at Levadeia, on the way to Delphi.[1]

Beyond the watershed between Attica and Boeotia the landscape becomes more continental, less Mediterranean. The vegetation is no longer confined to the olive, cypress and

1. In order to explore Boeotia thoroughly one can also stay at Delphi, where there is every kind of accommodation, from luxury hotels to rooms in village houses .The distance between Delphi and Levadeia is only fifty kilometres.

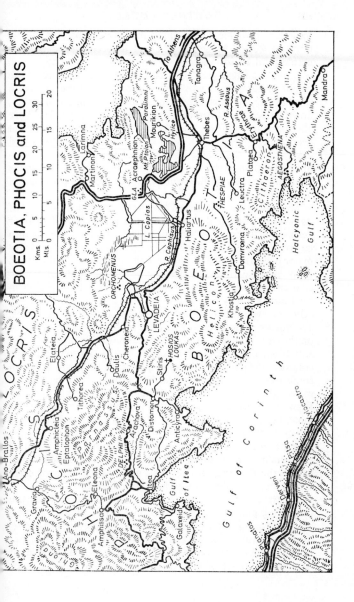

BOEOTIA, PHOCIS and LOCRIS

Kms. 0 ___ 5 ___ 10 ___ 15 ___ 20 ___ 25 ___ 30

Mls. 0 ___ 5 ___ 10 ___ 15 ___ 20

Lano-Brallos

L O C R I S

Larimna

Martinon

Paralimni

GLA Acraephnion

Mourikion

Mt. Ptoon

Hylice

Tanagra

Thebes

R. Asopos

ERYTHRAE

Graviá

Amphícleia
Eptalophon

Elateia

Tithorea

Daulis

Cheroneia

ORCHOMENUS

L. Copaïs

R. Cephisus

Haliartus

Leuctra

THESPIAE

Plataea

Cithaeron

AEGOSTHENA

Mandra

P H O C I S

Parnassus

Arachova

Distomon

LEVADEIA

R. Cephisus

Khostia

B O E O T I A

Helicon

Domvraena

Haliacmonic Gulf

Vlocastro

Amphissa

DELPHI

Eleona

Anticyra

HOSIOS LOUKAS

Stíris

Itéa

Galaxeidi

Gulf of Itéa

Gulf of Corinth

Derveni

Pisa

Vlocastro

oleander. The vine is sometimes restricted to back-plots and terraced ledges. Maize, cotton and tobacco take over. Flat agricultural plains succeed one another, flanked by barren foothills – austere grey on a cloudy day, fierce ochre at the height of summer – with hazy spruce-covered mountains in the distance, Parnassus towering above them all. The marshes, now drained and forming large tracts of wheat fields, once abounded in wildfowl, the lakes and streams in fish. Ancient geographers believed the subsoil to be full of hollows and caverns, and the whole country was famous for its mole-hills. The climate is one of extremes, and Hesiod complains about the severity of the winters. In summer the plains are a furnace.

The name Boeotia meant 'cow-land', so-called because of its pastures; and malicious Athenians often referred to their despised neighbours as 'Boeotian pigs', who were supposed to be gross, sensual and greedy. Nevertheless they produced two major poets: Hesiod and Pindar. Plutarch, too, was a Boeotian. In prehistoric times an obscure – we are told brilliant – civilisation flourished at Orchomenus. For a brief period in the fourth century B.C. Thebes was the first power in Greece, eclipsing even Sparta. The country also produced musicians. The auletic or flute reed, which had such a profound influence on the development of Greek music, grew in the marshes, and Amphion, the first harpist, taught the Lydian mode to the continental Greeks in Boeotia. Lying on the main invasion route from the north, Boeotia has witnessed the passage of many conquerors – Dorian, Persian, Macedonian, Roman, Frankish, Norman, Spanish, Turkish and German. Today the inhabitants are mainly devoted to agriculture. Remaining rooted to their fertile swamps, for the last two centuries they have produced no significant name, precipitated no event of consequence. Sometimes the grey skies and sudden chill winds, the flowering hedgerows and plum blossom of early spring are like a foretaste of Northern Greece.

The road runs westward across the Asopian plain. There are tantalising glimpses of the vivid blue streak of the Euripus, now approaching its narrowest point. Facing the channel is the bay of Aulis, where Agamemnon's fleet was becalmed and Iphigenia sacrificed (see p. 93). The ruins of the Temple of Artemis are too negligible to justify a visit. Tanagra, once

famous for its painted terracotta figurines,[2] has little to offer
but a military airport and the memory of the Triton, a sea-
monster with gills and a man's nose, the teeth of a beast,
sea-green eyes, the finger-nails of a shell-fish and a tail like a
dolphin's, which used to clamber up from the seashore, drink
quantities of wine and rob the local inhabitants of their cattle.
Beyond the airport there is a fork. The highway continues
westward. Another road turns east: to the Euripus and
Euboea. The third goes to **Thebes,** and 'no city in Greece', we
read in the Dictionary of Greek and Roman Geography,
'possessed such continued celebrity'. The celebrity is not
always to its credit.

Theban mythology is among the richest in Greece; Theban
history, if less distinguished, full of incident. But there is
practically nothing to see. Recalling its famous past, travellers
are drawn to the City of the Seven Gates, only to find themselves in a dreary provincial town with little to recommend it
except a good lightly resinated wine (rosé), a few ancient
stones and some dilapidated Turkish houses spreading across
a chain of hills overlooking the Cadmeian plain. But it is as
difficult to avoid Thebes geographically as it is to ignore the
fascination of its history and renown.

The centre of the town – a narrow main street with tavernas
and wine-shops – is on the highest hill, site of the ancient
acropolis, the Cadmeia. Cadmus came from Phoenicia; he
founded Thebes, colonised Boeotia and introduced letters into
Greece. Pindar says he married Harmonia 'with those full-
orbed eyes' and sowed the teeth of a dragon from which
sprang five warriors, ancestors of the Theban aristocracy,
including Labdacus, Laius and Oedipus. The city was built to
the accompaniment of music played by Amphion, father of
Niobe's luckless children, on a lyre, and the tunes were so
beautiful, according to Horace, that the stones moved of their
own accord and arranged themselves in perfect architectural
order. Here Cadmus' daughter, Semele, ravished by Zeus,
gave birth to Dionysus, who lost no time in planting the first
vine in this 'mother city' of his worshippers. Heracles, too,
was a Theban by birth; so was Teiresias, the famous seer,

2. Among the finest collections of painted terracotta figurines, often
called Tanagras, are those in the National Museum at Athens, in the
museum at Delphi and the British Museum.

whom Athena blinded because he caught a glimpse of her plunging naked into a stream on Mt Helicon. Afterwards she felt sorry for him and granted him the gift of inner sight.

Even in mythology, an aura of crime and pollution haunts the Theban palace, for an ancient prophecy had foretold that a son born of Laius and Jocasta would kill his father and marry his mother. Appalled by this prospect, the royal couple exposed their first-born child, a boy, with a spike thrust through his feet, on Mt Cithaeron. But a shepherd succoured the infant and took it to the Corinthian court, where it was given the name of Oedipus (Swell-foot), because of its swollen feet. One day, on his way back from Delphi, where he had been to consult the oracle, the young Oedipus met Laius and his suite in a narrow defile. In a scuffle with the royal attendants he accidentally killed the king. Unaware of the identity of his victim, he then crossed Boeotia, which was being ravaged by the Sphinx, a winged creature with a lion's body and a woman's head, and answered the monster's hitherto insoluble riddle, whereupon it fell off its rocky perch in dismay and died. As a token of gratitude, the Thebans proclaimed Oedipus king and offered him the hand of Laius' widow in marriage. So the prophecy was fulfilled and incest added to parricide. Years later another scourge swept the land. The plague, 'a fiery demon gripping the city', decimated the population because of the 'unclean thing born and nursed' in the soil of Thebes. In the charged atmosphere of pestilence and death the truth about Laius' murder leaked out, and the prophecy was confirmed by Teiresias. Undone by the gods, Oedipus gouged out his own eyes and Jocasta hanged herself. But the gods were not yet propitiated. The curse had to be visited upon that 'misbegotten brood', the children of Jocasta and Oedipus. After some years, their son, Polyneices, aided by his Argive allies, laid siege to the city, ringing its 'seven gates in a circle of blood', in a bid to deliver it from the tyranny of the usurper Creon. But Polyneices was killed in a brawl with his brother Eteocles and his body left unburied by order of Creon, who wished to make the consequences of armed revolt crystal-clear to his oppressed subjects. The stench of the corpse, 'eaten by dogs and vultures', filled the nostrils of the Thebans, and the air was polluted by the contaminated blood which Polyneices had inherited from Oedipus.

Defying Creon's order, Antigone, the dead youth's sister, secretly buried the body and poured libations over the grave, in conformity with religious practice. She also boasted of her action, invoking the gods as her champions. From this situation Sophocles develops the theme of his tragedy – the conflict between the laws of God, proclaimed by the self-willed heroine, and the laws of man, upheld by Creon, the stiff unbending bureaucrat. With the sacrifice of Antigone, buried alive 'in a strange cold tomb', the curse was finally expiated. For sheer tragic grandeur, dramatic unity and faultlessly worked-out plot there is little in Greek literature to match the Sophoclean version of these Theban legends.[3]

Of the ruins of the ancient city there are only some fragments of walls (south and west of the Cadmeia) between the streams of Dirce and Ismene, which provided the town with a copious supply of water that accounted for the quantities of mud, noted by Dicaearchus, a pupil of Aristotle, in the streets. Its monuments, though no doubt lavish, built of dark grey Boeotian marble which gave the city a sombre aspect, have never been described as beautiful. Traces of an imposing megaron, probably part of the palace of the Mycenaean age, where Laius, Oedipus and Creon held court, have recently been discovered and two strata of a palace annexe excavated in Pelopidas Street. Tablets found here are inscribed with Linear B dated to the thirteenth century B.C., a period associated with Creon's reign and the war of the Seven against Thebes.

The record of Thebes during the Persian Wars, when its army joined that of Mardonius in fighting the united Greeks, was beyond contempt. The slow-witted Thebans, obsessively jealous of the more lively Athenians, proved to be even more vindictive than the Spartans. After the Peloponnesian War, in which they sided with Sparta, they tried to persuade Lysander to raze Athens to the ground and sell the population into slavery. The Spartan leader, to his credit, refused. In the second half of the fourth century B.C., under the statesmanlike leadership of Epaminondas and Pelopidas, oligarchical Thebes appears in a more sympathetic light. But with the death of Epaminondas decline set in. After the Macedonian conquest, a revolt, instigated by the Athenian Demosthenes,

3. Sophocles, the *Oedipus Rex*, the *Antigone*.

who could be as meddlesome in politics as he was formidable in oratory, called down upon Thebes the fury of Alexander the Great. The future world-conqueror not only ordered his scarlet-coated soldiers to level the city to the ground, but also to slay six thousand Thebans and take thirty thousand prisoners. Arrian, his biographer and idolator, condones the action by pontificating, 'Thebes, at long last, had been punished for her treachery – she had paid the penalty for her betrayal of Greece in the Persian Wars.'

Alexander refused to sanction one sacrilege. His Aristotelian training may have inspired his decision to spare the house of Pindar, who was born here and is said to have begun his career as a lyric poet on a hot summer day when, pausing on the way to Thespiae for a rest, he fell into a deep sleep, whereupon a swarm of bees alighted on his face and covered his lips with wax. From then on he uttered nothing but honeyed words in bold dithyrambs that poured forth, declares Horace, 'like a river rushing down from the mountains and overflowing its banks'.

After Alexander's sack, the city sank into oblivion until the Middle Ages, when Benjamin of Tudela found it large and prosperous, full of Jewish silk-workers, whose lavish creations adorned Byzantine emperors and their consorts. The silk trade even survived the twelfth-century invasion of the Normans, who carried off numbers of Theban weavers to Palermo. The trade is dead now, but mulberry trees still grow around the town. With the arrival of the Frankish barons, Estives, as it was then called, became the seat of the de la Roches, who styled themselves 'Dukes of the Athenians and Thebans'. The plight of thirteenth century Athens must indeed have been tragic for them to choose this dreary humid place instead of the Attic city of light for their official residence. At the west end of Pindarou Street, there is one remaining vestige of the Frankish period: a fine squat tower, called Santameri (corruption of St Omer), part of the castle built by Nicholas de St Omer, part-lord of Thebes. Beside the tower is the **museum,** which possesses an impressive **Archaic Apollo** and curious **funerary stelae** of black stone with traces of painted bas-reliefs depicting Boeotian warriors in battle.

The normal axis of travel in Boeotia is east–west or vice-versa, with deviations into the foothills of the ranges flanking

the 'ribbon-like' plains. The first is to the south, along the old
Athens–Thebes road through undulating fields, home of the
Tulipa boeotica, a lovely bell-shaped red tulip with a black
centre in the form of a star. At the village of Erythrae, a third
of the way up the ascent of Cithaeron, a turning to the right
(west) leads to the site of **Plataea**. Boeotia has always been
the scene of violent armed clashes. None does more credit to
Greek arms than the third and decisive battle in the Persian
Wars.

A circuit of walls, about two and a half miles in circumference, can be traced round the cornfields sloping down
towards the stream of the Asopus. After Mardonius, the
Persian commander, had destroyed and evacuated Athens,
the allied contingents began to assemble in 479 B.C. on the
slopes of Cithaeron. It was a rare demonstration of Greek
unity – a fact that makes Theban perfidy appear all the more
contemptible. The Greeks, under the supreme command of
Pausanias, the Spartan general, a nephew of Leonidas,
numbered a hundred and ten thousand. Athens, a maritime
power, accepted second place with a good grace. Mardonius,
one of the principal architects of the grand design for the
Asiatic invasion of Europe, was torn between a premonitory
hunch to get out of Greece before the pincers closed round his
cumbersome army of three hundred thousand men and a
desire to avenge the humiliation of Salamis. Informed by his
scouts that the Greeks were massing at the Isthmus in order
to deploy into Boeotia, he resolved to make a decisive stand
on the Asopus, where his rear would be defended by friendly
Thebes.

From the foot of the low walls overlooking the valley, it is
possible, with the aid of Herodotus, to reconstruct the different
moves in this complex battle. While the Greek armies were
taking up their positions on the foothills, a bold cavalry
charge was made by Masistius, a distinguished Persian cavalry
officer, clad in a scarlet tunic and golden-scaled corselet. All
went well until Masistius was killed, whereupon the Persians,
says Herodotus, 'shaved their heads, cut the manes of their
horses and mules, and abandoned themselves to such cries of
grief that the whole of Boeotia was loud with their cries'. The
omens warned both armies to remain on the defensive. The
one that crossed the Asopus first was doomed. So for ten days

the opponents glared at each other across the stream. In the end, Mardonius, taken in by a series of Spartan and Athenian feints and a constant changing of the dispositions of allied units, believed the Greeks were preparing for flight. Ignoring the omens, he led a yelling ill-equipped rabble across the stream, where it was opposed by the highly professional, heavily armed Spartan units. Reinforced by the Athenians, the Spartans took a crippling toll of the barbarian levies. Mardonius, mounted on a white charger, fought bravely, but as soon as he was killed by a Spartan, panic seized the Persians, who fled in a disorderly rout towards their stockade, where the Athenians, masters in siege warfare, quickly surrounded them. The Thebans, too, fought with the fury of desperation. It was perhaps poetic justice that they should be slaughtered to a man by the Athenians, out of envy of whom they had betrayed Greece. In the great pursuit that followed, the allied contingents poured down the gullies and plundered Mardonius' sumptuous tent. The booty, equally divided among the allies, was fabulous in the eyes of helot and hoplite alike. There were not only enough silver tables, gold-inlaid couches, richly woven carpets to go round, but also wagons full of goblets, not to mention droves of camels, pack-animals and Persian women. The sight of so much opulence moved Pausanias, the Spartan general, to ask why such a wealthy people should have wanted to rob the Greeks of their only possession – their poverty. Glutted with triumph, plunder and slaughter, the Greeks returned to the agora of Plataea, where they sacrificed to Zeus Eleutherius (The Liberator). So 'the prophecy was fulfilled', concludes Herodotus, 'and Mardonius rendered satisfaction to the Spartans for the killing of Leonidas'. After Plataea the Great King made no further attempt to cross the Hellespont on a bridge of boats.

There are no vestiges of the ancient township, whose name derives, according to Strabo, from the word *plati*, a blade, because the Plataeans used oars when rowing across the swamps around the Asopus. On a terrace near the north-west wall there are foundations of a temple, possibly of Hera. There is no sign of the sanctuary of Demeter around which there was fierce fighting, but on whose holy ground no Persian corpse was found. Herodotus suggests that the goddess, remembering the barbarians' desecration of her most sacred shrine at Eleusis, prevented them from setting foot in her Boeotian temple.

Plataea has a noble record of fidelity to the Athenian alliance, dating from the late sixth century B.C. At Marathon they were the only state to send a contingent to assist the hard-pressed Athenians. During the Peloponnesian War they never wavered and withstood a famous siege for two years. When the depleted garrison was forced to surrender, the Thebans did not leave a single Plataean alive and they destroyed all the buildings. Plataea thus paid heavily for her loyalty to Athens. Philip of Macedon restored the city and Alexander the Great built the ramparts, which are now very ruined (best preserved on the west side); but one can walk for quite long stretches along a line of low walls overlooking the level meadows where so many Persian men, hopes and ambitions perished.

The next battlefield on the westward route represents a historical milestone of a very different character. Of the victory of Thebes over Sparta in 371 B.C. at Leuctra, Pausanias says it was 'the most famous ever won by Greeks over Greeks'. It is the familiar story of Greek tearing Greek to pieces. Spartan supremacy was unquestioned in the mid–fourth century. Thebes had replaced Athens as the second power in the country. Thebes therefore must be crushed. The Spartan helots were spilling over Boeotia when the clash came.

Just before re-entering Thebes from Plataea, a dirt road to the left (south-west) crosses a stretch of treeless but well-watered country to the hamlet of Leuctra on a low hill overlooking the battlefield. The site is marked by a modern plinth adorned with some ancient marble slabs.

At first the Theban leaders were nervous about engaging such a formidable foe on open ground, but Epaminondas, who had revitalised the state and glorified Theban arms, was confident, in spite of his inferiority in numbers, in the fighting qualities of the Sacred Band and the dash of the Boeotian cavalry. The omens, too, were auspicious. In Thebes temple doors opened of their own accord, and the arms in the shrine of Heracles vanished overnight – an indication that the demi-god himself had sallied forth to battle. A white spider's web was spun across the entrance to the sanctuary of Demeter, and while the debate – to fight or not – was going on, a frisky little mare cantered into the Theban camp. This was taken as a further favourable augury, and the mare was duly sacrificed.

The battle was fought north of a tumulus easily identified near the commemorative plinth. The victory was largely due to the brilliant tactics of Epaminondas. Instead of attacking along the whole line, he formed a wedge; behind followed a 'massed formation', says Xenophon, 'of at least fifty shields in depth'. A fierce charge made by this solid mass in echelon on the enemy right wing was completely successful, for the Spartans, though more numerous, were strung out in a line and therefore relatively thin on the ground at the point where the Theban thrust broke their ranks. The Spartans were utterly confused by these novel tactics, and, to make matters worse, Cleombrotus, their king, was killed early in the engagement. The Theban cavalry completed the victory by isolating and cutting the bewildered helots to pieces. The Spartan defeat came, in the words of Grote, 'like a thunderclap upon everyone in Greece . . .' It changed all military values and upset the balance of power between the city states.

The tumulus we now see is probably the Spartan sepulchre. There is little else. The plinth, we were told, is to be crowned by a statue of Epaminondas. I asked a peasant if there were any *archaia* (ancient things) nearby. He led me across a field, scrabbled among the corn and pointed to a stone slab, which might have formed part of a stele and was inscribed with the name MYPON, projecting out of the muddy soil. The inscription could not have referred to the sculptor, who, although a native of neighbouring Eleutherae, died about a hundred years before the battle. The slab was ploughed up, the man said, by a tractor in 1963.

West of Thebes, another dirt road crosses a hilly region as far as Thespiae, which, with Plataea, shares the distinction of being one of the two Boeotian cities that remained unrelentingly hostile to Thebes, refused to Medise and was consequently burnt by Xerxes.

The ruins, barely identifiable (foundations of a temple of the Muses), are scattered around the plain below the village. The deity worshipped here was Eros, hatched from the Cosmic Egg, a primeval deity, symbolising sexual vigour, armed with flaming torches which he aimed at gods and mortals alike. It is not until Hellenistic times that Eros is sentimentalised by poets and artists, becomes the son of Aphrodite and finally the plump little Cupid rendered so popular by Roman artists. The original Greek Eros was a more virile deity. A festival in his honour, known as the *Erotidia* (the Erotics), was held every four years, and the cult statue consisted of an erect monolith to which every bride offered a tress of her hair representing her youth and a girdle symbolising her virginity. In the fourth century B.C., Lysippus, most prolific of Greek sculptors, carved a famous Eros which still embellished the Sanctuary of Love at Thespiae in the time of Cicero and was later removed to Rome by Nero. Another statue of the god, the work of Praxiteles, was presented to the city by its most famous inhabitant, the courtesan Phryne. Of humble Thespian origin, Phryne gained a living by gathering capers until she realised the advantages that could be derived from her sublime beauty and accordingly became the most famous *hetaira* in Greece, grew immensely rich and inspired some of the great works of art of the period. Praxiteles was hopelessly infatuated with her, and his gold statue of her stood in the holiest sanctuary in Greece – that of Apollo at Delphi. No Greek considered this a sacrilege. On one occasion, standing on trial at the Areopagus in Athens, she bared her divine bosom and was promptly acquitted by the judges.

Near here, too, flowed the reed-fringed stream into which the youth Narcissus gazed so long and intently that he fell in love with his own image. How perverse, it seems, that a place so wholly devoted to the pursuits of love should retain so little to recall its erotic past.

Of the supposedly idyllic beauty of the Valley of the Muses (roughly two hours' drive and walk west of Thespiae) there is also little evidence. Only some wild almond trees, and the fir-covered slopes of Helicon above. There are traces of an altar and of the cavea of a theatre. On the way to the valley (to the right) a ruined Hellenic tower crowns a cone-like eminence, site of ancient Ascra, birthplace of Hesiod. South-west of Thespiae, a passable road leads to Thisbe, the Homeric 'haunt of doves', where there are polygonal walls north-west of the village and remains of classical towers on the plateau to the east.

Beyond the fork to Thespiae the main Thebes–Levadeia road leaves the melancholy Theban plain. The ground rises,

then dips down into the basin of the former Lake Copais: a
shimmering expanse of cotton fields, surrounded by cliffs and
mountains which, in early antiquity, rose sheer from the
shallow water's edge, intersected into squares and rectangles
by avenues of poplars and willows. The haunt once of cranes,
now of migratory storks, the lake or swamp – today the main
cotton-growing region of Greece – was reclaimed by French
and British engineers at the end of the nineteenth century.
Strabo's assertion that the whole basin had in fact been
drained by the inhabitants of ancient Orchomenus is borne
out by the discovery of a primitive but intricate system of
dykes and canals encircling the entire Copaïc 'lake', whereby
the various streams were channelled by an ingenious network
of canals into *katavothras* which disgorged their waters into
the Euboean channel. Archaeologists have located long low
mounds, the remains of ancient dykes, stretching across
considerable tracts of the plain, either in unbroken lines or
with gaps at intervals. Here, as indeed throughout most of
Boeotia, one is constantly aware of geology: of subterranean
channels coursing through limestone ranges; of curious
hump-shaped mounds of slate-grey rock emerging out of a
mirage of sun-drenched arable land; of lakes descending on
different levels like stepping stones towards the Euboean
channel.

At the south-east end of the basin, beyond Mt Sphingion,
a grim pyramidal rock, identified with the height off which the
Sphinx fell when Oedipus answered her riddle, lies Homer's
'grassy Haliartus', still surrounded by 'well-watered meadows'.
Pausanias found the eels of the lake here 'of great size and
very pleasant to the palate'. Below the city walls, Lysander,
the most powerful man in Greece after the Peloponnesian
War, met his end during the Boeotian War of 395 B.C., killed
by a native of Haliartus who 'bore on his shield the device of
a dragon', thus fulfilling a prophecy, says Plutarch, warning
Lysander to beware of 'the earthbound dragon following
behind'. Here, too, died Teiresias, the blind prophet, after a
life covering the span of seven generations, of a chill caught
from drinking ice-cold water from a spring.

At Haliartus the traveller has the choice of two routes.
One leads direct to Levadeia (and on to Delphi or northwards
into Central Greece), skirting the base of Helicon, whose

constantly changing outlines dominate much of the Boeotian landscape. Neither as grand as Taygetus nor as beautiful as Parnassus – and not nearly as high as either – it is often well-wooded, rugged but never forbidding. Its beehives produce a perfumed honey, and in antiquity the grasses and roots indigenous to its maquis-covered sides were said to be so sweet-tasting that they served as an antidote to the venom of vipers. George Wheler, roaming its thyme-scented slopes in the seventeenth century, picked quantities of golden-crowned polyanthus narcissus which grow in the protected valleys beyond Levadeia on the way to Delphi, and he climbed to a sufficient height to see 'great stores of the Male Fir tree . . . whose Turpentine is very fragrant . . . and some of the Leopard's bane, whose root is like a Scorpion', and arbutus, whose strawberry-coloured fruit he found delicious.

The other route, of greater interest, follows an arc round the plain, reaching Levadeia via Ptoion, Gla and Orchomenus (a long half-day). From Haliartus a dirt road cuts across the cotton fields to the north, intersected by poplar-lined canals, and reaches the main Athens–Salonica highway below a line of hills, whose rocky sides rise abruptly from the level board of the reclaimed swamp, and around which the local inhabitants used to sail in flat-bottomed boats in ancient times.

A miniature canyon cuts through the wall of cliff, opening out into a rugged little valley entirely enclosed by beige-coloured hills. Above the village of Acraephnion, where the Thebans took refuge after the destruction of their city by Alexander the Great, a track climbs the western slope of **Mt Ptoion** (the ancient Ptoom or Ptoon), which has a triple peak and was named after a son of Apollo. It is not easy to locate the ruins. A whitewashed chapel, shaded by a large holm-oak, is the landmark to look for. Behind it rise the three terraces of the **Sanctuary of Apollo,** an oracular seat, consulted among others by Mardonius on the eve of Plataea through a Carian interpreter, to whom the oracle replied in fluent Carian, to the bewilderment of his Theban guides. On the first terrace are the base of a tholos building and a rectangular cistern where consultants purified themselves before ascending to the second terrace, across which lie traces of stoas buttressed by a few courses of the retaining wall, and finally to the third, marked by foundations of a Doric temple of Apollo. Here was found the great Archaic statue of Apollo Ptoion, now in the National Museum at Athens (see p. 76). Pindar writes that Apollo, before choosing the site, whirled around in the heavens and 'passed over the land and over all the sea, and stood on the lofty watchtowers of the mountains, and explored the caverns, while he laid for himself the foundation of his groves . . .' There is no longer a grove: only aromatic shrubs and a few holm-oaks. Above the temple the foundations of a spring called Perdiko Vrysi (The Partridge Spring) that gushes out of the rock has been identified as the site of the oracle. The waters of the spring connect with the cistern below. Climbing from one terrace to another, one tends to sink ankle-deep into a soft mossy deposit seamed with trickles of water. It is as though the whole mountain, through which some of the main *katavothras* carve their way towards the sea, had a subsoil of underground rivulets. From a ledge slightly south-east of the ruins there is a fine view of the winding inlets of Lake Hylice below.

The lake itself, main water supply of Athens, is skirted by the Athens–Salonica highway. Obviously once a crater, on a lower level than the Copaïc basin, its configuration is of fascinating complexity – a series of figures of eight of different dimensions. Barren rocky banks rise from a succession of fiords of crystal-clear water. At times the conical summits and contorted volcanic shapes overlooking the winding shore give the impression of a lunar landscape; at others of Japanese prints. A *katavothra* connects Hylice with the smaller lake of Paralimni, the ancient Schoenus, which lies in an even deeper depression, and can be approached by a track off the highway which passes through the village of Mourikion and descends into a narrow shut-in basin, where the shallow water lies motionless in an elliptical expanse against a screen of slate-grey cliff. It is an astonishing sight: unexpected, desolate, bizarre.

Rejoining the highway and following a north-west course, one reaches the village of Castro. A track to the right, less than a mile long, runs across the fields to the so-called **Isle of Gla,** one of the strangest prehistoric sites in Greece. The 'isle' – it obviously was one once, washed by the shallow waters of the Copaic lake – is a natural curiosity: a low triangular eminence, with a ramp (one of the two means of entry) on the north, flanked by two defensive buttresses, and a two-mile circumference of Cyclopean walls without towers that follow the contours of the cliff. Dominating the north-east basin below Mt Ptoion, it may have been a Minyan principality, forming part of a system of fortifications guarding the shores of the lake. The cliffs, never higher than two hundred feet, are pitted with caves and *katavothras*. On the inner side of the gate to which the ramp leads there was a small courtyard. Below the north-east redoubt is another double gate. Moving north-west you reach the central redoubt; north of it are foundations of a palace with two wings (L-shaped), built of sun-dried bricks (the base is of stone), on the highest point of the eminence. There are traces of corridors, two megarons (one in each wing) and square apartments with anterooms common to Mycenaean citadels. Thirty-nine doors have been identified. All around, the countryside is dotted with rocky humps, like huge grey animals squatting on the cornfields of the drained marshland. Gla is one of the few ancient sites in Greece without a single mythological or historical association. This fact – more than the exiguous ruins – exercises a curious fascination. There is not a house, not a tree, not a browsing goat. Only the bees, the sage and the fennel.

Another dirt road runs alongside canals from Castro to the village of Orchomenus. Yellow water flag iris border the banks of the Cephisus, Aeschylus' 'many-distaffed river', which rises in the Phocian mountains and flows, says Hesiod, 'like a dragon . . . in winding courses', across the plain. Another stream, the Melas, issues out of a *katavothra* at the north base of Mt Acontium (the Javelin), a barren forbidding chain of hills guarding the approaches to this region of fens through which streams course sluggishly between banks of waving canes. Famous for its dark-coloured water (it is now called the Mavropotami, 'the black river'), the Melas, says Plutarch, 'augmented at the summer solstice like the Nile', and was the only stream in Greece navigable – presumably by flat-bottomed boats – at its source. Between the road and Mt Acontium extend traces of one of the oldest prehistoric sites in Greece.

Indeed so great was the antiquity of **Orchomenus**, capital of the Minyans (a people who had descended into Boeotia from Thessaly), that its golden age was little more than a memory in Classical times.[4] The legendary king of the country was Minyas, and the Argonauts, including Jason, were descended from his daughters, who were turned into bats because they refused to worship Dionysus. Thebes paid tribute to Orchomenus, and there is a legend that on one occasion the Orchomenian ambassadors, entering Theban territory to collect long overdue revenues, were confronted by a defiant Heracles, who cut off their noses and ears and then sent them back to Orchomenus with their dismembered features strung round their necks. This was too much for Orchomenian pride. In the war that ensued the Orchomenians were defeated by the Thebans, led by Heracles, whom Athena provided with divine armour.

The most impressive surviving edifice of Minyan civilisation is the **Treasury of Minyas,** claimed by Pausanias to be the first treasury ever built and 'a wonder second to none either in Greece itself or elsewhere . . .'[5] Situated just off the main road, this beehive tomb, excavated by Schliemann, is, like the Mycenaean royal mausoleum, with which it is probably contemporary, approached by a *dromos* (the sockets in the entrance platform can still be identified), cut through the hillside, leading to a tapering doorway with a formidable lintel of blue schist. The diameter of the vaulted rotunda, now roofless, is about 45 feet. Holes for bronze rosettes are discernible on the walls, of which eight courses survive. The fact that the circular chamber is open to the sky enables the spectator to get a better impression of the concavity of the structure than is possible in the Treasury of Atreus at Mycenae. On the other hand, there is a total absence of that atmosphere of centuries-old putrefaction which contributes so much to the macabre quality of the Mycenaean sepulchre. A corridor connects the rotunda with a small square funerary chamber, with palmettes and rosettes carved in low relief on the ceiling, where the original Minyas and later Hesiod (*c.* eighth century B.C.) were supposed to have been buried.

From the Treasury the way up to the citadel is steep and

4. The Boeotian Orchomenus should not be confused with the ancient city of the same name in Arcadia (see pp. 176-77).
5. One should ask at the Church of the Koimesis (Dormition) at Skripou (the modern agglomeration) for the guardian who has the key of the Treasury.

stony. One passes traces of buildings of the Neolithic, third millenium B.C. and pre-Archaic periods. The upper terraces were reconstructed by Philip and Alexander. On the final jagged outgrowth of rock are the remains of a square tower. The ramparts, best preserved on the south side, are of the fourth century B.C. Although by this time the greatness and wealth of Orchomenus were no more than a memory, Mt Acontium still possessed strategic value, dominating the bottleneck between the Cephisian and Chaeroneian plains.

The end of Orchomenus came in 364 B.C., as a result of the endemic feud with Thebes. Epaminondas was cruising with the fleet in the Hellespont, Pelopidas campaigning in Thessaly. Three hundred Orchomenian horsemen, aided by Theban traitors, prepared an attack on Thebes. The plot was betrayed and Orchomenus totally destroyed, its male population slaughtered and the women and children sold into slavery. This barbarous sack aroused the revulsion of neighbouring states and confirmed the reputation of cruelty earned by the Thebans.

Pindar and Theocritus refer to the Orchomenian worship of the Charites or Graces, at whose festival musical contests were held and poets and musicians from all over Greece took part. The reeds growing on the banks of the Cephisus provided the flutes which exercised so much influence on the development of Greek music. The plangent tone of the Epirot *clarino* can be traced back to the melancholy warble of the Cephisian flute-reed, most ancient of wind instruments. By modern standards, music in ancient Greece could never have been more than a subsidiary art form. In the scale of modulations and inequality of its tones, in the conservatism of its traditions and close associations with poetry, modern Greek folk music (including *bouzouki*) probably owes much to ancient scores, the notation of which consisted of small letters between the lines of a stanza inscribed on stone or marble. Of these scores few survive – none earlier than the fourth century B.C. The Greeks believed in the moral mission of music, in the exalted precepts contained in the words of a song. The instrumental section was a mere accompaniment, sometimes frowned upon as a distraction, even considered frankly immoral. Bowing was unknown. Gut-strings, however, were twanged or plucked, just as the wire strings of the *bouzouki* are today. The ear of the average modern Greek is still much more closely attuned to the lyrics than to the melody of a popular song.

The temple of the Charites is thought to have been situated east of the road, opposite the Treasury, probably on the site now occupied by the Byzantine church. The Charitis – Hesiod says there were three – were the personification of all that is most agreeable in life – love, beauty and grace. They were much given to laughter and very agile, not only simpering and singing, but also dancing and leaping about, bathing in streams and crowning themselves with garlands of roses. At the wedding of Cadmus and Harmonia they delighted the guests with their pretty songs. Pindar says they also aided Orchomenian runners to win races at Olympia.

The site of their revelry is now surrounded by cotton fields, canals and mud-flats, and their temple replaced by the Byzantine **Church of the Koimesis (Dormition of the Virgin)** of Skripou, the oldest cross-inscribed edifice in Greece. An inscription dates it to 874. Constructed out of large blocks of stone of unequal size, clearly of ancient origin (such as the drums of columns built into the interior west wall), the general effect, while one of spaciousness and sturdiness, is heavy and awkward. The architect, while employing the Greek Cross plan, retained certain features of the basilica: the three naves, for instance, and the triple windows of the narthex, each with two columnettes. More attractive are the courses of sculptural relief – a form of church decoration soon to disappear from Byzantine art – separating the three zones of the interior. In the apse we see sculptured grapes, vine leaves and donkeys, in the course round the base of the dome birds with worms in their bills. Marble reliefs also decorate the exterior: an ornamental inscription round the whole of the apse, a human-headed monster chasing a boar, a griffon pouncing on a stag. On the south wall a sundial, flanked by peacocks, is embedded in stone-work. Children play in the forecourt and old women sit in the sun, while hens peck desultorily among truncated pillars and sculptured marble slabs, one of which consists of the cornice of an iconostasis carved with effigies of birds and animals, crosses and stylised foliage.

There is a tailpiece to the story of Skripou. One day in October, 1943, a band of Greek Resistance fighters took refuge in the church. The autumn rains had set in, and the

Cephisus had overflowed its banks. A German armoured column rumbled down the road, with guns trained on the church; but as the tanks closed round, their chains sank in the mire. A pandemonium of guttural cries and martial orders broke out, while the thunder echoed in the defiles of Helicon and Parnassus. Suddenly an apparition of the Virgin, unaffected by the sheets of rain, appeared above the dome of the church. As soon as they had extricated themselves from the bog, the German tanks withdrew. Not a shot was fired. An ugly modern icon in the church commemorates the event.

Nearby (a few minutes' walk to the right of the church) there is a taverna called Pestropha (The Trout) where one can lunch on fried or grilled trout, whose spawn has been imported from Switzerland by the enterprising landlord. In his back garden sleek rainbow trout are bred in tanks filled with water from the Cephisian streams. They eventually find their way to the kitchens of the Hilton in Athens.

Close to Orchomenus lies **Levadeia,** chief town of Boeotia, its houses with red-tiled roofs spreading fanwise across the foothills of Helicon on either side of a narrow gorge. A clock tower, presented by Lord Elgin, is a conspicuous landmark. Behind the town rises a screen of spruce-covered heights. Westward towers Parnassus, misty blue in colour, its summit snow-capped from November to May, often wreathed in cloud. In its elevation, in the symmetry and harmony of its forms, in its dramatic upward surge from the plain, no other Greek mountain, except Taygetus, is more impressive. Levadeia, with a local trade in blanket-making, has an animated air. Scarlet, green and magenta blankets hang out to dry from wooden balconies, ramshackle dwellings spread across the slope of a rocky eminence crowned by a medieval castle, and streams cascade down the hill. Buses bound for Delphi stop on the main road which skirts the lower town, and passengers get out to buy *souvlakia* fried on wooden skewers from itinerant *restaurateurs.*

At the foot of the castle hill the **Hercyna** issues out of a sunless canyon. Plane trees form arbours over the ice-cold stream, which is spanned by a little arched Turkish bridge. The springs on the east bank flow into two pools: Lethe (Oblivion) and Mnemosyne (Remembrance). On the west bank niches for votive offerings have been carved out of the cliff-side. The largest of these forms a kind of stone chamber with rock-hewn seats, the favourite refuge of Turkish governors who came here to smoke their narghilehs or doze through long soporific summer afternoons. Everywhere there is water: oozing, trickling, gurgling. Below the rocky precipices, among the shady planes, there are open-air cafés and tavernas.

Nearby was the Oracle of Trophonius, consulted, among others, by Croesus and Mardonius, and by Plutarch in the second century A.D. when all other Boeotian oracles had fallen silent. The oracular chamber was in an underground chasm in a sacred grove containing a temple with a statue of Trophonius, a Minyan semi-deity, by Praxiteles. Leake, most reliable of nineteenth century topographers, placed the grove on the east bank of the Hercyna, but not as far as the upland plateau associated with the hunting-grounds of Persephone, to which the gorge ultimately leads.

The protocol of consultation is fascinating. For several days the consultant, lodged in a chamber sacred to Good Fortune, was not allowed to have a hot bath. He could, however, wash himself in the icy waters of the Hercyna. After being anointed and rubbed with oil by thirteen-year-old boys, he would be handed over to priests who made him drink from the waters of Lethe so as to forget everything he had ever known. Afterwards he would drink from those of Mnemosyne in order to remember what he heard in the oracular pit. Dressed in a linen tunic girdled with ribbons, he was conducted to the fissure which was in the shape of a bread-oven. On the night of his entry a ram would be sacrificed over the pit, the interior of which contained statues of local deities with serpents coiled round their sceptres.

The method of ingress and egress is described by Pausanias, himself a consultant. 'The descender lies with his back on the ground, holding barley-cakes kneaded with honey, thrusts his feet into the hole and himself follows, trying hard to get his knees into the hole. After his knees the rest of his body is at once swiftly drawn in . . . The return upwards is by the same mouth, the feet darting out first.' After this, priests took charge of the consultant again, placed him on the chair of Memory, which stood near the shrine, and questioned him as to what he had seen and heard. 'Paralysed with terror and unconscious both to himself and his relatives,' he was then handed over to his friends. Pausanias adds that he soon regained his faculties, as well as 'the power to laugh'.

To the right (west) of the gorge a high crag is crowned by the castle, the earliest Catalan monument in Greece. The ruined towers, walls and archways of the keep are reminders of a strange period of Spanish rule in Greece.[6] At the beginning of the thirteenth century Levadeia had become an apanage of the Frankish Duchy of Athens. But in the winter of 1311 a band of Catalan soldiers of fortune, originally hired by the Duke of Athens to fight the Greeks and who were owed extensive arrears of pay, descended into Boeotia, accompanied by an immense train of women, children and baggage, resolved to settle accounts with their Frankish debtors by force of arms. The knights were commanded by Walter de Brienne, Duke of Athens. The Marquis of Boudonitza, the Duke of Naxos, Thomas d'Autremencourt of Salona and the barons of the Morea and Euboea followed with their contingents. With such a host, Walter had thoughts of going on, after chastising the insolent Spaniards, to Constantinople and wresting the throne from the Byzantine emperor. A cruel surprise awaited him.

The Catalans, though outnumbered, had laid their plans with cunning and foresight. Flooding the fields between Skripou and Levadeia by digging canals into which the waters of the Cephisus flowed, they were defended by a quagmire covered with a carpet of scum that looked like grass. The Duke of Athens, waving his banner of a golden lion on an azure field sown with stars, personally led the attack, followed by his golden-spurred knights in coats of mail. Plunging their horses into the morass, they were unable to move forward or back, and men and beasts became sitting targets for the bolts and arrows of the Spaniards who bore down on them, yelling 'Aragon!' The massacre of the French was appalling. A Catalan chronicler claims that twenty thousand infantry and seven hundred knights were killed, including Walter de Brienne, whose severed head was paraded on a pikestaff in the Catalan camp. The battle was decisive. Frankish power in Central Greece was broken in a few hours, the Greeks opened

6. Fragments of watchtowers on the road between Thebes and Levadeia are also of Catalan construction.

the gates of Levadeia to the 'Fortunate Company of Catalans' and the road to Athens lay open. Henceforth Attica and Boeotia became the domain of Spanish (and later Florentine) overlords.

West of the Cephisian battleground lie Chaeroneia and Daulis. Both can be visited from Levadeia in a half-day. **Chaeroneia,** where Plutarch was born and died (A.D. 46–120) and wrote most of his works, lies in the narrow plain between Mts Acontium and Thurium. Astride the main invasion route from the north, it was a position of great strategic importance. In ancient times it was a flowery place, the Grasse of the Hellenic world, famous for the manufacture of therapeutic unguents distilled from lilies, roses and narcissus. The rose ointment, smeared on wooden images, prevented them from decaying.

The antiquities are visible from the road. The cavea of a little theatre, without the usual supporting walls at the side, is well preserved (the skene, however, has gone). Behind it fragments of ruined towers and walls, which enclosed the ancient city, ascend the hill. The marble **Lion of Chaeroneia** stands in a cypress grove a few minutes' walk from the centre of the village. Its artistic merit, if any, is overshadowed by its historical associations, for it surmounts the collective grave of the Theban Sacred Band, wiped out in a murderous combat with the young Alexander's phalanx at the battle of Chaeroneia. English travellers first discovered it in the early nineteenth century. In the War of Independence Odysseus Androutsos, most predatory of revolutionary leaders, hacked it to pieces in the hope of finding it full of treasure. Subsequent excavation of the tumulus on which it lay revealed over two hundred skeletons – presumably of the Theban Sacred Band. The Lion, put together at the beginning of the present century, now rests on its haunches, open-mouthed, staring fatuously from its marble plinth, against an imposing background of Parnassus.

Chaeroneia was a decisive battle. By the summer of 338 B.C. Philip of Macedon was ready to force the gateway into Boeotia and subjugate all continental Greece. On a blazing August day, the Macedonian army, well trained, admirably equipped and expertly commanded, faced an army of disunited Greeks, held together only by the exhortations of

Demosthenes, whose inflammatory oratory, says Plutarch, made even the Thebans choose 'the path of honour' this time. The Thebans and Athenians furnished the largest contingents; there were also Phocians, Corinthians and Achaeans. But no Spartan fought at Chaeroneia. It is interesting to speculate whether Spartan generalship would have tipped the scales. As it turned out, even Demosthenes, to whom the allied leaders looked for counsel, did not acquit himself with honour; in fact, in Plutarch's account, 'he fled, deserting his place disgracefully and throwing away his arms . . .'

Road and rail follow a parallel course across a stretch of level ground between the Cephisus and the village where the battle was fought. (I have failed to identify the oak trees, beside one of which Alexander pitched his tent.) After the engagement Philip is accused of indulging in unseemly mirth, of getting drunk on the field of battle and jesting in the most ribald manner as he inspected the corpses of his foes piled up in the blood-soaked streams. But he is said to have wept at the sight of the Theban dead, privileged members of the Sacred Band – 'young men,' Plutarch describes them, 'attached to each other by personal affection' – who went into battle in pairs of sworn friends. They had borne the brunt of Alexander's onslaught and fought with the courage and self-sacrifice that their predecessors had often shown in less worthy causes. They died to a man, all with chest wounds. When the news of the catastrophe reached Athens Isocrates died of anguish and Hyperides proposed draconian emergency measures. In time the battle – 'that dishonest victory,' fulminates Milton – acquired a kind of romantic aura, its outcome being identified by succeeding generations as the end of the democratic Greek city state.

In 87 B.C. another decisive battle, equally disastrous to Greek arms, was fought on the field of Chaeroneia. The Hellenistic world of Alexander the Great's successors was crumbling before the irresistible tide of Roman conquest. An army of Mithridates, King of Pontus, around whom Hellenism had rallied, put up a last stand in the Chaeroneian bottleneck. An ostentatious potentate, Mithridates was accustomed to having a figure of Victory holding a crown let down on his head by a mechanical device. One day the contraption fell just before reaching the king's head, and the crown rolled on the ground. The omen was clear. Sulla's legions accordingly passed 'like a torrent pouring over Boeotia', says Plutarch, and the forces of Mithridates were so totally annihilated that Sulla himself claimed Boeotia to be impassable for the piles of corpses.

West of Chaeroneia the foothills of Parnassus alternately advance and recede into the plain, forming a fascinating sequence of different perspectives. The first turning to the left (south) leads to the village of Ayios Vlasis and the acropolis of Panopeus, native city of Epeius, who built the Trojan Horse with the aid of Athena. There are remains of two well preserved gateways and six towers of the fourth century B.C. In a ravine nearby Pausanias saw large pale-coloured stones which smelled 'like the skin of a man' and were said to be composed of the original clay from which Prometheus fashioned the human race.

Another spur is crowned by **Daulis** (south-east of the main road) which is worth visiting, if only for its striking position. The name itself is evocative, derived from the wooded character of the district, *davlos* being the local variant of *dasos*, a wood. From the village one climbs a cultivated slope, dotted with water mills, to the acropolis, which is covered with evergreens and trailing shoots of *Vinca major* speckled with periwinkles. There are remains of a gate over ten feet wide between two towers – the one on the right is medieval. The square towers of the ramparts (polygonal and rectangular stone dressing), covered in holly-oak, overhang a torrent-bed strewn with huge boulders. The whitewashed Convent of Jerusalem, surrounded by cypresses, is perched on a ledge of Parnassus above the acropolis, just below the belt of firs. To the south-east a track leads across desolate contorted hills to the Cleft Way and thence to Delphi. The course of history has flowed past in the plain below, the never-ending armies from the north hardly ever pausing to desecrate this elegiac fennel-covered place. Only Philip of Macedon halted long enough to destroy the town, where the men, though few in number, were renowned for their height and strength. The fortress was rebuilt, we know, because Livy refers to the town's impregnable situation on its 'lofty hills'.

Mythology, on the other hand, has not by-passed Daulis. Here Tereus, the Thracian coloniser of Boeotia, partook of the gruesome meal prepared by his wife Procne. Having seduced his sister-in-law Philomela and fearing lest she betray him, he cut out her tongue. But Philomela, though mute, remained an expert needlewoman. Embroidering an account of her woes on a piece of cloth, she presented it to her sister. The outraged Procne then devised a macabre revenge. Slaying her son by Tereus, gutting him and boiling him in a copper cauldron, she served up the flesh and bones to her husband for his dinner. On discovering that he had devoured his own child, Tereus resolved to kill both his wife and sister-in-law; but he was suddenly transformed into a hoopoe, with a crest of gold feathers, which henceforth flew about the woods, crying *'pou? pou?'* ('where? where?'), as he sought the two sisters. At the same time Philomela was turned into a swallow and Procne into a nightingale who never ceased to lament the child she had slain in exquisite song.[7] Daulis is often referred to as the haunt of nightingales, and 'many of the poets,' says Thucydides, 'when they mention the nightingale call it the Daulian bird'.

7. Latin poets reverse the sisters' identities, making Procne the swallow, Philomela the nightingale. Other versions have Procne's tongue cut out, not Philomela's, as Procne is a prisoner and Philomela thinks she is dead.

CHAPTER SIXTEEN

The Way to Delphi: The Parnassus Country

❧

Tithorea – The Gravia Pass – Amphissa – The Sacred Plain –
Galaxeidi – The Cleft Way – Anticyra – Hosios Loukas

PARNASSUS dominates not only the country of the Boeotians, but also that of the Phocians and Locrians: an amorphous geological complex of spurs and foothills, narrow plains, sombre defiles and cup-shaped valleys. Few travellers are likely to visit all the places described in this chapter. They will pass some, ignore others, according to their chosen route. In the centre of it all is Delphi, which can be approached by several ways. I propose to describe these in two sections:
(i) An arc running from Tithorea through the Gravia pass to Amphissa and Galaxeidi on the Corinthian Gulf (easily accomplished in one day) – thence in reverse (about a third of the way) to Delphi.
(ii) A rough westward loop from Levadeia to the Monastery of Hosios Loukas,[1] with a deviation (south) to Anticyra, and on to Delphi (also easily accomplished in one day).

I

Tithorea, inhabited by Phocians, a warrior people who dwelt on Parnassus, is perched above the Cephisian valley at the end of a branch road parallel to the dirt road to Daulis.[2] Named

1. The average traveller visits Hosios Loukas, one of the most important Byzantine monuments in the country, on the way to Delphi. The journey Athens–Hosios Loukas–Delphi (or vice versa) is a comfortable day's journey, allowing for stops and deviations.
2. East of the Tithorea fork a track to the north crosses the Cephisus and leads to Elateia, once the most important place in Phocis after Delphi. Its capture by Philip in 339 B.C., followed by the victory of Chaeroneia, laid all Central Greece at the mercy of the Macedonian king. The ruins are vestigial.

after a nymph who grew out of an oak tree, it was famous for its olive oil, which was considered the finest in the Graeco-Roman world. Unguents of such rare quality were distilled from it that they were sent as gifts to the emperor in Rome. More spectacular, though less beautiful, than Daulis, Tithorea is protected to the south by vertical cliffs terminating in a huge three-cornered ledge of Parnassus which forms a backcloth to the village. To the east the precipice drops sheer into a desolate ravine. The town's ancient fortifications were strongest to the north and west, where the approaches were undefended by nature. Fragments of fourth–third-century B.C. walls of regular ashlar masonry, with low towers covered with moss and ivy, are scattered about the vegetable plots, forming an arc round the more exposed slopes. They are not always easy to locate. The base of what must have been a fine tower beside a modern war memorial is conspicuous at the entrance to the village.

Huddled round the base of the cliff, the village is picturesque and salubrious, with narrow streets interspersed with outcrops of ancient ivy-mantled masonry. The east end overhangs the ravine through which flows the Kakorevma (The Evil Torrent), whence the inhabitants fetched water in antiquity. The gorge winds inland, into the heart of Parnassus. On the right, just beyond the last houses, is a cave where the Tithoreans took refuge during Xerxes' invasion, and in which Trelawny, most irresponsible of nineteenth century English philhellenes, dwelt during the War of Independence with the brigand-patriot, Odysseus Androutsos, and whence he wrote to his mother, giving his address as 'The Cavern of Ulysses, M't Parnassus'. 'What a wonderful thing that we should correspond with that ancient and famous place,' was the ingenuous reply he received.[3] The two adventurers vied with each other in the filthiness of their personal habits, the Englishman making a great show of letting lice drop from his fingertips as he talked. He married, and afterwards abandoned, Androutsos' twelve-year-old half-sister. Later their verminous redoubt was found to be filled with gold looted by Androutsos from Greek peasants and rival chieftains.

Beyond Tithorea the road skirts the base of Parnassus. At Amphicleia, orgies, which Pausanias found 'well worth

3. Ann Hill, *Trelawny's Strange Relations*, Saxmundham, 1956.

seeing', were held in honour of Dionysus, locally worshipped as a curer of diseases treated through the medium of dreams, while a priest, divinely inspired, chanted oracles. The only ruin is a fragment of ancient wall in the cemetery. The tower base nearby is of Venetian origin. Formidable mountains, between four and eight thousand feet high, close round on all sides and the 'ribbon-like' plains contract into a narrow insulated valley. Road and rail ascend an eastern offshoot of Mt Oeta, sacred to Zeus. From Ano-Brallos a track leads to the site of the famous funeral pyre, where Heracles, his tormented body corroded by 'the garment of damnation', implored his son to

> '. . . cut down a pile of branches
> Of firm-set oak and robust wild-olive,
> Then lay my body on the pire, and kindle it
> With a flaming torch of pine. Do this in silence –
> I will have no weeping there, no lamentations – '[4]

His colossal limbs racked with pain, the 'sacker of cities', the symbol of incomparable masculine strength, ended his turbulent career on this lonely mountain top with more dignity than he showed in his relations with men and monsters. It remained for Sophocles to immortalise his ascent, amid peals of thunder and flashes of lightning, to the marble halls of Olympus where his father granted him immortality and a charming wife.

From Gravia, south of Ano-Brallos, a mountain road climbs to the village of Eptalophon, straggling across seven hills on different levels amid streams and boscages of poplars against a background of rugged cliffs remarkable for the perfection and symmetry of their forms. After reaching the watershed the road enters a silent world of fir forests, crosses a desolate plateau and winds down to Arachova (see p. 346) and the navel-shaped valley of the Pleistos, with Delphi perched on its bastion in the west.

Another road from Gravia, originally built by the Anglo-French army in 1917 with a view to shortening their lines of

4. Sophocles, *The Women of Trachis*. 'The garment of damnation' is the magic robe ,stained with the poisoned blood of the Centaur Nessus, unwittingly presented to Heracles by his wife Deianeira.

communication with the Macedonian front, runs between torrent-rent buttresses of Parnassus and Ghiona. Forests of ilex and firs spread across the higher slopes. At times the scenery is almost Swiss, but for the plane and wild-pear trees. Beyond the watershed, which connects Parnassus with the Locrian massif of Ghiona, there are glimpses of a vast sea of olive groves curling round the bases of rocky foothills and flat-topped mountain ledges. No village could be more idyllically situated than Eleona, amid a jungle of olive trees, with water cascading from one vine-covered terrace to another.

The descent ends at **Amphissa,** built around a tapering crag crowned by the ruins of a medieval castle, in the shadow of a crescent of mountains formed by Parnassus and Ghiona, whose smooth elephantine flanks are crowned by grandiose summits. In antiquity, Amphissa, lying at the head of the Crissaean plain, was the chief city of Ozolian Locris. In the fourth century B.C. its inhabitants acquired notoriety by daring to cultivate the neighbouring land, sacred to Apollo, whose oracle at Delphi overlooked the plain. This was taken as an act of provocation by the Amphictyonic League, the great religious federation of states, one of whose functions was to protect the god's property. Militant members of the Amphictyonic states, armed with pick-axes, marched across the plain, resolved to destroy this sacrilegious cultivation of holy soil. The Amphissans defended their crops, and the last of the Sacred Wars (see p. 350), fought at or around Delphi, broke out. The Amphictyons appealed to Philip of Macedon, who promptly answered their call, seized Amphissa for himself and made it a strategic linchpin for his conquest of the rest of Greece.

In the thirteenth century the d'Autremencourts of Picardy built a strong castle on the site of the classical fortress, of which there are vestiges of quadrangular and polygonal walls, and called it Salona (later Catalan conquerors called it La Sol). It had three enceintes, whose ruined ramparts (with subsequent Catalan additions) are now fringed with tall umbrella pines. The climb is steep, the medieval ruins exiguous. A fine monolithic lintel, probably of ancient origin, surmounts the entrance gate. A circular tower crowns the keep. There are also vestiges of two churches: Byzantine and

Frankish. Guarding the southern exit of the Gravia pass, the castle formed one of the bulwarks of Central Greece.

In the late fourteenth century the castle was ruled by the dowager Countess Helene, but the real power was wielded by her lover, a disreputable and libidinous priest who robbed the shepherds of Parnassus and debauched the girls of Delphi. The local bishop, alarmed by this medieval Rasputin's designs on his daughter (and her dowry), called upon the aid of Sultan Bayazit I, surnamed the Thunderbolt, who rode across the Locrian mountain passes, accompanied by several thousand hawkers, established his headquarters in the castle, delivered the dowager Countess to the insults of his soldiers and beheaded the nefarious priest. The supreme humiliation was reserved for the Countess's daughter, in whose veins ran the bluest blood of Byzantium and Aragon. Admitted into the Sultan's harem, she was unceremoniously thrown out when her physical charms were found inadequate.

South of Amphissa the road crosses the **Sacred Plain,** which is surrounded on all sides by lofty mountains. Peaks, ridges, slopes seem to develop organically out of the primeval convulsion. Each plane and volume, each detail – whether the meanderings of the olive groves or the windings of the land-locked bay – repeats the forms of the outer arena. A signpost points the way up to Delphi. The density of the olive trees is legendary, the gnarled trunks being among the most ancient in Greece. Somewhere along this silvery-green stretch – we do not know exactly where – lay the hippodrome of Delphi, the scene of epic chariot races run during the celebration of the Pythian Games (see p. 360). So sacred (to Apollo) were these equestrian contests that the gods themselves are said to have taken part in them. Often, too, they intervened in the results, reversing the umpire's verdict or snatching the reins from the hands of a victor who did not enjoy their favour. The chariot races, run at sunrise, began, says Sophocles in a description of an event in which Orestes competed with his Thessalian mares, with a blast from a bronze trumpet. Nothing is left to recall the turbulence of the race-track. The sun beats down on the silent groves; occasionally peasants turn over clods of reddish-brown earth. The road ends at Itea, the port of Delphi, at the head of a muddy gulf where cruise ships anchor. The place has a wasteland air, but there are two good hotels

Hosios Loukas. Mosaic in north transept. The main church, dedicated to the Blessed Luke, glows with 11th century mosaics. Austere figures of saints against gold backgrounds. Bottom: the Blessed Luke, thaumaturgical founder of the original 9th-century shrine. (p. 343).

Mosaic of the Virgin and Child at Hosios Loukas illustrates the intensity and serious side of Byzantine art which makes the church such an imposing example of an 11th century Byzantine church. (p. 343).

which are useful when there is no accommodation at Delphi. There is also a ferry-boat service to Aeghion on the Achaean coast (see pp. 298-99). A new road runs along the western shore of the gulf, startlingly barren after the shady luxuriance of the Sacred Plain. It ends (at present) at **Galaxeidi.**

Often called the future St Tropez of Greece, Galaxeidi is built on a headland flanked by a bay and a pine-fringed creek which provide excellent anchorages for yachts. There is a fine view across the inland sea towards Delphi and the escarpments of Parnassus. The houses, inhabited by caïque-builders, are picturesque without architectural distinction or historical associations. Skeletons of broad-beamed caïques litter the waterfront. The bathing is not good, for the rocks are spiky, the sea soupy; and at the height of summer there are swarms of flies. The seafaring Galaxeidians came into prominence in the eighteenth century, their sailors being among the ablest in Greece. They were also brave, patriotic and skilful fighters. For this reason, the Turks, soon after the outbreak of the War of Independence, tried to exterminate them. Ypsilantis sorrowfully watched the burning of the town from the Achaean coast.

Galaxeidi, however, has a thirteenth century Byzantine church.[5] Above the town the road ascends into the olive belt, circling a bluff overlooking the sea. Across the Corinthian Gulf rise the Peloponnesian ranges, slashed by great gorges. The **Church of Ayios Sotiras (The Saviour)** nestles in a cypress grove surrounded by olive trees. It was commissioned by Michael II Angelus, Despot of Epirus, as a thanksgiving for his deliverance from the wiles of a notorious sorceress. A transverse barrel-vault at the south end gives the impression of a dome (seen from the interior) which has been added to the basilica. The wall-paintings are too poorly preserved to merit attention. Reliefs in the exterior apse, probably from the iconostasis of an earlier church, are decorated with reversed stylised pine cones and cypress branches in the angles of the crosses.

A caïque service connects Galaxeidi with Itea. It is a short but memorable journey. The oily waters of the gulf, dotted with barren islets, like petrified porpoises, are ruffled only by

5. The traveller should ask at the police station where to get the key of the church, which is usually locked.

the caïque's wash. A silver haze hangs over the groves of the Sacred Plain, within the amphitheatre of tremendous mountains.

II

There is only one way from Levadeia to Hosios Loukas – the road to Delphi. It begins by winding round a series of rolling eroded hills in a wide trough between Helicon and Parnassus. From no other point I know is the perfection of form of Parnassus seen to greater advantage – a well ordered mass of soaring limestone, its buttresses and escarpments, square, rectangular, curvilinear, rent by deep ravines running in parallel vertical courses. Gradually it seems to occupy the whole of one's angle of vision. It is lonely country. There is only a Vlach hamlet, some sheep-folds, a *khani*, or resting place, shaded by great plane trees.[6] Goats scrabble among prickly shrubs on the precipitous slopes – a landscape, one feels, specially designed to guard the approaches to Delphi. On every side mountains soar above the Cleft Way, the ancient junction of the three roads from Delphi, Daulis and Thebes, where Oedipus met Laius and his royal suite.[7] In this grim silent place:

'. . . where two severed roads unite,
They met: the charioteer of Laius cried
In an imperious tone, "Give way to Kings,
Thou stranger": yet the silent youth advanced,
With inborn greatness fired, till o'er his feet
Distained with gore the steel-hoofed coursers trod . . .'[8]

A monument (left of the roadside) commemorates the exploits of an army officer who destroyed a notorious band of nineteenth century brigands. Some say the monument stands on a tumulus under which Laius and his attendants were buried. A Plataean king, according to Pausanias, found them and 'piled

6. The Vlachs, or Kutsovlachs, are nomadic mountaineers of Wallachian origin, speaking a form of Low Latin, who descend in winter into the lowlands of Central and Western Greece from the mountains of Northern Greece.

7. The Cleft Way is also known as the Schisté (The Divided Road) and the Triple Road.

8. Euripides, *The Phoenician Women*.

unhewn stones' over the bones. The tombs, he adds, 'were in the middle of the place where the three roads met' – a position which corresponds to that of the modern monument.

Soon there is a fork. The turning to the left (south) leads to Distomon, a centre of guerilla activity in the last war, where the walls of houses are painted with black crosses: reminders of a German reprisal in which one male member in every family was shot. Here there is another fork. The road to the south descends abruptly to the bay of Anticyra, on the Corinthian Gulf. The broken coastline is dotted with mining installations inhabited by the families of French engineers employed in an aluminium factory and bauxite works. A corniche runs eastward, and the shell of a little Byzantine Church of Ayios Panteleimon lies at the mouth of a stony valley. Fragmentary remains of the ancient walls of Anticyra are scattered across a bluff. Tombs have also been excavated. Anticyra was famous for its hellebore, which had medicinal properties, and in ancient times people flocked here to be cured of intestinal ailments. The flowers, usually green with tubular honey-secreting organs and large leaves divided into toothed segments, grew in profusion over the rocky hillsides. There were two varieties of hellebore: one cathartic, with a black root; the other emetic, with a white one. It was also used as a cure for madness, and later for gout.

The other road from Distomon (to the west) passes through Stiris, famous for its sheep's milk yoghourt of the richest quality, and runs along a ridge of windswept hills to the **Monastery of Hosios Loukas.** The church and its dependencies overlook a bowl-like valley with cultivated strips laid out in chequer-board fashion, enclosed on all sides by steep slate-grey spurs of Helicon.

The original chapel, dedicated to St Barbara, the legend of whose martyrdom was very popular in the tenth century, was built by the disciples of a holy man from neighbouring Stiris. He was called Luke – 'Hosios' being the Orthodox equivalent of a 'blessed man' in the Western Church – and the fame of his prophetic pronouncements, thaumaturgical powers and conversations with birds and animals soon spread beyond his native mountains. He died in the middle of the tenth century, and his humble shrine became a place of pilgrimage, and a monastery was founded. In Constantinople, Theophano, daughter of a cabaret-owner and wife of three successive emperors, heard of it and thought of embellishing it. Her son, the Emperor Basil II the Bulgar-Slayer, is believed to have added impetus to the enterprise in the course of his triumphant tour of Greece at the beginning of the eleventh century. The wars against the Bulgars had been successfully concluded. Throughout the Empire there was a surge of creative activity. It was the beginning of the Byzantine Golden Age. In the by no means negligible traces of its original opulence, Hosios Loukas remains a typical example of the Byzantine tradition of imperial patronage of remote monastic establishments.

The almond orchards and patchwork fields in the cup-shaped valley, owned by the once flourishing community of monks, now reduced to a handful of white-bearded old men, have been expropriated by the government. Until recently dilapidated outhouses spread across the rectangular terrace. Now there is a tourist shop and a modest little hotel. Where one sat on wooden benches under the great plane trees sipping ouzo offered by the monks, young men and women sprawl in plastic chairs, drinking Coca-Cola and Nescafé. But by seven o'clock the last motor coach has gone, the echo of the last transistor died away. The foothills of Helicon form a dark screen round the empty valley. In spring the air is heavy with the scents of broom, honeysuckle and lemon blossom.

The main church (eleventh century) is a tall, cross-inscribed edifice, with lavish brickwork exterior decoration (recently restored), surrounded by monastic cells and a refectory. The windows, which possess sculptural embellishments, are divided into three sections by columns of different coloured marbles – blue, green and white – and set in arched frames. The interior, probably decorated by Constantinopolitan artists, is one of the finest extant examples of the Byzantine effort to create a harmonious unity, echoing with praises of the Lord, out of colours, cubes, bricks, paste, stone and marble. The way in which each tessera, whatever its shape,

Church of Hosios Loukas

Key to Plate Numbers

1. Demetrius
2. Nicholas
3. Andrew
4. Peter
5. Mercurios
6. Luke of Stiris
7. Gabriel
8. Basil

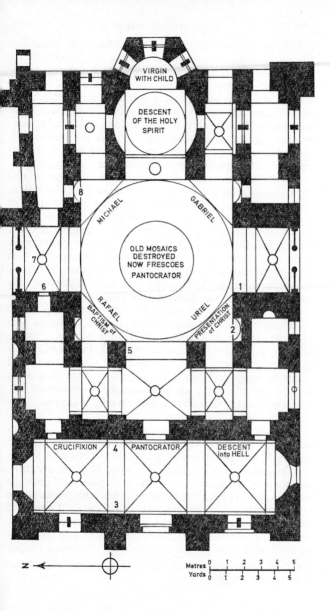

VIRGIN
WITH CHILD

DESCENT
OF THE HOLY
SPIRIT

8

MICHAEL
GABRIEL

OLD MOSAICS
DESTROYED
NOW FRESCOES
PANTOCRATOR

7

6

1

RAFAEL
BAPTISM of CHRIST

URIEL
PRESENTATION of CHRIST

2

5

CRUCIFIXION   4   PANTOCRATOR   DESCENT into HELL

3

N ←

Metres 0 1 2 3 4 5
Yards   0 1 2 3 4 5

colour or quality, reflected the light from the ground of cement in which it was embedded, acted as a stimulus to the perception of that unity. Bands of white sculptured marble divide the sumptuous multi-coloured revetments into two levels, the floor is of jasper and porphyry, the marble iconostasis elaborately carved and every inch of wall space in the narthex, dome, apses and transepts glows with sombre-hued mosaics against gold backgrounds (except for some unimportant frescoes of a later date), with radiant highlights reflected in the apices of deep niches under the cupolas.

The narthex comes first. A subtle and basic unity underlying the disposition of the figures of the apostles on the various arches is achieved through their attitudes – quarter-views or turning movements, so that they all ultimately point to the Pantocrator, whose image once filled the space above the door leading into the naos. Two of the most striking portraits are those of **St Peter** (east wall) and **St Andrew** (west wall) with lively expressions and disproportionately large heads. Among the scenes from the life of Christ the most impressive are the **Crucifixion** (left) and **Descent into Hell** (right) in shallow lunettes. The bulky figure with heavy tubular legs on the Cross is, in spite of its monolithic columnar quality, contorted with physical pain. In the Descent into Hell the swirling draperies of Christ's cloak are repeated in those of the mantle of Eve, as she is drawn out of Limbo. The decorative work of the arched frame is lavish and colourful. All the narthex decoration possesses a pliability, an expressiveness, even sensibility, which is absent in the more majestic severity of the mosaics in the main body of the church.

Here and in the side chapels the iconographic arrangement adheres strictly to the established programme – complex, yet organic in conception and execution. In the first zone (vaults and chapels), saints intermingle with ascetics, prophets, bishops and provincial holy men in a gallery of portraits which, at first, tend to overshadow the narrative scenes on the upper register. The prominence given to local saints is attributed to the provincial character of the church, and this emphasis, says Otto Demus, contributes largely to the 'spirit of monkish austerity' that prevails here.[9] Professor Grabar

9. Otto Demus, *Byzantine Mosaic Decoration*, Kegan Paul Trench Trubner, London, 1947.

goes further and says 'Byzantine art is unsmiling enough in general, but at Hosios Loukas we are confronted by its most ascetic and serious side'.[10] There are few concessions to grace, none to sentimentality. Among the portraits those of St Demetrius (south transept), St Basil (lunette in north-east transept), Mercurios, the soldier-saint, with sheathed sword (north-west arch, left on entering the nave) and a lively St Nicholas (lunette in south-west corner of the nave) are worth noticing. In the north transept there is a fine puce-footed puce-winged **Archangel Gabriel** and a **bust of the blessed Luke** himself, severe and monkish, his hands raised in worship. In numerous arches and vaults the Archangels and military saints act as guards of honour. The busts within medallions, unlike those of the apostles in the narthex, are portrayed frontally so that the impression of hieratic formalism is heightened. At Daphni (see pp. 107-10), where the style is more evolved, the same figures are depicted at more oblique angles, with the result that the portraits are rendered more as pictures.

High up above the world of holy men extends the sphere of divine beings, at the summit of which Christ Pantocrator (in this instance missing) dominates the universe. In the apse the **Virgin and Child** are represented seated on a cushioned throne decorated with elaborate inlay, against a concave gold background which creates an effect of immense spaciousness. Gold backgrounds, so much favoured by Byzantine mosaicists, were indeed intended to suggest space; they were also meant to reproduce the effect of light. In the dome of the sanctuary the twelve apostles are seated round the symbol of the Trinity, with the Dove perched on the throne of the Hetoimasia. Below the central cupola are the spandrels in which scenes from the *Dodecaorton* are depicted: a beautiful **Nativity,** in which the figure of Joseph with enormous black eyes and the animals leaning over the crib lend an extraordinary homely quality to the scene; a **Baptism,** in which Christ stands shoulder-high in the waters of the Jordan while two angels advance towards him bearing elaborately designed towels; a rather more crude **Presentation in the Temple,** where the usual left-right movement of the figures is reversed – conse-

10. André Grabar, *Greek Mosaics of the Byzantine Period*, Collins Unesco, 1964.

quently we have the Virgin walking towards the centre of the church, not out of it. This constant focus of movement towards a central point is one of the most individual features of the mosaic decoration of Hosios Loukas. Since it is not always easy to examine these lofty concave compositions satisfactorily from below, Byzantine artists, profoundly aware of the relation between optics and geometry, were constantly endeavouring to heighten the effect of light within a mosaic by creating an impression of depth in front of, instead of behind, the scene. As there is little differentiation in colour tones, which became such a striking feature of later Palaeologue wall-paintings, the austere mosaicist of the eleventh century at Hosios Loukas tends to overemphasise the modelling of his figures. The mosaics at Daphni are certainly more evolved and sophisticated in technique and execution, but Hosios Loukas, in its completeness, in the power and intensity of the figures crowding its walls, in its elaborate decorative detail and majestic proportions, remains a more imposing and convincing example of an eleventh century Byzantine church.

Below the church is the crypt of St Barbara, containing the tomb of the blessed Luke, painted with crude frescoes of the peasant school of Cappadocia which was rustic and didactic rather than aesthetic in purpose and flourished through the Empire in conjunction with the more refined art of the capital. Adjoining the main church is the chapel of the Virgin.

The monastery possessed many dependencies, two of which I have visited. They are well off the beaten track. One is the little ruined church of Ayios Panteleimon in the bay of Anticyra (see p. 321); the other, Ayios Nikolaos *eis tous kambous* (St Nicholas-in-the-Fields), situated in an undulating almond orchard, is reached from Orchomenus (see p. 339) along a mountain track, passable by car when it is not too muddy. It has some uncleaned frescoes of the tenth century.

CHAPTER SEVENTEEN

Delphi

❧

'The shrine that is the centre of the loudly echoing earth.'
                                        PINDAR, *Odes*, P. vi.

*Arachova – The Oracle – The Sanctuary of Apollo: The
Treasuries; The Stoa of the Athenians; The Temple of Apollo;
The Theatre - The Stadium – Marmaria: The Tholos; The
Temple of Athena Pronaea – Sybaris – The Corycian Cave –
The Museum*

ISOLATED by a ring of mountains, Delphi has always been
subject to violent climatic and geological pressures. Earthquakes and landslides are common. Shadows of clouds that
dissolve and reform drift across the olive groves. Torrential
showers blot out the landscape, and thunder echoes in the
hollows of the valley. In summer the heat is trapped within
the arena of refractory limestone, and the cliffs, pitted with
primeval fissures, reflect a peculiar radiance which seems to
derive its glow from the interior of the rock. Travellers have
never ceased to be impressed by the dramatic quality of the
scene. Only Byron was disappointed and sighed 'o'er Delphi's
long deserted shrine'.

Several ways of approaching the sanctuary have been
described in Chapter 16. But the direct route from Athens
through Levadeia is the one most travellers take: the one
originally followed by pilgrims who walked or rode in chariots
– others came by sea, disembarking at the ancient port of
Cirrha, in the Gulf of Itea. After the fork to Distomon (see
p. 338) the road climbs between jagged peaks. Fir trees spread
across the higher slopes. Every outline acquires a razor-edge
sharpness, the atmosphere a rarefied quality, the blue of the
sky a new intensity. One has a sensation of approaching a
place of immense significance in the affairs of men. At the
top of the pass the curtain is raised with a tremendous

flourish. The gorge lies below, the mountains crowding round to complete the famous umbilical effect. In the distance a buttress of cliffs, concealing the sanctuary, juts out to meet another wall of rock; beyond it there is a tantalising glimpse of the olive groves of the Sacred Plain.

In the immediate foreground a double-peaked bastion of Parnassus, over 3000 feet high, is crowned by the grey stone houses of **Arachova,** its clock tower perched on the summit of a crag overhanging cultivated strips descending in terraces to the bottom of the gorge. So beautiful is the position of this mountain eyrie that the inhabitants, anxious to cherish and prolong every moment of existence, are said to live longer than elsewhere in Greece. Shops display local handicrafts: woollen bags, carpets, blankets. The colours are crude and gaudy, but some of the bedspreads, runners, mats, tablecloths embroidered with old regional designs and fleecy hearth-rugs called *flocatas* are attractive. Formerly the women of Arachova wore national costumes, now preserved as heirlooms, and in the seventeenth century George Wheler was struck by their elaborate head-dress. 'The Women,' he says, 'wear round their Faces small pieces of Money; and likewise round their Neck and Arms: Their Hair combed back, and curiously braided down their Backs; at the ends of which hang Tassels of Silver Buttons.' This type of headgear is a feature of several regional costumes. In the difficult days of the Turkish occupation, the Greeks had the ingenious idea of preserving and bequeathing money by stringing coins of different currencies, Turkish, Austrian, Italian, on chains, ostensibly as ornaments. The red wine of Arachova is good, if rather heady. The local cheese, made from goat's milk, its wax rind moulded in the design of a wickerwork basket, is more of a curiosity than a delicacy. Arachova is the starting-point for the ascent of Parnassus (a local guide is indispensable), for the visit to the Corycian Cave (see p. 363) by car, and for the drive across Parnassus to Gravia (described in reverse on p. 334).

Beyond Arachova the road descends, between shelving ledges planted with almond trees, into the vine belt. The gorge narrows. The ruins of an ancient necropolis herald the approach. The road loops round a huge projecting bluff and enters the inner amphitheatre of rock. The ruins of the sanctuary – broken columns, polygonal walls, grey stone tiers, red-brick Roman rubble – are splayed across the steep hillside. Unfortunately, the most prominent architectural feature is the modern building of the museum, with sheet glass windows, surrounded by shrubs and flowerbeds. A wall of cliff rises sheer from the ultimate ledge of the sanctuary, and hawks and vultures – ancient writers say eagles – hover overhead. In the valley below olive trees of immense antiquity mantle the precipitous banks.

Hotels and tourist shops line the main street of the village, which clings to another great projection of rock. The original hamlet, built over the sanctuary, was removed stone by stone to its present position when the excavations began at the end of the last century. All the hotels have magnificent views. One lunches and dines on terraces, shaded with awnings, overlooking the gorge. The yoghourt of Parnassus is rich and creamy, probably the best in Greece; so are the dark fleshy olives of the plain of Amphissa. The smart hotels (Vouzas, Amalias) have good bars. Shopping is much the same as at Arachova, a bit more expensive, with a lot more junk thrown in. Oddly enough, there is no chemist in this sanctuary of the father of the god of healing. On Sundays and feast days shepherds with complexions tanned by sun and wind to a rich golden hue come down from mountain sheepfolds to drink coffee and listen to the news in the cafés. Sometimes, in the evening, flushed with ouzo or wine, they perform a lively *tsamiko*, to the accompaniment of a wailing clarinet. A tourist pavilion, where local and foreign youth dance on summer nights, is perched 2000 feet above the Sacred Plain. The antiquities are confined to two areas: the Sanctuary of Apollo above the main road, and the Marmaria, in an olive grove below the Castalian Spring. These (and the museum) can be rushed through in one long exhausting day. A longer stay is unlikely to be regretted.

It is only five minutes' walk to the Sanctuary of Apollo. The earliest references to it are purely mythical. They tell of roving shepherds suddenly seized by an uncontrollable frenzy as potent exhalations issued from a fissure in a rocky ledge and pouring forth garbled prophecies in the name of Apollo. In time a temple was raised to the god above the sacred pit. Symbol of youth, light and beauty, Apollo, who, on the fourth day after his birth, asked for bows and arrows, is the most consistently Greek of Olympian deities. Although vain, uxorious and narcissistic, he has many attractive qualities: an affection for flocks, an interest in medicine and astronomy, a love of music and poetry – he played on a golden lyre with seven strings, whose sounds, when plucked, corresponded to the seven vowels of the Greek language. Sometimes he is public-spirited; occasionally he even exercises moderation. In his amorous intrigues he often transforms himself into different shapes – a tortoise or a snake that hisses. In all his personal traits he reflects the anthropomorphic nature of Greek religion.

Musaeus, the mythical poet, claimed that the oracle was originally owned by Ge (Earth) and Poseidon (Sea) in conjunction. Ge gave her portion to Apollo, who offered Poseidon a maritime station in exchange for his share. Before taking possession, he was obliged to slay Python, a Chthonian monster who had persecuted his mother before his birth, with the golden arrows specially made for him by his half-brother, Hephaestus. Travelling across Thessaly to the Vale of Tempe, he purified himself in the waters of the Peneius and was crowned with the laurel which possessed therapeutic qualities and became the emblem of his Delphic shrine. He then tamed the Muses who dwelt in the solitude of Mt Helicon, brought them to Delphi and led them in ritual dances. Nomadic by nature, the god visited Delphi every spring in a chariot drawn by swans, and departed in the autumn accompanied by priests carrying lighted torches. During the winter the oracle fell silent.

The Apolline cult developed rapidly and a priestess, the Pythia, was installed in the temple, where she chanted the ambiguous riddles that exercised such a powerful influence over men's actions for ten centuries. In the *Eumenides* Aeschylus says it was the god himself who interpreted 'his father's word and will' to mankind through the agency of the Pythia. As a panhellenic sanctuary, Delphi possessed a far more profound religious significance than Olympia, and four Sacred Wars were fought for its preservation. From the beginning, the sanctuary's purpose was wholly oracular, existing solely for communicating the counsels of the gods to mortals. Strabo believes 'the position of the place added something. For it is almost in the centre of Greece . . . and people called it the navel of the earth.' He goes on to quote Pindar as saying 'that the two eagles (some say crows), which had been set free by Zeus met there, one coming from the west and the other from the east'. Thus nature and the gods conspired to render the place sublime.

The oracle was administered by five elected priests who claimed descent from Deucalion. They had complete control of administration, were responsible for the Pythia's political brief and were represented in Athens and elsewhere by agents. The fame of the prophecies was established as early as the eighth century B.C.; by the sixth, votive gifts were pouring in from every part of the civilised world. Croesus alone presented the shrine with a gold statue of a lion, a gold mixing-bowl that weighed a quarter of a ton, a silver wine vessel that held five thousand gallons, four silver casks and two silver sprinklers for lustral water. As though that were not enough, the Lydian king added all his wife's necklaces and girdles, and ordered the sacrifice of three thousand animals. As an instrument of policy, the oracle's influence was by no means negligible. In the Persian Wars it tended to be defeatist, in the Peloponnesian War it showed a pro-Spartan bias. It was consulted among others by Oedipus, Agamemnon, Cleomenes, Philip of Macedon and Alexander the Great. To the latter the priestess cried, 'My son, none can resist thee!'

The oracles, delivered in hexameters, were generally extremely equivocal.[1] Can one blame Croesus, when told he would destroy a mighty empire if he crossed the Halus, for failing to realise that the empire in question was his own? How many Athenians, instructed to put their trust in 'wooden bulwarks', imagined that Athens would be saved by the ships at Salamis? Was Philip of Macedon particularly obtuse, on receiving the cryptic warning 'Crowned is the bull, the time is full, the sacrificer comes', not to identify the 'sacrificer' as his own assassin? Sometimes the oracle would express a personal opinion, as when it described Socrates as a wiser man than either Sophocles or Euripides. Little is known of the relations between priests and politicians, but there can be little doubt that string-pulling went on behind the scenes. Consultants had to be pure in heart and without evil design, and the order in

1. After the 4th century B.C. the oracles were delivered in prose.

which they entered the holy chamber was fixed by lot. Most of the problems, upon which they sought the god's arbitration, related to cultivation of crops, love affairs, intended marriages, journeys, loans, the sale of slaves. They had to pay a fee and sacrifice a goat, sheep or ox. Before the animals were slaughtered it was necessary to ensure that they were in good health. To test their appetites oxen were given barley, sheep chick-peas. Goats were doused in cold water and only if they shivered were they considered worthy of being led to the sacrificial altar.

At an early stage Delphi was admitted into the Amphictyonic League, one of whose main responsibilities was to safeguard the sanctuary's interests and treasure. But the inhabitants of neighbouring Crissa grew increasingly envious and rapacious; they exacted heavy tolls from consultants approaching the oracle, and their assaults on female pilgrims scandalised the Delphians. The first Sacred War (c. 590 B.C.) broke out and Crissa was razed to the ground by troops of different states determined to uphold the sanctity of this *estia*, or 'common hearth', to all Greeks. In the second Sacred War Athens and Sparta sparred over the ownership of the sanctuary, the former supporting the Phocians' claim, the latter the Delphians'. In the mid-fourth century, the Phocians, out for loot, seized the sanctuary, thus provoking the third Sacred War. They melted down much treasure and their leader distributed precious objects from the temple, including a necklace worn by Helen, to his favourites. In the last Sacred War the aggressors were the Locrians of Amphissa, who wanted to cultivate their lands, until then undefiled by spade or ploughshare, which the League considered sacred to Apollo. Aeschines, the Athenian orator, whipped up public opinion against this sacrilege. In the end Philip of Macedon had to be called in to put an end to Locrian profanity (see p. 335).

In the third century B.C. bands of Gauls descended on the sanctuary. Handicapped by unfavourable auguries, the invaders also had the elements ranged against them: not only frost and snow, but also earthquakes followed by landslides. Scrambling down the precipices of Parnassus, the Greeks attacked them in the rear. Thunderbolts and boulders fell from above. Panic broke out and, in their frenzy, the Gauls slaughtered each other by the hundreds. It was left to Sulla,

two centuries later, to plunder the shrine with his usual
appalling thoroughness. After him the insatiable Nero carried
off five hundred bronze statues to Rome. The philhellenic
Hadrian and the Antonines did what they could to restore
Delphi to its former splendour, but it was too late. The god's
utterances no longer carried conviction. Acceptance of bribes
by priests was rife, and the charlatanism suspected by
Thucydides, and denounced by Euripides, exposed. Consultants became sceptical, and the Early Christian Church
believed the oracle was inspired by the devil. In the fourth
century Constantine the Great removed many works of art to
Constantinople. During the brief reign of Julian the Apostate,
himself one of its last consultants, the oracle predicted its own
end in a moving if timely swan song. The sanctuary was
closed down by the Emperor Theodosius in his famous edict
of 393.

In time a hamlet grew up on the ancient deposits. In the
seventeenth century Wheler observed traces of marble tiers on
the terrace of the stadium and identified niches for statues
beside the Castalian Spring. On the site of the sanctuary he
only found 'a *Kan*, or Place of Entertainment, to Passengers',
and 'Two hundred Houses, and those very ill built'. Between
1892 and 1903 the French School of Archaeology at Athens
excavated the sanctuary and the Marmaria.

The sanctuary is screened by a semi-circle of cliffs, the
rose-coloured Phaedriades, mottled with tufts of evergreens.
Aesop, whose comic fables delighted fifth century B.C. Athenian literary circles, was hurled from their summit by the
outraged Delphians, who suspected him of embezzling funds
belonging to the temple. Later the oracle proved him to be
innocent, and they had to compensate his grandson. Stunted
pedestals and foundations of treasuries spread across a hillside
covered with vetch, mullein and cistus. The bronze and marble
statues have long since vanished: looted by Roman and
Byzantine emperors or hacked to pieces by Goths and Visi-
goths. To the east the Castalian stream issues out of a rocky
cleft and flows into the hollow valley, enclosed within a ring
of mountains that no human hand could have fashioned with
a more perfect sense of symmetry. Across the gorge a zigzag
mule track climbs the arid wall of Mt Cirphis like some crude
graffito scratched by the hand of a giant. Hundreds of feet

below the Pleistos trickles sinuously between olive groves towards the Sacred Plain.

There is not a ruin in the sanctuary that is not Graeco-Roman. The Sacred Way, a steep narrow ramp in the form of a double hairpin, begins at the lowest (east) end of the enclosure, beside the brickwork remains of a small square-shaped Roman agora, identified by two unfluted Ionic columns, once crowned with pilgrims buying talismans and other religious trinkets. Plutarch complains of the tiresome solicitations of guides. The paved ramp climbs between bases of statues and treasuries which once jostled against each other on the steep incline. It is all very congested and confusing, and there is none of the spaciousness or shade of the Olympian Altis. The fact that the sanctuary is built on a succession of narrow ledges further complicates the layout. In summer the sun is scorching and cicadas drone relentlessly among parched shrubs. There was little of the holiday atmosphere of Olympia, the proceedings being carried out with a solemnity consistent with the religious nature of the place. Bacchylides speaks of oxen lowing on their way to sacrifice, of golden tripods glittering at street corners, Euripides of the air filled with fumes of frankincense streaming 'upward to the temple's height'. Priests, versed in diplomacy and foreign languages, acted as guides and ushers. The political knowledge which they amassed was enormous, and the sanctuary became a kind of central office of information for the whole of Greece.

On the right lie the foundations of the rectangular ex-voto of the Lacedaemonians, dedicated by Lysander in commemoration of the victory of Aegospotami, with traces of a parapet once adorned with statues of Spartan admirals, against the interior wall. So close to it as almost to constitute an act of deliberate provocation, the Arcadians placed a row of bronze statues of national heroes notorious for their hostility to Sparta. On the west side, an imposing exedra, embellished with statues of Argive kings (the bases have been restored) who traced their descent from Heracles, was raised by the Argives, also eager to pay off old scores, to commemorate the foundation of independent Messene. Next come the treasuries which contained the archives and national treasure of the various states. On the left are the foundations of the Treasury of Sicyon, followed by the substructure of the Treasury of

General view of the Theatre and Temple of Apollo at Delphi surrounded by a ring of mountains.

North frieze of the Treasury of Siphnos, Delphi (6th century B.C.) – the battle of the gods against the giants. (p. 352).

The Bronze Charioteer — belonged to a quadriga (chariot) placed on the terrace of the temple, the gift of a Sicilian tyrant in the 1st half of the 5th century B.C. (p. 366).

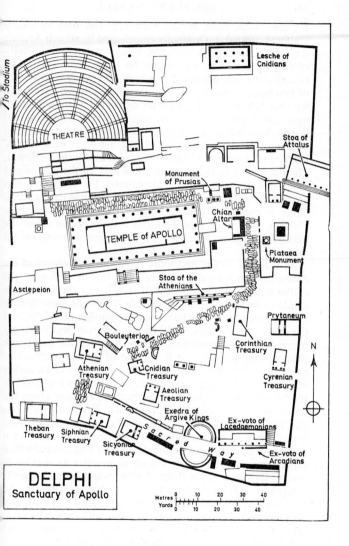

DELPHI
Sanctuary of Apollo

To Stadium

THEATRE

Lesche of Cnidians

Stoa of Attalus

Monument of Prusias

Chian Altar

Plataea Monument

Asclepeion

Stoa of the Athenians

Prytaneum

Bouleuterion

Corinthian Treasury

N

Athenian Treasury

Cnidian Treasury

Aeolian Treasury

Cyrenian Treasury

Theban Treasury

Siphnian Treasury

Sicyonian Treasury

Exedra of Argive Kings

Sacred Way

Ex-voto of Lacedaemonians

Ex-voto of Arcadians

Metres 0 10 20 30 40
Yards 0 10 20 30 40

Siphnos, with slabs carved with egg and dart moulding scattered around it. Originally embellished by superb Archaic sculptures, now in the museum, this remarkable little sixth-century B.C. edifice, measuring no more than twenty by twenty-eight feet, consisted of a cella and porch with statues of two women standing on plinths, each holding a fruit and wearing tall basket-shaped hats decorated with sculptured figures and surmounted by an echinus carved with scenes of lions killing bulls. The frieze of Parian marble was composed of figures carved in high relief, the acroteria of sphinxes' heads; and a winged victory was placed above the pediment. The doorway was richly ornamented and all the figures and sculptured designs were brightly painted. The visible remains are negligible, but there is a partial restoration in the museum. Other treasuries – Theban, Megarian, Potidaean, Aetolian, Cnidian, Syracusan, even Etruscan – are scattered about the hillside. To the unprofessional eye they are no more than a mass of rubble, wholly incomprehensible.

At the apex of the first loop, the restored **Treasury of the Athenians** stands on a prominent ledge, one of the landmarks of the sanctuary. Only 33 by 20 feet, it was the first Doric edifice to be built entirely of marble. The walls grow thinner as they ascend in order to convey the illusion of height, and the effect of squatness made by the low roof was probably relieved by an acroterium of an Amazon on horseback surmounting the gable. It is not one of the masterpieces of classical architecture. A third century B.C. copy of an earlier inscription, 'The Athenians dedicated to Apollo the spoils of the Medes after the battle of Marathon', running along the south and west walls of the triangular forecourt, indicates that the trophies captured from the Persians were displayed here. The gold on the offerings is supposed to have been pecked off by crows just before Alcibiades' disastrous Sicilian expedition. Auguries were indeed as popular as oracles in ancient Greece, and the flight of birds would be meticulously studied by a general about to go into battle. Socrates and Euripides, among others, however, were more sceptical, and Socrates probably reflects enlightened opinion when he says: 'The augur should be under the authority of the general, and not the general under the authority of the augur.'[2]

2. Plato, The *Laches*.

The Sacred Way now slants obliquely up the hill between foundations of votive edifices. On the left are the remains of the Bouleuterion, or Senate House, where the committee of five transacted business and formulated policy. Beyond it is the rock, reinforced by modern masonry, from which the Sibyl Herophile, who alternately called herself wife, daughter and sister of Apollo, chanted the first oracles. Pausanias attributed her confusion of mind to the 'frenzy' which seized her 'when possessed of the god'. A natural fissure in the ground nearby is said to be the entrance to the lair where the serpent Python dwelt. Three steps lead up to the Stoa of the Athenians, in which the spoils captured from the Spartans in the Peloponnesian War were displayed. Three of the original eight miniature Ionic columns, sufficiently slender and elegant to have supported a wooden roof, are ranged against the massive stone-dressing of a great polygonal wall. The interlocking irregular-shaped stones have a smooth honey-coloured surface and were designed to reinforce the god's temple, which was situated directly above the wall, in the event of earthquakes. Opposite is the open space of the *halos*, or threshing-floor, where Apollo's victory over Python was celebrated every seven years.

At the apex of the second loop a sharp ascending turn to the left (north) leads to the round pedestal of the votive offering set up by all the states who fought at Plataea. The central support, which was of bronze and in the form of three intertwined serpents, inscribed with the names of the victorious states, was removed to the hippodrome in Constantinople. Facing it is the altar of the Chians, also commemorating the Greek victory over the Persians, composed of rectangular slabs of grey-blue marble – a conspicuous but uninspiring monument, twice restored during the present century at the expense of wealthy Chian shipowners. Beyond it is a rectangular plinth with a garlanded frieze once crowned by an equestrian statue of Prusias II, a vicious physically deformed Bithynian king of the second century B.C., much given to vulgar ostentation.

Vertical cliffs rise above the high-lying terrace. A modern ramp climbs the east entrance of the stylobate of the **Temple of Apollo,** which commands a prospect of the whole precinct and the stupendous circular panorama. The perspective is enhanced by the restoration of three massive Doric limestone columns which reflect the changing light – grey, brown or gold – according to the time of day, their huge calcified drums conveying an impression of the scale of the building which was almost as large as the Parthenon. The immense stylobate stands out like an embodiment of the native rock on which it rests. The origins of the temple lie buried in a tangle of whimsical legend. According to the oldest version, it was made of laurel leaves; in another it was composed of ferns interwoven with stalks; in yet another it was put together by bees and birds out of wax and feathers. At this point the height of whimsicality seems to have been reached, and it is a relief to learn that Hephaestus was the architect and that he built the temple entirely of bronze.

Of the historical origins little is known, except that the Archaic temple was gutted by fire. In the late sixth century B.C. it was replaced by a splendid edifice raised by the Amphictyons, restored in the fourth century after an earthquake. The existing foundations and stylobate belong to the later construction. But it is the sixth century Amphictyonic temple that acquired such fame. A panhellenic subscription was raised to obtain the necessary funds and the tender was offered to the Alcmonidae – an influential family which counted Cleisthenes among its contemporaries, Pericles and Alcibiades among its descendants – who had been driven out of Athens by the odious dictatorship of Hippias, the last of the tyrannical Peisistratae. But it was neither the émigré politics of the Alcmonidae nor the desperate attempt of the youth Harmodius and his protector, Aristogeiton, to assassinate Hippias that brought about the downfall of the Peisistratae. A more practical agency was invoked in the oracle's repeated injunction to Cleomenes, the Spartan king: 'Athens must be liberated.' Herodotus says the Alcmonidae actually bribed the priestess to tell the Spartans to free Athens. Subsequent events underline the irony. Dictatorial Sparta was to expel the Athenian tyrant and make Athens safe for the democratic reforms of Cleisthenes. The aura of distinction attached to the name of the Alcmonidae, whom Pindar describes as 'Those citizens of Erectheus, who in divine Pytho made thy temple, O Apollo, a marvel to behold', added immense prestige to this enterprise of nationwide proportions.

A massive peripteral temple of the Doric order on a three-tiered stylobate of bluish marble, its front was adorned with marble columns, several drums of which still survive. The terms of the contract had stipulated a stone frontage, but the Alcmonidae personally bore the expense of a front of Parian marble, which introduced a lighter touch in Greek architecture, foreshadowing the marble masterpieces of the fifth century.

Euripides in the *Ion*, in which he angrily denounces the quibbling machinations of the oracle, has left a memorable description of the interior of the temple and its storehouse of sumptuous objects: the ancient omphalos, the holy navel-stone 'hung with wreaths and the carved Gorgons on either side'; the tapestries adorning tents on festive occasions; the curtains captured by Heracles as spoils from the Amazons, with their design of Heaven assembling the stars in the sky; the woven stuffs depicting sea battles between Greeks and Persians, Centaurs chasing deer and stalking lions and Cecrops in the form of a coiled serpent. Garlands of laurel festooned the ceiling of the cella, and the temple servants swept the sacred hearth with sheaths of:

> '. . . fresh and lovely leaves
> Gathered from the immortal laurel-groves,
> Sacred foliage fed by unfailing waters
> That gush from myrtle-thickets . . .'

Little remains of the sculptures of the temple – only some truncated limbs from the pediment, now in the museum. Among the most famous was the gold effigy of Apollo, behind an altar of eternal fire fed by piles of fir-wood. Other precious objects included the wrought-iron statue of Heracles struggling with the Hydra, which Pausanias thought 'marvellous', the iron chair in which Pindar sat when composing his Pythian odes, and the bronze effigy of a wolf that howled nightly outside the sanctuary in order to draw attention to the whereabouts of a cache of treasure stolen from the temple. The maxims of the Seven Sages, including the famous Γνῶθι σαυτὸν (Know thyself) and Μδηὲν ἄγαν (Nothing in excess), were inscribed on the walls of the pronaos. What influence these counsels of moderation had on a people as prodigal in love and intemperate in hatred as the Greeks can only be conjectured. The seat of the oracle was in the adytum, a chamber penetrated only by priests. The fissure from which the exhalations emanated has not been identified. The priestess – Pindar calls her 'the Delphic bee' – was a young virgin, until, on one occasion, she was raped by an impious lecher. After that only older and less attractive women were employed. No further impropriety is recorded. The Pythia sat on a gold tripod above the fissure, which had a narrow mouth. She thus had no contact with the ground, and 'the holy influence of the god', says Pausanias, 'could come beneath her and enter her.' In a state of frenzied exaltation, munching laurel leaves, she then recited the equivocal conundrums which the bewildered consultants interpreted with the aid of qualified advisers. Sometimes the effect of the exhalations on the priestess was so great that she would leap dementedly from her tripod, suffer from convulsions and die within a few days.

Above the temple a Roman stairway mounts to the **theatre** (originally fourth century B.C., of white marble, restored in grey limestone by the Romans). The cavea has only thirty-three tiers, divided by a paved diazôma, but they are well preserved: so is the orchestra, which is composed of irregular slabs and surrounded by the usual water conduit. No Greek theatre is a more perfect expression of an architectural creation in relation to its setting, the sweeping forms of the stone tiers repeated in the rocky hemicycle of the Phaedriades. The highest tier is the loveliest viewpoint. In the late afternoon the glow of the Phaedriades is reflected on the slopes of the encircling mountains which turn pink, mauve and finally a deep cobalt blue. Hawks and buzzards hover over the auditorium. The valley fills with obscure shadows. For all its grandeur, it is an intensely serene landscape. Occasionally the sound of goat-bells rises from the gorge. Neither the motor coaches parked along the main road nor the guided tours trailing across the esplanade of the temple can detract from the profound harmony of the scene. In 1927 the American-born wife of the poet, Angelos Sikelianos, organised a Delphic festival which included a performance of the *Prometheus Bound* of Aeschylus, the first ancient tragedy performed in this theatre since the Edict of Theodosius. It launched a fashion. Theatrical companies now tour the ancient sites of the country, and the works of the Attic tragedians are good box office from Epidaurus to Dodona. I once attended a performance of the *Oedipus Rex* of Sophocles here. It was a late afternoon in August. The calamities that befell the house of Labdacus were followed by the provincial audience with audible emotion. Like their ancient ancestors, the Greeks have a genuine love of the theatre and they easily identify themselves with the epic figures of ancient tragedy. I remember the moment when the blinded Oedipus stumbled out of the palace, crying:

> 'O dark intolerable inescapable night
> That has no day!'

The rose-coloured light had just faded from the Phaedriades. Grey shadows spread across the mountains. It was brilliant timing.

To the right of the theatre, beyond the dried-up stream of Cassiotis, which watered the sacred groves of laurel and myrtle and flowed through a secret channel into the adytum of the temple, where the Pythia drank from its waters before prophesying, a path leads to the site of the Lesche of the Cnidians. Its walls were of unburnt brick, and the interior was in the form of a rectangular atrium. Four stone socles for wooden columns which supported the wooden roof are all that remains of this famous rest-house, where pilgrims sought shade and shelter. Within the atrium the celebrated paintings of Polygnotus, depicting scenes from the Trojan War, were exhibited on boards. None survive. But recalling the great collection of painted vases in the National Museum in Athens, the organic relation between composition and detail that characterises them, and the felicitous sense of order created by the disposal of figures in constant motion on successive bands – puce, black or white – one feels that no other landscape can have exercised a greater influence on Greek painters than that of 'hallowed Pytho'; for none other so completely illustrates the faultless disposition of nature's complementary forms.

From the theatre another path climbs (left) between bushes of arbutus and blackberry to an astonishing altitude – beyond the boundaries of the Sanctuary proper – where the **stadium**, culminating point of the ancient city, extends across a terrace immediately below the Phaedriades. The best preserved of Greek stadia, it once seated seventeen thousand spectators.

Built in the mid-fifth century B.C., it probably did not possess stone accommodation until the fourth. Most of the existing tiers are of the Antonine period. The entrance is from the south-east. Of the Roman triumphal arch there remain four pillars. Here began the procession of athletes which made a circuit of the race-track, past the tribune where seats with backs were reserved for representatives of the Amphictyonic League. As at the Olympic stadium, the *aphesis* (with grooves for the runners' toes) and *terma* are preserved. The expense of maintaining a race-track accommodating seventeen runners at such an altitude must have been considerable, and a mid-third century B.C. inscription refers to the cost of clearing and levelling the track, of digging the jumping pit, of putting up fencing and turning posts and carrying up enormous quantities of sand required for the surface. On the north bank, against the cliff-side, are twelve well preserved tiers divided into as many sections by stairways; on the west and south, where there is a sharp declivity buttressed by a polygonal wall supporting the mountain shelf, only six. A slight concavity in the centre was intended to prevent the spectator's view from being obstructed by his neighbours. A niche near the semi-circular end led to a fountain where the audience could refresh themselves with ice-cold water.

Like the Olympic Games, the Pythian festival, also a pan-hellenic celebration, was held every four years. It opened with the recitation of the Hymn to Apollo, to the accompaniment of a lyre, celebrating the god's victory over Python. The athletic programme was the same as at Olympia, with the addition of a long race for boys and, last and most spectacular of all, a race in bronze armour. Chariot races were held in the Sacred Plain (see p. 336). Victors were crowned with wreaths of laurel plucked by small boys. There was no other reward, except the adulation so dear to the Greek heart. The honour of a victory at the Pythian Games was second only to that of an Olympic award. A typical instance was that of Doreius, a popular athlete captured by the Athenians while commanding a hostile fleet during the Peloponnesian War, but promptly released because of the prestige he had acquired in a succession of Pythian victories. In one point the programme differed from that of Olympia. Music played an important part. There were singing and flute solo compositions, and later lyre-playing. Pindar calls the flautist's melody 'that glorious incentive to contests', a 'many-headed tune' which resembled the hissing of serpents. Pausanias, however, says flute-playing competitions were finally dropped because 'the tunes of the flute were most dismal and the songs sung to the tunes were lamentations'. Greek musicians are still often inspired by the most melancholy sentiments, which find expression (in popular music) in the *myrologoi*, funeral laments chanted by peasants over the dead; only the clarinet has now replaced the flute.

From the stadium there is a short cut to the centre of the village. It is more rewarding, however, to zigzag down through the Sanctuary, regain the main road and, walking east, reach the Castalian Spring. Although now a parking place for motor coaches, this remains an idyllic spot. Large plane trees shade the stream issuing out of a ravine which cleaves the Phaedriades in two. The source, whose water is ice-cold and extraordinarily clear, is the site of an ancient cult-worship. Greek visitors, with their passion for water of the purest quality, are constantly drinking from it. Above the spring is the niche of an old shrine. Consultants and athletes purified themselves by washing their hair (only convicted murderers bathed their whole bodies) in Castalia's lustral water before proceeding to the temple and the stadium. Roman poets were said to be inspired by their muse after drinking it. A path leads a short way into the gloomy ravine between the Phaedriades, strewn with huge boulders, pitted with unsuspected crevices. Rocks, propelled by no human agency, occasionally crash down from above.

Beyond the café below the road a path winds down to the **Marmaria**, Sanctuary of Athena Pronaea. The first complex of ruins is the fourth century B.C. gymnasium, with Roman additions, distributed on different levels and buttressed by supporting walls. This was the practice-ground for athletes entered for the Pythian Games, with a covered race-track in the form of a colonnade (used in bad weather) running parallel to the open-air one. Among the weeds and thistles lies a stone slab with a groove and socket, believed to have been a practice start, equipped with a husplex, a mechanical device that made a loud noise as it fell, thus giving the signal for the start. In the *Phaedrus*, Plato compares sprinters rearing back from the husplex, waiting for the report of the falling arm, to charioteers reining in their horses just before the race. On the lower level of the palaestra is an open once colonnaded court, with remains of a round basin (probably a bath) and openings for showers at regular intervals in the supporting wall.

The path slants down the hill under shady olive branches to the Sanctuary of Athena Pronaea, less spectacular than Apollo's, but no less beautiful. Carpeted in spring with grape-hyacinths and bee-orchids, it extends across a rectangular shelf below the eastern projection of the Phaedriades. Chameleons slither along ruts and cracks in the hacked masonry; bees swarm in the sweet-smelling bay trees. First comes the stylobate of an austere fourth century B.C. Temple of Athena, guardian of the precinct. Foundations of other temples and buildings, slabs of bluish limestone and fragments of broken drums litter the terraced olive grove. But the pride of the sanctuary is the **Tholos,** a circular fourth century B.C. edifice on a three-stepped platform. A work of extreme elegance, it had an outer ring of twenty Doric and an interior one of ten Corinthian columns and was crowned by a conical roof. The gutter of the entablature had a rich ornamentation, including lion-head spouts, one of which is preserved above a restored metope. Three stout yet graceful Doric columns, surmounted by a lintel and fragments of metopes, rise from the stylobate. What purpose the temple served is not known. It certainly remains a lovely ruin, and the setting, with the valley contracting to its narrowest point, is peaceful and bucolic – shady, scented, with insects humming in the bushes of cistus. There is none of the overcrowding that creates such a jigsaw puzzle effect in the Sanctuary of Apollo.

Beyond the Tholos are the substructures of two treasuries: the first, that of Marseilles, is thought, judging from several courses of the base, to have been an elegant little building in the Ionic style, contemporary with the Treasury of Siphnos. Next comes the debris of the early fifth-century B.C. Temple of Athena Pronaea, built of tufa on the site of a much earlier edifice. This is where thunderbolts, Herodotus affirms, fell on a Persian detachment about to plunder the sanctuary on the eve of Salamis, and 'two pinnacles of rock, torn from Parnassus, came crashing and rumbling down . . .' Seized by panic, the Persians fled. The story is one of the rare examples of a display of family loyalty among the Olympians. Generally they tend to undermine each other's interests. In this instance, Athena offered her temple, demolished in the landslide, as a buffer to protect her half-brother's more precious shrine. The goddess of wisdom did not always show such magnanimity. Three thick Doric columns still survive at the north-west corner and two enormous boulders, lying across the stylobate, provide evidence of the repeated landslides. Beyond the Marmaria lies the necropolis of the ancient city.

Several paths descend through terraces of olive groves to the bed of the Pleistos. Vestiges of the polygonal masonry of supporting walls are discernible. In autumn donkeys carrying huge panniers filled with olives clamber up the stony tracks. There are few dwellings: only an occasional chapel, ruined or abandoned. At the bottom of the gorge the feeling of isolation is complete. The stream of the Pappadia trickles down from the Castalian Spring, and there is a grotto, surrounded by contorted boulders, said to be the ancient Sybaris, where the Lamia, a sphinx-like monster that ravaged the countryside, dwelt in a subterranean lair. The walk takes about two hours.

A longer walk or ride (about six hours there and back) is to a more famous grotto, the **Corycian Cave.** The path climbs the southern wall of the Phaedriades behind the village to a highland plateau of stones and stunted pines dominated by the summit of Parnassus. Black mountain-goats hop vertiginously from boulder to boulder, led by flaxen-haired shepherds carrying sheepskin gourds. The cave, to which the track ultimately leads (it is essential to have a guide) is at the north-west end of the plateau below the fir belt. I confess I cannot share the enthusiasm of Pausanias, who found it, of all the caves he had ever seen, the finest. Euripides extols its 'mountain-chambers', of which there are said to be forty, their damp walls shining with pink and green reflections. The light of a candle reveals stalactites and stalagmites. The cave was named after the nymph Corycia, beloved of Apollo, and was sacred to the nymphs and Pan. On these heights dwelt the wild Thyad women, whose 'flaming torch held high in the night', lit up the sombre solitude as Dionysus leapt swiftly 'onwards among his frenzied followers'.[3] The base of the final ascent to the cave (twenty minutes' hard climbing) can also

3. Euripides, the *Ion*.

be reached by car along a rough road from Arachova (see p. 346).

The **museum,** its barrack-like façade somewhat incongruous in this most classical of landscapes, is situated halfway between the Sanctuary of Apollo and the village. Before entering it is worth looking at two fourth-century A.D. floor mosaics (right of entrance). During the late Roman period mosaic floors were found to be less costly as embellishments of country villas than pavements of polychrome marbles, and the fashion spread throughout the Mediterranean. The decoration of the two pavements at Delphi is largely composed of birds: parrots, red-legged partridges and spotted guinea-fowl. The larger one, however, has a wider zoological range, and the mosaicist has reproduced a number of stylised animals, including a horse, camel, greyhound and wild boar.

The interior of the museum is spacious and well lit, but few of the precious fragments are numbered. At the top of the flight of stairs stands an ovoid stone object, a copy of the original sacred stone, the omphalos or so-called navel of the earth, with its interlocking marble fillets symbolising the continuity of life, which was placed in the adytum of the Temple of Apollo. From here on the arrangement is more or less chronological.

In Room 1 are displayed bronze shields and a small seventh-century bronze kouros. Room 2 is full of interest. The **Naxian Sphinx,** a heraldic work of the mid-sixth century B.C., towers up on a marble plinth crowned by an Ionic capital. Seated on her hind paws, with scythe-shaped wings and a bosom ornamented with stylised feathers, she gazes imperviously into space. Yet her high-cheek-boned face is compellingly human. The crouching position recalls the monolithic lions of Delos: also products of a Naxian but probably earlier workshop. There is a feeling of an aristocratic tradition about these works. They radiate order, taste, authority.

Fascinating fragments of the **frieze of the Treasury of Siphnos** are ranged along the walls. Dated to the sixth century B.C., the figures are without the least trace of crudity. The sculptures, though battered, quickly come to life. In the battle of the gods against the giants (north side) a tornado of agitation galvanises the figures into action. The gods are depicted on the left, the giants on the right. Spears, swords and boulders are used as weapons. A lion digs its fangs into the exposed torso of a helmeted giant. Apollo and an exultant Artemis aim arrows. A stocky-limbed Ares, smirking with self-confidence, takes on a couple of giants over the prostrate body of a third. Hera dispatches another. It is like a curtain-raiser to the far greater battle of the Centaurs and Lapiths at Olympia. The east side depicts seated gods debating the issue of the Trojan War: Athena, Hera and Hebe, the pro-Greek faction, on the right; the pro-Trojan Ares, Aphrodite and Artemis, and Apollo who turns to address them, on the left. They are obviously taking an enormous interest in the quarrel. The detail of the frieze is fascinating. Both the pliability of the stylised drapery and the difference in texture between the naked flesh and the long ringlets of the head-dresses point to the chisel of a master sculptor. Particularly beautiful are the filleted manes and tails of the horses in the south frieze which describes the story of the abduction of the twin sisters, Phoebe and Hilaira, by the twin Dioscuri. The west frieze (in a poor state of preservation) depicts the Judgement of Paris. The reliefs ran round the entire building, framed between decorative fillets. In its entirety, with its crowd of agitated figures and prancing horses, the frieze must have been a masterpiece of refinement, liveliness and sophistication.

Room 3 is dominated by two crude and impressive early sixth-century B.C. figures of **Cleobis and Biton,** the Argive boys who, in the absence of oxen, harnessed themselves to a chariot and bore their mother across the plain to the Temple of Hera, where she was chief priestess. For their pains, the goddess rewarded the youths with eternal sleep. Cleobis (right), who is better preserved than his brother, possesses all the 'inner mobility' associated with later, more polished Archaic kouroi. Tough, stocky, with short muscular arms, an expression of expectancy on his slightly parted lips, he is endowed with remarkable tension, ready to spring forward and harness himself to his mother's chariot. An interesting feature is the absence of toes on the feet of both figures. This is believed to imply that they once wore high-heeled shoes. The five stone metopes of the Treasury of Sicyon, depicting the exploits of the heroes, are damaged almost beyond recognition.

Rooms 4–8 contain fragments of metopes from the

Athenian Treasury (labours of Heracles, exploits of Theseus); hacked figures (with uncompleted backs) from the Temple of Apollo; metopes and coffers from the ceiling of the Tholos. In Room 7, besides two bronze kalpis (elegantly shaped ewers with three handles), there is a fine stele of an athlete extending his arms to the right, while a bereaved child, no doubt his servant, gazes up from the right hand corner. The modelling of the athlete's arms and torso is in the best classical tradition. Unfortunately both figures are headless.

In Room 9 the **Column of the Dancing Girls,** an unusual monument of the Hellenistic period, soars towards the ceiling. The shaft, about 30 feet high, was so carved as to resemble a gigantic acanthus stalk, the foot of each drum being surrounded by luxuriant foliage. Grouped round the highest tier of leaves are the three girls performing a hieratic dance. In spite of the fundamental awkwardness of the composition, the girls' drapery is loose and flowing and they possess much of the life and grace which the more solemn Caryatids of the Erectheum lack. The nude athlete, the **Thessalian Agas,** winner of fourteen awards at panhellenic festivals, is a good late fourth century B.C. marble copy of a bronze work by Lysippus.

The bronze **Charioteer** stands – very properly, very excitingly – alone in Room 10, against a pale grey background. He could not be more effectively exhibited. The life-size figure, made up of seven separately cast parts, belonged to a quadriga placed on the terrace of the temple, the gift of a Sicilian tyrant in the first half of the fifth century B.C. Only the shaft and yoke of the chariot survive. The tail and hind legs of a horse have also been found. The team, probably depicted at the moment of the finish (some scholars believe it to be the start), commemorated a victory in a chariot race. Although the charioteer's arm and hand, holding a rein, are muscular and powerful, the expression of his face, with the high cheekbones and long full chin, which is slightly asymmetrical (indicating that it was meant to be looked at diagonally), is gentle, and the marvellously preserved eyes of onyx and magnesium are limpid. The head, turned to the right, is adorned with a fillet with a meander pattern, and the spiral locks of the nape are so finely chiselled that one almost senses the dampness of the matted hair. The veined, beautifully modelled feet are set close together. The heavy tubular drapery of the tunic, perfect in its symmetry and rhythm, creates a columnar effect that distinguishes this work from all other Greek statues. From all angles, the figure remains stately, if disproportionate, for the sculptor, possibly a Magna Graecian, was endeavouring to correct the distortion which is inevitable when life-size figures are viewed from below. As a person, however, the Charioteer lacks the authority of the Poseidon of Artemisium or the Piraeus Apollo, the two other bronze masterpieces of the fifth century B.C. One suspects he may have been just a good-looking stable boy with a nice nature and little personality. He is certainly not a god.

Room 11, although not without interest, is an anti-climax. A well preserved Antinoos represents the Roman era: a gentle flaccid figure. Among the small objects are bronze bats and crouching lionesses, the head of a greyhound and geo-metric horses. One of the terracotta figurines depicts a female figure, naked to the waist, leaning on a column, another a fully and stylishly dressed lady, with traces of paint. In their coquettish eighteenth century elegance they might have stepped out of a painting by Fragonard.

Passing out of this last hall, marvelling at the incomparable blend of skill and rapture with which Greek sculptors reproduced the forms of the human body, with which they drew skin over bone and drapery over flesh, created a rhythmic organisation of hips, thorax and abdomen and related the turn of the head to the movement of the legs, one is suddenly confronted with a staggering view of the Phaedri-ades framed within sheet-glass windows. Russet-coloured, they tower up on either side of the ravine that slashes them into two separate but complementary volumes; on the periphery, the olive groves, watered by rivulets of the Castalian Spring, shelve down into the valley, and purple shadows shift across the outer ring of mountains 'whence Apollo twanged his bow . . . in the world's centre'.[4] The spirit of harmony that must have existed between the creative genius of the Greeks and the external visible world in which they dwelt is not now beyond the bounds of comprehension.

What is more difficult to understand is how that colossal

4. Euripides, *The Phoenician Women*.

hoax, the Delphic oracle, could have taken in so many people for so long.

For some travellers Delphi may be the end of the journey. But it is not the end of Greece. North and west of Parnassus lies all continental Greece: different in character, more varied in landscape, historical associations and extant ruins. But never again is the shape and feel of things the same. Here, at Delphi, the seal of Classical Greece, of that ideal of perfectionism of form, so consistently reflected in the light and landscape – whether in the rocky coasts of Attica, the radiant shut-in plains of the Peloponnese or the sculptural contours of Parnassus – seems to be as indelibly stamped as it was on the Acropolis at Athens, where this journey of Pausanias' Greece began.

Appendices

❧

Some Practical Suggestions

Seasons

JANUARY–FEBRUARY can be cold and wet, with intervals of brilliant winter sunshine. A period of cloudless skies and calm seas in early January corresponds to the ancient Halcyon Days: breeding time of the mythological halcyon birds. Brief falls of snow are not uncommon in Attica and Boeotia (high mountains are snow-covered November–April). Woodcock shooting. Almond blossom and first wild flowers (anemones).

MARCH, unpredictable, as everywhere. Hillsides covered with wild flowers. Mid-March to mid-April ideal period for botanists.

APRIL can be showery or idyllic. Good season for travelling with lengthening days. Dirt-roads sometimes impassable after spring rains. Scent of lemon and orange blossom intoxicating in orchard country.

MAY, generally fine and warm. Occasional rain. Flowers in profusion.

JUNE, good month for travelling. Not too hot. Sometimes cloudy in the middle of the day.

JULY–AUGUST, very hot. Hordes of tourists. Season of fruits. Crystalline light emphasises structural quality of landscape. Barren mountains the colour of gunmetal turn a glowing purple in late afternoon. North-east etesian winds.

SEPTEMBER, still full summer, but not as hot as July–August. Fewer tourists; fewer local trippers. Quail-shooting.

OCTOBER, in spite of the first rains, generally lives up to the tradition of a 'golden autumn'. Hillsides covered with cyclamen and autumn crocus.

NOVEMBER, unpredictable. Can be a prolongation of the 'golden autumn' or a foretaste of December. Dirt roads often impassable after autumn rains.

DECEMBER, inclined to be cloudy, raw, but not very cold, with some fine spells and magnificent winter sunsets.

Museums

Hours of opening, which are liable to alter and are certainly not uniform throughout the country, should be checked on the spot (hotel receptionists have all the up-to-date pamphlets).

Museums at small ancient sites (often no more than shacks serving as store-rooms) have no regular hours of opening. The *phylax* (guard), who is generally on the spot, has the keys.

All museums throughout the country (including the Acropolis at Athens, the Sanctuary of Apollo at Delphi, the Altis at Olympia and other major archaeological sites) are shut on 1st January, 25th March (Independence Day), Good Friday (Orthodox), Easter Sunday (Orthodox), Christmas Day.

Countryside Churches and Chapels

These, even when of considerable historical or artistic interest, are often locked. The keys are generally kept by the local *pappas* (priest) or unofficial *phylax* (the owner of the main café in the nearest village will send a child to fetch either). The child will also show you the way to the church, return the keys to the responsible person and be pleased to receive a tip.

Communications (for the non-motorist)

Inquiries about bus and train timetables can be made at all hotels and travel agencies. Buses are plentiful. The remotest mountain villages are connected with the nearest town by a daily service. Due, perhaps, to the successive hairpin bend ascents and descents Greek passengers are inclined to be car-sick (nylon bags are provided).

Taxis or private cars (for long journeys) are parked in the main squares of small provincial towns. Prices are not exorbitant, but should be fixed in advance.

In Athens there are plenty of car-hire agencies (with or without driver). Travel agents and hotels have all the addresses.

The railway network does not cover the whole country. One can make a complete (more or less coastal) tour of the Peloponnese, touching inland at Tripolis and Megalopolis (there is also a branch line from Pyrgos to Olympia), and one can go from Athens to Salonica, and thence to Jugoslavia or Turkey, but one cannot cross the Pindus spine which runs vertically down the length of mainland Greece.

The non-walker who wishes to visit some ancient site, castle or church, to which no passable road leads, may hire a mule or donkey. As usual, the owner of the café in the nearest village is the person to approach for information. Mule- or donkey-riding is one of the most agreeable ways of seeing the countryside, although the saddle-bags are sometimes flea-ridden. Riding is particularly recommended when visiting Frankish castles, the keeps of which are perched on precipitous crags.

Travel Agencies

Although the American Express (2 Ermou Street) and Cooks-Wagons Lits (8 Ermou Street) make all the necessary arrangements for tours, travellers are likely to receive more personal attention and obtain more precise information (hotels, condition of roads, motor coach tours, time involved, etc.) from one of the smaller travel agencies in Athens. Among these are:

HELLENIC TOURS, 3 Stadiou Street (Stoa Calliga)
HEL-PA, 18 E. Venizelou (Panepistimiou) Street
HERMES EN GRÈCE, 4 Stadiou Street

KOSMOS, 1 Mitropoleos Street (Syntagma Square)
NICOLOUDES TOURS, 9 Valaoritou Street

Beaches

It would require a small volume to list these. In most parts of the country, the beaches, whether sand, shingle or pebbly, are superb. Those which I consider outstanding are mentioned in the relevant passages in the text.

Transliteration of Place Names

On the highways and main roads the motorist will find signposts in English as well as Greek (off the beaten track there are often no signposts, and one has to keep asking the way). The official transliteration of Greek place names seems to be both arbitrary and quixotic. 'Pireefs' for 'Piraeus', for instance, and 'Olimbia' for 'Olympia'. The present tendency (in Greece) to try to equate the English spelling of place names with modern Green pronunciation is all very well, but 'Delfoi' and 'Mikinae' look odd, to say the least. In writing this book, I have aimed at keeping usage and common sense as my principal guides in the transliteration of all names.

Hotels

Both in Athens and the provinces, hotels are being built so fast that any list given here would be out-of-date (certainly incomplete) by the time this book is published. Nevertheless, the names of a few hotels are mentioned in the text: largely because of their outstanding position.

The monthly publication, *Key Travel Guide for Greece and the Middle East* (obtained from any travel agent), gives a complete list of hotels (when built or restored), with prices, number of rooms, private bathrooms, whether air-conditioned, etc. It contains similar information regarding pensions and service flats (Athens only), bungalows and holiday camps. Any travel agent will also provide more accurate up-to-date information than is likely to be contained within the compass of a book of this kind.

There may be two opinions about the official classification of hotels by the Greek Ministry of Tourism. By Western standards there are only two real luxury hotels in Athens, the Grande Bretagne and the Hilton, and not eight as at present officially listed. The tendency is to up-grade the various categories. Nevertheless, second and, in many cases, third class hotels are perfectly adequate. Most bedrooms have a shower, if not a bath. The hotels of the government-subsidised Xenias group, found at all the tourist sites, are superbly situated, generally on the periphery of the town or village. Signposts direct the traveller.

Restaurants, Tavernas, Cafés

The average Greek has never been a fastidious gastronome. The works of ancient authors contain few references to their repasts. Homeric kings live on bread, wine, olive oil and roast kid. No elaborate dishes are mentioned by the great dramatists or by Plato when Socrates and his companions converse round the dining-table. The same applies to Byzantium. No Byzantine chronicler has left any record of the meals served in the imperial palace or the houses of the Byzantine aristocracy.

The main ingredients in modern Greek cooking are olive oil, tomatoes, onions, garlic, synthetic fats. Most dishes are of Turkish (romantics say Byzantine) origin. In private houses, where the quality of the materials (butter, oil, fats) is good, several dishes can be delicious, such as pilaff, the ubiquitous *mousaka* (minced meat between layers of fried aubergines and onions, with a crust of béchamel at the top) and vegetables (tomatoes, peppers, aubergines, vegetable marrows) stuffed with rice, herbs and minced meat.

The lack of interest in the quality, temperature and presentation of food is not conducive to a demand for a wide range of restaurants. The traveller is likely to be amazed at the paucity of restaurants in a city the size of Athens. Tavernas provide occasions, often delightful, for dining in a relaxed informal atmosphere, but the food (at which Greeks peck leisurely and without the Western concept of an ordered sequence of dishes) is seldom memorable – veal or lamb chops, fried potatoes (soggy), *horiatiki* salad (sliced tomatoes, with peppers, olives, onions and chunks of goat's milk cheese), sometimes a tepid *mousaka*, and, with luck, the delicious smoky flavoured *melintzanosalata* (aubergines worked with oil – occasionally with yoghourt – into a pulp and flavoured with onions).

Travellers with queasy stomachs had best keep to grilled meat (and fish, when obtainable). Most restaurants (but not tavernas) are indoor, even at the height of summer. Service is slapdash, but waiters can be friendly. They often lose their heads, but seldom their sense of humour.

Wines, both red and white, are fair to good, and rapidly improving. So are the cheeses: Fontina (Port Salut type), Cretan Gruyère, Serres (Parmesan type), Kasseri (the Turkish *kaskaval*), Manouri (Mozarella type). The summer fruits (May–September) – strawberries, cherries, plums, yellow peaches, grapes, figs and melons – are beyond praise. Greek beer (lager type) is excellent.

A comprehensive list of restaurants and tavernas would certainly be out of date by the time this book is published. A restaurant (and/or taverna) with certain pretensions may be open one year, shut the next. A selective list of restaurants is published in the daily English-language newspaper *Athens News* and the weekly pamphlet *The Week in Athens*, which can be bought at any kiosk in the central area of Athens.

The following are a few restaurants and tavernas which seem to be permanent fixtures in Athens (no restaurant or taverna in the provinces of Southern and Central Greece is worth mentioning).

Restaurants

CORFU, 6 Kriezotou Street, Corfiot and semi-international cooking. Moderate prices.

DELFOI, 13 Nikis Street. Mainly Greek dishes. Cheap.

DIONYSOS, 43 Roverto Galli Street (opposite Theatre of Herodes Atticus). Superb view of the Acropolis. International cuisine. Expensive.

FLOCA, 9 E. Venizelou Avenue. Cafeteria atmosphere. International cooking. Expensive.

L'ABREUVOIR, 51 Xenocratous Street. Open-air in summer. French cuisine. Expensive. Best restaurant in Athens.

VASILIS, 14A Voukourestiou Street. Greek and semi-international cooking. Moderate prices.

YEROPHINOIKAS, 10 Pindarou Street, Restaurant-cum-taverna. Wide selection of Greek and oriental dishes. Expensive.

ZONAR, 9 E. Venizelou Street. Central. Cafeteria atmosphere. International and Greek cooking. Expensive.

Tavernas

KOSTOYANNI, 37 Zaimis Street. Specialities: Greek hors d'œuvre (well presented); prawn (or crab) salad. Moderate prices.

O YEROS TOU MOURIA, 27 Mnesicleous Street. Orchestra. Situated in most picturesque part of the Plaka (see p. 51). Very popular with tourists. Expensive. Noisy.

PLATANOS, 4 Diogenes Street (near Tower of the Winds – agreeable setting). Greek cooking. Unpretentious and cheap.

TA TRIA ADELPHIA, 7 Elpidou Street. Specialities: Greek hors d'œuvre (well presented). Moderate prices.

XINOU, 4 Angelos Yerondas Street. Orchestra. Most Greek dishes (and grills). Probably best all-round taverna in Athens.

ZVINGOS, 41 Ayia Zoni Street. Specialities: pork, lamb and chicken roasted on the spit.

The larger brightly illuminated tavernas of the Plaka (Athens) – Erotocritos, Vakhous, Palaia Athena, Kastro, etc. – have elaborate floor-shows. The food is indifferent and expensive.

With few exceptions, tavernas do not serve luncheons.

The fish restaurants (taverna type) outside Athens are agreeable – particularly at Tourcolimano (see p. 87) and Glyphada (see p. 89). Here luncheons are served.

It might be worth noting that all luxury, first, second and some third class hotels in Athens, and all the Xenias group in the provinces, have restaurants.

Cafés (both indoor and open-air) – they are also confectioners – proliferate all over the capital, suburbs and provincial towns. The confectionery element is the more popular with Greeks, who have a very sweet tooth. The range of cream-cakes is staggering. The ices are generally good. Many open-air cafés are open until well after midnight.

As in many Mediterranean countries, café life has always played a large role in shaping the people's and country's destinies. In many of the downtown cafés of Athens contracts are drafted, debts contracted and settled, dowries discussed, important new contacts made and plots to overthrow the government hatched.

There is no need to list the cafés. They are there for all to see: in the capital, at every street corner; in small provincial towns, in the main square.

Shops

Athens is not a capital for the fastidious shopper, although the quality of goods on sale (both local and imported) is improving rapidly. A weekly pamphlet, published in English and French, on sale at all kiosks in the centre of the city, lists chemists, department stores, discothèques, florists, hairdressers, jewellers, photographers, lingerie shops, perfumeries, etc.[1]

The principal shopping areas are Ermou Street (drapers, lingerie, perfumes) and Stadiou Street (stores, shoes, men's haberdashers). There are expensive boutiques in the Kolonaki and Syntagma Square areas.

Antiques and local handicrafts are more likely to interest the traveller. The best antiquaries are:

MARTINOS, 50 Pandrossou Street (icons, silverware, ancient ceramics, figurines, etc.).

MEZIKIS & PARIGORY, 5 Neophytou Vamva Street (carpets, silverware, furniture).

ZOUMBOULAKIS, Antiquities, 7 Kriezotou Street (jewellery, coins, figurines from ancient tombs, icons).

Travellers should obtain an export licence from the shopkeeper for any purchase of value (if an antique) which they intend to take out of the country. Failure to do so may result in confiscation and payment of a fine.

The best selection of handicrafts are found at:

DIPLOU PELEKIS (The Double Axe), 23b Voulis Street (scarves,

1. *The Week in Athens* also contains useful addresses (Embassies, Consulates, banks, car repair services, as well as ferry-boat schedules, timetables of sailings to islands, air flights, etc.).

bags, handwoven rugs, tablecloths, ashtrays and vases of Cretan alabaster).

VASILIKI PRONOIA (Their Majesties' Fund) – 24a Voukourestiou and 10 Stadiou (Stoa Lemou) Streets (handwoven rugs and carpets with old island and Byzantine designs; stoles, tablecloths, bags, embroidered slippers).

Tourist shops, filled with imitation vases, modern icons and plaster casts of famous statues, are centred round the Syntagma Square area. Here are also displayed *tagharia* (woollen bags) and tablecloths, etc., woven with peasant designs. The show-cases in the Hilton Hotel give a general idea of the high standard of workmanship of ancient Byzantine jewellery (for addresses of jewellers see *The Week in Athens*). Some of the modern icons (copies of old Byzantine ones) are also of a high standard.

There is a brisk trade in furs. The main furriers in Athens are:

FUR HOUSE, George M. Trakos, 7 Philhellinon Street
VOULA KITSAKOU LTD, 7 Mitropoleos Street
SISTOVARIS FRÈRES, 9 E. Venizelou Street.

The traveller will be impressed by the number of English bookshops, well stocked with standard works and all the latest publications. The main ones are:

ATLANTIS, 8 Korais Street
CACOULIDES, 39 E. Venizelou Street
ELEUTHEROUDAKIS, 4 Nikis Street (the largest)
KAUFMANN, 11 Voukourestiou Street (mainly books on Greece; also old prints)
PANTELIDES, 11 Amerikis Street
LES AMIS DU LIVRE, 9 Valaoritou Street (rare editions of English and French books on Greece).

English and foreign newspapers are on sale at about 8 o'clock in the evening, the Sunday papers around 11 o'clock in the morning, at all kiosks in the Syntagma Square and Kolonaki areas.

Outside Athens (and Salonika in Northern Greece) there are no shops worth mentioning. Villages specialising in regional handicrafts are mentioned in the text.

Feasts and Holidays

1st January. Public holiday. Feast of St Basil, one of the most distinguished Early Christian Fathers of the Church. *Vasilopitta* (the cake of St Basil), a kind of large round brioche, is eaten in every Greek house. It contains a coin which brings good luck to the finder.

6th January. Epiphany. Public holiday. Blessing of the Waters. An official ceremony is held at the Piraeus, attended by high-ranking prelates, flanked by acolytes bearing banners, cabinet ministers and representatives of the armed forces. As the officiating priest throws the cross into the sea and the waters are blessed, ships' sirens hoot and youths dive into the water to recover the cross. Throughout the country wells and springs are blessed.

At Ephiphany the earth is rid of *Callicantzari*, puckish demons with red eyes, monkey's arms and cleft hooves, who run amok during the twelve days after Christmas and are probably a Christian version of the boisterous and equally grotesque Satyrs and Sileni who danced attendance on Dionysus. Among the *Callicantzaris'* favourite pranks are riding piggy-back on frightened mortals, polluting food, making water on fires and flinging pitch on front doors.

February–March
(a) Carnival (the three weeks before Lent). During the three week-ends of the period, children in fancy dress roam the streets, and gypsies, accompanied by performing monkeys, bang on tambourines (into which pedestrians drop coins) at street corners. In Athens, the tavernas of the Plaka are crowded. Streamers and confetti litter the pavements. The most lively Carnival procession takes place in Patras during the third week-end (see p. 294).

(b) *Kathari Deutera* ('Clean Monday' – Monday after last Sunday of Carnival). A public holiday. So-called because it is the first day of Lent. There is a general exodus into the country, and the occasion is one for picnics. Kite-flying begins. In some villages dumb-shows are staged by itinerant mummers. At Thebes there is a lively parody of a peasant wedding, a thinly veiled spring fertility rite, at which the relatives arrive riding donkeys backwards. The bride (a man disguised as a woman) is bedecked with clanging bronze bells round her neck.

'Clean Monday' diet (meatless and served cold) consists of *phasolia piaz* (beans dressed with olive oil and sprinkled with slivers of onion), *taramosalata* (a pinkish paste made of cod's roe, bread-crumbs and olive oil, to which chopped onions and dill may be added), *yalantzi dolmadhes* (rice, currants and pine-nuts cooked in olive oil and wrapped up in vine leaves, flavoured with onion), and *laghana*, flat loaves of un-leavened bread.

25th March. Independence Day. Public holiday. Anniversary of the day when Bishop Germanos raised the standard of revolt against the Turks at Kalavryta in 1821 (see p. 302). Military parades are held in all towns and villages. The feast of the Annunciation is also celebrated in all churches.

The Easter Cycle[2]
Maundy Thursday. Housewives dye the red eggs which will be cracked and eaten on Easter Day. The first egg placed in the dye belongs to the Virgin; it is regarded as a talisman and must not be eaten. The colour red is supposed to have pro-tective powers. Interiors of churches are decorated with black, purple and white shrouds, and church bells toll throughout the evening.

Good Friday. A day of complete fast, kept by the overwhelming majority of Greeks. Brown wax candles are sold at street corners. Church bells toll and funeral marches and religious music broadcast on all radio networks. Cemeteries are crowded with private mourners laying wreaths on graves.

At about nine in the evening (earlier in the villages), the Epitaphios, the funeral of Christ, the most moving and beautiful ceremony in the Orthodox calendar, begins. Behind

2. Orthodox Easter generally falls within the second half of April, seldom before, occasionally in early May. The weather can be showery, but the flowers are at their most prolific, the gardens heavy with the scent of lilac, wistaria, Banksia roses and stocks.

the Cross, the body of Christ, in the form of a gold embroidered pall, smothered with wreaths woven out of scented flowers,
is borne under a gilded canopy through the main streets of
towns and villages. Priests (ranging from mitred bishops in
lavish vestments to black-frocked deacons) shuffle behind it,
flanked by acolytes in coloured shifts, carrying banners.
Then come the officials (civil and military) followed by a
crowd of silent dark-clothed worshippers, lighted candles
cupped in their hands. The procession halts at every street
corner where a short prayer is said. By about ten o'clock,
when the beflowered bier is borne back to the church and the
pall has been kissed by the faithful, all places of entertainment,
including many cafés and restaurants, are shut (for a description of the Epitaphios procession in Athens, see p. 48).

Easter Saturday. Nothing could be more striking than the
contrast between the solemnity of the Epitaphios and the
liveliness of the Anastasis, the Resurrection service, the
greatest feast in the Orthodox Church. Throughout the afternoon funereal drapings are removed from churches and
replaced with branches of laurel and myrtle, while sprigs of
rosemary are strewn across the floor of the naos. White (no
longer brown) candles, decorated with white or blue ribbons
(the national colours) are sold at open-air booths.

The service begins in a dim incense-laden atmosphere.
Gradually more lights are turned on until the whole church
is brilliantly illuminated. On the stroke of midnight the priest,
in a soaring triumphant tone, chants the words '*Christos
Anesti!*' ('Christ is risen!'). The doors of the sanctuary open
amid a blaze of light, and the bier, only yesterday borne to the
grave, is seen to be empty. Christ has risen. Church bells ring,
children shout and let off squibs in the street. Members of the
congregation shake hands or exchange the kiss of Resurrection,
murmuring 'Christ is risen!' All personal quarrels are (supposed to be) forgiven and forgotten.

The crowds then disperse, homeward bound, holding their
candles – it is a good omen to reach the house with the taper
alight – and break their fast with a dish of *mayeiritsa* (egg-
lemon soup with rice and chopped lambs' liver and entrails,
seasoned with dill – rich but delicious) and red-dyed hard-
boiled eggs.

Easter Sunday. A day of national rejoicing. In Athens the Head of State and the Cabinet attend the doxology in the Cathedral, while the cannon on Mt Lycabettus fires thunderous salvoes. The paschal lamb is roasted on a spit in gardens and open places, and red eggs are cracked by tapping one against the other. Houses are decorated with lilac: *paschalia*, the flower of Easter.

Easter Monday. Public holiday.

Friday after Easter. Feast of the Virgin Mary who is represented as the *Zoodochos Pighi*, 'The Source of Life'. In villages where the church is dedicated to the Life-Bearing Spring a procession headed by a priest carrying an icon of the Virgin winds through the streets in the late afternoon, as at Acharnae, twelve kilometres north-west of Athens (see p. 103). The procession is sometimes followed by folk-dancing.

23rd April. St George's Day. The young Eastern martyr is one of the most popular saints in the Orthodox calendar. Like the no less venerated Demetrius, he represents a Christian reincarnation of the noble ephebe of antiquity.

At Arachova, near Delphi (see p. 346), St George's Day is celebrated with a religious procession, the performance of folk-dances to the accompaniment of drums and bagpipes and athletic contests.

30th April. On the eve of May Day wreaths of flowers – stocks, roses, lilies, pansies – symbolising the advent of summer, are hung above the front doors of houses, where they remain, brown and withered until the feast of St John the Baptist, 24th June.

Athenians flock to the suburb of Ano-Patissia, where fireworks crackle and much wine is drunk in tavernas. There is little to eat except hacked pieces of (rather tepid) lamb roasted on open-air spits. The streets are lined with booths, where wreaths of flowers are sold, and late at night the pavements are littered with bruised blooms.

May Day itself may or may not be a public holiday, according to the party line taken by the government in office.

21st May. Feast of SS Constantine and Helena. Public holiday. The feast's importance derives from the aura of veneration attached to the figures of Constantine the Great, founder of the Byzantine Empire, and his pious mother, Helena.

Whit Monday. Public Holiday.

June–July. Festival of ancient drama at Epidaurus (see p. 165).

24th June. St John the Baptist's Feast. The summer solstice. Bonfires are lit in villages on the eve of St John's Day, and the inhabitants dance round the pyre into which the May Day wreaths are cast and leap over the embers, thus purifying themselves of their sins. The cinders, which possess protective and divinatory properties, are collected by housewives. Sea-bathing and the eating of water melon (cheapest and most popular of summer fruits) begin 'officially' on St John's Day, and the proverb runs 'Do not swim before you see water melon peel floating on the sea.'[3]

17th July. St Marina's Feast. The saint was martyred in Antioch in the third century and her feast ushers in the season of grapes. Peasants flock to the vineyards to cut the first bunches and bear offerings of fruit to the churches.

A fair is held outside the Church of Ayia Marina in the Theseum quarter at Athens, where the saint is worshipped as protectress against smallpox (she is also the scourge of all insects).

20th July. Feast of the prophet Elijah, patron saint of thunder, lightning and rain, worshipped on hill-tops crowned with whitewashed chapels where bonfires are sometimes lit (as on Mt Taygetus) and associated with the prophet's ascent to Heaven. As Lord of the Thunder (his thunderclaps are attributed to the rolling of the chariot wheels), he represents a Christian counterpart of Zeus.

3. George A. Megas, *Greek Calendar Customs*, Athens, 1963.

15th August. Assumption of the Virgin. Public holiday. After Easter and Christmas the most important religious holiday in the Greek calendar, a symbol of the Orthodox veneration of the Virgin. 1st–15th August is a period of fast, which Greeks keep with varying degrees of strictness.

Two great religious pilgrimages are made on 15th August: to the Aegean islands of Tinos (the Lourdes of Greece) and Paros.

29th August. Anniversary of the beheading of St John the Baptist. The malarial fevers that until recently ravaged many of the plains, especially during the torrid month of August, were supposed to be the manifestations of the shock or spasm suffered by the Baptist when he was beheaded to please Salome (a scene much favoured for reproduction in rustic icons). Fairs (*paneghyria*) are held in villages where the main church is dedicated to St John the Baptist.

September. Wine festival at Daphni, near Athens. Entrance charge covers unlimited wine-tasting. Rather bogus folk-dances (see p. 110).

14th September. The Exaltation of the Cross. An important Orthodox feast. In churches a priest presents the congregation with sprigs of basil as a token of the herb that sprouted at the foot of the Cross.

26th October. Feast of St Demetrius, one of the most popular saints in the calendar. All churches dedicated to St Demetrius, a gallant young convert martyred by Galerius in a public bath at Thessalonica, are brilliantly illuminated on the nights of 25th and 26th October.

The weather is usually fine and the last week in October is referred to as 'the summer of St Demetrius' – the Greek Indian Summer. The saint's name day is the occasion for the tasting of new wine.

28th October. Public holiday. Anniversary of the Italian invasion of Greece in 1940, in the course of which a small Greek army routed Mussolini's numerically superior but ill-equipped divisions. Commonly known as '*Ochi*'-day ('No'-

day) from the simple negative uttered by the Prime Minister, Ioannis Metaxas, when presented with the Fascist ultimatum by the Italian Ambassador.

6th December. St Nicholas' Day. Commonly regarded as the first day of winter. The saint, patron of sailors, is often represented in popular hagiography dressed in clothes covered with brine, sea-water dripping from his long white beard, after rescuing sailors from sinking ships in winter storms. His affinity with Poseidon is obvious, but he is more benign, less violent, than the Lord of the Trident. He prefers to pacify tempests rather than to rouse them.

Every Greek ship, from the largest ocean-going liner to the smallest caïque, possesses an icon of the saint covered with votive trinkets in the shape of vessels.

Chapels dedicated to St Nicholas abound in the islands and maritime districts of the mainland.

12th December. Feast of St Spyridon. The embalmed mortal remains of the Cypriot bishop, martyred during Diocletian's reign, and borne overland from Constantinople to Corfu after 1453 in order to escape Ottoman desecration, are now displayed in an ornamental silver coffin in the Church of St Spyridon at Corfu. The saint, patron of Corfu, is greatly venerated throughout the country.

The name Spyridon derives from the word *spyri*, a pimple, and, according to popular superstition, the wonder-working properties of the saint's relics act as an antidote against smallpox, rashes and skin diseases.

24th December. Little boys ring doorbells and ask: '*Na ta poúme*' ('Shall we tell them?') – in other words, should they sing the *kalanda* (the Greek equivalent of Christmas carols), while they beat a miniature hammer on a little metal triangle, in return for a small gratuity.

In Athens the sale of holly, mistletoe, Christmas trees, turkeys and other Christmas fare follows the Western pattern.

25th–26th December. Public holidays.

31st December. Singing of *kalanda* as on Christmas Eve. In the evening all Greeks play cards. It is considered a breach of tradition (if not of etiquette) not to try one's luck at the gaming-table on the threshold of the New Year.

Glossary

Some technical terms and untranslatable Greek words

abacus – slab crowning capital of a column.

acroteria – sculptured ornamental effigies or mouldings placed at either end of pediment in ancient Greek architecture. Modified form of acroteria may still be seen in some modern Greek architecture (particularly nineteenth century).

adytum – inner sanctuary and holiest chamber of a temple where oracles were delivered.

agora – a Greek market place. Equivalent to Roman forum.

aphesis – starting-post of an ancient Greek race-track.

aryballos – ancient flask (swollen in the centre) with a round base, used as a perfume container.

cavea – Latin for Greek Κοῖλον: the whole part of an ancient theatre reserved for spectators.

chiton – sleeveless tunic, fastened over the shoulder by clasps and round the waist with a girdle, worn by men and women in ancient Greece.

chlamys – oblong outer raiment, smaller than the himation (see below) and even more ornamented, hung from the neck.

choregic – pertaining to a choregus, administrator and financer of a chorus. Choregoi were wealthy citizens responsible for the training of members of the dance-chorus.

deme – geographical unit for local government purposes in ancient Greece.

diazôma – horizontal passage between the tiers of an ancient theatre which served as a foyer.

Dodecaorton – The Twelve Feasts, the principal scenes from the lives of Christ and the Virgin, which (either in mosaic or fresco) decorate the walls of all Byzantine churches.

Dormition – religious art term applied to funeral of holy personages, particularly the Virgin.

dromos – a public way, often lined with statues, temples, etc.

echinus – cushion-like moulding (ovolo moulding) fitted on top of a column immediately below the abacus. So-called because it resembled the shell of an *echinos* (sea-urchin).

entasis – a convexity of the shaft of a column: an intentional distortion designed to obviate the optical illusion whereby a straight column appears thinner in the centre than at the top or bottom.

ephor – Spartan magistrate.

epitaphios – flower-bedecked bier of Christ borne in procession in towns and villages throughout the country on the evening of Good Friday (also a gold-thread embroidery representing the body of Christ after the Deposition).

exedra – apsidal (sometimes rectangular shaped) recess with seats (classical architecture).

ex-voto – votive gift.

Glycophilousa – a type of icon of the Virgin and Child (The Sweetly-Kissing One) in which the Child is depicted resting his cheek against the Virgin's.

hammam – Turkish bath.

helot – Spartan serf who formed backbone of Spartan army.

hetaira – a courtesan in ancient Greece.

Hetoimasia – preparation of the Throne for the Second Coming.

himation – cloak of varying texture, colour and embroidered decoration, worn by both men and women in ancient Greece.

Hodeghetria – a type of icon in which the Virgin holds the Child with her left arm and points to him with her right hand. 'Hodeghetria' literally means 'indicator of the way'.

hoplite – heavily-armed ancient Greek infantryman.

hydrophorus – bearer of pitcher filled with water.

in antis – two porch columns between two prolongations (*antae*) of the side walls of the cella of a temple.

katavothra – subterranean stream flowing under hard lime-stone rock of many Greek mountains.

koré – an ancient Greek maiden. Term commonly applied to statues of young women of Archaic period.

kouros – an ancient Greek youth. Term commonly applied to statues of young men of Archaic period.

krater – a vessel with wide mouth in which liquids, chiefly wine and water, were mixed.

kokkineli – slightly resinated rosé wine.

lecythos – a slender vessel (derived from the domestic oil-flask) with long spout-like mouth, used at fifth-century B.C. funerals. The base is sometimes rounded.

mandorla – almond-shaped aureole surrounding depictions of holy personages in Christian art.

megaron – Homer's term for the great hall of a palace.

naos – the main chamber, or inner shrine, of a Greek temple, in which the effigy of the deity was kept. Also the main body of a Byzantine cruciform church, entered through the narthex.

nargileh – synonym for hookah.

odeum – concert hall.

oinoche – an ancient jug for pouring; with handle.

opisthodomos – back chamber of a temple, serving as a treasury.

orchestra – circular space below the lowest tier of an ancient theatre where the chorus chanted and performed dance patterns. A small segment of the circle was generally occupied by the narrow stage (see proscenium).

pancration – one of the most popular events in ancient athletic contests. A combination of boxing and wrestling (at Sparta all-in wrestling, including biting and scratching). Said to have been invented by Theseus when grappling with the Minotaur.

Pantocrator – The All-Ruler (Christ), an effigy of whom is depicted in the central cupola of most Byzantine churches.

parados – one of two side entrances into the orchestra of a Greek theatre used by the chorus only. The *parodoi* often had architectural embellishments.

pentathlon – one of the principal contests in Greek athletic competitions, consisting of a group of five events: long jump, discus and javelin throwing, foot race and wrestling.

peplos – fifth-century B.C. dress (ankle-length, belted up) worn by women on ceremonial occasions. Often elaborately embroidered.

peristyle – colonnade surrounding a temple or court.

phylax – guard, custodian.

pronaos – outer chamber (sometimes a portico) of a temple, in front of the naos.

propylaea – entrance way (generally a monumental gateway) to a sacred enclosure.

proscenium – narrow stage of an ancient theatre on which the protagonists, but not the chorus, performed.

prostyle – colonnaded portico in front of an ancient building.

protome – bust.

quadriga – chariot drawn by four horses.

skene – back wall of stage of ancient Greek theatre. Sometimes used loosely to mean the whole stage and its embellishments.

souvlakia – pieces of lamb, veal or pork grilled on a skewer.

sphendone – semi-circular end of race-track in a Greek stadium.

steatite – soapstone.

stele – upright stone or marble tablet, often sculptured, placed above ancient graves.

stylobate – continuous base or substructure from which the columns of a temple rise.

terma – finishing post of an ancient Greek race-track.

tholos – a circular building, generally a temple.

tholos tomb – circular mausoleum with a monumental approach and a conical beehive roof, covered with earth so as to form a tumulus.

triglyph – block of stone or marble carved with three vertical bars placed in the entablature of temples of the Doric order.

Chronological Table

B.C.
Neolithic Period (? *c.* 3200)

Early Helladic Period (*c.* 3200–1900)
c. 3000–2000   Early Bronze Age. Minoan civilisation in Crete.

Middle Helladic Period (c. 1900–1575)
c. 1900–1575   Middle Bronze Age. Achaeans settle at Mycenae.

Late Helladic Period (c. 1575–1100)
c. 1575–1100   Late Bronze Age.
c. 1400–1200   Mycenaean ascendancy on the mainland.
c. 1400   Destruction of Knossos and Phaestos in Crete.
c. 1250–1200   Trojan War.

Early Iron Age (c. 1100–750)
c. 1100–1000   Dorian invasion. Destruction of all Mycenaean cities.
c. 900–800   Legislation of Lycurgus at Sparta.
c. 800–700   Fame of Delphic oracle established.
776   First panhellenic games held at Olympia.

Archaic Period (750–480)
c. 750–700   Homer.
c. 730–10   First Messenian War.
c. 700–650   Megarian colonists found Byzantium.
c. 635–20   Second Messenian War.
594–93   Solon's social reforms in Athens.
582   Pythian festival at Delphi transformed into panhellenic celebration.
560–10   Tyranny of the Peisistratae in Athens.
530–15   Temple of Apollo at Delphi rebuilt by the Alcmonidae.
514   Conspiracy of Harmodius and Aristogeiton.
510   Expulsion of Hippias from Athens.
508–07   Democratic reforms of Cleisthenes at Athens.
490   Persian expedition led by Datis against Greece. Battle of Marathon.
480   March of Xerxes across Greece. Battle of Artemisium. Leonidas defends Thermopylae. Xerxes in Athens. Destruction of the Acropolis. Battle of Salamis.
479   Battle of Plataea. Persians leave Greece.

Classical Period (479–323)

476–60	Aggrandisement of Athens under leadership of Cimon abroad and Aristides at home.
472–71	Ostracism and flight of Themistocles.
468–56	Building of Temple of Zeus at Olympia.
464–59	Third Messenian War.
462–60	Rise of Pericles.
447–38	Construction of Parthenon.
437–32	Building of the Propylaea.
431	Outbreak of Peloponnesian War.
430	Plague in Athens.
429	Death of Pericles.
429–27	Siege and reduction of Plataea by Peloponnesian allies.
425	Siege of Sphacteria.
421	Peace of Nicias. Dedication of Temple of Niké Apteros.
420	Rise of Alcibiades.
419	Resumption of hostilities between Athens and Peloponnesians.
418	First battle of Mantinea.
415	Mutilation of hermae at Athens. Athenian expedition to Sicily. Recall of Alcibiades.
413	Spartans occupy Deceleia in Attica.
c. 408	Completion of Erectheum.
405	Lysander commander of Spartan fleet. Battle of Aegospotami. End of Athenian naval supremacy.
404	End of Peloponnesian War. Surrender of Athens. Destruction of Long Walls.
403	Thrasybulus overthrows the Thirty Tyrants. Restoration of democracy in Athens.
401	March of the Ten Thousand under Xenophon.
399	Trial and death of Socrates.
371	Battle of Leuctra. End of Spartan hegemony. Ascendancy of Thebes under Epaminondas and Pelopidas.
371–69	Foundation of Megalopolis and Messene.
362	Second battle of Mantinea. Death of Epaminondas.
356	Birth of Alexander the Great.

338	Battle of Chaeroneia. Philip II master of Greece. End of Greek democracy.
336	Assassination of Philip II. Accession of Alexander the Great.
334	Alexander crosses into Asia.
324	Alexander's divinity proclaimed at Olympia.
323	Death of Alexander.

Hellenistic Period (323–146)

323	Outbreak of war between the Diadochi.
323–22	Lamian War. Greeks revolt against Macedonian tyranny.
307	Demetrius Poliorcetes master of Athens.
281	Formation of Achaean League.
226	War between Sparta and Achaean League.
222	Battle of Sellasia. Sparta defeated by armies of Macedonia and Achaean League.
168	Battle of Pydna. Defeat of Perseus by Aemilius Paulus. End of Macedonian monarchy.
146	Sack of Corinth by Mummius. Supression of Achaean League. Greece and Macedonia become a Roman province.

Roman Period (146 B.C.–A.D. 330)

88–87	War between Rome and Mithridates, King of Pontus, in Greece.
86	Sack of Athens by Sulla.
48	Julius Caesar in Greece. Battle of Pharsalia.
42	Battle of Philippi.
31	Battle of Actium.
A.D.	
c. 50–53	St Paul's mission to Greece.
66–67	Nero visits Greece.
125–29	Hadrian visits Athens.
132	Completion of Temple of Olympian Zeus at Athens.
313	Edict of Milan. Toleration of Christian worship.
330	Constantine the Great transfers capital of the Empire to Constantinople.

Early Byzantine Period (330–843)

392	Edict of Theodosius the Great proscribing paganism. Sanctuaries of Delphi and Olympia closed down.
395	Gothic invasion of Greece.
467–77	Invasion of Vandals.
588	Slav invasion of the Peloponnese.
726–80	First Iconoclast period.
802–42	Second Iconoclast period.
843	Proscription of Iconoclasm by seventh Council of Nicaea.

Middle Byzantine Period (843–1261)

1018	Byzantine victory over Bulgars. Emperor Basil II makes triumphal tour of Greece and visits Athens.
1054	Schism between Roman and Eastern Churches.
1081–84	Normans under Robert Guiscard invade Greece.
1204	Fourth Crusade. Capture and sack of Constantinople by Crusaders. Establishment of Latin Empire. Geoffroy de Villehardouin lands at Methone.
1205	Othon de la Roche first Latin Duke of Athens. Conquest of the Morea by Geoffroy I de Villehardouin and William de Champlitte.
1248	Siege of Monemvasia by William de Villehardouin.
1259	Battle of Pelagonia. Decisive defeat of Franks by Byzantine army.
1261	Greeks recapture Constantinople. End of Latin Empire of Constantinople.

Late Byzantine Period (1261–1453)

1311	Battle of the Cephisus. Franks routed by Grand Company of Catalans.
1311–87	Catalan rule in Athens.
1348	Manuel Cantacuzenus first Despot of Mistra.
1393–1414	Turkish conquest of Central Greece.
1402–56	Florentine Acciajuoli Dukes of Athens.

1427–32	Byzantine campaign against Latins in the Morea.
1439	Emperor John VIII Palaeologus and Patriarch of Constantinople attend Council of Florence.
1453	Fall of Constantinople.

Turkish Period (1453–1832)

1459	Fall of Mistra. End of Despotate of Mistra.
1499–1500	Venetians surrender maritime stations on Greek mainland to Turks.
1686–1715	Morosini expedition.
1687	Destruction of Parthenon during Venetian siege of Athens.
1801	Lord Elgin obtains firman to remove sculptures from the Acropolis.
1809–11	Byron in Athens.
1821	Standard of revolt against Turks raised by Bishop Germanos at Kalavryta.
1824	Arrival of Byron at Misolonghi. Death of Byron.
1825	Ibrahim Pasha devastates the Morea.
1827	Battle of Navarino. Destruction of Turkish fleet.
1828	French army under General Maison liberates the Morea.
1832	Protocol of London. Greece declared an independent kingdom. National Assembly at Nauplia ratifies election of Prince Otho of Bavaria as King of Greece.

Modern Kingdom of Greece (1833–   )

1833	Arrival of King Otho at Nauplia, capital of new kingdom.
1834	Capital transferred to Athens.
1875–81	German archaeologists excavate Olympia.
1876	Schliemann excavates Mycenae.
1892–1903	Site of Delphi excavated by French School of Archaeology.
1896	First revived Olympic Games held at Athens.
1912–13	First and Second Balkan Wars.

1916	Venizelos proclaims provisional government at Salonica. Greece enters the war against the Central Powers.
1919–22	Graeco-Turkish campaign in Asia Minor. Expulsion of Greek population from Asia Minor.
1924	Establishment of Greek republic.
1935	Restoration of monarchy.
1940	Italian invasion of Greece.
1941	Landing and evacuation of British Expeditionary Force.
1941–44	German-Italian-Bulgar occupation of Greece.
1944–45	First Communist rebellion.
1947–49	Second Communist rebellion.
1967	Establishment of military dictatorship. King Constantine II leaves Greece.

Table of Latin Rulers and Greek Despots (Mistra)

PRINCES OF ACHAEA

William de Champlitte, 1205–10.
Geoffroy I de Villehardouin, 1210–18.
Geoffroy II de Villehardouin, 1218–46.
William de Villehardouin, 1246–78.
Charles I of Anjou, 1278–85.
Charles II of Anjou, 1285–89.
Isabelle de Villehardouin, 1289–1307)
   (with Florent of Haunalt, 1289–1301)
   (with Philip of Savoy, 1301–7).
Philip I of Taranto, 1307–13.
Matilda of Hainault (with Louis of Burgundy), 1313–18.
John of Gravina, 1318–33.
Catherine de Valois (with Robert of Taranto), 1333–46.
Robert of Taranto, 1346–64.
Marie de Bourbon, 1364–70.
Philip II of Taranto, 1370–4.
Joanna of Naples, 1374–6.
Otto of Brunswick, 1376–7.
Knights of St John, 1377–81.

Jacques de Baux, 1381–83.
Mahiot de Coquerel, 1383–86.
Bordo de S. Superan, 1386–1402.
Maria Zaccaria, 1402–4.
Centurione Zaccaria, 1404–32.

DUKES OF ATHENS (alternatively known as *Megaskyr*, i.e.
'the great gentlemen', Lords of Athens, Dukes of Athens
and Thebes)
House of de la Roche
Othon de la Roche, founder of French house, 1205–25.
Guy I, 1225–63.
John I, 1263–80.
William, 1280–87.
Guy II, 1287–1309.
House of Brienne
Walter of Brienne, 1309–11.
Catalan Grand Company and House of Aragon
Roger Deslaur, founder of the Spanish house, 1311–12.
Manfred, 1312–17.
William, 1317–38.
John of Randazzo, 1338–48.
Frederick of Randazzo, 1348–55.
Frederick III of Sicily, 1355–77.
Pedro IV of Aragon, 1377–87.
John I of Aragon, 1387–88.
House of Acciajuoli
Nerio Acciajuoli, founder of Florentine house, 1388–94.
Period of government by Venetian *podestà*, 1394–1402.
Antonio I (restoration of Acciajuoli), 1402–35.
Nerio II, 1435–39.
Antonio II, 1439–41.
Nerio II (restored), 1441–51.
Francesco, 1451–55.
Franco, 1455–56. (Lord of Thebes only, 1456–60).

GREEK DESPOTS OF MISTRA
Manuel Cantacuzenus, 1348–80.
Matthew Cantacuzenus, 1380–83
Theodore I Palaeologus, 1383–1407.
Theodore II, 1407–43.

Constantine Dragases, 1428–48
 (later last Emperor of Byzantium, Constantine XI Palaeologus, 1448–53).
Thomas, 1432–60.
Demetrius, 1449–60.

Some Books on Greece

This selective list is not a bibliography; it may, however, be of some use to travellers who want to learn more of the people, motives, political forces and artistic achievements that make up the four-thousand-year-old story of Greek ascendancy, decline and regeneration.

HISTORY

Ancient

A. R. BURN, *The Pelican History of Greece*, Penguin Books, 1966. Covers the ground from earliest to Roman times.

J. B. BURY, *A History of Greece* (to the death of Alexander the Great), Macmillan, London, 1951 edition. Standard work. Handy.

GEORGE GROTE, *A History of Greece* (to the wars of the successors of Alexander the Great), 8 vols., John Murray, 1862. Standard work. A major piece of historical writing.

W. W. TARN and G. T. GRIFFITH, *Hellenistic Civilisation*, Edward Arnold, London, 1952.

LORD WILLIAM TAYLOR, *The Mycenaeans*, Thames & Hudson, London, 1961. A useful introduction to the prehistoric age.

E. VERMEULE, *Greece in the Bronze Age*, University of Chicago, Chicago, 1964. A general account.

Medieval

CHARLES DIEHL, *Figures Byzantines*, 2 vols., Librairie Armand Colin, Paris, 1930. Fascinating account of outstanding Byzantine personalities.

GEORGE FINLAY, *A History of Greece* (146 B.C. to A.D. 1864), 7 vols., Oxford University Press, 1878. An historical and literary *tour de force*.

EDWARD GIBBON, *History of the Decline and Fall of the Roman Empire*, John Murray, London, 1855.

WILLIAM MILLER, *The Latins in the Levant*, John Murray, London, 1908. The standard, if not only, work in English on Frankish and Venetian Greece.

SIR STEVEN RUNCIMAN, *Byzantine Civilization*, Edward Arnold, London, 1933. A scholarly general account.

DAVID TALBOT RICE, *The Byzantines*, Ancient Peoples and Places Series, Thames & Hudson, London, 1962. Useful introduction for the beginner.

A. A. VASILIEV, *History of the Byzantine Empire*, Basil Blackwell, Oxford, 1952. A definitive general history.

Modern

JOHN CAMPBELL and PHILIP SHERRARD, *Modern Greece*, Ernest Benn, London, 1968. A succinct objective account, covering every aspect of the Greek character.

ART AND ARCHITECTURE

Ancient

PIERRE DEVAMBEZ, *Greek Painting*, Contact Books, Weidenfeld & Nicolson, London, 1962. A useful introduction.

A. W. LAWRENCE, *Greek Architecture*, The Pelican History of Art, Penguin Books, 1957. An invaluable work of reference.

R. LULLIES and H. HIRMER, *Greek Sculpture*, Thames & Hudson, London, 1960. Introductory but useful, and magnificently illustrated.

G. M. A. RICHTER, *A Handbook of Greek Art*, Phaidon Press, London, 1959. Comprehensive and well arranged.

Medieval

KEVIN ANDREWS, *Castles of the Morea*, American School of Classical Studies, Princeton, N.J., 1953. The only scholarly work on this much neglected subject.

O. M. DALTON, *Byzantine Art & Archaeology*, Clarendon Press, Oxford, 1911. The standard work in English.

ANDRE GRABAR, *Byzantium, Byzantine Art in the Middle Ages*, Art of the World Series, Methuen, 1963.

GERVASE MATHEW, *Byzantine Aesthetics*, John Murray, London, 1963. A theoretical interpretation.

DAVID TALBOT RICE, *Art of the Byzantine Era*, The World of

Art Library, Thames & Hudson, London, 1963. Useful for the beginner.

MYTHOLOGY

ROBERT GRAVES, *The Greek Gods*, 2 vols., Penguin Books, 1967. Exhaustive, discursive, imaginative.

J. C. LAWSON, *Modern Greek Folklore and Ancient Greek Religion*, University Books, New York, 1964 (first published by the Cambridge University Press, 1909). Standard work.

H. J. ROSE, *A Handbook of Greek Mythology*, Methuen, London, 1928. The most useful work on the subject.

TRAVEL AND TOPOGRAPHY[4]

EDWARD LEAR, *Journals of a Landscape Painter in Albania, Illyria, etc.*, reprinted under the title of *Edward Lear in Greece*, William Kimber, London, 1965. Witty, astute and brilliantly written.

ROBERT LIDDELL, *The Morea*, Jonathan Cape, London, 1958. Indispensable to the traveller in the Peloponnese.

PATRICK LEIGH-FERMOR, *Mani, Travels in the Southern Peloponnese*, John Murray, London, 1958. A penetrating study of Greek lore, character and landscape.

GENERAL

SIR MAURICE BOWRA, *The Greek Experience*, Weidenfeld & Nicolson, London, 1957. An appreciation of the ancient Greek achievement.

H. D. F. KITTO, *The Greeks*, Penguin Books, 1951. Useful account of the Hellenic achievement in the social and artistic spheres.

MISCELLANEOUS (special aspects)

OLEG POLUNIN and ANTHONY HUXLEY, *Flowers of the Mediterranean*, Chatto & Windus, London, 1965. For the botanist. Illustrated with colour plates and line drawings.

4. With the exception of Lear, all the great travel writers (who were also scholars) of the 19th century, Leake, Mure, Curzon, W. J. Woodhouse, etc., are out of print.

PHILIP SHERRARD, *The Marble Threshing Floor*, Valentine Mitchell, London, 1956. The post-War of Independence literary scene.

TIMOTHY WARE, *The Orthodox Church*, Penguin Books, 1963. Useful to the Byzantinist.

LIGHT LITERATURE

EDMOND ABOUT, *Le Roi des Montagnes*, Amis du Livre, Paris, 1961 edition. Shrewd novel about Greek brigandage and party politics in the nineteenth century.

LEONARD COTTRELL, *The Bull of Minos*, Pan Books, London, 1955. An account (for the average reader) of Schliemann's and Sir Arthur Evans's archaeological discoveries at Troy, Mycenae and Knossos.

MARY RENAULT, *The Last of the Wine*, Longmans Green, London, 1956. Romantic but authentic novel about life in ancient Athens during the Peloponnesian War.

GUIDEBOOKS

The 1909 Baedeker is still the best of all factual guidebooks: erudite, precise and handy. But information regarding communications is hopelessly out-of-date; furthermore, it is out of print (second-hand copies sometimes obtainable). The French *Guide* Bleu (Librairie Hachette, Paris, English translation, 1964) is good on ancient sites, but sketchy on Byzantine and medieval ruins. The *Blue Guide* (Benn, London, 1967) is reliable, up-to-date, even indispensable. Less detailed but also good and reliable is Nagel's *Greece*, Geneva, English translation, 1963).

Index

❧